AA
Habermas
(Whi)

Each v[...]   [...]s contains specially
commi[...]   [...]al team of scholars,
together with a substantial bibliography, and will serve as a
[...] for students and nonspecialists. One aim of
[...]imidation such readers often
[...] the work of a difficult and challenging thinker.

Jürgen Habermas is unquestionably one of the foremost
philosophers writing today. His notions of communicative
action and rationality have exerted a profound influence
within philosophy and the social sciences. This volume examines the historical and intellectual contexts out of which
Habermas's work emerged and offers an overview of his
main ideas, including those in his most recent publications.
Among the topics discussed are his relationship to the
Frankfurt School of critical theory and Marx, his unique
contributions to the philosophy of the social sciences, the
concept of "communicative ethics," and the critique of postmodernism. Particular attention is paid to Habermas's recent work on democratic theory and the constitutional
state.

New readers and nonspecialists will find this the most
convenient, accessible guide to Habermas currently available. Advanced students will find a conspectus of recent developments in the interpretation of Habermas.

THE CAMBRIDGE COMPANION TO

HABERMAS

The Cambridge Companion to
HABERMAS

Edited by Stephen K. White

Virginia Polytechnic Institute and
State University, Blacksburg

CAMBRIDGE
UNIVERSITY PRESS

Published by the Press Syndicate of the University of Cambridge
The Pitt Building, Trumpington Street, Cambridge CB2 IRP
40 West 20th Street, New York, NY 10011-4211, USA
10 Stamford Road, Oakleigh, Melbourne 3166, Australia

First published 1995

Printed in the United States of America

Library of Congress Cataloging-in-Publication Data
The Cambridge companion to Habermas / edited by Stephen K. White.
   p. cm.
   Includes bibliographical references and index.
   ISBN 0-521-44120-X – ISBN 0-521-44666-X (pbk.)
   1. Habermas, Jürgen. I. White, Stephen K.
B3258.H324C36   1995
193 – dc20   94-28826
                              CIP

A catalog record for this book is available from the British Library.

ISBN 0-521-44120-X hardback
ISBN 0-521-44666-X paperback

CONTENTS

v

CONTRIBUTORS

KENNETH BAYNES is Associate Professor of Philosophy at the State University of New York at Stony Brook. He is the author of *The Normative Grounds of Social Criticism: Kant, Rawls and Habermas* (State University of New York Press, 1992) and a co-editor of *After Philosophy: End or Transformation?* (MIT Press, 1987).

SIMONE CHAMBERS is Assistant Professor of Political Science at the University of Colorado at Boulder. Her main interests lie in the study of ethics and democratic theory. Her book *Discourse and Procedural Ethics* is forthcoming from Cornell University Press.

ROMAND COLES is Assistant Professor of Political Science at Duke University. He is the author of a book on Augustine, Foucault, and Merleau-Ponty entitled *Self/Power/Other: Political Theory and Dialogical Ethics* (Cornell University Press, 1992) as well as numerous articles. He is currently completing a book entitled *Critical Theory and Difference: Toward a Post-Secular Caritas.*

JOHN S. DRYZEK is Professor of Political Science at the University of Oregon. His books include *Rational Ecology: Environment and Political Economy* (New York: Blackwell, 1987) and *Discursive Democracy: Politics, Policy, and Political Science* (Cambridge University Press, 1990). He writes mostly in the areas of critical theory, environmental politics, democratic theory, policy analysis, philosophy of social science, and political science history.

AXEL HONNETH is Professor of Political Philosophy at the Free University of Berlin. His books in English translation include: *Social Action and Human Nature* (together with Hans Joas; Cambridge

vii

University Press, 1988); *Critique of Power* (MIT Press, 1990); and *Struggle for Recognition* (Polity Press, forthcoming).

NANCY S. LOVE is Associate Professor of Political Science at Pennsylvania State University. She is the author of *Marx, Nietzsche, and Modernity* (Columbia University Press, 1986) and articles on critical theory and postmodernism. Her current project is a study of the role of music in the development of social movements.

J. DONALD MOON is Professor of Government at Wesleyan University. Among his publications are *Constructing Community: Moral Pluralism and Tragic Conflicts* (Princeton University Press, 1993), "The Logic of Political Inquiry" in the *Handbook of Political Science* (Addison-Wesley, 1975), and articles on the philosophy of social inquiry and the political theory of the welfare state. He is a co-editor of *Dissent and Affirmation* (Bowling Green University Press, 1983) and editor of *Responsibility, Rights, and Welfare* (Westview, 1988).

MAX PENSKY is Assistant Professor of Philosophy at Binghamton University. He is author of *Melancholy Dialectics: Walter Benjamin and the Play of Mourning* (University of Massachusetts Press, 1993) and translator of Habermas's *The Past as Future* (University of Nebraska Press, 1994).

FRANK ANDREAS SPOSITO is finishing a dissertation in political theory at the University of California, San Diego, on the implications for liberalism of the romantic critique of the Enlightenment.

TRACY B. STRONG is Professor of Political Science at the University of California, San Diego, and editor of the journal *Political Theory*. His books include *Friedrich Nietzsche and the Politics of Transformation* (University of California Press, expanded ed., 1988) and *The Idea of Political Theory: Reflections on the Self in Political Time and Space* (University of Notre Dame Press, 1990).

GEORGIA WARNKE is Professor of Philosophy at the University of California, Riverside. She is the author of *Gadamer: Hermeneutics, Tradition and Reason* (Stanford University Press, 1987), *Justice and Interpretation* (MIT Press, 1993), and articles on critical theory, hermeneutics, and feminism.

MARK E. WARREN is Associate Professor of Government at Georgetown University. He is author of *Nietzsche and Political Thought* (MIT Press, 1988) as well as articles on Marx, Weber, Habermas, Nietzsche, and democratic theory. He is now working on a book entitled *Democratic Transformations of the Self*, which draws on continental political thought to rethink concepts of the self in democratic theory.

STEPHEN K. WHITE is Professor of Political Science at Virginia Tech. His books include *The Recent Work of Jürgen Habermas* (Cambridge University Press, 1988); *Political Theory and Postmodernism* (Cambridge University Press, 1991); and *Edmund Burke: Modernity, Politics, and Aesthetics* (Sage, 1994).

Part I

INTRODUCTION

1 Reason, modernity, and democracy

One of the most distinctive features on the intellectual landscape of the last decades of the twentieth century is the intensity with which doubts have been raised about the conceptual foundations of Western modernity. Hard questions have emerged about the predominant modern understandings of reason, subjectivity, nature, progress, and gender. With the exception of the last topic, one might argue that these questions emerged in this century in their most powerful form within two streams of German philosophical reflection. In the immediate post–World War II years, Martin Heidegger wrote his "Essay on Humanism" (1946) and "The Question Concerning Technology" (1949), and he continued for the next thirty years to articulate a thorough critique of most of what the modern West has held dear.[1] In 1947 Theodor Adorno and Max Horkheimer published their *Dialectic of Enlightenment*, developing the claim that the systematic pursuit of enlightened reason and freedom had the ironic long-term effect of engendering new forms of irrationality and repression.[2] These critiques had an immense impact both on the initial shape of the work of Jürgen Habermas and on its continued evolution.

The very extremity of these critiques, as well as their association with fascism in Heidegger's case and Marxism (however unorthodox) in Horkheimer and Adorno's, made them highly contentious from the start. Their real effect – and it was often achieved at second or third hand – was never one of convincing a large audience to embrace some new, alternative moral-political vision; rather, it brought prevailing interpretations of reason, progress, nature, and subjectivity to a new level of explicit questioning. These intellectual assaults, coupled with shattering world events of the mid–twentieth century,

3

have ensured that modernity's self-understanding will never have the level of self-assurance that it once possessed.

For Heidegger, the loss of confidence was virtually complete, and many of those influenced by him, especially contemporary post-structuralists and postmoderns, lean in the same direction. Similarly, Horkheimer and Adorno felt little reason for optimism when they considered the intellectual and political resources the West could bring to bear to heal its self-inflicted wounds. The choices seemed to be either strutting self-confidence or total loss of confidence. And yet, in *Dialectic of Enlightenment* one could still detect an appeal being made to some ideal of reason and freedom that might provide the illumination, however weak and uncertain, necessary for finding a path out of modernity's difficulties.[3] Neither Horkheimer nor Adorno wanted, or was able, however, to make this gesture more convincing in the years that followed.

Their appeal to reason and freedom had its roots in the pre–World War II era, when they had been among the founders of the Institute for Social Research in Frankfurt. The institute members carried out a wide range of philosophical and social investigations sharply critical of the economics, politics, and culture of Western societies. Although they considered themselves to be on the left politically, their attachment to Marxism became looser and looser, especially as the character of Stalin's regime in the Soviet Union became increasingly apparent. Horkheimer coined the term "critical theory" in the 1930s to describe their stance.[4] As originally conceived, critical theory would have the role of giving new life to ideals of reason and freedom by revealing their false embodiment in scientism, capitalism, the "culture industry," and bourgeois Western political institutions.

The members of the institute were forced to flee Nazi Germany, and most of them settled in the United States. It was during this time in exile that the *Dialectic* was written. After the war, Horkheimer and Adorno reestablished the institute at the University of Frankfurt. Among the young philosophers who became associated with it was Jürgen Habermas. During this period, Horkheimer and Adorno became ever more disillusioned about the world around them. Adorno began to articulate a mode of thinking he called "negative dialectics" that resisted any affirmative thinking whatsoever about ethics and politics.[5] And Horkheimer was drawn increasingly toward theology.[6] Habermas, however, resisted these changes of direction.

Beginning in the 1960s, he charted a course for himself which, in its spirit and deepest moral commitments, has not changed in any fundamental sense.[7] He was convinced that one could retain the power of his predecessor's critique of modern life only by clarifying a distinctive conception of rationality and affirming the notion of a just or "emancipated" society that would somehow correspond to that conception.

Thus Habermas's philosophical journey begins with a departure from the positions of Horkheimer and Adorno's later years; but it is a departure that Habermas has always felt better retains the spirit of the Frankfurt School's prewar period. The tension with Adorno's later work is especially interesting. For Habermas, his growing pessimism and the totalization of his critique of Western modernity constituted something of a failure of nerve. In this regard, there is a subtle and disturbing affinity between Adorno and Heidegger. From the depths of such a total critique, what sort of politics is likely to capture the imagination? Heidegger's early association with Nazism and his lifelong refusal to renounce it thoroughly carry, for Habermas, a lesson that cannot be forgotten or downplayed. When his *Philosophical Discourse of Modernity* appeared in the 1980s, the list of those who threatened too extremely the continuity of that discourse included not only Nietzsche, Heidegger, Foucault, and Derrida, but also Horkheimer and Adorno.[8] In this regard, one finds certain resonances in the present volume between some of the issues raised in the first essay by Romand Coles concerning Adorno, and those raised in the last two essays concerning the challenge to Habermas from postmodernism.

Many readers of *The Philosophical Discourse of Modernity* are perplexed at the intensity and relentlessness of Habermas's attack on his opponents. Adding to the perplexity is the fact that one of the hallmarks of his career has been an extraordinary openness to critical discussions. Such perplexity can be at least partially dispelled if one remembers that the stakes involved with totalized critiques of modernity are very high for a German who, like Habermas, has historically rooted worries that certain figures of thought may either lend themselves (even if unwittingly) to desparate forms of politics or provide insufficient resources for effective resistance to them. One simply cannot understand Habermas's work as a whole without attending to this historical rootedness. Max Pensky's contribution to this volume draws this connection out in its various dimensions.

Habermas's project, as it emerged in the 1960s, had two major components. First, he set himself the daunting task of developing a "more comprehensive" conception of reason, by which he meant one that was not reducible to the instrumental-technical or strategic calculations of an essentially monadic, individual subject.[9] Moreover, it was only in terms of such a broader conception that one could begin to sketch the outlines of an "emancipated" or "rational" society.[10]

The effort to think about reason differently bore its first fruit in 1965, in "Knowledge and Human Interests: A General Perspective," his inaugural lecture delivered upon assuming a professorship at Frankfurt. The thesis was soon expanded into a book of the same name.[11] There he postulated the existence of three anthropologically deep-seated interests of human beings, to which three categories of knowledge and rationality correspond. We have "knowledge-constitutive interests" in the technical control of the world around us, in understanding others, and in freeing ourselves from structures of domination: a "technical," a "practical," and an "emancipatory" interest.[12] Following Horkheimer and Adorno, Habermas found that modern society has fostered an unbalanced expansion of the technical interest in control: The drive to dominate nature becomes a drive to dominate other human beings. Habermas's speculation upon how to alleviate this distortion revolved around reasserting the rationality inherent in our "practical" and "emancipatory" interests. Entwining these two interests in a distinctive fashion, Habermas announced that a rational basis for collective life would be achieved only when social relations were organized "according to the principle that the validity of every norm of political consequence be made dependent on a consensus arrived at in communication free from domination."[13]

This idea became the guiding thread of Habermas's project. He soon found, however, that it could not be adequately fleshed out using the epistemological framework of knowledge-constitutive interests.[14] He decided instead to pursue his aims through an exploration of the ongoing "communicative competence" displayed by all speakers of natural languages.[15] The heart of this endeavor was an explication of the implicit mastery of rules for raising and redeeming "validity claims" in ordinary language. Insofar as actors wish to coordinate their action through understanding rather than force or manipulation, they implicitly take on the burden of redeeming claims they raise to others regarding the truth of what they say, its normative rightness, and its sincerity. When claims are explicitly challenged, they can only be redeemed in, respectively, "theoretical discourse," "practical discourse," or further interaction that reveals whether the speaker has been sincere.[16] The fundamentals of this "linguistic turn" in Habermas's work – the turn to the theory of communicative rationality and action – are laid out in Georgia Warnke's essay.

With this shift, Habermas established a conceptual framework out of which he has continued to work until the present. There have been many modifications and elaborations, but as he says, "my research program has remained the same since about 1970."[17] The task of making plausible the theory of communicative action and rationality is an enormous one, and his writings from this point on are best seen as pursuing various but interrelated paths toward this goal. For Habermas, there is no single, straightforward line of argument that will make his case in knockdown fashion. Plausibility at this philosophical level is gained only piecemeal, by showing in a variety of contexts how the theory of communicative action and rationality generates more conceptual, moral, and empirical insight than alternative approaches.[18] Four contexts are particularly important: methodological discussions in the social sciences, accounts of the character of modernity and the societal rationalization associated with it, controversies in contemporary moral philosophy, and contending views about the legitimacy of the liberal, democratic state.

In the broadest methodological sense, Habermas's account of reason and action offers a new conceptual "core" to the research tradition of critical theory. It thus provides a means of generating coherence across a broad terrain of research in the social sciences. At the end of his monumental two-volume work, *The Theory of Communicative Action*, he explicitly harkens back to the institute's efforts in the 1930s to pursue a wide range of interconnected, interdisciplinary studies.[19] John Dryzek's essay explores the general implications of Habermas's approach for the philosophy of the social sciences.[20]

The Theory of Communicative Action is best known, however, for the striking perspective it provides on how we should understand modernity. An underlying goal of the book is to elaborate how the communicative approach to reason and action helps us both to critique certain aspects of modernity and yet to clarify the value of other aspects in such a way as to give us some grounds for "self-reassurance."[21]

Habermas offers a two-level interpretation of the modern world, in which a distinction is drawn between the rational potential implicit in "cultural modernity" and the selective or one-sided utilization of that potential in "societal processes of modernization."[22] The cultural potential of modernity constitutes the critical standpoint from which particular aspects of Western modernization can be judged negatively. What Habermas means by this is that modern culture has made available a "rationalized lifeworld" – one in which actors consistently carry the expectation that the various validity claims raised in speech are to be cognitively distinguished, and that they have to be redeemed in different ways. As such a lifeworld emerges, an increasing number of spheres of social interaction are removed from guidance by unquestioned tradition and opened to co-ordination through consciously achieved agreement. Simultaneously with this advance in communicative rationalization, there also occurs an advance in the rationality of society as measured from a functionalist or systems perspective. This latter sort of rationalization means that there is an expansion of social subsystems that coordinate action through the media of money (capitalist economy) and administrative power (modern, centralized states). The initially beneficial expansion of these media has progressed to the point, however, that they increasingly invade areas of social life that have been or could be coordinated by the medium of understanding or "solidarity." Modernization in the West has thus generated a pathology: an unbalanced development of its potential. Habermas refers to this phenomenon as a "colonization of the lifeworld" that brings in its wake a growing sense of meaninglessness and dwindling freedom.[23]

This imbalance is one that can be resisted; it is not an unbreakable "iron cage" in Max Weber's sense. Habermas sees palpable signs of the rejection of the smooth unfolding of functionalist reason in various new social movements that have emerged since the 1960s, whose common denominator is their concern not so much with "problem of *distribution*, but [with] questions of the *grammar of forms of life*."[24] Whether the questions arise in the form of a critique of productivist civilization as in the ecological movement, or in the form of a rejection of scripted identities as in feminism or the gay and lesbian rights movement, they all constitute resistance points to further colonization. Such opposition is of course conceived by Habermas to be progressive only to the degree that its concerns can be articulated in ways that accord with the universalist normative bent of communicative rationality; that is, only to the degree that resistance to colonization of the lifeworld is carried out so as to build upon the cultural potential of modernity rather than reject it, as is the case with exclusivist appeals to national identity.

The strong, universalist position on rationality and morality, and the claim that the modern West – for all its problems – best embodies these values, has, not surprisingly, run into intense opposition. For a broad array of poststructuralist, postmodern, and feminist thinkers, this sort of universalism is merely a sophisticated variant of earlier, deleterious forms. And, like them, it functions merely to blind the West to the ways in which it both drives itself in ever more disciplinary directions and engenders "others" who fall short of the demands carried by its criteria of reason and responsibility. Such critiques are sometimes premised on a fairly significant misunderstanding (sometimes nonreading) of Habermas's work – but not always. The two essays in this volume that engage such issues do so from a position of adequate understanding and no small degree of sympathy. Tracy Strong and Frank Sposito raise the problem of the "other" of reason from within the Kantian tradition of philosophy as a whole and suggest that its shortcomings have to be more adequately confronted by anyone who, like Habermas, draws so deeply upon that tradition. Axel Honneth's essay carries a similar tone. He surveys various critiques of Habermas that have emerged out of postmodern and feminist concerns and shows how they contain ethical insights to which Habermas has failed to do full justice. (The last part of Nancy Love's essay is also relevant to these issues.)

In the somewhat less hostile context of analytic moral philosophy, Habermas has exhibited a great willingness to elaborate his universalist perspective and defend it at length against alternative positions. He has tried to show generally why a communicative ethics provides the best way of comprehending the universalist core of the Western understanding of morality. This has necessitated, first, defending the priority he grants to a deontological approach to morality, which delineates "the moral point of view" in terms of procedural justice and rights, over a teleological one, which understands morality as oriented first and foremost around a substantive notion of the good. Second, Habermas has had to distinguish his own deontological view from those of Kant and contemporary philosophers such as John Rawls.[25] The essays by Warnke and J. Donald Moon survey these efforts and assess their success.

Even as the importance of the communicative approach to reason and ethics was becoming more widely recognized in the 1980s, a persistent criticism of Habermas remained in regard to what was perceived as his failure to address adequately institutional, political questions. His ethical perspective and critique of Western rationalization seemed to distance him radically from the existing institutions of liberal democracy. That was acutely evident in his *Legitimation Crisis*, written in the early 1970s.[26] Like many other critics of the legitimacy of liberal democracies written in that decade, Habermas contended that such systems were beset by difficulties likely to drive them into a crisis resolvable only by radical democratization. But the precise shape of this more just society – what he had earlier called "emancipated" – remained obscure. Up through the early 1970s, Habermas continued to think in terms of a fundamental transition from a liberal, constitutional state to some sort of socialist system with more radicalized democratic institutions.[27] By the time *The Theory of Communicative Action* appeared in German in 1981, however, it was clear that this perspective was undergoing substantial modification.[28] As said earlier, Habermas there affirms certain modes of resistance in advanced industrial societies, but such opposition is never conceived as directed toward a wholesale replacement of liberal states. The primary image one is left with is struggle at the margins. Healthy democratic impulses seem largely confined to the periphery of organized politics; from there they merely try to resist further systemic encroachment. The force of communicative reason, as manifest in new social movements and other upwellings of radical "public spheres," can, in effect, only hurl themselves against an administrative Leviathan.

Even though the precise institutional implications of Habermas's conception of democracy remained unclear through the 1980s, there were other aspects of it that were developed in enough detail to permit a fruitful engagement with various issues in democratic theory. Mark Warren's essay investigates how a discursive perspective brings about something of a "paradigm shift in how we think about the location and legitimacy of radically democratic expectations" (see Chapter 8).

The broad suggestiveness of Habermas's perspective for democracy has finally been brought into the context of a more detailed analysis of political institutions with the publication of his *Between Facts and Norms: Contributions to a Discourse Theory of Law and Democracy*, which appeared in German in 1992.[29] In *The Theory of Communicative Action*, Habermas had certainly regarded the emergence of modern law, with its universalism and orientation to individual rights, as a significant evolutionary step in moral-practical learning. But this positive quality was seen largely as something that has kept us from recognizing the degree to which law in the welfare state has in fact become a vehicle for expanding administrative power (a problem Habermas treated under the theme of "juridification" [*Verrechtlichung*].[30] Thus, although modern law is understood in that book as deeply ambivalent, its negative side is what receives the most distinctive treatment. This one-sidedness is corrected in *Facticity and Validity*. The essays by Kenneth Baynes and Simone Chambers explore the various issues raised by this significant addition to Habermas's corpus.

Within the new perspective, law's role as an instrument of stability and social control is retained; only now that capacity is displayed as being in perpetual "tension" with the distinctive and positive normative quality it takes on in modern politics.[31] The institutions of modern law, such as basic rights and constitutions, provide a means by which actors can maintain, in a historically new way, a collective sense of "validity" and "solidarity" no longer adequately carried by traditional institutions. The former institutions can assume this role because they can be understood as representations of the idea of a self-determining community of free and equal subjects who wish to guide their collective life through binding rules. In a general sense, such a philosophical reconstruction of the self-understanding of modern politics is quite familiar. Habermas, however, wants to show how communicative rationality can provide a novel way of reconceptualizing this figure of thought. Previous articulations of the idea of a political community of free and equals have foundered on their inability to resolve the conflict between private and public autonomy. Either individual rights are given priority over collective autonomy (as in Kant and liberalism), or collective autonomy is given priority over the individual (as in Rousseau, republicanism, and communitarianism). The problem, according to Habermas, is that both positions are rooted in notions of *subjectivity*, individual or collective. If political theory is rooted instead in a notion of *intersubjectivity* fleshed out in communicative-rational terms, then we can understand the "equi-primordiality of private and public right [*Recht*]." This is so because, in Habermas's terms, public autonomy is reconceived as the availability of a differentiated "network" of communicative arrangements for the discursive formation of public opinion and will; and a system of basic individual "rights provides exactly the conditions under which the forms of communication necessary for a politically autonomous constitution of law can be institutionalized."[32]

This "discursive" conception of democracy links up with other recent efforts to tie legitimacy more closely to the quality of deliberation exhibited in political processes. Democratic legitimacy, for Habermas, is measured not just in terms of law being enacted by a majority, but also in terms of the discursive quality of the full processes of deliberation leading up to such a result. Discursively healthy processes, from the most diffuse and informal to the most structured and formal, are what maintain a sense of validity and solidarity among a "constitutional community" (*Rechtsgemeinschaft*); they alone allow law to be structured not just by the systemic "needs" of control, expressed in the autonomous expansion of "administrative power," but also by needs arising from the lifeworld of actors, expressed in "communicative power" (here Habermas borrows heavily from Hannah Arendt). When the democratic constitutional state is functioning well, it continually "translates" communicative power into administrative power.[33]

Between Facts and Norms thus presents us with some substantial shifts in Habermas's views about politics in the liberal state. First, and most evident, any notion of a socialist democracy seems to have receded almost completely from view. Although Habermas does not wish to renounce totally his socialist roots, it is not entirely clear what is really left of them. Nancy Love's essay wrestles with this aspect of Habermas's heritage.

The picture of politics in *Between Facts and Norms* also constitutes a modification of the one offered in *The Theory of Communicative Action*, which envisioned a radical alterity between a normatively obtuse, monolithic, administrative state and the discursive claims arising in civil society. Now the picture is of a differentiated state whose multiplicity of sites for deliberation and decision making is broadly warranted by communicative rationality. Each site, however, must be judged carefully in terms of "the discursive level of public debates" occurring there. Discursive democracy thus requires a continual and variegated "interplay" between a multiplicity of "public spheres" emerging across civil society and a broad spectrum of formal political institutions.[34]

Habermas's detailed elaboration of his discursive, deliberative model constitutes a major contribution to the debates in contemporary democratic theory. This model contends with liberal variants, on the one side, and republican and communitarian ones, on the other. For Habermas, the former neglect the need for a social solidarity obtainable only by a radicalization of public communication processes, while the latter seek to constitute such solidarity around notions of community that are too thick. These claims no doubt will be the subject of intense controversy for the next few years.

This reference to a new opening in debate is the appropriate place to end this introduction. Habermas's pace of philosophical contribution has not slackened. Conclusions remain, hopefully, a long way off.

NOTES

1 Martin Heidegger, "Essay on Humanism," in *Basic Writings*, edited and with introduction by David Krell (New York: Harper & Row, 1977), pp. 189–242; and *The Question Concerning Technology and Other Essays*, translated and with introduction by William Lovitt (New York: Harper & Row, 1977).

2 Max Horkheimer and Theodor W. Adorno, *Dialectic of Enlightenment*, trans. John Cumming (New York: Seabury, 1972).

3 Ibid., see Introduction.

4 See esp. Horkheimer, "Traditional and Critical Theory," in *Critical Theory: Selected Essays*, trans. Matthew J. O'Connell et al. (New York: Seabury, 1972), pp. 188–243.

5 Adorno, *Negative Dialectics*, trans. E. B. Ashton (New York: Continuum, 1973).

6 For this turn in Horkheimer's thought, see Habermas, "To Seek to Salvage an Unconditional Meaning without God Is a Futile Undertaking: Reflections on a Remark of Max Horkheimer," in *Justification and Application: Remarks on Discourse Ethics*, trans. Ciaran Cronin (Cambridge, Mass.: MIT Press, 1993), pp. 133–46.

7 I would draw a distinction between this deepest level of commitment and the philosophical framework intended to make good on it. The former has not changed essentially; the latter, however, has been modified significantly.

8 Habermas, *The Philosophical Discourse of Modernity*, trans. Frederick Lawrence (Cambridge, Mass.: MIT Press, 1987), ch. 5.

9 Habermas, "The Analytical Theory of Science and Dialectics," in Adorno et al., *The Positivist Dispute in German Sociology*, trans. Glen Adey and David Frisby (New York: Harper & Row, 1976), p. 143; and "A Positivistically Bisected Rationalism," in the same volume, pp. 198–99, 219. Cf. also *The Theory of Communicative Action*, Vol. I, *Reason and the Rationalization of Society*, trans. Thomas McCarthy (Boston: Beacon Press, 1984), p. 10.

10 See Habermas, *Toward a Rational Society: Student Protest, Science, and Politics*, trans. Jeremy Shapiro (Boston: Beacon Press, 1970).

11 Habermas, *Knowledge and Human Interests*, trans. Jeremy Shapiro (Boston: Beacon Press, 1971). The inaugural lecture is included as an appendix.

12 Ibid., p. 308.

13 Ibid., p. 284.

14 Habermas, *Theory of Communicative Action*, Vol. I, p. xxxix.

15 Habermas, "Toward a Theory of Communicative Competence," in *Patterns of Communicative Behavior*, ed. Hans Dreitzel (New York: Macmillan, 1970), pp. 115–48.

16 Habermas, "What Is Universal Pragmatics?" in *Communication and the Evolution of Society*, trans. Thomas McCarthy (Boston: Beacon Press, 1979), pp. 1–68; *Theory of Communicative Action*, Vol. I, pp. 8–42; and *Moral Consciousness and Communicative Action*, trans.

Christian Lenhardt and Shierry Weber Nicholsen (Cambridge, Mass.: MIT Press, 1990).

17 Habermas, *Justification and Application*, p. 149.

18 Habermas, *Faktizität und Geltung: Beiträge zur Diskurstheorie des Rechts und des demokratischen Rechtstaats* (Frankfurt: Suhrkamp, 1992), p. 9; "Interpretive Social Science versus Hermeneuticism," in *Social Science as Moral Inquiry*, ed. Norma Hahn et al. (New York: Columbia University Press, 1983), p. 261; and "Philosophy as Stand-in and Interpreter," in *After Philosophy: End or Transformation*, eds. Kenneth Baynes, James Bohman, and Thomas McCarthy (Cambridge, Mass.: MIT Press, 1987), pp. 310–11; and *The Theory of Communicative Action*, Vol. II, *Lifeworld and System: A Critique of Functionalist Reason*, trans. Thomas McCarthy (Boston: Beacon Press, 1987), pp. 398–403.

19 Habermas, *Theory of Communicative Action*, Vol. II, pp. 378ff.

20 Cf. also Dryzek's *Discursive Democracy: Politics, Policy, and Political Science* (Cambridge: Cambridge University Press, 1990), intro. and ch. 10.

21 See Habermas, *Theory of Communicative Action*, Vol. II, ch. 8; and *Philosophical Discourse of Modernity*, ch. 1.

22 Habermas, *Theory of Communicative Action*, Vol. I, pp. 157–85, 221–22.

23 Ibid., pp. 183, 239–40; and Vol. II, pp. 292–93, 422, 452, 470–88.

24 Habermas, *Theory of Communicative Action*, Vol. II, pp. 576, 579.

25 Habermas's most recent reflections on these issues are contained in *Justification and Application*.

26 Habermas, *Legitimation Crisis*, trans. Thomas McCarthy (Boston: Beacon Press, 1975). The German edition appeared in 1973.

27 Habermas, "Further Reflections on the Public Sphere," in *Habermas and the Public Sphere*, ed. Craig Calhoun (Cambridge, Mass.: MIT Press, 1992), p. 443.

28 So as not to make the mistake of thinking that he simply changed his mind as a result of the collapse of communism in the Soviet Union, it is important to note that Habermas's views on socialism were shifting already in the early 1980s.

29 Cited in n. 18. An English translation of this volume entitled *Between Facts and Norms: Contributions to a Discourse Theory of Law and Democracy*, trans. William Rehg, is forthcoming from MIT Press.

30 Habermas, *Theory of Communicative Action*, Vol. II, pp. 357ff.

31 *Faktizität und Geltung*, pp. 37, 109.

32 Ibid., pp. 134–35, 151, 207–09.

33 Ibid., pp. 181–87.

34 Ibid., pp. 369, 448. It should be noted that attention to the leavening influence of "public spheres" on politics is a theme that has been present, in one form or another, since his *Habilitationschrift*, which was published in German in 1962. The English translation is entitled *The Structural Transformation of the Public Sphere: An Inquiry into a Category of Bourgeois Society*, trans. Thomas Burger with the assistance of Frederick Lawrence (Cambridge, Mass.: MIT Press, 1989).

Part II

HERITAGE AND CONTEXT

2 Identity and difference in the ethical positions of Adorno and Habermas

One can explore the overlaps and tensions between Adorno and Habermas on diverse and related themes concerning instrumental reason, the potential for crises in contemporary capitalist democracies, the prospects for historical transformation, the relationships between critical theory, social science and analytic philosophy, the normative positions of critical theory, and so on. Depending upon one's thematic focus, assessments of proximities, distances, advantages, and disadvantages will vary markedly. In this essay my analysis of the relationship between Adorno and Habermas is limited to questions concerning the normative character of critical theory. On my reading Adorno provides a more interesting and promising position than Habermas recognizes, and both illuminates and gestures beyond some of the most important weaknesses of Habermas's communicative ethics.

Habermas once noted with a certain melancholy that his writing had not succeeded as much as he would have liked in "awaken[ing] the hermeneutic willingness requisite for its reception."[1] Ironically, given Habermas's often harsh and repeated criticisms of Adorno, there is a sense in which Habermas may indirectly contribute to just such an awakening for the reception of Adorno's work. For the former's emphasis on communicative ethics has contributed to an interrogative framework – a set of compelling questions concerning ethics and dialogue – which illuminates and brings into sharper focus themes that are often missed because of their oblique, sometimes illusive (though persistent and promising) treatment in Adorno's work. Thus illuminated, Adorno appears to raise the question of whether Habermas's self-proclaimed movement beyond him

19

is not more adequately to be characterized as "one step forward, two steps back."

I begin by summarizing Habermas's account of Adorno concerning the question of normative foundations, and then sketch the central contours of Habermas's effort to move beyond problems he perceives in Adorno by developing discourse ethics. In the next half of the essay I develop a dialogical ethics of nonidentity that runs throughout Adorno's work and criticize Habermas's position from this vantage point.

I. HABERMAS'S CRITIQUE OF ADORNO

While the tradition of ideology critique stemming from Marx differentiates between knowledge and power, and undermines false claims to the former by showing them to be sustained in fact only by the latter, according to Habermas,[2] Adorno and Horkheimer undermine even the privileged position of ideology critique by turning the suspicion of the power-drenched bankruptcy of truth back upon critique itself in a totalizing manner, seemingly undermining all constructive outcomes. However, in contrast to Nietzsche and twentieth-century Nietzscheans who develop totalizing critiques of reason and then attempt in various ways to deny, skirt, or slip out of the "performative contradiction" involved in continuing to make validity claims while claiming to undermine all legitimate conditions of possibility for making such claims, Adorno elaborates a totalizing critique that stands and thinks resolutely in the face of this contradiction. "*Negative Dialectics* reads like a continuing explanation of why we have to circle about within this *performative contradiction* and indeed even remain there."[3] Without hope in the enlightenment that Adorno is nevertheless unwilling to surrender, he permits reason to "shrivel" to a mimetic impulse that must, but cannot, be recovered. "In the mimetic powers the promise of reconciliation is sublated. For Adorno that then leads to *Negative Dialectics* – in other words to Nowhere."[4] Without rational normative foundations critique becomes a vicious circle, ad hoc, self-defeating.

"How," he wonders in a question that is at once interesting and scolding, "can these two men of the Enlightenment . . . be so unappreciative of the rational content of cultural modernity that all they perceive everywhere is a binding of reason and domination?"[5] In his view, it is because even as unyielding critics of subjectivity as "self-preservation gone wild," they remained trapped within the modern paradigm of subjectivity and were thus condemned to its aporias. Insofar as this framework holds sway, the "two attitudes of the mind" are limited to "representation and action." Our representations are fundamentally tied to the possibility of instrumental efficacy, which in turn requires this knowledge. Even critical theory remains within this violent and oblivious structure, and hence it cannot articulate any notion of reconciliation that might guide its criticism, for this would require an impossible access to something beyond instrumental reason. Yet precisely the reconciliation that is inconceivable from the perspective of an out of balance instrumental subjectivism is also exaggerated and demanded by the out-of-balance Nietzschean aesthetic subjectivism by which Adorno and Horkheimer "let themselves be inspired."[6] This aestheticism simply overwhelms normative questions with a "longing for an unspoiled inward presence," a yearning for the transitory and constrained, through which *all* practices necessarily appear as subjugative.[7] At once permanently revoked and radically invoked, reconciliation, and Adorno's normative impulse more generally, must remain far beyond the realm of discursive thought in a (philosophically useless) presupposed "original relation of spirit and nature [that] is secretly conceived in such a way that . . . truth is connected with . . . universal reconciliation – where reconciliation includes the interaction of human beings with nature, with animals, plants, and minerals"[8] – in short, "the utopia of a long since lost, uncoerced and intuitive knowledge belonging to a primal past."[9]

In spite of the utterly flawed character of this project, Adorno appears as a *relatively* good philosopher when compared to the other post-Nietzscheans dealt with in *The Philosophical Discourse of Modernity*, and Habermas even hints at a debt owed to Adorno. For the utter integrity of Adorno's thought leads him to remain steadfast within – and develop to an agonizing degree – the contradictions spawned by epistemological, normative, and aesthetic monological subjectivism. In so doing, Adorno makes visible problems that lesser philosophers conceal, and thereby "furnishes us with reasons for a *change in paradigm* within social theory."[10] Indeed, in response to Adorno's elusive passage about how "the reconciled state . . . would find its happiness in the fact that the alien remained distinct and remote within the preserved proximity, beyond being either heterogeneous or one's own," Habermas writes:

Whoever meditates on this assertion will become aware that the condition described, although never real, is still most intimate and familiar to us. It has the structure of a life together in communication that is free from coercion. We necessarily anticipate such a reality . . . each time we want to speak what is true. The idea of truth, already implicit in the first sentence spoken, can be shaped only on the model of the idealized agreement aimed for in communication free from domination.[11]

In short, Adorno clarifies the insurmountable difficulties of subjectivism and unwittingly gestures in directions that "whoever meditates will become aware" lead toward Habermas.

II. HABERMASIAN COMMUNICATIVE ETHICS

The theory of communicative rationality and discourse ethics is an "unfinished project" that has developed increasing complexity and undergone subtle shifts and revisions. In this section I strive only to sketch the version endorsed in his recent writings, focusing on those themes that best illuminate his differences from Adorno.[12]

To comprehend discourse ethics, we must begin by analyzing Habermas's understanding of everyday "normal" communicative action, for discourse, or "argumentative speech," is but "a special case – in fact, a privileged derivative – of action oriented toward reaching understanding," and only by conceiving of the former in terms of the latter "can we understand the true thrust of discourse ethics."[13] Normal communicative practice (drawing upon Meade, Austin, Searle), is fundamentally structured around the imperatives of a species dependent upon linguistically coordinated actions. Concisely: "Under the pressure for decisions [a frequently used phrase] proper to the communicative practice of everyday life, participants are dependent upon agreements that coordinate their actions."[14] Normal speech acts facilitate our *"carrying on the world's business – describing, urging, contracting, etc. – "*[15] insofar as they strive to reach agreements concerning the objective and normative worlds that can stand up to the ongoing tests posed by the ever-present idealizing supposition of a consensus sustainable through "open criticism on the basis of validity claims."[16] Through the "constraints" of these context-transcending idealizations, everyday communication can develop a sense of legitimacy in which an "illocutionary binding force" provides "a mechanism for coordinating action."[17] It is this character of communication, Habermas claims, that allows us to transcend strategic action and the fateful world of power, and act according to the "unforced force" of obligations based upon mutual understanding.

In short, the "pressure to decide" in everyday communicatively coordinated action engenders "constraints" within which participants must strive toward an idealized consensus that facilitates such action. These pressure-engendered idealizations manifest themselves as a "concern to give one's contribution an informative shape, to say what is relevant, to be straightfoward and to avoid obscure, ambiguous, and prolix utterances," and they structurally determine the character of everyday communication such that learning processes with independent logics can develop that allow us increasingly to master the world's difficulties.[18]

However, not all speech takes place in this everyday manner. The pressures of everyday communication can be dropped in a way that, far from releasing us from normal idealizing suppositions (as in poetic speech), allows them to come into their own and gain fullest sway over our speech acts. When the pressure to act is "minimized" or "relieved," the hypothetical attitude of argumentative speech or "discourse" can emerge in which validity claims can be tested solely in light of the idealizing assumptions of an achievable pure consensus.[19] What Habermas implies here is that the very pressures that initially engender idealizing presuppositions also frequently work to undermine or pollute their operation, insofar as temporal pressures for action truncate processes of communication and thereby allow contingent interests and powers to skew agreements. This means that while the *legitimacy* and *unavoidability* of subjecting one's serious speech to the guidance of consensual suppositions stems from the rootedness of communication in pressure-laden everyday social action, the *fullest sway* and clearest appearance of these suppositions requires the rescindment of precisely those pressures. Thus, "discourse" is the medium in which the ethical aspects of our idealizing suppositions are most transparent and easily reflected upon, while the "true thrust" of discourse ethics can only be grasped – in terms of its depth and ubiquity – when it is not forgotten that "argumentation is a reflective form of communicative action and the structures of action oriented toward reaching an understanding always already presuppose those very relationships of reciprocity and mutual recognition around which *all* moral ideals revolve in everyday life no less than in philosophical ethics."[20]

The idealizing suppositions discussed throughout Habermas's work lead, in his view, to the principle of discourse ethics which states: "Only those norms are valid that meet (or could meet) with the approval of all affected in their capacity *as participants in a practical discourse.*" This principle in turn presupposes that it is possible to justify a norm, and this possibility rests on the principle of universalization, which is a rule of argumentation requiring that: "All affected can accept the consequences and the side effects its *general* observance can be anticipated to have for the satisfaction of *everyone's* interests (and these consequences are preferred to those of known alternative possibilities for regulation)." Both of these principles are meant to guide participants (all on equal footing) in argumentation, "with the aim of restoring a consensus that has been disrupted."[21] They are not arbitrary rules, in Habermas's view, but rather rules we cannot deny without committing performative contradictions. Nevertheless, he acknowledges that his efforts explicitly to reconstruct this pretheoretical knowledge have an ineliminable hypothetical and fallible quality.

The idea of "restoring a disrupted consensus" is one that occurs repeatedly in Habermas's work, and it deserves further elaboration here insofar as it indicates the status that the discordance among particulars and that between particulars and various claims to universality acquires in light of consensual universalistic idealizing suppositions. Drawing upon early Hegel, Habermas objects to Kant's understanding that such discordance is due to the absence – this side of infinity – of any preestablished harmony between bodily impulses, desires, pleasures, and experiences on the one hand, and moral universality on the other. Rejecting the idea of fundamental discrepancies, Habermas argues that this alienation stems from a "dirempted totality" in which "one part isolates itself and hence also alienates all other parts from itself and their common life" of symmetry and reciprocity. It is this which "first *generates* the subject–object relationship . . . introduced . . . into relationships that by nature follow the structure of mutual understanding among subjects."[22] This latter idea is crucial, for if discordance is the result of dirempted relations that "by nature follow the structure of mutual understanding," then the problem has nothing to do with an excess of rationality, but simply a deficit. Contra-Adorno and others who "let themselves be inspired by Nietzsche," reason is perceived here as devoid of any essentially tragic, oblivious, violent moment. Hence, when the repression of "unconstrained communication and the reciprocal gratification of needs" gives rise to a "causality of fate" operating through "split-off symbols and reified grammatical relations,"[23] the path beyond this alienation emerges only when hardened opposites resume their efforts at mutual understanding based on rational consensus. In short, agonism is a privative "fallen" condition in light of communicative suppositions, one that calls for the rehabilitating effects of consensual striving.

The imperative consensuality and formalistic universalizing impulses of Habermas's communicative rationality have disturbed many who are animated by concerns about nonidentity, difference, otherness, the dangers of homogenizing normalization, and so forth. The fear is that real differences would wither in the process of this insistent striving toward rational agreement that is the supposed telos of our communication. Habermas has always viewed this fear as misguided: "Nothing makes me more nervous than the imputation . . . [that] the theory of communicative action . . . proposes, or at least suggests, a rationalistic utopian society. I do not regard the fully transparent society as an ideal. . . ."[24]

While he has reiterated this claim on numerous occasions, one of his strongest defenses lies in the essays in *Postmetaphysical Thinking* that elaborate the insight that "repulsion towards the One and veneration of difference and the Other obscures the dialectical connection between them."[25] This connection receives important development in his appropriation of Meade's work on speaker and hearer perspectives. In the idealizing supposition of a consensus open to criticism, the possibility of diverse voices on a given issue is not repressed, but rather the very condition of possibility for the legitimacy of the agreement. "The intersubjectivity of linguistically achieved understanding is by nature porous, and linguistically attained consensus does not eradicate from the accord the differences in speaker perspectives but rather presupposes them as ineliminable."[26] Under the constraint of the pragmatic idealizations of communicative striving toward truth, the "I" is bound to maintain an openness toward the possible criticisms of everyone of the "others" in the unlimited communication community. Hence in the insistent consensual demands, Habermas sees not only an impulse toward truth as unity, but also the requirements of an ineliminable openness to the infinite nonidentical "thous" with whom one coexists. This recognition is key to the distance Habermas maintains from the monologicism of Rawls. Analogously, just as the differences of others are presupposed even as they are drawn toward unity, the ego is individuated in the process of making claims it deems worthy of consensus. For as the "I" submits to the idealizing constraints of universal discourse, it "projects the context of interaction" in which the addressees recognize it as an "irreplaceable and unique" alter ego – it returns to itself as a differentiated "me" through the others in the postconventional context of a community operating under the "idealizing supposition of a universal form of life."[27]

These different speaker perspectives infuse intersubjective accord with a "porosity" that is more than hypothetical, for in spite of idealizing suppositions of identical ascriptions of meaning and agreement, the "shadow of difference is cast" by "the fact that the intentions of speakers diverge again and again from the standard meanings."[28] This point is bolstered by his reflections on the effects of the movement toward greater universalism, the most important of which he summarizes in the following: "The transitory unity that is generated in the porous and refracted intersubjectivity of a linguistically meditated consensus not only supports but furthers and accelerates the pluralization of forms of life and the individualization of lifestyles. More discourse means more contradiction and difference. The more abstract the agreements become, the more diverse the disagreements with which we can *nonviolently* live."[29]

Of course, universality and difference are utterly entwined for Adorno too, who, like Habermas, insists on holding on to each as internally necessary for the existence of the other. Yet the relative absence of agony and paradox in the connection Habermas describes between universality and difference, the lack of raw tensions – even wounds – in the "profane rescue of the nonidentical" which he thinks he accomplishes through communicative rationality and ethics, the analytical calm – all this is in such contrast with the agitated aporetical compositions of Adorno. And so we must delve now into the tumultuous texts of the latter and attempt to discern whether the tumult is due to an erroneous paradigm now surpassed or, rather, whether it is the essence of a wisdom not so much salvaged as it is buried in Habermas's "turn" toward "communication."

III. ADORNO: NEGATIVE DIALECTICS AS DIALOGICAL ETHICS[30]

The world that surrounds and includes us is, Adorno claims, irreducibly nonidentical, which is to say always more and less than we think, persistently exceeding our grasp. "The name of dialectics says no more, to begin with, than that objects do not go into their concepts without leaving a remainder. . . . Dialectics is the consistent sense of nonidentity."[31] This observation leads Adorno repeatedly to draw attention to the violent, eclipsing, arbitrary aspect of concepts *as such*. These observations animate negative dialectics: "My thought is driven to [a "sense of nonidentity"] by its own inevitable insufficiency, by my guilt of what I am thinking."[32]

Questions about the status and philosophical underpinnings of such thoughts immediately spring forth, and perhaps no one has critically probed this terrain more provocatively than Albrecht Wellmer.[33] Since Adorno's possible response to Wellmer's Wittgensteinian/Habermasian critique is vital to our effort to clarify and appreciate Adorno's ethical alternative, I introduce Adorno's position through this lens.

Wellmer's "metacritique" hinges upon two key insights: First, Adorno's description of the "rigidity" and fixed monotonous generality of concepts, which is central to his "totalizing" critique of the violence of concepts as such, remains tied to the "rationalistic fiction" from which it seeks to distance itself. In contrast to this position, Wittgenstein illustrates that "words can be used in many and various ways," and their character – far from being closed, world-clubbing universals – is better evoked in "the image of family resemblance, and also, that of the rope that consists of a multiplicity of fibres . . . this multiplicity of ways of using a word reflects the openness of linguistic meanings."[34] As multiplicitous, flexible, and capable of productive and open-ended extension, language *as such* can hardly be described as violent. Rather only, *particular uses* of concepts can be thus depicted – "specific disturbances, blockages, or limitations of communication,"[35] that stand out against the intralinguistic normative backdrop of unimpeded communicative practice. Second, accompanying Adorno's "rationalist fiction," is a "residue of naivety" through which Adorno tacitly adopts a position *outside* the linguistic realm in order to condemn the latter's relation *as such* to the extralinguistic. For from no other perspective could Adorno assert the injustice of "the identifactory concept."[36]

Considering Wellmer's first point, it is wrong to attribute a "rationalist fiction" theory of concepts to Adorno, not simply because he repeatedly criticizes this view (which is tacitly engendered by all reifying practices), but moreover because he has always participated in and thought about – in the affirmative interstices of his work – the world of language from a very different perspective. The multiplicity, flexibility, and openness of concepts is integral to Adorno's central idea of the "constellation," of which he writes: "the model for this is the conduct of language. Language offers no mere system of signs for cognitive functions. Where it appears essentially as language, where it becomes a form of representation, it will not define its concepts. It lends objectivity to them by the relation into which it puts the concepts, centered about a thing. Language thus serves the intention of the concept to express completely what it means."[37] Concepts express different things depending upon the constellational context. Expressing the open character of language, radically different constellations, such as those Adorno sought to compose, change the categories within, and "when a category changes . . . a change occurs in the constellation of all categories, and thus again in each one."[38] Hence Adorno, by other paths, seems to have arrived at a view of language's being and possibility "as language" that is close – at least in terms of its multiple, flexible, open, and practiced possibilities – to that of the Wittgensteinian paradigm Wellmer claims Adorno lacks.

In spite of this, Adorno attributes to concepts and language as such an unshakable violent and unjust quality. Yet he does so not from a position outside language, but rather firmly rooted in the – ever-repeated – knowledge that "there is no peeping out,"[39] and that "I have no way but to break immanently." Returning to an earlier mentioned passage that dialectics is "the sense" (*Bewusstsein*, also, awareness or consciousness) of nonidentity, Adorno immediately adds that, dialectics "does not begin by taking a standpoint."[40] It does not originate from a stable extralinguistic ground, but from my "own inevitable insufficiency, my guilt of what I am thinking." Phenomenologically, the awareness of nonidentity emerges as a *personal* ("my") and *privative* sense, not as an impersonal positive consciousness. The privation is made conscious *immanently* as one endlessly discovers excesses, differences, depths, that one or others previously transgressed.[41] In this repetition one does not finally "peep out" and see affirmatively and transparently that language as such is violent. Rather one is driven to an *"awareness"* (expressing a sense that is more experiential, less completely determinate, positive, singular) of the transgressive aspect of our relationship to nonidentity. This awareness is certainly not deductive; and it is not exactly inductive, insofar as what is repeatedly sensed are *different* qualities whose only essential commonality is that they were all *absent* in previous thoughts. Rather it is a negative sensibility, an experientially rooted generalization that emerges as one – driven in part by repeated guilt – reflects upon one's connection to that which appears again and again as a more-having-been-taken-for-less.

Certainly the "more" always appears within the linguistic realm: "What would lie beyond makes its appearance only in the materials and categories within."[42] Yet this circumstance need not confine us to an understanding of identity and difference as something that concerns only the linguistic. Instead, we can, through our experiences of and reflections upon the perpetual discovery of the limits of every concept and constellation of concepts, become aware of an extralinguistic surplus that is endlessly eclipsed and transgressed by our words, even as no particular eclipse is positively beyond our limits to rescind. In this general sense, that which lies beyond and appears obliquely and privatively "within," is the existence of a "more" that is always partly damaged by linguistic thought, while no specific damage is immutable. The importance of the *oblique* and *privative* character of this knowledge is indicated in Adorno's defense of relativism (of which he was otherwise very critical) against critics who accuse it of assuming "one absolute, its own validity." These critics "confuse the general denial of a principle with the denial's own elevation to affirmative rank, regardless of the specific difference in positional value of both."[43] Something similar could be said of Wellmer vis-à-vis Adorno: He confuses the latter's position rooted in a general denial of pure identity and harmony with an affirmative position rooted in a positive absolute view from without.

For Adorno, the linguistic realm is entwined with and permeated by a nonidentical extralinguistic existence that is "always already" and "not yet." The nonidentical is "always already" because our linguistic consciousness emerges from and is colored by a dense and specific corporeality with multiplicitous material relations with the world. "The somatic moment as the not purely cognitive part of cognition is irreducible – Physicality emerges . . . as the core of that cognition," displacing the dream of a conscious or intersubjective constitution of the body.[44] The nonidentical is "not yet" insofar as linguistic thoughts "point to entities" which they have not posited, and whose fundamental nonidentity cannot "be abolished by any further thought process."[45] As conceptual thought moves toward the world it seeks better to interpret that which eludes it.

Now, our entwinement with nonidentity is of great significance for Adorno. For (in contrast with Habermas's appropriation of early Hegel's critique of Kant) it implies that the discrepancy between particular and general – between perceptions, inclinations, pleasures, desires, on the one hand, and more general socially and personally imposed conceptual and practical orders on the other – is not due *simply* to the diremption of a totality from which reason has separated itself, but is moreover an *ineliminable characteristic* for our inscription in this world. While many specific discrepancies, blindnesses, and transgressions arise *from* the process Habermas describes – and no specifically identifiable violence is absolutely immutable, on Adorno's reading, our relations appear to be characterized as well by an elemental nonidentity between general and particular, that we cannot escape in toto. New blindnesses and violences will accompany our best efforts to remedy those that now appear to us. Somewhat paradoxically, this insight is for Adorno more a source of hope than despair. For to become "aware" of this tragic finitude is to begin to address a hubris (institutional as well as personal) that otherwise madly proliferates a blindness and violence that enslaves and devitalizes the surrounding world as well as the self in a parodic reciprocity. It is this awareness that unendingly solicits and is vital to the enlightenment that "accommodates reflection on its recidivist element," the enlightenment from which "social freedom is inseparable," "a positive notion of enlightenment," announced in *Dialectic of Enlightenment*.[46] It is because "the force of consciousness extends to the delusion of consciousness"[47] – both in terms of specific delusions and in terms of thought's general "awareness" of its ineliminable delusive aspect – that negative dialectics can "serve the end of reconcilement . . . dismantle the coercive logical character of its own course"[48] and "change this direction of conceptuality, to give it a turn towards nonidentity."[49]

The dissipation of the blindness and violence that crosses back and forth between people – as well as the possibility of a greater degree of insight, freedom, and the wealth that stems from experiencing and engaging others in their subtlety and specificity – hinges upon committing oneself with a dialogical generosity to the reception of and engagement with others and otherness.[50] Yet this dialogical ethical activity, negative dialectics as a "morality of thinking,"[51] is not governed by the singular imperative to strive toward consensus, nor does it aim single-mindedly at healing a dirempted totality. Rather, an awareness of the nonidentical extralinguistic moment that permeates linguistic intersubjectivity draws Adorno toward an understanding of dialogue as agonistically guided by contrary solicitations: We can best fashion our voices and open our ears in the tension-laden constellation of forces pulling us at once in the direction of consensuality and in the direction of dissent. In fact, it is the lively tension between these two pulls – not either alone – that constitutes the dialogical life of enlightenment as an unending effort at achieving – in both thought and action – a nonidentical reciprocity.

In spite of the problems regarding nonidentity that are engendered by the notion of "system," nevertheless its accompanying themes of "unity and unanimity are at the same time an oblique projection of pacified, no longer antagonistic conditions."[52] Far from simply rejecting the idea of and impulse toward unanimity, Adorno cultivates a consensual moment as one important point of illumination and gravity in the ethical constellation woven by his texts – a point that draws us toward criticism of oblivious hostile relations of reciprocal enslavement. Hence this critic of identity repeatedly draws attention to the utopian aspect of identification, which, in approaching and seeking to mark the object, also seeks "to be marked by the object. Nonidentity is the secret *telos* of identification."[53] He solicits us to venture in directions that might decrease violence by drawing upon the nonsubjugative impulse of identification that is evoked when we speak "not of identifying an object, but of identifying with people and things."[54] Beyond both homogenization and antagonism, this sort of identity would be "a togetherness of diversity" – a difference-embracing consensuality that we can surrender in our relations with ourselves and others only at great cost to all.[55]

Yet consensuality is simultaneously an ideal that is dangerous and engenders its own blindness and violence, for every subject is also an object and "objects do not go into their concepts without reminder."[56] Whatever the terms of our agreements, no matter how ideal, aspects of the self and others are eclipsed. When elevated to the rank of a sovereign regulative principle, the ideal of striving toward unanimity understood as embracing a togetherness of diversity, tends toward forgetfulness of this element of blindness and transgression that accompanies the finitude of subjectivity and intersubjectivity. It conceals the impossibility of its own completely nonviolent realization, the costs of unification. It hides an awareness that for humans, resistance, transgression, and agonism are fundamentally vital ideals that are as deserving of our fidelity as those ideals that pull us together, lest our somnambulism is to begin again to proliferate violence. It submerges the awareness that there are few positive accords that rise completely beyond concealments and exclusions that demand our dissenting explorations: That for beings of finitude, the ideal of dissent is no more transitory or secondary than that of consensuality, that the cultivation of thoughtful dissent in our voices and characters is as important for the existence of dialogical relationships in which we might thrive as is the ideal of agreement.

It is for those reasons that Adorno's texts so resolutely develop and inhabit the *tension* between the best moments of identity's striving toward peaceful differential unity on the one hand, and the ineliminably transgressive aspect of our thought and lives which engenders the ideal of relentless negation, on the other. Juxtaposed with the former yearning, Adorno harangues us endlessly to recall "the untruth of identity"; to remember that "life purely as a fact will strangle other life";[57] to search ever anew for the specific fissures in every order; to keep in mind that even for art "harmony is unattainable, given the strict criteria of what harmony is supposed to be";[58] to strive to look the unavoidable moment of tragic violence of one's own voice, art, praxis in the face and "not try to erase the fractures left by the process of integration, preserving instead in the . . . whole the traces of those elements which resisted integration";[59] to resist the singular imperative of unity and consensuality even as one seeks to position one's voice and ears in audible proximity to this demand.

Life that lives, dialogical intelligence, and the highest degree of freedom and well-being we can develop emerge only as we struggle to keep those very different but equally vital pulls in mind. Powerfully soliciting us to inhabit a paradox we tend to eclipse, both points are evoked in a radical manner meant to shock us out of our dazed complacency. Yet even as Adorno illuminates the extremes, he does not view the latter as positivities that are only externally related. Rather, like many oppositions he elaborates, both "keep faith with their own substance through their opposites,"[60] and they "are linked by criticizing one another, not by compromising."[61] Through reciprocal critique each insight "keeps its substance" insofar as its antithesis helps illuminate and disempower the blindness that obscures its moment of insight and undermines its efficacy for the practice of freedom. In this process, each pull is transfigured and this transfiguration is elaborated in its own right. Thus, in agonistic juxtaposition with the voice of reconciliation, the insight into the ineliminably transgressive dimension of thought and existence rises beyond a potentially hopeless despair or even a mindless participation in the inevitable, to solicit the deployment of thought's resistant transgressive relation to the world against oblivion and violence itself. "Accompanying irreconcilable thoughts is the hope for reconcilement"[62] Similarly, the mythical eclipsing aspect of the reconciling dimension of our dialogical relation with the world is transfigured in its proximity with its opposite in the direction of a *resolutely critical transgressive* insistence that total reconciliation is always transcendent and not yet. Juxtaposed with its other, "the idea of reconcilement forbids the positive positing of reconcilement as a concept."[63] Just as the sense of the transgressive moment is drawn toward realization of the hope for peace, the reconciling moment finds its sense as a permanent agitation resisting the ever-present subjugations. This insight is poignantly evoked in *Aesthetic Theory:* "Dissonance is the truth about harmony."[64]

Significantly, Adorno's "morality of thinking" (conveyed in the form of an ethically solicitous agonistic constellation), is defensible against the charge of "performative contradiction" that Habermas levels against those who depart from "communicative ethics." For Adorno does not *deny* the crucial role of the ideal of consensuality and reconcilement in dialogue, but rather situates it agonistically in juxtaposition with the competing pull of dissent. Both points constitute necessary ideals in order to animate the most promising dialogical relations. Adorno would not so much reject Habermas's insight on consensuality, as he would convict it of eclipsing additional insights, without which it is insufficient for soliciting what is highest in humans – namely a more receptive dialogical activity. For Adorno, the drive toward consensus extends to discover the illusive moment of consensuality itself, and must make space for the drive toward dissent in order to remain closest to its own substance. Adorno calls us to this paradox not in order to despair, nor magically to invoke a "mindfulness of nature,"[65] but to situate us in a position where a patient negative dialectical labor might illuminate dangers and possibilities for freedom.[66]

From Adorno's perspective, the hegemony of consensual presuppositions in Habermas's work, along with its diminution of the problems and paradoxes posed by extralinguistic nonidentity,[67] represents more than the idiosyncracies of a single theorist. Rather it manifests a sense of communication as it so often functions in modern society (in lifeworld as well as system) and expresses a significant spirit of the age of which Adorno was relentlessly critical.

His attacks are sometimes delivered with a rhetorically exaggerated edge aimed at disrupting a complacent acceptance of the centrality and dignity of "communication": "Without exception, what is called communication nowadays is but the noise that drowns out the silence of the spellbound."[68] While on a quick reading this is easily dismissable by a Habermasian, it contains something important that calls for further exploration. For it is a critique of "communication" in the name of communication. It is a critique of "communication" on the basis of the role it plays in concealing this particular silence – this lack of communication. And it is clear that, for Adorno, "communication" not only *conceals* the communicationless "silence," but plays an important role in *engendering* it as well.

"Communication" hampers dialogue and engenders spellbound silence, insofar as "what is called [phrase repeated] 'communication' today is the adaptation of spirit to useful aims and, worse, to commodity fetishism."[69] One might want to confine the legitimacy of this claim to the realm of systemic steering media, but Adorno clearly thinks it has broader significance. As "communication" is adapted to utility and instrumentality – *and as our understanding of what "communication" is and ought to be similarly adapts –* the role of consensuality is magnified to the point of exclusive sovereignty. For the spirit of utility, broadly construed, demands that consensus become the primary objective in order to coordinate social action. This pressurized spirit insists that our voices and ears be subjected perpetually to those constraints. In order for communication to engender useful coordination, the moment of idealized identical ascriptions of meaning and consensuality must be overemphasized – in short, the dimension of exchangeability in dialogue must be fetishized. Adorno is clear that he does not want simply and completely to reject the idea of exchangeability, but to situate it in an agonistic constellation with other insights that transfigure its sense (n.d., pp. 146–48). Outside of this constellation the insistence upon consensual identity becomes a normalizing force, leading to a "communication" in which "the straight line is now regarded as the shortest distance between two people, as if they were points. Just as nowadays house walls are cast in one piece, so the mortar between people is replaced by the pressure holding them together. Anything different is simply no longer understood."[70] This pressure holding us together for useful coordination demands that our statements (and those we accept) be direct, defined, totally reproducible, without hesitations and ambiguities: It demands the silencing, the cessation, of so much communication.

One doesn't have to stretch far to see here a critique (even if sometimes exaggerated) of Habermas that has substantial force. For Habermas's understanding of communication is rooted fundamentally in its role in coordinating action through agreements deemed legitimate. The pressure for decision in the context of social action generates constraints to strive toward consensus: a "concern to give one's contribution an informative shape, to say what is relevant, to be straightforward and to avoid obscure, ambiguous, and prolix utterances."[71] His understanding of discourse ethics is rooted in this situation.

Of course, Habermas has in mind *criticizable* validity claims, but the question is really whether there is sufficient space within these pressures and constraints – and moreover whether the essential vitality of the critical agonistic moment is sufficiently illuminated and solicited in his work – for the dimension of criticism to flourish there in a way adequate to beings whose dialogues are so thoroughly permeated with ineliminable nonidentity. Habermas is certainly correct to gesture, in his recent work, toward the entwinement of identity and difference, but it is doubtful that he depicts sufficiently the character of this entwinement. In light of Adorno's thoughts, it is not enough to gesture toward a space for the possibility of difference within abstract agreement, nor say that as a "fact" meanings will diverge from our idealizing suppositions, nor simply to assert that "more discourse means more difference." For whether these points are true depends largely upon the character, direction, and textures of communication, which are in turn influenced by the way we understand what we are and ought to be doing when we speak with, listen to, and engage one another. Adorno's claim is that the capacity to speak of and hear differences is one that requires far more solicitation and nurturing, both of which ought to be lodged in our very interpretations of dialogue. While he certainly does not deny the importance of linguistically mediated actions and the role of communication in social coordination, Adorno questions whether we ought to take communication directly rooted in the imperatives of social coordination as emblematic of "communication *as such*" and the ethical situation, or rather, whether we ought not view this as a privative – or at least only one – mode when compared to the more receptive, farther reaching agonistic dialogical activity that is not only possible, but necessary, to resist the dangerous tendencies of communication harnessed primarily to the "spirit of utility." The ethical-political question is whether this farther-reaching dialogue ought not be given far greater reign to impinge upon, contest, guide, and restrain the "communication" that is more singularly and directly tied to action-coordinating imperatives. Here we can imagine another boundary conflict in addition to that between system and lifeworld provocatively described by Habermas.

A Habermasian might question whether Adorno's focus on otherness has much normative substance. Aren't there many kinds of otherness – from Hitler to insane/brilliant artists who pace the night, cut off their ears, and paint with a depth that radically transfigures our perception? Can Adorno suggest ways of discriminating here that might ethically inform – and perhaps even guide – our responsibility to act in a world with radically discrepant manifestations of and possibilities for otherness? Or is he at best an important voice calling us to attend to the nonidentity truncated by social orders, but ultimately in need of an ethical position that must be generated primarily in the domain of social coordination? This would seem to be the position of Stephen White, who articulates a sympathy with those who, like Adorno, illuminate a "responsibility to otherness" that he would like to hold in tension with the Habermasian "responsibility to act" that he persistently – but not thoroughly – favors.[72]

In response to such an interpretation, two points are crucial to note. First, Adorno's ethics is not most fundamentally a simple and unmediated "responsibility to otherness," but a "responsibility to proliferate respectful agonist dialogical relations within which a responsibility to otherness can flourish." This articulation delineates the centrality of the performative reciprocal dialogical conditions of possibility for a responsibility to otherness, and Adorno makes ethical judgments of specific others throughout his work regarding their degrees of compatibility and incompatibility with these porous yet significantly directional performative preconditions. He most esteems those dimensions of otherness capable of receptively engaging the world and is most critical of those that appear to be thoroughly other-obliterative in their fundamental make-up (though he attempts to expose the scars of his own judgments through irony, paradox, and unpolished discord). Second, this ethics, as performative, is always already a "responsibility to act" in light of an ideal of nonidentical reciprocity. Though even in much more desirable circumstances the pressures of social coordination will accent the moment of consensuality in many communicative practices and institutions, Adorno's ethics calls us to permeate and loosen – where we cannot supplant – this accent at least in certain dimensions or during certain periods of time, in order that these practices may be informed by the processes and substantive insights of a more agonistic receptive dialogue. For the aim of production and government ought to be, finally, to encourage – make more possible and likely – social practices that pursue the contours of an ethics of receptive generosity. *This* dialogical coexistence is what is highest, though it must exist in tension with domains of action coordination that exaggerate consensuality in ways that both serve and jeopardize it. If we make pressurized communication the norm, we erode this tension and increase the consensual moment's already strong tendency to proliferate the concealment of a freer, richer, and higher, dialogue.

But does Adorno really embrace a notion of dialogue? Hopefully this essay begins to make such an interpretation plausible. I want briefly to address why Adorno – so very dialogical – is so persistently oblique in his development of this position, in order further to articulate his understanding of the textures of dialogical activity.

The dialogical bent of Adorno's thinking seems to be at once affirmed and negated by the following passages in *Negative Dialectics:* "If the thought really yielded to its object . . . the very objects would start talking under the lingering eye." He describes constellations as "interventions" through which objects might "come to speak."[73] These passages are dialogical insofar as they illuminate and solicit our efforts to make audible and hear other voices, to guide our voices and lives with this receptivity – implying both *receiving and being received by the other* – in mind. However – thinking now only of other humans – these passages perhaps appear, as undialogical insofar as they constitute the other not as another subject, but as an object; not an other with a voice of its own, but one that needs the self's intervention to "come to speak." In perceiving others thus, does not Adorno botch his effort to *receive* the other? And, shifting to a related question, doesn't a theory of dialogue miscarry in light of Adorno's frequent apparent dismissal of all concern for how one is *received by* others?

Regarding the first question, far from truncating dialogical receptivity, Adorno's frequent reference to the other as object, is part of an effort to infuse the relations between self and other, self and self, and other and other with an awareness of distances – that might loosen the constraints and decrease the pressures of utility-governed "communication" that suffocate receptive dialogue. In referring often to the other as an object, Adorno draws attention to the transgressive moment of our reception of others: to the fact that in spite of our efforts to be present to others, they remain significantly concealed. In spite of our best attempts to understand the other as a specific "you," our reception of others is always confusedly entwined with a process of objectification in which so much of the other disappears. Reference to the other as an object is intended to recall this moment of disappearance so that we might ever again renew our receptive efforts. At the same time it indicates the other's nonidentity with itself, the other's lack of sovereignty. In this sense, other-as-object calls us to efforts at receptivity that aim beyond the intentional expressions of the other, in an effort to give voice to that which the other's subjectivity silences. For Adorno, the activity of receptive respect for others requires that we negotiate the delicate paradoxes of a generosity that calls us at once to humility and audacious efforts to transfigure.

Regarding Adorno's apparent lack of concern for the other as recipient, here too, I think that his critics too often confuse Adorno's emphatic emphasis on the necessarily oblique and difficult character of this relation – in order for it to succeed – with a dismissal of the importance of the relation itself.[74] Adorno often calls us to "move away from any concern for the viewer,"[75] to "free [ourselves] of all concern for the sensibilities of the recipient."[76] This "turning away" from a pressurized intersubjectivity is in part an effort to open up distance, a space where an experience worth expressing to another might occur; a space that is discontinuous with the others' expectations. Yet this turning away is, though not without a moment of autonomy, agonistically connected with a – difficult and oblique – "turning toward" the others such that they might receive something beyond the confines of a schematizing conformism. This paradoxical entwinement is expressed repeatedly in *Aesthetic Theory*, when Adorno writes: "*The manner in which art communicates with the outside world is* . . . *also a lack of communication.*"[77] "Works of art . . . are not created with the recipient in mind, but *seek to confront the viewer* with artistic objectivity."[78] Similarly, "the *only way to get through to reified minds* . . . is to shock them into realizing the phoneyness of what pseudo-scientific terminology likes to call communication. By the same token art maintains its integrity by refusing to go along with communication."[79] By rejecting a notion of receptivity as constant, Adorno seeks to "communicate the uncommunicable," and thereby open the possibility of dialogue with a greater degree of nonidentity. Ultimately, art and philosophy must fetishize neither autonomy nor expression, but rather mediate their agonistic tensions in a manner exemplified by a work like Picasso's *Guernica*.

IV. CLOSING REFLECTIONS

Adorno calls us to a dialogical ethic that seeks to articulate a respect for others through an agonistic generous receptivity. Defying the constraints and pressures of a communication rooted in the hegemony of social coordination, he solicits our paradoxical efforts to engage the nonidentical. The dialogue that Adorno describes and solicits has a greater space and desire for the ambiguous, the prolix, the paradoxical, the oblique; and Adorno's participation in this dialogue often manifests these qualities. As a result, Adorno's reflections on *dialogue itself* are frequently oblique and paradoxical to the point of being unrecognizable to those – like Habermas – guided more exclusively by the constraints of straightforward consensual striving. My own elaboration of Adorno's thought in this essay – developed in a process of negotiating between pulls toward expressing the integrity of Adorno's thought, the desire to express it in a manner hopefully more intelligible (though still disturbing) to those closer to Habermasian terrain, as well as the insistences of my own sensibility and voice – aims to unsettle the comfortable narrative within which Habermasians situate Adorno, to cut short this mythical monologue and provoke a dialogue.

One could say that the ethic articulated and exemplified in Adorno's work[80] ultimately concerns the political in the following sense: Like art it "calls for externalization . . . [It] is practical in the sense that it defines the person who experiences it as a *zoon politicon* by forcing him to step outside himself."[81] As I see it everything boils down to the specific textures of this paradoxical effort to step outside and engage – as well as judge – others through and in light of this activity. Both Habermas and Adorno are pulled by a moment of ethical universalism which has this aim in mind. But such an accord is necessarily abstract. Finally, the substance and sense of each theorist's universalism is engendered and articulated in the way each narrates, solicits, and practices the activity of respecting others. In the difficult *activity* of stepping outside, Adorno seeks continually to root respect in, and return respect to, our awareness of our entwinement with nonidentity. Habermas, too, seeks to mutually articulate universalism and difference. More questionable, however, is whether his texts adequately illuminate and solicit the activity of and performative conditions of possibility for caring for the latter, or whether such activity and care is not eclipsed more than it should be by an overly and singularly insistent consensuality. If this rhetorical question has any merit, it might help explain the flaws in Habermas's paradigm which contribute to his poor communication with Adorno.

NOTES

1 Jürgen Habermas, "A Reply to My Critics," in *Habermas: Critical Debates*, ed. John B. Thompson and David Held (Cambridge, Mass.: MIT Press, 1982), p. 219.

2 Other theorists follow the contours of this critique quite closely; see, for example, Seyla Benhabib, *Critique, Norm, and Utopia: A Study of the Foundations of Critical Theory* (New York: Columbia University Press, 1986), Alex Honneth, "Communication and Reconciliation: Habermas's Critique of Adorno," *Telos* 39 (1979), Thomas McCarthy, *The Critical Theory of Jürgen Habermas* (Cambridge, Mass.: MIT Press, 1978), and Albrecht Wellmer, *The Persistence of Modernity: Essays on Aesthetics, Ethics, and Postmodernism* (Cambridge, Mass.: MIT Press, 1991), though Wellmer's critique deviates somewhat and is more subtle. There are resonances between Habermas's critique and Leszek Kolakowski's far more damning analysis in *Main Currents of Marxism*. Vol. III. *The Breakdown* (Oxford: Oxford University Press, 1970).

3 Jürgen Habermas, *The Philosophical Discourse of Modernity*, trans. Frederick Lawrence (Cambridge, Mass.: MIT Press, 1987), p. 119.

4 Jürgen Habermas, in *Autonomy and Solidarity: Interviews*, ed. Peter Dews (London: Verso, 1986), p. 90.

5 Habermas, *Philosophical Discourse of Modernity*, p. 121.

6 Ibid.

7 Ibid., p. 123.

8 Jürgen Habermas, *The Theory of Communicative Action*, Vol. I, *Reason and the Rationalization of Society*, trans. Thomas McCarthy (Boston: Beacon Press, 1984), p. 381.

9   Habermas, *Philosophical Discourse of Modernity*, p. 186. In this, the previous citation, and elsewhere, Habermas cites Herbert Schnädelbach, "Dialektic als Vernunftkritik," in *Adorno-Konferenz 1983*, ed. Ludwig Von Friedeburg and Jürgen Habermas (Frankfurt, 1983).

10 Habermas, *Theory of Communicative Action*, Vol. 1, p. 366.

11 Jürgen Habermas, *Philosophical-Political Profiles*, trans. Frederick G. Lawrence (Cambridge, Mass.: MIT Press, 1983), pp. 108–09. Theodor Adorno, *Negative Dialectics*, trans. E. B. Ashton (New York: Continuum, 1973), p. 191.

12 I discuss these and other themes in Habermas and Adorno in far greater detail in a book I am completing entitled *Critical Theory and the Question of Difference: Toward a Post-Secular Caritas*.

13 Jürgen Habermas, *Moral Consciousness and Communicative Action*, trans. Christian Lenhardt and Shierry Weber Nicholsen (Cambridge, Mass.: MIT Press, 1990), p. 130.

14 Habermas, *Philosophical Discourse of Modernity*, p. 198.

15 Ibid., p. 201, affirmatively quoting R. Ohmann.

16 Ibid., p. 199.

17 Ibid., p. 196.

18 Ibid., p. 204.

19 Habermas, *Moral Consciousness and Communicative Action*, pp. 158 and 187.

20 Ibid., p. 130.

21 Ibid., pp. 65–67.

22 Habermas, *Philosophical Discourse of Modernity*, p. 29.

23 Jürgen Habermas, *Knowledge and Human Interests*, trans. Jeremy Shapiro (Boston: Beacon, 1971), pp. 56–59.

24 Habermas, "A Reply to my Critics," p. 235.

25 Jürgen Habermas, *Postmetaphysical Thinking*, trans. W. M. Hohengarten (Cambridge, Mass.: MIT Press, 1992), p. 140.

26 Ibid., p. 48.

27 Ibid., pp. 186–87.

28 Ibid., pp. 47–48, my emphasis.

29 Ibid., p. 140.

30 Other efforts to draw out the ethical implications of Adorno's work include Robert Hullot-Kentor, "Back to Adorno," *Telos* 81 (1989): 5–29; Drucilla Cornell, "The Ethical Message of Negative Dialectics," *Social Concept* 4 (1987): 30–36; and Fred Dallmayr, *Twilight of Subjectivity: Contributions to a Post-Individualist Theory of Politics* (Amherst: University of Massachusetts Press, 1981) and *Between Freiburg and Frankfurt: Toward a Critical Ontology* (Amherst: University of Massachusetts Press, 1991). Although Cornell and Dallmayr insightfully explore

receptivity and difference in Adorno, their interpretations place less emphasis on the agonistic dimension of his work; and too, I think Dallmayr's reading may have to go further to address some of Richard Bernstein's questions concerning universality, in "Fred Dallmayr's Critique of Habermas," *Political Theory* 16, no. 4 (1988): 580–93.

31 Adorno, *Negative Dialectics*, p. 5.

32 Ibid.

33 Much of Wellmer's *The Persistence of Modernity: Essays on Aesthetics, Ethics, and Postmodernism*, trans. David Midgley (Cambridge, Mass.: MIT Press, 1991) addresses these and related issues. The most sustained discussion occurs in "The Dialectic of Modernism and Postmodernism: The Critique of Reason since Adorno," pp. 36–94.

34 Ibid., p. 71.

35 Ibid., p. 74.

36 Ibid., p. 73.

37 Adorno, *Negative Dialectics*, p. 162. Cf. Max Horkheimer and Theodor W. Adorno, *Dialectic of Enlightenment*, trans. John Cumming (New York: Seabury, 1972), p. 15, where it is claimed that through the dynamic entwinement of identity and nonidentity "language is transformed from tautology to language." Susan Buck-Morss probingly explores Adorno's transfiguring employment of concepts in *The Origin of Negative Dialectics: Theodor Adorno, Walter Benjamin and the Frankfurt Institute* (New York: Free Press, 1977), esp. pp. 57–62, as does Gillian Rose, *The Melancholy Science* (New York: Columbia University Press, 1978), ch. 2.

38 Ibid., p. 166.

39 Ibid., p. 140.

40 Ibid., p. 5. German: *Negative Dialektik* (Frankfurt: Suhrkamp, 1973), p. 15.

41 The essentially immanent, active, performative aspect of this awareness is one of the main reasons Adorno warns against making nonidentity just another ontology. Cf. *Negative Dialectics*, pt. 2.

42 Ibid., p. 140.

43 Ibid., pp. 35–36.

44 Ibid., pp. 193–94.

45 Ibid., pp. 135–36.

46 Horkheimer and Adorno, *Dialectic of Enlightenment*, pp. xiii and xvi.

47 Adorno, *Negative Dialectics*, p. 148.

48 Ibid., p. 6.

49 Ibid., p. 12.

50 My present focus is limited to elaborating an ethics of generous receptivity – Adorno's dialogical ethic – in terms of humans. I extend these

thoughts in the direction of an ecological ethic in "Ecotones and Ecological Ethics: Adorno and Lopez" in *In the Nature of Things*, ed. William Chaloupka and Jane Bennett (Minneapolis: University of Minnesota Press, 1993).

51 Theodor Adorno, *Minima Moralia*, trans. E. F. N. Jephcott (London: Verso, 1978), pp. 73–74.

52 Adorno, *Negative Dialectics*, p. 24.

53 Ibid., p. 149.

54 Ibid., p. 150.

55 Ibid., p. 151.

56 Ibid, p. 179. Cf. "Subject and Object," in *The Essential Frankfurt School Reader*, ed. Andrew Arato and Eike Gebhardt (New York: Continuum, 1985), pp. 502ff.

57 Ibid., p. 364.

58 Theodor Adorno, *Aesthetic Theory*, trans. Christian Lenhardt (London: Routledge and Kegan Paul, 1984), p. 161.

59 Ibid., p. 10.

60 Adorno, *Negative Dialectics*, p. 15.

61 Ibid., p. 61.

62 Ibid., p. 19.

63 Ibid., p. 145.

64 Adorno, *Aesthetic Theory*, p. 161.

65 Habermas, *The Philosophical Discourse of Modernity*, p. 119.

66 However, Adorno saw little actual political space for this knowledge to have much broad transformative impact.

67 I am thinking particularly of the discussions of external nature (ch. 2) and inner nature (ch. 10) in *Knowledge and Human Interests*. For Joel Whitebook's insightful analysis of some of the difficulties with these discussions, see "The Problem of Nature in Habermas," *Telos* 40 (1979) and "Reason and Happiness: Some Psychoanalytic Themes in Critical Theory," in *Habermas and Modernity*, ed. Richard Bernstein (Cambridge, Mass.: MIT Press, 1985). Habermas gestures toward but does not develop the role of the aesthetic dimension in engaging nonidentity in "Questions and Counterquestions" in Bernstein, *Habermas and Modernity*, p. 201. Stephen K. White's *The Recent Work of Jürgen Habermas: Reason, Justice and Modernity* (Cambridge: Cambridge University Press, 1988) develops passages such as these to fortify Habermas's ability to respond to postmodernists, yet this provocative effort fails to allow difference sufficiently into the heart of our understanding of intersubjectivity.

68 Adorno, *Negative Dialectics*, p. 348.

69 Adorno, *Aesthetic Theory*, p. 109.

70 Adorno, *Minima Moralia*, p. 41.

71 Habermas, *The Philosophical Discourse of Modernity*, p. 204.

72 In *Political Theory and Postmodernism* (Cambridge: Cambridge University Press, 1991). For an alternative reading of Foucault, see my "Communicative Action and Dialogical Ethics: Habermas and Foucault," *Polity* 25, no. 1 (1992). On Nietzsche and Derrida, see my "Storied Others and the Possibility of *Caritas:* Milbank and Neo-Nietzschean Ethics," *Modern Theology* 8, no. 4 (1992).

73 Adorno, *Negative Dialectics*, pp. 27 and 29.

74 An example of this misreading is Wellmer's "Truth, Semblance, Reconciliation: Adorno's Aesthetic Redemption of Modernity," in *The Persistence of Modernity*.

75 Adorno, *Aesthetic Theory*, p. 136.

76 Ibid., p. 281.

77 Ibid., p. 7, my emphasis.

78 Ibid., p. 374, my emphasis.

79 Ibid., p. 443, my emphasis.

80 Tragic as it is that Adorno died before writing his work on moral philosophy that was to complement *Negative Dialectics* and *Aesthetic Theory* (cf. Gretel Adorno and Rolf Tiedemann, "Editors' Epilogue" in *Aesthetic Theory*, p. 493), there is an ironic appropriateness about this fact, given Adorno's preference for oblique and performative treatments of ethical issues over direct declarative approaches.

81 Adorno, *Aesthetic Theory*, p. 345.

3 What's left of Marx?

The liberal interpretation is not wrong. It just does not see the beam in its own eye.

With the bankruptcy of state socialism, [welfare state liberalism] is the eye of the needle through which everything must pass.[1]

These passages, from Jürgen Habermas's "What Does Socialism Mean Today?," surely sound strange. Biblical allusions to blindness and to heaven? From one who promotes communicative rationality as the "completion of the modern project"? From one who explicitly rejects nostalgic, romantic, and utopian visions of socialism? Yet they provide clues that help explain Habermas's continued commitment to socialism. Socialism is not dead, nor will it rise again. In response to recent events, Habermas suggests a different, less dialectical, approach to resurrection. The possibilities of "actually existing socialism" are exhausted, but "socialism-as-critique" remains a source of hope.[2] It retains the "intuitions" and "impulses" of a humanity that makes its history with conscious will. For Habermas, socialism is to be sustained as a "discourse-in-exile." What's left of Marx in this is the tradition of Jewish mysticism.

Any attempt to separate Habermas's Marxism from the other strands of social theory – Weberian, Parsonian, social interactionist, and genetic structuralist – with which he interweaves it will oversimplify. Even to sort out his debt to Marxism, which he acknowledges in a variety of contexts, is a daunting task. To do so by claiming a common heritage in Jewish mysticism further complicates the situation. These remarks, then, should not be taken as a comprehensive interpretation of Habermas's Marxism. Instead, they are an effort to explain why, despite his criticisms of Marx's historical materialist method, including his analysis of capitalist society, Habermas remains a socialist.

I begin with Habermas's interpretation of Marx's theory of history, focusing on the relationship of crisis and critique. Then, I examine Marxist concepts – reification and alienation – which assist Habermas in his analysis of crisis potentials in late capitalism. Last, I assess unacknowledged influences of Habermas's lifeworld on his theory of communicative rationality. Consciously embracing socialism as a "discourse-in-exile," I conclude, also removes "the beam in Habermas's eye."

I. CRISIS AND CRITIQUE IN HISTORY

In an early work, Habermas argued that Marx's critique of capitalism presupposes the logic of Hegel's philosophy of history, which has its roots in Jewish and Protestant mysticism, specifically the Gnostic-inspired story of salvation.[3] As Habermas retells it, God created the world not by manifesting or externalizing Himself, but rather by going into exile within Himself, by emigrating into His own bottomless foundations, and becoming His Other. God's original self-abasement made it possible for Adam and Eve to disobey him, leading to their expulsion from Eden. The result was that humanity was left alone in history to redeem itself and, thereby, God. Human estrangement from God is extremely painful. Activities once performed joyously became desperate efforts to survive; basic needs for love and work often remained unfulfilled. However, only by learning to be human can people become God's partners in creation again. In a fascinating interpretation of alienation as exile, Dennis Fischman links the stories of Creation and Eden to another: the tower of Babel.[4] The men who constructed the tower hoped to avoid the difficult process of human growth and to make themselves gods instead. When God destroyed the tower, he completed the exile of humanity. By fragmenting their shared speech, he prevented them from finding common purposes.

Habermas argues that this story of self-exile (he excludes Babel from his account, a point to which I return) provides the basis for Hegel's understanding of world history as a crisis complex in which God actualizes, recognizes, and returns to Himself in man-as-spirit. In his critiques of Hegel and the Left Hegelians, Marx explicitly rejects theological and anthropological interpretations of history. However, his theory retains the same basic structure, and not only in his early philosophical writings, though the parallels may be clearest there. Habermas draws them as follows:

Just as that God, in a mythical act of unfathomable egosim, alienated Himself from His essence by withdrawing within Himself, so the "egoistic" relationship which is established together with private property is interpreted by Marx as the "encapsulation" within which the essential human forces are concentrated and estranged from the human beings themselves.[5]

This Hegelian-inspired dialectic of labor still operates in Marx's scientific critique of political economy, which traces the contradictions of capitalism to the relation between wage-labor and capital. Class conflict is made possible by the prior identification of labor as a commodity, that is, by the translation of a human power into an exchange value. In the labor theory of value, Marx reveals the connections between alienated labor and commodity fetishism. Again, Habermas makes the association:

Only with the appearance of the free wage laborer, who sells his labor power as his sole commodity, has the historical condition been established under which the labor process confronts man in its independence, as a process of exploitation, in such a manner that the production of use values seems to disappear entirely within a kind of self-movement, an automatism, of capital.[6]

According to Marx, political economists objectify the aspects of alienated labor in corresponding commodity fetishes. Regarding alienation from productive activity, the reality is that laborers sell their labor-power to capitalists who control whether or not and the conditions under which they work. The related commodity fetish is that all sorts of human labor have a quantitative equivalent form or exchange-value that obscures the qualitatively different social utility of various sorts of labor. Under capitalism, human beings are also alienated from their products. This is because workers produce and capitalists appropriate not as part of a collective effort, but as isolated, private, individuals. The corresponding commodity fetish is that, given the equality of all sorts of human labor, all products have a quantitative equivalent form or exchange-value equal to the labor-power required to produce them. The fetish obscures the qualitatively different social use-value of various commodities. Last, as this implies, people are alienated from one another and, hence, from their species-being. The reality here is that individuals interact only in exchange. The corresponding commodity fetish is that "the mutual relations of the producers, within which the social character of their labor affirms itself, take the form of a social relation between the products." This fetish obscures the social character of human labor.[7]

Under capitalism, then, workers are in exile, unable to claim their powers and to satisfy their needs, including the need to make sense of the world. Indeed, Fischman argues that capitalism itself is a society in exile, an inversion of human reality. Critique, in this context, refers to "a theory developed with the practical intention of overcoming the crisis."[8] When Marx demystifies commodity fetishes by revealing their origins in capitalist class relations, he does not mean to imply that political economists misrepresent reality. On the contrary, the appearances they portray are distortions because reality is itself distorted. By exposing these distortions, Marx fosters the class consciousness necessary for a socialist revolution. Socialism becomes a "politics of return," the reunion of humanity with itself. But it is not our reunion with God – and the distinction is important. If Hegel's crisis resolution parallels the Christian story of incarnation, then Marx's reaffirms a Jewish commitment to "hallow the world" even, perhaps especially, in the absence of God.

Although he dismisses Hegel's dialectic, Habermas finds the "possibility of a philosophy of history with practical intent" in Marxism. However, Marx fails adequately to situate his critique of political economy in its context, i.e., a crisis of capitalism. Instead of recognizing history as a "variable source of experience provided by the socially concrete life-world," Marx retains residues of "First Philosophy," that is, Hegel's logic of history.[9] These appear in three problematic assumptions: (1) that labor is the act of human self-creation; (2) that societies are totalities; (3) that history is progressive. In his reconstruction of historical materialism, Habermas challenges each in turn.

First, Habermas questions Marx's Hegelian-inspired concept of labor as human's self-creative activity. Through labor, people learn how to dominate the natural world and develop instrumental or technical knowledge. However, it is social interaction that is our distinctively human capacity. Interaction requires intersubjective recognition of roles and norms, or the social integration of internal nature. Habermas argues that individuals and, by analogy, societies undergo a process of moral-cognitive development from pretraditional through traditional to posttraditional consciousness. Current levels of learning are reflected in their basic structures and core values. According to Habermas, expansion of the productive forces cannot explain the development of intersubjective capacities. Interaction (or communicative action) follows its own evolutionary path. This means that class conflict no longer is the motive force in history. Societies are now the bearers of evolution and individuals are integrated into them. With his focus on production, Marx missed the potential for emancipation – and domination – in the sphere of interaction. He confused mastery of external nature with human freedom, and neglected social repression of internal nature.

This brings us to Habermas's second criticism of historical materialism. Societies are not totalities whose parts are even ultimately determined by the level of development of their productive forces. Habermas distinguishes between lifeworld and systems, each of which he further divides into private and public spheres. The lifeworld is the locus of moral-practical knowledge or relations of meaning shared in families and workplaces (private) and in political actions and opinions (public). It is coordinated through communicative action – that is, action oriented toward reaching self- and mutual-understanding. In contrast, political (states) and economic (markets) systems are coordinated through the steering media of money and power. As we will see, Habermas argues that Marx failed to anticipate both the stability of capitalism and the bankruptcy of socialism because he lacked these distinctions. They enable Habermas to distinguish the steering problems of economic and political systems from lifeworld problems of motivation and meaning, and to assess the different problem-solving capacities offered by systems media of money and power, and the lifeworld medium of communication. The differentiation of modern societies is, of course, a mixed blessing. It offers the potential for a legitimation crisis in late capitalism and for the iron cage of bureaucratic socialism.

Third, and implied earlier, Habermas argues that Marx confuses the dynamic with the logic of historical development. Societies do evolve, and Habermas regards the development of posttraditional identities manifest in universal principles of morality and justice as progress. However, these developments are not the unfolding of reason in history. As Habermas puts it, "Historicizing the knowledge of an essence . . . only replaces the teleology of Being with that of History. The secretly normative presuppositions of theories of history are naturalized in the form of evolutionary concepts of progress."[10] The result is to minimize the uncertainties of theory and practice, and thereby to encourage totalizing knowledge and vanguard politics – that is, "the conditions for an abuse, or even a total inversion of what was originally intended."[11] In contrast, Habermas maintains that moral-cognitive developments only create the logical space for new forms of social organization. The capacity of a society to adjust and to grow, which is established by its boundary conditions and learning capacities, determines when, indeed whether, fundamental changes occur. What those changes are, that is, the meaning of freedom, must be determined by the participants themselves. Habermas insists that "in a process of Enlightenment there are only participants."[12] It is the convergence of knowing and doing, the self-conscious creation of a socialist society, which ends human exile. The task of critical theory is limited to identifying the formal conditions which make emancipation possible.

According to Habermas, by conceptualizing humans as producers, societies as totalities, and history as progress, Marx reverts to a Hegelian-inspired theology and anthropology. Habermas identifies the salvation story as the vehicle for Marx's "false extrapolation" from a specific historical context to the structure of human history. Habermas reconstructs historical materialism, in part, to expose this "peculiar disproportion" between Marx's "practical inquiry" and his "philosophical self-understanding."[13] Of course, one can ask whether Habermas makes a similar move. Is he sufficiently reflective about the origins of his theory of communicative rationality in his lifeworld? Or, does Habermas tell another, admittedly less confident, version of the same story? I return to this issue after examining Marx's continued influence on Habermas's critique of late capitalism.

II. CRISIS POTENTIALS IN LATE CAPITALISM

The labor theory of value is the centerpiece of Marx's critique of capitalism, and a site of the unresolved tension between his Hegelian categories and historical materialism. That theory presents capitalist society as a fetishistic totality originating in living labor; that is, it translates human capacities into commodity form, class conflict into market relations. Although accurate for early capitalism, Habermas insists that empirical analyses cannot rely on value theory or a similar translation tool. His critique of late capitalism replaces Marx's "monism" with multiple interchanges between media-steered subsystems and the lifeworld. However, the real abstractions that value theory helps Marx identify – alienation and reification – persist. Habermas agrees that "any civilization that subjects itself to the imperatives of the accumulation of capital bears the seeds of its own destruction, because it . . . blinds itself to anything, however important, that cannot be expressed as a price."[14] Here lies the crisis potential of late capitalism – or, the beam in liberalism's eye.

Habermas suggests that these "[real abstractions] can be gotten at through an analysis that at once traces the rationalization of lifeworlds *and* the growth in complexity of media-steered subsystems, and that keeps the paradoxical nature of their interference in sight."[15] Unpacking this statement, examining the processes it identifies, illustrates how system imperatives thwart lifeworld potentials in late capitalism.

Since Habermas regards mutual understanding as the inherent telos of human speech, he argues that a rational society is coordinated to achieve this end. A lifeworld is correspondingly rationalized "to the extent that it permits interactions that are not guided by normatively ascribed agreement but – directly or indirectly – by communicatively achieved understanding."[16] Although this rationalization process is never complete, less rational lifeworlds do presuppose more. As Habermas puts it, "The more cultural traditions predecide which validity claims, when, where, for what, from whom, and to whom must be accepted, the less that participants themselves have the possibility of making explicit and examining the potential grounds on which their yes/no positions are based."[17]

Modern societies offer participants that possibility because they are decentered. They distinguish between three worlds and adopt distinct attitudes to each, that is, an instrumental-technical attitude to nature, a moral-pragmatic attitude to society and an aesthetic-expressive attitude to self. Since individuals are distinct from their objective and intersubjective worlds, they can be reflexive about them. Decentration allows them to deal "with the world of facts in a cognitively objectified manner and with the world of interpersonal relations in a legally and morally objectified manner."[18] In contrast, decentration counters attempts to objectify individuals' desires and feelings. Rational individuals interpret their needs "in the light of culturally established standards of value, but they also adopt a reflective attitude to the very value standards through which desires and feelings are interpreted."[19] In keeping with this, speakers use different criteria to evaluate claims in each of their worlds. They ask: Are certain statements about objective conditions true? Are certain actions right given social norms? Are certain expressions sincere for this individual? Communication is rational when they base their answers only upon "the peculiarly constraint-free force of the better argument."[20]

Habermas spells out the preconditions for rational communication in his theory of communicative competence. He derives them from the "performative aspects of speech which are presupposed by the ability to utter, not any particular speech-act, but speech acts as such" – or, what he calls, "universal pragmatics."[21] As the term suggests, speech-acts have a double structure: Speakers simultaneously say something (assert a proposition) and do something (establish a relationship). Habermas recognizes the importance of linguistic competence, that is, mastery of language-specific rules and words, in formulating understandable propositions. However, speakers' natural languages are always (re)presented through "dialogue-constitutive universals," such as verb forms (assertions, interrogatives, imperatives) and personal pronouns (I and You, We and They), and so forth. These reveal the intersubjective factors – reflexivity and reciprocity – that make mutual understanding possible. Competent speakers must be able to give reasons for their claims and be willing to grant others the same rights as themselves. According to Habermas, speakers demonstrate communicative competence through mastery of the ideal speech situation. He defines ideal speech as "intersubjective symmetry in the distribution of assertion and dispute, revelation and concealment, prescription and conformity among the partners of communication."[22] Habermas presents these symmetries as linguistic conceptions of truth (unconstrained consensus), freedom (unimpaired self-representation), and justice (universal norms), respectively. When these symmetries exist, communication is not hindered by constraints arising from its own structure – it is rational.

In terms of historical development, communicative competence and ideal speech represent the posttraditional identities and democratic structures that characterize a rationalized lifeworld. However, democracy competes with another principle of social integration in modern lifeworlds – capitalism. "Unpolitical class rule" is the organizational principle of capitalism, and it corresponds to interactions coordinated by syndromes of civil and familial-vocational privatism. Familial-vocational privatism involves an achievement orientation, the belief that markets reward merit, which Habermas traces to the Protestant ethic. Status symbols – consumer goods, leisure time, and so forth – serve to indicate personal success. Civil privatism appears in the closely related "depoliticizing" of the public sphere. Economic status is officially separated from political power, and ostensibly free markets exist alongside formally equal rights, obscuring the capitalist interests behind liberal constitutions. As long as government can stabilize markets without seeming to do so, citizens accept the economic status quo and express little interest in politics. A prebourgeois authoritarianism is successfully (con)fused with a bourgeois participatory ideology.

From a lifeworld perspective, the tension between capitalism and democracy is promising. It indicates a potential transition from traditional to posttraditional forms of social integration. However, since modern societies are differentiated, we must also consider this tension from a systems perspective. According to Habermas, economic and political systems interact with the lifeworld through media of money and power. The economic system pays wages for labor and provides goods and services to meet consumer demand. The administrative system funds organizational performances with taxes and makes political decisions to sustain mass loyalty. These interchanges suggest corresponding roles: employee and consumer, client and citizen. To translate these roles into the systems media above is already to abstract from their lifeworld contexts.[23] Habermas's description of this process is worth quoting at length, especially given the parallel he draws to Marx:

Just as concrete work has to be transformed into abstract labor so that it can be exchanged for wages, use-value orientations have to be transformed, in a certain sense, into demand preferences, and publicly articulated opinions and collective expressions of will have to be transformed into mass loyalty, so that they can be exchanged for consumer goods and political leadership.[24]

This translation process distorts less with employee and client roles, since they are already legally and organizationally dependent – the creations of private enterprises and public bureaucracies. In contrast, consumer and citizen roles originate in the liberal-capitalist lifeworld syndromes – that is, in free contracts and equal rights. At least in theory, they are vehicles for satisfying personal needs and expressing social values chosen through processes of mutual understanding. With the development of welfare state policies to stabilize economic markets and sustain political loyalties, consumer and citizen roles are also colonized by systems imperatives.[25] Habermas argues that their functions of cultural (re)production cannot be replaced by steering media. As these roles are "split off from the symbolic structures of the lifeworld," the class interests behind the welfare state compromise become increasingly obvious.

Systems imperatives, then, both exacerbate lifeworld tensions and frustrate lifeworld potentials. The conflicts between a rationalized lifeworld and increasingly complex media-steered systems have two unfortunate results: a loss of freedom and a loss of meaning. Marx's concepts of real abstractions – reification and alienation – help Habermas to characterize them. The loss of freedom takes the form of a reification of communication processes. As the lifeworld is colonized, citizens become more "conscious of the contingency not only of the *contents* of tradition, but also of the *techniques* of tradition."[26] However, they simultaneously experience the overwhelming complexity of economic and political systems. The result is a "de-moralization of public conflicts" because "only opportunistic behavior towards the system seems to offer a way of finding one's bearings."[27] There is a corresponding loss of meaning. Since cultural traditions cannot be administratively produced, "once their unquestionable character has been destroyed, the stabilization of validity claims can succeed only through discourse."[28] Yet a colonized lifeworld offers citizens only "an alienated mode of having a say in matters of public interest."[29] The gap between state-sanctioned and culturally supplied meanings leads to fragmented, rather than false, consciousness. Alongside the reification of communication processes, personality structures disintegrate, as individuals are alienated from their capacity to make sense of their world(s).

Although Habermas applies Marx's concepts of real abstractions to late capitalism, he does so with some reservations. According to Habermas, Marx's latent Hegelianism causes him to confuse differentiation with reification and individuation with alienation. Unlike Marx, Habermas argues that levels of system differentiation are distinct from their class-specific institutionalizations. This means that complexity does not necessarily conflict with democracy. Instead, reification of communication should be seen as a class-specific, system-induced deformation of the lifeworld. Marx's other confusion is closely related. Since Marx bases his concept of alienation on the destruction of traditional forms of life, he cannot distinguish the rationalization of modern lifeworlds from the reification of post-traditional ones. Habermas, who rejects Marx's vision of species-being, insists that the pain of individuation, of integrating personality structures and social roles, is not alienation. The communication processes of rationalized lifeworlds offer individuals adequate opportunities to form social connections, to create solidarity. The task of a critical theory of late capitalism is to examine "the conditions for recoupling a rationalized culture with an everyday communication dependent on vital traditions."[30]

Socialism, with its conviction that "the socially integrating force of solidarity should be in a position to stake its claim against the other social forces, money and administrative power, through a wide range of democratic forums and institutions," represents lifeworld potentials.[31] New social movements, which arise at the seam between system and lifeworld to challenge the reification of communication, are its expressions. Habermas distinguishes their efforts from colonized forms of participation: "The issue is not primarily one of compensations that the welfare state can provide [of redistribution], but of defending and restoring endangered ways of life."[32] The socialist hope, that human beings will reclaim their powers, will become obsolete only when society "allows the full significance of everything that cannot be expressed as a price to be perceived and taken seriously."[33]

III. BEAMS AND LIFEWORLDS

Near the end of his *Theory of Communicative Action*, Habermas quotes Marx:

even the most abstract categories, despite their validity – precisely because of their abstractness – for all epochs, are nevertheless, in the specific character of this abstraction, themselves likewise a product of historical relations, and possess their full validity only for and within those relations.[34]

Habermas has claimed that Marx failed fully to see how this insight applied to his own category of abstract labor and his related theory of value. With Habermas's critique of late capitalism in mind, we can now return to the question I set aside: Is Habermas sufficiently reflective about the origins of his theory of communicative rationality in his lifeworld? Indeed, we might even ask: Does Habermas have the courage of Marx's convictions? To answer, we must examine Habermas's concept of the lifeworld, including his own, in greater depth.

Habermas defines the lifeworld as "the intuitively present, in this sense familiar and transparent, and at the same time vast and incalculable web of presuppositions that have to be satisfied if an actual utterance is to be at all meaningful, i.e., valid *or* invalid."[35] Lifeworlds are, then, always simultaneously achieved and ascribed, or situation and background, even conscious and unconscious. Less rational lifeworlds may presuppose more, but no society – or theory – is fully rational. For this reason, Habermas disavows foundationalist and transcendentalist claims: "Insofar as it [the theory of communicative rationality] refers to structures of the lifeworld, it has to explicate a background knowledge over which no one can dispose at will. The lifeworld is at first 'given' to the theoretician (as it is to the layperson) as his or her own, and in a paradoxical manner."[36] According to Habermas, "the development of society must *itself* give rise to the problem situations that *objectively* afford contemporaries a privileged access to the general structures of the lifeworld."[37]

Habermas applies this insight to his theory – to a point. He claims that deformations of the lifeworld take the form of reified communication only in late capitalist societies, and that system challenges to lifeworld structures explain their increased accessibility to us. However, he is less clear about the historical specificity of the lifeworld potentials he identifies. His distinctions among new social movements help to illustrate this confusion. Habermas distinguishes between revolutionary and reactionary movements based, most simply, on whether they seek to create a rationalized lifeworld or to preserve particularistic values. By this criterion, feminism is the only contemporary emancipatory movement because it alone "follows the tradition of bourgeois socialist liberation movements" and pursues "the realization of a promise that is deeply rooted in the acknowledged universalist foundations of morality and legalism."[38] Leaving aside, for the moment, feminists' differences with bourgeois and socialist liberation movements, this statement remains problematic. My concern is not whether Habermas's reconstructive method can be distinguished from foundationalism, quasi or otherwise. For present purposes, I grant his claim that communicative rationality is a "critical," that is, historically specific, theory.[39] Indeed, that is the problem here. Habermas does not adequately acknowledge its lifeworld precedents, specifically the tensions between socialist and liberal concepts of democracy. Socialism does reveal the beam in liberalism's eye, and it is one Habermas shares.

These tensions manifest themselves in Habermas's understanding of ideal speech as symmetrical intersubjectivity or in the idea of equivalences between individuals. An instructive comparison can be made here between proletarian dictatorship and ideal speech. They represent realizations, economic and communicative, respectively, of equal rights. Marx says that the dictatorship of the proletariat recognizes no class differences. There are no laborers, no capitalists because all are laborers, all are capitalists: "Both sides of the relationship are raised to an imagined universality – *labor* as state in which every person is put, and *capital* as the acknowledged universality and power of the community."[40] The ideal speech situation analogously recognizes no communication differences. Indeed, there are no sides, such as classes, genders, races, to be transcended here, except perhaps the separation of individuals from society (a point to which I return). Following Marx, speech is a role in which every person is put, and justice is the acknowledged universality and power of the community.

The problem with these equivalences – or symmetries – is that they treat different people by the same standard. That is, they abstract from concrete individuals' specific abilities and needs, to establish relations of "formal reciprocity" between "generalized Others."[41] For this reason, Marx argues that equal right, like every right, is inevitably unequal:

Right by its very nature can consist only in the application of an equal standard; but unequal individuals [and they would not be different individuals if they were not unequal] are measurable only by an equal standard in so far as they are brought under an equal point of view, are taken from one definite side only . . . everything else being ignored.[42]

Marx concludes that the dictatorship of the proletariat still carries the "birthmarks" of liberal-capitalism. The "higher phase" of communist society crosses "the narrow horizon of bourgeois right in its entirety" and inscribes on its banner: "From each according to his ability, to each according to his needs."[43]

Habermas recognizes the problem posed by translating different needs into equal rights and, as we have seen, argues that Marx fails to solve it. He claims that his empirical critique of late capitalism does not require, indeed, cannot include, a vehicle for translating lifeworld values into system imperatives. This is true, if one interprets "translate" as determine. Communicative action follows its own developmental logic, and Habermas refuses to posit a revolutionary subject or to prescribe a rational society. However, in other respects, universal pragmatics parallels the labor theory of value as a translation tool. Habermas admits that all media translate real qualities into abstract categories, though he maintains that they do so in fundamentally different ways. The systems media of money and power are "artificial languages" that colonize the lifeworld. In contrast, universal pragmatics mediatizes natural languages and behavioral roles – both of which are lifeworld structures.[44] But what lifeworld structures does it mediatize?

According to Habermas, language "presents inalienably individual aspects in unavoidably general categories."[45] Yet it is also how individual identities, which are always also intersubjective, are formed: "The ego knows itself not only as subjectivity but also as something that has always already transcended the bounds of subjectivity in cognition, speech, and interactions simultaneously."[46] The problem is that "the ego can enter into and penetrate beyond structures of interaction only if its needs can be admitted into and adequately interpreted within the symbolic universe."[47] Since all needs cannot be so interpreted, Habermas explicitly disavows a "fully transparent" or "a homogenized and unified" society as an ideal. Instead, he maintains that cultural traditions, including languages and roles, always serve a dual purpose. They are the "stencils" by which "needs are shaped," and the "medium" in which "needs can seek and find alternative interpretations."[48] Rather than ascribe needs "to individuals as natural properties," Habermas allows for their discursive interpretation through ideal speech – but only if they are "generalizable."[49]

Although Habermas might prefer a qualified comparison to higher communism, this suggests that his theory of communicative rationality is ultimately more liberal than socialist. From a systems perspective, Habermas's concept of a translation process looks even more like a form of colonization. It requires that competent speakers develop a "dual consciousness." In a recent essay on Kierkegaard, Habermas grappled with this problem and asked "how intersubjectively shared life contexts must be structured in order not only to leave room for the development of exacting personal identities but also to support such processes of self-discovery." Cultural traditions, he concluded, will not suffice: They are too integrative, too unreflective. Instead, he reaffirmed "autonomous and publicly conducted debate" as the intersubjective complement to "the responsible assumption of one's life history."[50]

In a different context, Iris Young conveys the inadequacy of this (re)solution well: "The *achievement* [emphasis mine] of formal equality does not eliminate social differences, and rhetorical commitment to the sameness of persons makes it impossible even to name how those differences presently structure privilege and oppression."[51] According to Habermas, this may be the best we can do: "At least the public sphere is an attempt to exclude violence, if only to reproduce some sort of violence internally again but in a criticizable fashion."[52] After the fall of Babel – to return to my opening theme – politics is a form of self-exile; at least, if liberalism is the "eye of the needle through which everything must pass. . . ."

But is it? What is left of Marx in Habermas's theory? How does Marx's legacy reflect Jewish mysticism? In a critical vein, we might now conclude that Habermas, like Marx, tries to rebuild the tower of Babel. The parallels drawn between proletarian dictatorship and ideal speech, and between labor and language, imply as much. Unlike Marx in his more Hegelian moments, Habermas knows that his efforts cannot succeed. Rationalized lifeworlds prevent the reconciliation of individual and society, though they also anticipate it whenever speakers genuinely seek mutual understanding. In other words, Habermas knows that humans are not gods and he mourns our losses, especially the violence we do to ourselves and others.[53]

However, Marx also leaves a more positive legacy that Habermas has not yet fully embraced. Marx understands that liberal politics, as well as capitalist economics, leaves humanity in exile. This is partly because it asks us to be gods, to abstract from our creaturelike aspects. In this context, I want to return to Habermas's praise for the feminist movement. Habermas does situate feminism in the tradition of bourgeois socialist liberation movements. But he also affirms particular values, specifically, the "ethic of care," often associated with it:

The emancipation of women means more than the merely *formal* attainment of equality and elimination of male prejudices. It means the toppling of concrete life styles determined by male monopolies. The historical legacy of the sexual division of labor, to which women were subjected in the nuclear bourgeois family, also gives them access to virtues, to a set of values that are both in contrast and complementary to the male world and at odds with the one-sided rationalized praxis of everyday life.[54]

The feminist "ethic of solidarity" suggested here goes beyond the liberal principle of equal rights: It allows individuals to embrace cultural traditions, to express their specific needs, and to speak in their own voices.

Such an ethic seems more consistent with Marx's principle "From each according to his ability, to each according to his needs." Without making too much of what is, for Habermas, an uncharacteristic passage, is this also Marx's legacy? Dennis Fischman makes a similar connection between feminism, Marxism, and Judaism: They teach us that "being a specific person is not less than being a self-defining subject, but more." He concludes that "if liberal politics at its best is designed to make subjects free, but not people, not you and me, then we need a new politics, one that aims to overcome our specific alienation and to emancipate us as distinct human beings: in short, to return us from exile."[55]

In the present context, I can offer only a few speculations about how consciously embracing socialism as a "politics of return" might transform Habermas's theory of communicative rationality. The liberal tradition of equal rights would remain important. But, it would now include the recognition that only by expressing differences, by forming a "heterogeneous public," can we overcome oppression. That is, justice would require applying different standards to different people, or a greater sensitivity to the diversity and complexity of life.[56] Such sensitivity would develop alongside greater acceptance of natural languages – that is, of group-specific "categories of meaning" and "standards of significance."[57] This requires greater attention to a relatively undeveloped category in Habermas's universal pragmatics: the cultural universal. It is the intersubjective – and substantive – twin to dialogue-constitutive universals, and the vehicle for cross-cultural comparisons between world systems, such as for kinship relations, color categories, and so on. Increased recognition of differences in communication styles and roles, what might be called a "natural pragmatics," is also necessary. This suggests how Habermas might complete the blank box in his fourfold table of action types. To the three he identified, the instrumental, strategic, and communicative, he might add empathic action to characterize individual efforts to understand others. Empathy might be seen as the necessary complement to sincerity. Together they require us to listen carefully in order to understand and to speak clearly in order to be understood.[58]

Not surprisingly, given their emphasis on "care," feminists also prove helpful in suggesting a corresponding speech situation. According to Carol Gilligan, Annie Rogers, and Lyn Mikel Brown, the musical concept of point–counterpoint "offers a way to listen to many voices, as themes and variations on themes, and to correct for not listening to particular themes."[59] The political analogy (which they do not draw) is con-sensus. The hyphen conveys its original meaning "'feeling or sensing together,' implying not agreement, necessarily, but a 'crossing' of the barrier between ego and ego, bridging private and shared experience."[60] Con-sensus, like a fugue, is an elaborate design, a harmony simultaneously disrupted and ordered. The contrapuntal themes are not at war or in conflict, but they come together without becoming the same. Different voices cross, even while they respect, distinct boundaries.

A "politics of return" as a politics of difference is not nostalgic or romantic; it rejects intuitive and rational impulses to unify. But are these, admittedly tentative, suggestions utopian? Is this what ultimately remains of Marx? I think not, unless any source of hope seems utopian today. According to Habermas, socialism preserves "the hope that humanity can emancipate itself from self-imposed tutelage."[61] Ultimately, what is left of Marx is the conviction that "people can be more human than their society permits."[62] In this respect, Habermas's socialism remains a "discourse-in-exile."

NOTES

1 Jürgen Habermas, "What Does Socialism Mean Today?" in *After the Fall: The Failure of Communism and the Future of Socialism*, ed. Robin Blackburn (New York: Verso, 1991), pp. 45, 31.

2 Jürgen Habermas, *The Theory of Communicative Action*, Vol. II, *Lifeworld and System: A Critique of Functionalist Reason*, trans. Thomas McCarthy (Boston: Beacon Press, 1987), pp. 374–403.

3 Jürgen Habermas, *Theory and Practice*, trans. John Viertel (Boston: Beacon Press, 1973), p. 215.

4 Dennis Fischman, *Political Discourse in Exile: Karl Marx and the Jewish Question* (Amherst: University of Massachusetts Press, 1991), ch. 5.

5 Habermas, *Theory and Practice*, p. 236.

6 Ibid., p. 221.

7 For a more extensive discussion of Marx's epistemology, see Nancy S. Love, "Epistemology and Exchange: Marx, Nietzsche, and Critical Theory," *New German Critique* 41 (Summer 1987): 71–94.

8 Habermas, *Theory and Practice*, p. 214.

9 Ibid., p. 243.

10 Habermas, "What Does Socialism Mean Today?" p. 35.

11 Ibid.

12 Habermas, *Theory and Practice*, p. 40.

13 Jürgen Habermas, *Knowledge and Human Interests*, trans. Jeremy Shapiro (Boston: Beacon Press, 1971), p. 42.

14 Habermas, "What Does Socialism Mean Today?" p. 32.

15 Habermas, *Theory of Communicative Action*, Vol. II, p. 378.

16 Jürgen Habermas, *Theory of Communicative Action*, Vol. I, *Reason and the Rationalization of Society*, trans. Thomas McCarthy (Boston: Beacon Press, 1984), p. 70.

17 Ibid.

18 Ibid., p. 216.

19 Ibid., p. 20.
20 Ibid., p. 26.
21 Ibid., p. 51.
22 Jürgen Habermas, "Toward a Theory of Communicative Competence," *Inquiry* 13 (1970): 371.
23 Habermas provides a useful diagram of these interchanges in his *Theory of Communicative Action*, Vol. II, p. 320.
24 Ibid., p. 322.
25 Ibid., p. 323.
26 Jürgen Habermas, *Legitimation Crisis*, trans. Thomas McCarthy (Boston: Beacon Press, 1973), p. 72.
27 Habermas, "What Does Socialism Mean Today?" p. 43.
28 Habermas, *Legitimation Crisis*, p. 72.
29 Habermas, *Theory of Communicative Action*, vol. II, p. 350.
30 Ibid., p. 356.
31 Habermas, "What Does Socialism Mean Today?" p. 42.
32 Habermas, *Theory of Communicative Action*, Vol. II, p. 393.
33 Habermas, "What Does Socialism Mean Today?" p. 45.
34 Habermas, *Theory of Communicative Action*, Vol. II, p. 403.
35 Ibid., p. 131.
36 Ibid., p. 400.
37 Ibid., p. 401.
38 Ibid., p. 393.
39 For a more extensive discussion of my position, see "Politics and Voices: An Empowerment/Knowledge Regime," *differences: A Journal of Feminist Cultural Studies* 3 (Winter 1991): 97–98. For opposing views, see John B. Thompson, "Universal Pragmatics," in *Habermas: Critical Debates*, ed. John B. Thompson and David Held (Cambridge, Mass.: MIT Press, 1982), pp. 116–133, and Fred R. Dallmayr, "Lifeworld and Communicative Action: Habermas," in *Critical Encounters: Between Philosophy and Politics* (Notre Dame, Ind.: University of Notre Dame Press, 1987), pp. 73–100.
40 Karl Marx, Economic and Philosophical Manuscripts of 1844, in *The Marx–Engels Reader*, ed. Robert C. Tucker (New York: Norton, 1978), p. 83.
41 Seyla Benhabib makes this now familiar distinction in her *Critique, Norm, Utopia: A Study of the Foundations of Critical Theory* (New York: Columbia University Press, 1986), p. 341.
42 Karl Marx, "Critique of the Gotha Program," in *Marx–Engels Reader*, p. 530.
43 Ibid., p. 531.
44 Jürgen Habermas, "Concluding Remarks," in *Habermas and the Public*

Sphere, ed. Craig Calhoun (Cambridge, Mass.: MIT Press, 1992), p. 473. I am indebted to one of my graduate students, Mark Bower, for this concept of a translation process.

45 Jürgen Habermas, "On Systemically Distorted Communication," *Inquiry* 13 (1970): 211.

46 Jürgen Habermas, "Historical Materialism and the Development of Normative Structures," in *Communication and the Evolution of Society,* trans. Thomas McCarthy (Boston: Beacon Press, 1979), p. 100.

47 Jürgen Habermas, "Moral Development and Ego Identity," ibid., p. 91.

48 Ibid., p. 93.

49 Ibid., p. 90.

50 Jürgen Habermas, "Historical Consciousness and Post-Traditional Identity," in *The New Conservatism: Cultural Criticism and the Historians' Debate,* ed. and trans., Shierry Weber Nicholsen (Cambridge, Mass.: MIT Press, 1990), pp. 261–62.

51 Iris Marion Young, *Justice and the Politics of Difference,* (Princeton, N.J.: Princeton University Press, 1990), p. 164.

52 Habermas, "Concluding Remarks," in Calhoun, *Habermas and the Public Sphere,* p. 479.

53 Johann Baptist Metz calls upon Habermas to do this. See his "Anamnestic Reason: A Theologian's Remarks on the Crisis in the *Geisteswissenschaften,*" in *Cultural-Political Interventions in the Unfinished Project of Enlightenment,* ed. Axel Honneth, Thomas McCarthy, Claus Offe, and Albrecht Wellmer (Cambridge, Mass.: MIT Press, 1992), pp. 189–96.

54 Habermas, *Theory of Communicative Action,* Vol. II, p. 394.

55 Fischman, *Political Discourse in Exile,* p. 117.

56 Iris Young coins the term "heterogeneous public" and develops a group-specific concept of justice in her *Justice and the Politics of Difference.* Habermas also recognizes the need for such a concept in another uncharacteristic passage: "This necessary disregard for the complexity of concrete life . . . calls for specific compensations that make good the deficits with regard to the application and realization of moral insights." "Questions and Counterquestions," *Habermas and Modernity,* ed. Richard Bernstein (Cambridge, Mass.: MIT Press, 1985), p. 210.

57 Fischman makes this point in a discussion of dual consciousness. Nancy Fraser has also argued for a concept of solidarity based on recognition of "concrete collective others" in "Toward a Discourse Ethic of Solidarity," *Praxis International* 5, no. 4: 425–29.

58 Habermas, *Theory of Communicative Action,* Vol. I, p. 285.

59 Carol Gilligan et al., "Soundings into Development," in *Making Connections: The Relational Worlds of Adolescent Girls at Emma Willard*

School, ed. Carol Gilligan, Nona P. Lyons, and Trudy J. Hammer (Cambridge, Mass.: Harvard University Press, 1990), p. 320.

60 N. N. Holland, *Five Readers Reading,* quoted in Mary Kay Belenky et al., *Women's Ways of Knowing: The Development of Self, Voice, and Mind* (New York: Basic Books, 1986), p. 223.

61 Habermas, "What Does Socialism Mean Today?" p. 45.

62 Fischman, *Political Discourse in Exile,* p. 108.

4 Universalism and the situated critic

It has long been a curious feature of Jürgen Habermas's reception in the English-speaking world that, for all the intense and exhaustive scrutiny of his critical social theory, Habermas's role as a politically engaged intellectual, polemicist, and essayist in the political public sphere has received relatively little attention. Given the consistency with which Habermas himself has worked toward a normative theory of political participation – and also given the fact that, over the last decade or so, Habermas has rather unobtrusively emerged as Germany's most prominent *intellectual* as well as its most influential social theorist – this lack of interest in Habermas's "moonlighting role as an intellectual" seems difficult to explain.[1]

In what follows, I would like to sketch in very broad strokes the major focus of Habermas's activity as a politically active intellectual over the past few years, in order to suggest that, to an unrivaled degree, Habermas has single-mindedly worked to bring his theoretical and his political writings into a steadily closer relation with each other. The *universalism* that lies at the heart of Habermasian theory remains an empty abstraction unless it can be reconstructed within the context of a concrete lifeworld; it thus cannot be disassociated from the *particular* fate of universal *mentalities* – what Habermas calls "constitutional patriotism" – in the Federal Republic. Conversely, Habermas's political writings on the Federal Republic are unified by the single-minded project of protecting and cultivating a form of republican commitment that only makes sense insofar as there is a corollary theoretical justification of moral-political universalism. I believe that it is this – the extent to which Habermas's work situates itself in the particularities of the German situation since the 1940s – that underlies the peculiar imbalance on the side

67

of theory that has characterized Habermas's reception in English-speaking countries.

For those who have experienced the birth and unsteady growth of a democratic state in the former German *Reich*, the "Federal Republic" has always appeared more as a value than a fact; more as a verb than a noun. Rather than referring to a cultural reality to be taken for granted, German republicanism – and the bedeviling question of what form of state organization could best realize it – connotes an ongoing project, a continuously withheld historical ambition, with historical roots stretching from the *Vormärz* period of nineteenth-century German liberalism, through Germany's unification under Bismarck, and extending to its rise to a position of predominance in "middle Europe," the Weimar years, Germany's subsequent descent into a fascist nightmare, its partition, and now its deeply ambiguous reunification.

The development of a truly democratic, "universalist" political culture from out of the particular historical experience of moral and political catastrophe continues to define the challenge of a German *Bundesrepublik*. Since 1949 this task has taken the paradoxical shape of a nation (in the former West Germany) attempting to accustom itself to the principles of a universalist democracy under the rule of law that was foisted upon it from the outside – and since 1990, the larger Federal Republic is once again obliged to ask itself whether or not its past will continue to rule its present, and whether or not its self-understanding as a cultural and political reality is to be defined through universal conceptions of citizenship in a multicultural, porous society, or through specifically German conceptions of *Volk*, of destiny, soil, and blood.

The question of the self-identity of the *Bundesrepublik* – whether *universalist* principles and mentalities will succeed in providing a durable collective identity for the *situated* Germans – defines the relation of universal and particular in Habermas's polemical writings as well. Habermas has been the single most consistent, energetic, and imaginative intellectual defender of Germany's fragile and paradox-ridden tropism toward a democratic *way of life* in which commitments to postnationalistic, postconventional institutions and values are firmly rooted within the lifeworlds of political agents. The irony is that Habermas has become *the* intellectual of the Fed-

eral Republic by consistently championing precisely those universalistic democratic political ideals that seek to oust Germany's long-
held and calamitous fascination with characteristically German
forms of collective national identity. Insofar as it takes its bearings
from the particular historical and cultural *situation* of postwar Germany, Habermas's theoretical and political work is highly particular.
And yet, because the dynamic that it derives from its own particular
context has impelled Habermas's thought toward a thoroughgoing
political universalism, he has become a *German* intellectual precisely by working against the Germanness of the political culture of
the Federal Republic.

This irony, what one might call this *dialectic of universality and
situation* in Habermas's work, underlies the complex relation between theoretical and polemic writing that Habermas has produced
over a career that, so far, has run exactly parallel to the curriculum
vitae of the Federal Republic from its first hours to the moment of
unification. "Universalism" is an abstract moral-political principle
that nevertheless can be embodied only in particular cultural and
political situations.

In what follows, then, I would like to understand "universalism"
as a normative mentality that can receive a convincing explanation
only from within the concrete situation of a Federal Republic still
struggling, after nearly half a century, to develop its own distinctive
political culture, its own conception of national identity, and its own
concrete set of cultural, historical, and ethical problems.

I

The universalist kernel of Habermas's moral and political writing
has been the object of more criticism than any other aspect of his
work. The central claim that there is *always* a preexistent intersubjective context for any morally relevant question translates the moment of universality in collective political life to the basic *attributions* and *expectations of reasonableness* that speakers and hearers
in modern, rationalized societies can make of each other's discursive
conduct, in situations when needs and problems have to be collectively settled. "Universalism" is itself not so much a concrete political value as it is a collectively shared *mentality;* a sense of solidarity
inhabiting a public space that is distinct from political or economic

institutions. It is a locationless network of competencies; the ability to approach one's own situated needs and interests reflectively; to take the position of the other at least to the extent that one is willing to recognize that the other's needs are at least potentially legitimate; that one attributes value and comprehensibility to the other's needs and interests.[2] A universalistic mentality cannot adjudicate questions of the good life, for such questions are inextricably particular. But a collectively shared universalist mentality does enforce the principle that norms are only just insofar as they can meet with the considered approval of all those who will be affected by their implementation.[3] For Habermas, universalism is the only formal criterion of the *rightness* or justice of collective norms that is available, and hence the *only* recourse that modern societies have for opening up a sphere in which particular questions of the good life can even be addressed.

In this sense, "universalism" means something like the basic shared mentality that allows individuals to conceive of themselves as *citizens* of a democratic state, one in which citizenship consists of a constellation of interlocking duties and rights that together form an abstract level of popular sovereignty subsisting below – and making possible – the spectrum of particularistic kinds of identity operating within a diverse society. In democratic societies, the capacity for mutual recognition and the generalization of norms must install itself as an attitude that can reflectively separate from the particular fabric of their own interests.

The sense of an abstract version of relations of solidarity consists in separating the symmetries of mutual recognition that are the premise of communicative action, and that make the autonomy and the individualization of sociated subjects possible, on the one hand, from the concrete ethical life of organic relations of interaction on the other, and of generalizing these symmetries in the reflexive forms of understanding and compromise, as well as securing them through legal institutionalization.[4]

Such a mentality has always underwritten the Western, enlightenment conceptions of popular sovereignty, citizenship, and the democratic rule of law first brought to philosophical expression in Rousseau and Kant. In this way the rational constitution of a democratic state is the embodiment of a preestablished, decontextualized social contract, an expectation on which all particular consenses and compromises must be based:

> In a pluralistic society, the constitution expresses a formal consensus. The citizens want to regulate their collective lives through principles that, because they lie in the same interests of all, can find the reasoned agreement of all. Such an association is structured through relations of reciprocal acknowledgement, in which each can expect to be respected as free and equal.[5]

Such a popular sovereignty, moving restlessly between its moments of abstract expectations of reasonableness and its unthematizable sets of culturally specific problems and needs, "finds its placeless place [*ortlosen Ort*] in the interactions between democratically institutionalized will formation and culturally mobilized public spheres."[6]

The vision of a "placeless place," where practical discourse can at least introduce the possibility of a reasoned consensus on collective norms and needs, entails the fundamental claim that the institutions and principles of democratic government contain a universal normative demand for full, continuous, multifarious, and serious public political communication; a demand that, empirically speaking, has "no place," insofar as it cannot correspond, in any sense at all, to a particular cultural *situation.*

This notion of "universalism" as a collectively shared mentality offers a way of bridging the formalistic and abstract conceptions of universality in Habermas's theoretical works with the task of anchoring republican attitudes more firmly in the Federal Republic, the major leitmotif of Habermas's political writings. In describing universalism as a mentality, I am referring in essence to a mode of conduct with its accompanying capacities for self-deliberation, for self-examination and self-criticism. While necessarily distinguishing itself from particular cultural forms of life, such a mentality is of course of no significance at all unless it can root itself firmly within a *particular* cultural milieu.

Individual and collective life histories and identities are always concrete. They are woven from strands of cultural, linguistic, familial, and personal experiences and choices, from traditions and norms, that cannot be reduced to abstract formulas. The question is

whether, and if so in what manner, universalist principles can dura-
bly and meaningfully install themselves in democratic societies –
not just formally, as in abstract constitutional principles, but in the
characteristic attitudes and motivations of "normal" citizens. "Constitutional principles," writes Habermas,

can only take shape within social practices, and can thus become a driving
force for the dynamic project of constructing an association of free and
equal individuals, if these principles are situated within the context of the
history of a nation of citizens in such a way that they enter into a binding
relationship with the motives and attitudes of the citizens themselves.[7]

Particular life practices alone can anchor universalist principles,
thus transforming them into regular attitudes and expectations. "A
particularistic anchoring *of this sort* would not take away one bit
of the universalist significance of popular sovereignty and human
rights. . . . Democratic citizenship does not need to be rooted in the
national identity of a people; however, without view to the multiplicity of different cultural life forms, it does demand the socialization of all citizens in a common political culture."[8]

What, then, does universalism mean? That one relativizes one's own form
of existence in relation to the legitimate claims of other forms of life, that
one attribute the same rights to the strangers and the others, along with all
their idiosyncrasies and incomprehensibilities, that one not insist on the
generalization of one's own identity, that the realm of tolerance must become endlessly larger than it is today: all this is what moral universalism
means today.[9]

II

The "placeless place" of consensual-communicative popular sovereignty has never had much luck surviving long in situ in Germany.
Whether decked out with the irrationalist dithyrambs of *Heimat,
Volksgeist,* soil, and destiny, or uncut as Germany's power-political
obsession with its geographical destiny and its multiple territorial
ambitions, a particularist political mentality and a preoccupation
with the meaning of place has always played an inordinately large
role in the historical fate of Germany and its neighbors. Ever since
the *Vormärz* period, the republican, cosmopolitan attitudes en-

joined by universalist moral-political principles have run up against the dream of a German cultural-linguistic national entity that has always existed more in collective fantasy than in reality, and whose scattered attempts at realization have led to disastrous results.

From its founding in 1949 to its unification with the former *Deutsche Demokratische Republik* (DDR) in 1990, the West German *Bundesrepublik* (BRD) has been conditioned through and through by this inveterate and specifically German tension between the republican form of state organization and the strongly irrationalist currents that see the nation as a prepolitical magnitude rooted in the "imponderables of the soul of the people," as Brigitte Seebacher-Brandt has said. Born from the collective experience of unparalleled moral and political catastrophe, the Federal Republic's political culture – and the unmasterable, haunted family of political anxieties, insecurities, and sensitivities characteristic of it – have been generated from this tension as well.

The Federal Republic itself arose concretely from the perceived need of the wartime Allies to respond to the threat of Soviet expansion by establishing a recognized political entity in the German territories under Allied control. This historical fact grounded a doctrinary anticommunism as the cornerstone political ideology of the early Federal Republic. Anticommunism and the reconstructionist mentality served not only to link West Germany firmly into a Western alliance under Adenauer and to seal the German–German division as a durable source of self-understanding in the West, but also acted as a measure for paving over the Federal Republic's relation with its own recent past.

As Habermas and others have argued, the resolute repression of any discourse on collective guilt and responsibility in the early Federal Republic went hand in hand with the rise of a "Deutschmark Nationalism" as the only acceptable form of collective political identity. An entire generation in the *Adenauer-Zeit* bracketed off the question of the Nazi past – and of politics altogether – to focus stubbornly on economic success. *"Vergangenheitsbewältigung,"* the "management" of the past itself, was the key term under which this complicated motion of repression and displacement was discussed in the 1950s. The term itself captures the peculiar amalgam of collective psychology and political economy, of public pride and its private secrets, of a whole baleful constellation of stubborn silences and irremediable discontents, that are so characteristic of the political culture of the former West Germany.[10]

Repressed and sublimated into a system of collective tics and affects, the meaning of the Nazi past did not lead the early Federal Republic into anything approaching a collective moral discourse on what sort of nation it wanted to be. An influential 1959 study revealed that economic success, anticommunism, and thoroughly *volkisch* conceptions of Germanness still dominated the political culture of the Federal Republic long after the "zero hour" of its birth.[11] It was, ironically, only on the state level of political organization that the effects of the recent Nazi past asserted themselves in a formative way. The basic political commitments that founded the Federal Republic consisted of an attempt to respond self-consciously to "the particularist element" of the German political imagination that "finally became inflated into the ideal of the racial supremacy of one's own people."[12] One of the first and most durable products of this attempt was the Basic Law (*Grundgesetz*), in whose nineteen human rights articles, Habermas has written, "there sounds the echo of injustice that has been suffered," and that is "negated word for word. These constitutional articles not only achieve a determinate negation in the Hegelian sense; at the same time, they sketch out the contours of a coming social order."[13]

The Basic Law is one of the most liberal, universalistic, and democratic constitutions ever devised. In distinction from a "constitution" (*Verfassung*) the authors of the Basic Law had envisioned it as a provisional document, designed for what was then understood to be the very temporary status of a separate West German state. Nevertheless, the document has survived every vicissitude of West German history from German partition through reconstruction, the student revolts of 1968, left-wing terror and the "German Autumn" of 1977, through the right turn of 1982 and German unification.

At the same time, however, the fact remains that, in large measure due to its origin as a provisional document, the Basic Law was never discussed or voted on by the citizens of the Federal Republic themselves. The universalistic political mentality that it demands, above all, the dismantling of a particularly German conception of the *Obrigkeitsstaat* (the strong, centralized authoritarian state as the ultimate source of political sovereignty) and its replacement by a federal republic and by the rule-governed and proceduralistic conception of popular sovereignty, never received a popular mandate.[14] Hanging over the heads of the citizens that it creates, the Basic Law has occasionally seemed more like a collective superego than a collective constitution; more like what Hegel criticized as the abstractness of Kant's "tyranny of the pure ought" than the organic act of national self-creation.

Like all universalist constitutions, the Basic Law has served to place democratic demands on empirical political institutions that are difficult if not impossible to fulfill completely.[15] But, in the case of the Federal Republic, where the universalist philosophy underlying the Basic Law could only have been apprehended as one imposed from without, the particular situation of the adoption of the Basic Law also established the primary *task* of political culture in the Federal Republic as each German citizen's continuing attempt to embrace and incorporate these democratic principles; using them as the material from which a durable individual and collective self-understanding can be made, turning them into influential sources of political judgment and deliberation and allowing them to put down roots within the German lifeworld deep enough that these principles themselves could serve as cultural-political resources for the identification and adjudication of collective problems.

This *incorporation* of the spirit of the Basic Law on the level of motivations and mentalities (the political correlate of what Habermas's theoretical writings have described as the universalistic component of the discourse ethic) has for forty years been the primary question of Habermas's polemical writings. These have been guided by the consistent purpose of defending the fragile growth of "constitutional patriotism" in the Federal Republic from all threats. In speaking of a "constitutional patriotism" – the term is borrowed from Dolf Sternberger – Habermas argues that an identification with the principles of a republican constitution is the only form of patriotism that is *morally* permissible for German citizens.

A fundamental tension between postconventional forms of collective identity and the particularistic currents of nationalism is basic to modernized societies. In the case of the Federal Republic, however, Habermas argues that the Nazi past imposes *particular* parameters on this problem. In the "Historians' Debate" of the mid-1980s, Habermas attacked the neoconservative project of *strategically* reinvigorating traditional precatastrophe forms of national identity, a plank in what Habermas perceived as the broader neoconservative project of easing the burden of legitimation incumbent on modernized economic and political institutions by shoring them up with essentially antiquated, "conventional" forms of collective meaning.[16]

Emboldened by the Kohl administration's dogged if often maladroit efforts to "normalize" the Federal Republic's abnormal past with ceremonial peace-making rituals (Bitburg), neoconservative historians wondered aloud if it were not time to disburden Germany of "the past that won't go away" by placing the Holocaust in the broader context of the history of totalitarianism, in which case Auschwitz might appear as a reaction to the "asiatic deed" of Stalin's purges (Ernst Nolte), or by empathetically taking the perspective of the downtrodden *Wehrmacht* trooper on the Eastern Front, hoping only to save his Fatherland from the Russian hordes (Andreas Hillgruber). In both cases what the conservative historians regarded as a necessary "historicization" of the Holocaust, others, Habermas included, regarded as an inadmissible *relativization* of Auschwitz, in which professional historical research now applied itself to the ideological support of the ruling administration by essentially lowering the barrier of a singular moral catastrophe that stood between the Federal Republic's present and the reservoir of meaning-giving nationalist yearnings and traditions lying in its prewar past.

While the Historians' Debate quickly swelled into a professional dispute concerning the validity of comparison as a methodological strategy for the historiographical sciences, Habermas from the beginning insisted on regarding the heart of the debate to concern the struggle between neoconservative and republican mentalities for the hearts and minds of the citizens of the Federal Republic. In 1987 Habermas argued that Auschwitz provided and continued to provide the true north that oriented the spiritual-political development of political culture in the Federal Republic. An incomparable rupture in the fabric of human solidarity linked West Germany indelibly to its recent past. But it also served, on Habermas's argument, as a moral-political *filter*, a structural and collective psychological inhibition for the *uncritical* reappropriation of prewar conventional forms of national identity. Thus, for Habermas, the rare commodity of constitutional patriotism in the Federal Republic is a universalistic attitude that was only brought about by the particularity of Germany's fascist nightmare:

Our patriotism cannot deny the fact that it was only after Auschwitz – and in a certain sense only after the shock of this moral catastrophe – that democracy was able to sink roots into the motivations and the hearts of German citizens, at least those in the younger generations.[17]

In 1987 Habermas's criticisms of neoconservative attempts to reverse this trend and strategically reintroduce elements of German nationalism are tempered by the optimistic assessment that, over the last decades, constitutional patriotism had succeeded in displacing the complex of repression, opportunism, and pragmatic DM-nationalism of the Adenauer years as the primary form of political self-identification in the Federal Republic; that is, that universalism was finally "taking root," and that citizens were incorporating republican principles and attitudes, rather than merely accustoming themselves to a republican constitution. Many of the causes for such a "universalization" of political attitudes in Germany lay, predominantly, in economic developments that went beyond specifically German concerns: in the dynamic of late-capitalist expansion itself, and the growing irrelevance of national boundaries for the features and problems of a global economy; in the growth of a global communication network and a nationless mass culture, and in the economically motivated patterns of mass human migrations that steadily eroded the ethnic foundation for "inside–outside" national distinctions.[18] And yet Habermas's chief counter to the neoconservative interventions in collective memory was the claim that a process of denationalization in the Federal Republic, however fragile, was a departicularization of German political culture from its own impetus as well. And the short-term conclusion to be drawn from the "Historians' Debate" was that both in professional circles and in the public sphere, the neoconservative historians had been unable to generate much support for their efforts at moral revisionism; a sign, perhaps, that the process of *Vergangenheitsbewältigung* in the Federal Republic had incrementally succeeded in establishing a normatively robust sense of republican identity. As Habermas put it in 1987, the steady growth of postconventional attitudes was the only signal "that we have not completely wasted the opportunity that the moral catastrophe could also represent."[19]

Indeed Habermas could cite his colleague M. R. Lepsius that, notwithstanding West Germany's right turn in 1982, the 1980s had seen "an essential transformation in the political culture of the Federal Republic," that is, "the acceptance of a political order which determines and legitimatizes itself in constitutionally concrete forms through rights of individual participation." Thus the "crystallization of constitutional patriotism" is for Lepsius the "central result of the delegitimization of German nationalism."[20]

And yet, Habermas's optimism in 1987 was decidedly guarded:

> Beneath the debate on the question in what sense the Nazi mass crimes were unique lies the deeper question of what attitude we want to take toward the continuities of German history – whether we can affirm our political existence while maintaining a clear awareness of a break with our more sinister traditions. Can we, and do we want to, give up the comforts and dangers of a conventional identity that is incompatible with a *critical* appropriation of traditions? Nationalism is as virulent as ever. This question, I am afraid, has not yet come due.[21]

III

As it turned out, this question came due far earlier than Habermas or anyone else could have predicted. The revolutions of 1989 and the unification of the two German states in October 1990 brought the nationalist challenge to posttraditional conceptions of citizenship to a crisis point. The possibility, mode, and tempo of the unification process produced vocal and vigorous public debates among Germany's intellectual class, and once again Habermas took a leading role.

From the beginning, Habermas's position was marked by the resolute refusal even to entertain the notion that unification could permissibly mean the recovery of a peculiarly German conception of nationhood. This nonnegotiable opposition to a resurgent German nationalism put Habermas at odds with many if not most of his intellectual colleagues, particularly those old enough to have retained some sense of the "normalcy" of a unified German nation.[22] While never opposing unification outright, Habermas voiced intense concern and not a little pessimism over the normative implications of unification while it remained a possibility. Since 1990 his assessments – and not just his – of the fact of a unified Germany have grown increasingly disillusioned, centering on the many opportunities for truly valuable collective normative achievements that were missed by the manipulative mode and the hurried tempo of the unification process.

The vision of a process to reforge the network of political-cultural relationships between East and West Germans had, in addition to its obviously high potential for resurgent nationalism, a universalist content as well. In Habermasian terms, West and East both came into a new kind of relationship at the end of 1989 with communicative issues to settle. Each could have found in the other not only a chance to offer a kind of discursive assistance to a communicatively disadvantaged fellow citizen, but could also have found in the other a mirror, or perhaps better a lens, through which discursive distortions particular to its own society could have been seen and acknowledged.

For the "Ossis" of the former DDR, the communicative damage was obvious: Indeed the last years of the DDR, with the gradual consolidation of state control over what remained of a political public sphere and the surreally large, gruesomely efficient network of snitches set up by the STASI, were a nightmarish mirror image of the Habermasian form of universal unrestrained communication. East Germans had, one way or another, accommodated themselves – and whatever personal commitment they still had to "real existing socialism" – to an omnipresent state apparatus based upon the opposite of democratic participation. Gradually, even the counterfactual expectation of political participation withered, and the frozen relation of domination between state bureaucracies and everyday life was normalized.[23] As political communication between the public sphere and the state trickled to a stop, a "niche society" of individual strategies of refuge and meaning developed, and private life took on an increasingly overburdened role as the locus of the communicative dimension of the lifeworld. Political discourse within the pockets of publicity that remained had to adapt selectively to peculiar conditions, evolving a characteristic gift for misdirection, irony, and sarcasm, and double- or triple-entendres – political semiotics and parodic modes of communicative miscommunication that have never found much resonance in Habermas's straightforward model of political communication in Western societies.

The mandatory and inflexible antifascism of the DDR – the ideology that East Germany's relation to Nazism was one of uncomplicated heroism – served to squash even the possibility of a collective moral discourse about the recent past in the DDR even more effectively than the anticommunist reconstruction mentality of the early Federal Republic. The durability of this ideological wish delayed a process of *Vergangenheitsbewältigung* comparable to that which was carried out in West Germany, thus deepening a kind of inveterate discursive incapacity when it came time for the East Germans to confront their own national history, above all the excessively large part that the repressions of the STASI had played in it. Apart from the incessant images of material excess that they absorbed from massive amounts of American television, most East Germans had no cultural resources with which to make sense out of the new experience of a democratic capitalist society when the wall between them and their *Landsleute* collapsed. They entered into a new political reality with extraordinarily detailed images of economic success, but little experience of how such dreams could or could not be reconciled with the abstract principles that grounded political participation in a diverse multicultural society with interlocking constellations of different and often irreconcilable interests. West Germans' initial sympathy for the endearingly naive East Germans as they tried to navigate a lifeworld of extreme material abundance quickly cooled to an often irritable condescension.

But the West Germans came to the table with communicative problems of their own: the "inner colonization of the lifeworld" may take a very different shape in capitalist societies than it does in "real existing socialism," but the effect is in a basic sense the same. For West Germany, the dynamism of an open political public sphere had long been offset by the paralyzing effect of the unbridled development of its economic subsystem. The "history of success" of the Federal Republic's economy had brought about a serious imbalance between communicative solidarity, on the one hand, and the "steering media" of political and economic institutions on the other. While public attitudes toward democracy and a decentralized federal government remained strong up to unification,[24] the 1980s had nevertheless been plagued by an increasingly unsteady economy and a gradual ossification of government bureaucracies. A series of political scandals throughout the 1980s drew comparisons to Weimar, even from nationally prominent politicians.[25] Torn between the incessant anti-Western propaganda of their own state and the equally incessant fantasy land of material bliss offered by Western television, East Germans were often shocked by the frenzied pace of life in the Federal Republic, and by what they regarded as the shallowness and spiritual vacuity of their West German fellow citizens.

The inauguration of a new constellation of communicative relationships between the former West and East was from the beginning beset by the sheer historical fact that a forty-year separation, artificial though it may have been, nevertheless resulted in significant *cultural* differences. "Wessis" and "Ossis" had different attitudes, motivations, and perceptions; they had different collective patterns and standards for the interpretation of experience, different communicative habits and expectations. New communicative relations would have had to develop slowly and carefully, and could not have reasonably expected the production of a simple or easy consensus concerning the meaning of unification for either side.

But the tangle of miscommunications and misunderstandings that have long characterized East–West German discourses – the strange symbiosis of mutual recognition and mutual incomprehensibility captured so well by Peter Schneider[26] – are a part, perhaps even a necessary part, of a communicative relationship. A slow and steady development of this communicative relationship, one that placed normative weight on the careful cultivation of the communicative strengths of both sides, might have allowed the West to help the East in the adoption of the democratic principles of an open society. They could have opened up avenues for a discourse about the possibility of a *multicultural* Germany in which "Germanness" finally meant something like the common status of citizens of the Federal Republic, with all the corresponding rights and duties. The Easterners, on the other hand, could have thematized their own legitimate reservations about the excessive amounts of personal sacrifice necessary for material success in the hurry-up economy of the old Federal Republic. They could have used a particularly East German sensitivity for the priority of interpersonal relationships to assist a broader conversation about the ongoing task of balancing the costs of capitalist modernization for the fragile network of intersubjective relations that form the network of social solidarity. In collective discourse about the political and cultural differences that their separate histories had bequeathed them, East and West might have been required to take up once again the relation between a republican present and a Nazi past: The West might have been able to gently help the East at least begin its own process of *Vergangenheitsbewältigung*; a process that could only refocus a collective discussion on the significance of shared historical continuities and their corresponding responsibilities for the future.

From very early on, however, Habermas was already voicing the suspicion that the unification process would not enable the citizens of East and West to attempt such collective explorations. In an open letter entitled "The Hour of National Feeling: Republican Conviction or National Consciousness?" written two weeks after the collapse of the Berlin Wall in November of 1989, Habermas reflected on the two fundamental options open to the Federal Republic. Opting for "reunification" – indeed, during those last days of 1989, the choice between using the term "unification" and using "reunification" was already a crucial political commitment – risked introducing a fatal split in the self-identification of German citizens, who now had to reconcile their tenuous republican convictions with the resurgence of particularist national feeling. The citizens of the Federal Republic, Habermas wrote, had never had the opportunity to experience the transition from ethnic nationalism to universalism as a foundation for collective identity as an autochthonous achievement. One result of this peculiarity has been the absence, since the *Zusammenbruch*, of any *legitimate* form of self-expression apart from DM-nationalism. The possibility of a German–German unification, if worked for in purely ethnic, nationalistic terms, thus constituted a grave danger to the shallow roots of republican mentality, a threat of *relapse* into a kind of nationalist particularism that is historically off-limits for Germans. "What Adenauer had paved over is now showing cracks."[27]

By the beginning of 1990 Habermas was convinced that even this choice would not be made available: The Kohl administration had determined a *Deutschlandpolitik* that insisted on an all-out attempt to accelerate the unification process, on the premise that the "favorable hour" of history and the imminent economic collapse of the DDR made any delays unacceptable. On Habermas's view, the unification process was thus from the beginning plagued by an administrative strategy of *minimizing* the discursive, hence normative dimension of the situation as much as possible, and of circumventing any collective discourse on the possibility of the postconventional significance of an expanded German citizenship by strategic appeals to conventional forms of particular national identity. "Lambsdorff, Kohl and their fixers conceived of the unification process as the task of the legal-administrative reorganization of a self-running economic mechanism."[28]

Using the pressure of the political advantage of the ruling Christian Democratic Party (the CDU) in the East, a policy of early parliamentary elections, promises to finance unification without raising taxes (later known as the "tax lie"), currency union and forceful international diplomacy, the government was successful in the astonishing feat of bringing about the official union of the two German states less than a year after the opening of the Berlin Wall. As a means to this end, the conservative administration did not shy away from supplementing the already strong resurgence of national feeling with strategic nationalist calls of its own: Kohl's incessant appeals for the unity of the German *Vaterland* not only associated German unity with the CDU in the eyes of many new Eastern voters, but helped to supplant any discussion of different political or social options for the new German political entity with the old, "normal" image of an ethnic-linguistic German nation-state. Thus heavy-handed politics quickly cemented the meaning of what Habermas has called the "remedial revolution" of 1989 as a final triumphant grasp of the elusive brass ring of German nationhood.

For Habermas the consequent efforts to blur the distinction between nation as a society of citizens versus nation as a prepolitical community of *Volk* became the single most dangerous precipitate of this forced unification.[29] In 1990, as in 1987, Habermas argued that the commonality of moral catastrophe was a historical filter through which any *uncritical* reappropriation of a fictive German cultural nation-state would not pass.

Auschwitz can and should remind the Germans, no matter in what state territories they may find themselves . . . that they cannot count on the continuities of their own history. Because of that horrible break in continuity the Germans have given up the possibility of constituting their identity on something other than universalist principles of state citizenship, in the light of which national traditions can no longer remain unexamined, but can only be critically and self-critically appropriated. Post-traditional identity . . . *exists* only in the method of the public, discursive battle around the interpretation of a constitutional patriotism made concrete under particular historical circumstances.[30]

For Habermas, this fast-forward, hyperadministered unification operation deprived Germans on both sides of an irreplaceable opportunity for a collective moral discourse on the meaning of German citizenship. The result is what Habermas has called the "normative deficit" of German unification, the "utter moral impoverishment that the hurry-up tempo of the unification process has left us."[31]

The mode and the tempo of the unification process have been dictated by the Federal Government. The most striking physiognomic feature of this is the instrumental character of the administrative procedure itself. Despite all the carefully installed foreign-policy cushioning, despite all the tailoring to economic imperatives, this procedure never won any *democratic* dynamic of its own . . . Kohl and his kitchen cabinet achieved their goals with the same kinds of virtues and vices that one would have only expected from the narrow political infighting over some issue of domestic policy. By the instrumental use of international treaties, policies of self-imposed deadlines and the commandeering of the organizational networks of the bloc parties, they managed to out-maneuver both the deeply divided opposition and the public sphere. They set the course for a process that proceeded primarily in the categories of economic organization – without ever having made the political alternatives into a theme for discussion.[32]

The result of this strategic dampening of communicative possibilities is that "unification hasn't been understood as a normatively willed act of the citizens of both states, who in political self-awareness decided upon a common civil union."[33] The "normative deficit" of unification is thus

a complaint about the reckless intervention in our political culture, and thus about long-term damages to it that the political parties dangerously ignored in their election tactics, and the bureaucrats ignored with the administrative institutionalization of an economic system. The institutions provided for by the Basic Law can only function as well as they are allowed by the civic consciousness of a population accustomed to institutions of freedom. Political culture is made up of a delicate fabric of mentalities and convictions that can neither be invented nor manipulated through administrative measures. What we're objecting to is the reckless treatment of incalculable and exhaustible moral and cultural resources; resources that can regenerate themselves only spontaneously, and not according to a prearranged path. Self-understanding, the political self-consciousness of a nation of citizens, forms itself only in the medium of public communication. And this communication depends on a cultural infrastructure that is at this moment being allowed to fall into ruins in the new states.[34]

In his frequent calls for a collective discourse on the status of German citizenship during the unification process, Habermas of course had more in mind than the happy model of a spontaneously generated communicative encounter within the public sphere. While it is true that East–West dialogue did flourish in the extrainstitutional formats of print media, colloquia, and all manner of informal discussion groups, Habermas was also thinking of a concrete possibility for collective discourse mandated by the Basic Law itself.

Article 146, the final article of the Basic Law, expresses the provisional nature of the document – that is, the difference between it and a constitution – by stipulating that the Basic Law as a whole "loses its validity on the day that a new constitution takes effect, concluded by the German people in free decision." Such a legally mandated process of "free decision" could mean nothing else than a (truly Habermasian) collective moral-political discourse, a "popular referendum on the constitution"[35] that would necessarily move freely between different institutional structures and fora, that would demand open and nonstrategic expectations, attitudes, and procedures, and that would extend to a collective process of will-formation concerning a collective political identity. In other words, the invocation of Article 146 would not only have given the East Germans a period of time to catch their breath, but would also have finally *allowed* all Germans to decide once and for all whether they chose to define themselves according to universalistic principles or nationalistic conceptions. Constitutional patriotism itself, on this reading, demanded that the unification process consist of the *formal* enactment of the very sorts of popular sovereignty that Habermas was championing:

Identification with the principles and the institutions of our constitution demands . . . an agenda for reunification which gives priority to the freely exercised right of the citizens to determine their own future by direct vote, within the framework of a non-occupied public sphere that has not already been willed away. This means, concretely, that the will of the voting public is given precedence over an annexation cleverly initiated but in the final analysis carried through only at the administrative level – an annexation which dishonestly evades one of the essential conditions for the founding of any nation of state-citizens: the public act of a carefully considered democratic decision taken in both parts of Germany.[36]

Thus the *constitutional* side of the Kohl administration's strategy was the plan to avoid – at virtually any cost – the kind of public constitutional forum demanded by Article 146 of the Basic Law itself, on the presupposition that public attitudes toward a slower and more circumspect process of state unification, brought out in a process of public communication, could well throw a wrench into a process that for reasons of political expediency the Christian Democrat–Christian Socialist (CDU–CSU) coalition government wished to accomplish as quickly as possible.

The answer that the government arrived at was to read the Basic Law *strategically:* With a good deal of public support, the Kohl administration fastened upon the possibility of invoking Article 23 of the Basic Law as a means to circumvent the demand for public communication of Article 146. Article 23 guarantees the validity of the Basic Law for unspecified "other parts" of Germany upon their entrance to the Federal Republic, in effect providing a simple shortcut for the admission of new states. The authors of the Basic Law had been thinking primarily of the Saarland, which entered the Federal Republic by means of Article 23 in 1957. Kohl's *Deutschlandpolitik,* and the "Alliance for Germany" engineered by the federal government for the March 1990 East German parliamentary elections, both strongly emphasized a recourse to Article 23 as a speedy and uncomplicated constitutional medium for the unification process, justifying this approach by appealing to the (as yet unvoiced) collective will of the East German population as well as the rapid collapse of the East German economy. "The constitutional discussion," Habermas has written, "was regarded as an obstacle to the smooth operation of the administration, and pushed to the side."[37] "Via Article 23, citizens can merely *suffer* the process of unification."[38]

If we do not free ourselves from the diffuse notions about the nation-state, if we do not rid ourselves of the prepolitical crutches of nationality and community of fate, we will be unable to continue unburdened on the very path that we have long since chosen: the path to a multicultural society, the path to a federal state with wide regional differences and strong federal power, and above all the path to a unified European state of many nationalities. A national identity which is not based predominantly on republican self-understanding and constitutional patriotism necessarily collides with the universalist rules of mutual coexistence for human beings. . . .[39]

IV

Half a decade after unification, this prophesy of a collision has come depressingly true: The issues that have gripped German political culture since 1990 have been in large measure the precipitates of the *refusal* to take the slow and steady, discursive path toward unification that Habermas had urged. Apart from the severe economic problems arising from the costs of unification and global recession, the new, larger Federal Republic has been preoccupied with a bitter political and social struggle over how best to address the stubborn economic and social disparities that persist between the former West and East.

More important – certainly more visible internationally – the question of German identity is now raised by the status of asylum seekers, the mounting right-wing and skinhead violence against them in both the former East and West, and the growing political success of right-wing political parties. All three of these trends cannot be traced back directly to the consequences of the particular mode of unification in 1990. But, consonant with Habermas's concerns, all three point unmistakably to the possibility that the gains in universalist mentality and postconventional collective identity have been and continue to be sharply reversed in the new Federal Republic.

More shocking than right-wing violence itself, Habermas has written, is the "recognizable syndrome of prejudices" that the violence is awakening in the broader population: the past as future.[40] Resurgent national pride now takes the form of silent approval of the violent attacks against Turks and asylum seekers:

The problem isn't the Skinheads but the police who either weren't there or who looked on without intervening; the prosecuting authorities who . . .

proceeded only with hesitation; the courts that were lacking in comprehensible judgments; the *Bundeswehr* officers who throw practice grenades against the asylum shelters; the political parties who are trying to divert attention away from a wrongly engineered unification process with their unspeakable asylum debate, making themselves into the accomplices of the dullest, most resentment-laden portion of their electorate.[41]

Perhaps even more than violence against foreigners, however, the debate over asylum rights itself has for Habermas the most deeply troubling implications for the future of collective identity in the Federal Republic.[42]

The response to the tide of immigration and its right-wing backlash in the Federal Republic has, up until now, taken the form of a gradual concession to the antiforeigner sentiments. While Chancellor Kohl noticeably absented himself from the many demonstrations against antiforeigner violence (as well as the funerals of its victims), the major political parties gradually reached a consensus that the only politically viable solution to the immigration problem was to change the article (16) of the Basic Law assuring all those politically persecuted safe haven and financial aid in the Federal Republic until their cases could be decided. After a first attempt to supplement Article 16 with special conditions intended to hobble it, the *Bundestag* ultimately voted in May of 1993 to recast the constitutional guarantee of political asylum altogether, bringing the Federal Republic in line with other West European countries.

Habermas has attacked the government's constitutional solution to the asylum question as a transparent ploy to stop the hemorrhage of conservative voters from the CDU to Franz Schönhuber's radical right-wing *Republikaner*, and has castigated the scandal-rocked SPD for caving in to the pressure from the right.[43] But he also sees the asylum debate as a whole as a means for the strategic *reintroduction* of the most virulent strain of German ethnic particularism.

And thus we meet once again the same theme: The Federal Republic is balanced on the line of a decision between Republic and *Volksnation* that it seems destined never to conclude. In the case of asylum rights, this tension once again traces back to the context of the Basic Law: One of the true oddities of the Basic Law is the particularism that lingers in its own conception of citizenship. While citizenship is defined according to legal standards, German nationality remains based on bloodline, thus simultaneously denying citizenship to generations of Turks born and raised in Germany as well as granting citizenship to "Status Germans," ethnic Germans from Eastern Europe and the former Soviet Union who often have no linguistic or cultural relation with their ancestral land. The rights of naturalization in the Federal Republic are correspondingly narrow.

This paradox between ethnic and legal conceptions of citizenship lies at the heart of the *political* significance of the asylum debate, which for Habermas is a mask, behind which questions about German identity that were repressed during the unification process continue to fester. Yet again: "reactions to the resurgence of right-wing violence – and in this context the asylum debate as well – have given rise to the question of whether the *expanded* Federal Republic today will continue on the path of political civilization, or whether it will renew the old special consciousness in a new form."[44]

The postunification Federal Republic has witnessed a profound change in its political culture. The achievement of national unity, the sudden exposure of former East Germans to the challenges of a multicultural society, lingering economic recession, and immigration pressures have combined to lower the collective threshold of inhibitions for the expression of resentment and frustration.[45] The Federal Republic's customary "DM-Nationalism" is beginning to congeal into the very explosive admixture with irrationalist currents from Germany's prewar past that Habermas most fears.

It is too soon to tell whether the colder political climate in the Federal Republic represents an ugly if comprehensible letting off steam, or whether a true reversal of the gradual trend toward republican forms of political identification has occurred. Habermas argues that the present woes of the Federal Republic are all, in one sense or another, consequences of the "big lie" *(Lebenslüge)* on which the march toward discourse-free unification was based: that a unified German state could win back the chimerical "normalcy" of a conventional nation-state.[46]

One way or another, the old Federal Republic is gone for good. Habermas's polemical attempts to cultivate a universalist mentality from out of the ashes of Germany's irrationalist past will from now on be directed toward a nation with a far more complicated – and volatile – constellation of political attitudes. Mass antifascist demonstrations in virtually all of Germany's major cities still inspire confidence that "behind the coffins of the victims of right-wing violence, republican consciousness seems to be awake once again."[47] Popular sovereignty may still prove itself better than its own government. If so, it will be a truly historic triumph for the force of the better argument.

In *The Question of German Guilt*, Karl Jaspers proclaimed that "Germany cannot come to [regain consciousness] unless we Germans find the way to communicate with each other."

We want to learn to talk with each other. That is to say, we do not just want to reiterate our opinions but to hear what the other thinks. We do not just want to assert but to reflect connectedly, listen to reasons, remain prepared for a new insight. We want to accept the other, to try to see things from the other's point of view; in fact, we virtually want to seek out opposing views. Finding the common in the contradictory is more important than hastily seizing on mutually exclusive points of view and breaking off the conversation as hopeless.[48]

That was 1945. Jaspers already recognized that the "situation" could offer only ashes, and more ashes, to any more grand designs to set Germany up once again as a "community of fate." In the simplest openings of human discourse, the unavoidable solidarity of talking and listening, he sensed the only possibility for a "purification" of German guilt – a word that still resonated with all that Jaspers had set out to condemn – but also the only possible foundation for a German identity worth having.

Nearly a half century after this beginning, Habermas's consistent calls for civic spirit are increasingly being drowned out by other kinds of shouting, both from the pages of the feuilletons and from the streets. In the present political climate, as the journalist Jane Kramer has recently written, "A philosopher like Jürgen Habermas talking about the social contract . . . can sound like a voice from some other country."[49] Perhaps sounding foreign is the only way for *this* German identity to survive today.

NOTES

1 "Keine Normalizierung der Vergangenheit," in *Eine Art Schadensabwicklung, Kleine Politische Schriften VI* (Frankfurt: Suhrkamp, 1987), p. 17.

2 This Meadean sensibility for universalism as the ability to understand one's own and other's needs from an abstract standpoint is developed most clearly in "Discourse Ethics: Notes of a Program of Philosophical Justification," in *Moral Consciousness and Communicative Action* (Cambridge, Mass.: MIT Press, 1990): "True impartiality pertains only to that standpoint from which one can generalize precisely those norms that count on universal assent because they perceptibly embody an interest common to all those affected. It is these norms that deserve intersubjective recognition" (p. 65).

3 See *The Theory of Communicative Action*, Vol. II, *Lifeworld and System: A Critique of Functionalist Reason* (Boston: Beacon Press, 1987), p. 94, and "Discourse Ethics," pp. 57–76.

4 "Nachholende Revolution und linker Revisionsbedarf. Was heisst Sozialismus heute?" in *Die nachholende Revolution. Klein politische Schriften VII* (Frankfurt: Suhrkamp, 1991), p. 196.

5 "Staatsbürgerschaft und nationale Identität," in *Faktizität und Geltung. Beiträge zur Diskurstheorie des Rechts und des demokratischen Rechtsstaats* (Frankfurt: Suhrkamp, 1992), p. 638.

6 "Was heisst Sozialismus heute?" p. 196.

7 *Faktizität und Geltung*, p. 642.

8 Ibid., p. 643.

9 Interview with J. M. Ferry, in *Philosophy and Social Criticism* 14, nos. 3–4 (1988): 436. Translation edited.

10 In his 1990 article, "Yet Again: German Identity – A Nation of Angry DM-Burghers?" Habermas agrees with the historian Wolfgang Mommsen that "the self-confidence of a successful economic nation . . . forms the core of the political self-understanding of the population of the Federal Republic – and a substitute for a national pride that is widely lacking." In *When the Wall Came Down: Reactions to German Unification*, ed. Harold James and Marla Stone (New York: Routledge, 1992), p. 88. Hereafter referred to as "Yet Again."

11 See the study by Gabriel A. Almond and Sidney Verba, cited in H. Honolka, *Die Bundesrepublik auf der Suche nach ihrer Identität* (Munich: C. H. Beck, 1987), p. 104.

12 "Historical Consciousness and Post-Traditional Identity," in *The New Conservatism. Cultural Criticism and the Historians' Debate*, ed. and trans. Shierry Weber Nicholsen (Cambridge, Mass.: MIT Press, 1989), p. 255.

13 "Über den doppelten Boden des demokratischen Rechtsstaates," in *Die nachholende Revolution. Kleine politische Schriften VII* (Frankfurt: Suhrkamp, 1990), pp. 18–19.

14 The ratification by popular plebiscite originally proposed for the Basic

Law (in the London Conference of 1948), was, under pressure from the minister-presidents of the old German states in the American, British, and French zones, changed to a ratification by two-thirds of the state parliaments.

15 See "Über den doppelten Boden des demokratischen Rechtstaates," p. 20.

16 At the beginning of the 1980s Habermas had written that neoconservatives' strategic (read: nondiscursive) reappropriation of cultural traditions, meant to operate as a "compensation for damages" [Schadensabwicklung] for social modernization, "focuses upon the 'courage for the past' in schools, the family, and the state. The neoconservatives perceive their task, on the one hand, in the mobilization of shared pasts that are capable of being accepted approvingly; on the other, in the moral neutralization of other pasts that could only provoke criticism and rejection." "Die Kulturkritik der Neokonservativen in den USA und in der Bundesrepublik," in Die neue Unübersichtlichkeit (Frankfurt: Suhrkamp, 1985), p. 41.

17 "Grenzen der Neohistorismus," in Die nachholende Revolution, p. 152.

18 Cf. "Grenzen der Neohistorismus," in Die nachholende Revolution, p. 150.

19 "Apologetic Tendencies," in The New Conservatism, p. 227.

20 M. R. Lepsius, "Das Erbe des Nationalsozialismus und die politische Kultur der Nachfolgestaaten des 'Grossdeutschen Reiches,'" in Kultur und Nation, ed. M. Haller (Frankfurt, 1989), 254ff, cited in Habermas, "Yet Again?" p. 90.

21 "Political Culture in Germany since 1968: An Interview with Dr. Rainer Erd for the Frankfurter Rundschau," in The New Conservatism, p. 193.

22 Particularly instructive in this regard is Habermas's ongoing feud with Karl Heinz Bohrer, who had argued strongly in favor of a rapid recovery of a volkisch German nation-state, countering the "moral argument" against unification – that Auschwitz had made such an achievement morally impermissible – with a bizarrely literal reading of the old task of "coming to terms with the past" according to which Germany had concretely discharged its debt to the past by giving up its eastern territories in Silesia and East Prussia. ("Why We Are Not a Nation – And Why We Should Become One," in James and Stone, When the Wall Came Down, p. 66. In "Yet Again: German Identity: A Unified Nation of Angry DM-Burghers?" and Vergangenheit als Zukunft, Habermas attacked Bohrer's argument as a mendacious rehashing of the old German irrationalist conservatism of the generation of Schmitt and Heidegger – that is, an antiquated importation of prepolitical or aesthetic, neo-Romantic and irrationalist concepts into pragmatic political

choices. See "Yet Again?" pp. 99–100, and *Vergangenheit als Zukunft* (Zurich: Pendo Verlag, 1990), pp. 42–45.

23 For an interesting portrait of the everyday life in the last years of the DDR, see John Borneman, *After the Wall: East Meets West in the New Berlin* (New York: Basic Books, 1991).

24 The European Community's "Eurobarometer" survey for late 1988 showed 30 percent of West Germans dissatisfied with a democratic state – a rise from the 20 to 25 percent opposition from the early 1980s, but significantly lower than the 47 percent dissatisfaction rate for the European Community as a whole, 50 percent for Great Britain, and 53 percent for France. A long-term Allensbach survey, also from 1988, showed 71 percent of West Germans in favor of a federal over a centralized form of government, up from 17 percent in 1952. See David Marsh, *The New Germany at the Crossroads* (London: Century, 1989), pp. 351, 379.

25 For an account of the Flick and Barschel affairs and political reactions, see Marsh, *New Germany at the Crossroads*, ch. 4.

26 Peter Schneider, *Der Mauerspringer*. Translated as *The Walljumper* (New York: Random House, 1983).

27 "Die Stunde der nationalen Empfindung: Republikanische Gesinnung oder Nationalbewusstsein," in *Die nachholende Revolution*, p. 162.

28 *Vergangenheit als Zukunft*, p. 57.

29 See, for example, "Yet Again?" p. 98.

30 Ibid., p. 99.

31 *Vergangenheit als Zukunft*, p. 93.

32 Ibid., p. 56.

33 Ibid., p. 59.

34 Ibid., pp. 62–63.

35 "Yet Again?" p. 97.

36 James and Stone, *When the Wall Came Down*, p. 96.

37 *Vergangenheit als Zukunft*, p. 59: "Is it too much to demand that an effort be made in the medium of public communication, so that a *new* Federal Republic, composed of such unequal parts, can anchor itself in the consciousness of its citizens as something shared – and not experienced just as the byproduct of the forced construction of an expanded currency zone?"

38 "Yet Again?" p. 97.

39 Ibid., p. 97.

40 "Die Asyldebatte (Parisier Vortrag vom 14. Januar 1993)" unpublished manuscript, p. 5.

41 "Die zweite Lebenslüge der Bundesrepublik," expanded unpublished manuscript, p. 5.

42 See *Faktizität und Geltung*, p. 652: "The asylum problem exposes once again the latent tension between citizenship and national identity."

43 See "Die zweite Lebenslüge der Bundesrepublik: Wir sind wieder 'normal' geworden," *Die Zeit*, no. 51, Dec. 11, 1992.

44 "Die Asyldebatte," p. 14.

45 Cf. ibid., p. 16.

46 "The 'big lie' that was launched from above in the Adenauer years, and that we had to deal with back then, went: We're all democrats. It took the Federal Republic a long time to get over this; it required a youth revolt to liberate it from the devastating sociopsychological consequences of this self-deception. If a *second* big lie is in the process of emerging since 1989, it's more one that we "have finally become normal again." "Die zweite Lebenslüge der Bundesrepublik," p. 13.

47 "Die Asyldebatte," p. 21.

48 Karl Jaspers, *The Question of German Guilt*, trans. E. B. Ashton (New York: Dial Press, 1947), pp. 11–12.

49 Jane Kramer, "Letter from Germany," *The New Yorker*, June 14, 1993.

Part III

COMMUNICATIVE
RATIONALITY:
SOCIAL SCIENTIFIC AND
ETHICAL IMPLICATIONS

5   Critical theory as a research program

Critical theory is often dismissed (inasmuch as it is ever contemplated at all) by empirically inclined social scientists as an obscure, speculative, and unscientific philosophical enterprise. Such dismissal is not reserved for critical theory alone, often extending to social and political theory more generally. It must be admitted that there are often good reasons why these social scientists should scorn the efforts of their more philosophically inclined colleagues.[1] But here I shall argue that the critical theory of Jürgen Habermas stands out from most of what now passes for political and social theory in its ability to engage empirical social science in fruitful dialogue.

This dialogue is not just a matter of critical theory issuing philosophical and methodological guidance for the practice of social science, though any social science taking critical theory seriously could hardly emerge from the encounter unaltered. Critical theory can also provide a context and a frame for making sense of existing social science findings. Moreover, the street is a two-way one: Critical theory itself is rightly dependent on social science findings, and Habermas himself has made good (if somewhat sporadic) use of such findings. My discussion begins with the program for social science proposed in Habermas's earlier epistemological and methodological work. I shall then turn to the more productive influence of Habermas's later work on communicative action. I conclude with an examination of how critical theory can assimilate and make sense of more established social science research programs.

For suggestions and comments, I thank Kenneth Baynes, Amber Cole, and Hans-Kristian Hernes. For hospitality while writing this chapter, I am grateful to the Research School of Social Sciences and Graduate Public Policy Program at Australian National University.

97

I. HABERMAS'S PHILOSOPHY OF SOCIAL SCIENCE

Habermas's own distinct conception of critical theory first crystallized in the 1960s in the context of his work on the philosophy of social science, most notably in *On the Logic of the Social Sciences* and *Knowledge and Human Interests*.[2] Reflecting on this work in 1982, Habermas remembers that "I was convinced for a time that the project of a critical social theory had to prove itself, in the first instance, from a methodological and epistemological standpoint."[3] Now, to move from epistemology and methodology to social theory is one thing (and often difficult enough), the further movement to actual practice of social science quite another. To what extent have such moves been made by Habermas himself or by social scientists who took his methodological and epistemological standpoint seriously?

To approach an answer through reference to the "negative" aspect of Habermas's critique of social science, anyone who accepted his condemnation of positivism (the idea that the essence of science is the deduction of causal laws, which are then verified through empirical test) would presumably have to abandon the search for empirically verified causal explanation of social phenomena. However, two factors blunt the force of this condemnation of positivism. The first is that it is hardly original or unique to Habermas. The second is that even though social scientists have often preached positivism they have rarely practiced it. As Terence Ball notes, the actual practices of political scientists at least can be more readily assimilated to an interpretive or hermeneutic philosophy of social science, in which the primary task is coming to grips with the logic of particular situations constituted by human subjects.[4] This generalization holds even though many of these practitioners talk a positivist line and regard hermeneutics as something alien.

In his epistemological work of the 1960s (and in his subsequent dispute with Hans-Georg Gadamer) Habermas also discusses and criticizes this interpretive model of social science. Just as he believed that the positivist model is appropriate to the practice of natural science and its ultimate interest in manipulating and controlling the natural world, so Habermas believed that the interpretive model is appropriate to cultural sciences such as history and anthropology, whose interest is in grasping and understanding complexes of subjectively formed ways of life. But when it comes to social science, Habermas thought that both the "technical" interest in control and the "practical" interest in understanding are properly subordinate to an "emancipatory" interest in liberation.

In this light, the task for the social scientist is first to understand the ideologically distorted subjective situation of some individual or group, second to explore the forces that have caused that situation, and third to show that these forces can be overcome through awareness of them on the part of the oppressed individual or group in question. Thus a critical social science theory is verified not by experimental test or by interpretive plausibility, but rather by action on the part of its audience who decide that, upon reflection, the theory gave a good account of the causes of their sufferings and effectively pointed to their relief. In *Knowledge and Human Interests,* Habermas celebrates Freudian psychoanalysis in these terms as a model for the social sciences.[5] His critics were quick to point out that psychoanalysis in practice often involves substantial manipulation on the part of the analyst, not to mention the imposition of a dubious theoretical framework. Yet an idealized psychoanalysis involving an egalitarian encounter in which the patient comes to a self-understanding and then decides for himself or herself what shall be done to overcome his or her neuroses might still stand as a methodological model.

This model can be deployed quite straightforwardly to interpret Marxism as a (failed) critical theory concerned with the determinants of the false consciousness of proletarians, and how the workers might achieve emancipation from these ideological forces. Such an account would also expose the error of Marxists who have tried to cast their theory of society in the image of natural science (replete with supposed laws of history), or as economic determinism, or (most recently) in terms of the economically rational choices of individuals whose consciousness was never constrained by ideology, and who need no emancipation. Other social and political theories that can be interpreted as critical theories in Habermas's epistemological terms include feminism, Paulo Freire's pedagogy of the oppressed, dependency theory in international relations, liberation theology,[6] and perhaps Ralph Hummel's account of how social life is deformed under *The Bureaucratic Experience.*[7]

Habermas himself showed little interest in any such examples of critical theory in practice, preferring to confine his discussion of critical social science to the epistemological and metatheoretical level. Referring to his predecessors in the Frankfurt School, Habermas takes them to task because they "never really took the theoretical contributions of the social sciences . . . seriously," such that they "took refuge in an abstract critique of instrumental reason and made only a limited contribution to the empirical analysis of the over-complex reality of our society."[8] But Habermas's epistemological work is itself vulnerable to criticism on precisely these grounds, which is doubly ironic given his own belief that in his own work and beyond, philosophy and social science should rightfully be conjoined.

Habermas's epistemological work, which culminated in *Knowledge and Human Interests*, can, then, provide a context for the interpretation of a number of existing social and political theories, and a metatheoretical frame for social science in general. Yet it is probably fair to say that this idea of emancipatory social science never really inspired much in the way of empirical work, though in this respect the model is far from alone in the philosophy of social science. It may be a bit embarrassing, but it should probably be pointed out here that a conspicuous exception to such lack of impact may be found in the epistemological work of Habermas's adversary in the *methodenstreit* in German social science in the 1960s, Karl Popper. Popperian ideas about fallible causal knowledge necessitating controlled experimentation in connection with piecemeal social engineering have inspired a number of policy experiments, and a still greater number of chapters in policy evaluation textbooks.

II. COMMUNICATIVE ACTION AS A FRAMEWORK

The impact of critical theory's epistemology upon the practice of social science (as opposed to social theory) has, then, proven limited. A far greater impact is achieved with Habermas's turn toward communication and an emphasis on general competences embedded in the capacity for language, which began around 1970 and culminated in *The Theory of Communicative Action*.[9] With this turn, Habermas himself starts to look a bit more like a social scientist and a bit less like a philosopher. Indeed, in the *Theory* he refers several times to his project as a "research program" for social theory, and so presumably for empirical social science too.

The *Theory* is itself partially grounded in the developmental psychology of Lawrence Kohlberg and Jean Piaget, who postulate stages in the development of individual moral (Kohlberg) or operational (Piaget) thought. Habermas attempts to extend this kind of developmental account to society as a whole. This connection suggests that critical theory might profitably engage the traditions of empirical work associated with Kohlberg and Piaget. Along these lines, Shawn Rosenberg sketches a program for a "social psychology of politics."[10] This program is essentially Piagetian, in that its essence is the exploration of how subjective or ideological factors develop in reasoned encounters between the individual and his or her social environment. But Rosenberg notes that an emphasis on the *social* in social psychology is more consistent with Habermas than with Piaget, for Habermas stresses that meaning is constructed intersubjectively, rather than by the subject in isolation.[11] If Piaget's own work can be interpreted as critical theory operating at the level of individual psychology – perhaps more plausibly than can Freudian psychoanalysis, which I discussed earlier – then a Piagetian social psychology can obviously contribute to a critical theory of society, inasmuch as it is in a position to unmask and criticize factors that block developmental processes.

Beyond such possibilities in social psychology, the concepts of communicative action, communicative rationality, and systematically distorted communication can and do provide orientation for empirical study. Just how they might do so is not always entirely clear in *The Theory of Communicative Action* itself, which proceeds in the context of an engagement with some classics in social theory, rather than encounters with real-world cases of communicative action. A more empirical, if much less theoretically developed, inquiry into communicative practice may in fact be found in Habermas's much earlier work on the rise and decline of the early bourgeois public sphere, published in 1962.[12] But let me now discuss a few pieces of social science research inspired by Habermas's more recent ideas about communicative action.

To begin, Habermas's contrast between strategic and communicative action, and the associated distinction between system and lifeworld, provide a frame for the interpretation of many kinds of social phenomena. For example, Habermas himself interprets new social movements in terms of their defense of a threatened lifeworld against encroachments by the forces of state and capital.[13] On this account, systemic imperatives to destroy ecosystems, militarize society, and subjugate women meet with not just strategic resistance upon the part of aggrieved individuals, but also the development of ecological, peace, and women's movements whose internal politics can best be understood in terms of communicative action and a general commitment to principles of free discourse. With their general lack of interest in securing a share of state power, and their persistent debate on their own identity, such movements are not easily analyzed in the categories of more traditional political science and sociology. Postmodernists have also laid claim to these movements, but critical theorists would aver that these movements embody "a selective radicalization of 'modern' values," as Claus Offe puts it, rather than a rejection of modernity.[14] Along these lines, and directly inspired by Habermas's account of communicative action, Jean Cohen and Andrew Arato have developed a broader analysis of civil society as a locus for democratization.[15] To Cohen and Arato, civil society is an autonomous realm of association and discussion where influence over the state is at issue, but where a share in state power is not sought. Empirical support for their analysis is provided by both new social movements in the West and the politics of opposition in Eastern Europe which culminated in 1989.

Habermas's own account of the encroachment of systemic imperatives upon the lifeworld, and resistance through new social movements, is couched in fairly general terms. But more focused empirical analysis along these lines is possible. So, for example, Nancy Fraser conducts an analysis of gender-related needs interpretation in the U.S. welfare system, which, as Jane Braatan notes, fits well with Habermas's notions of communicative action.[16] Fraser contrasts women's needs as defined by welfare administrators with the needs that women themselves might construct if they were allowed to develop a communicative practice of need definition. The matter is not just one of administrators ignoring real needs, but rather of their construction of welfare recipients in certain ways: as objects of state administration, in need of treatment.

To take another example here, Carol Hager draws upon Habermas in her analysis of West German energy policy as a clash between entrenched government bureaucracies and grassroots citizen opposition.[17] Citizen action here sought not just to develop "counterexpertise" and block particular energy projects, but also to establish the rightful supremacy of participatory democracy over bureaucratic authority in determination of the ends and means of policy. The issue, then, becomes one of the appropriate form of legitimation for governmental action: technical expertise or consensus based on communicative interaction. There is more going on here than an ordinary political clash of particular interests.

One of the more ambitious social scientific applications of Habermas's ideas concerning communicative action may be found in Michael Pusey's analysis of Australian politics, which has proven a popular as well as an academic success in that country.[18] At one level, Pusey's book is simply an empirical study of the aggressively economistic and market-oriented attitudes of members of the Senior Executive Service in the central agencies of the Australian federal government in the late 1980s, and a demonstration of their hold over policy making. But Pusey situates these findings in a Habermasian analysis of rationalization and modernization. In this light, economic rationalism in Canberra manifests the increasingly one-sided rationalization of Australian society, in which the "systemically coordinated behavior" of the market displaces "communicatively coordinated action."[19] Pusey compares this relatively recent development with the more discursive and participatory political style that he believes characterized Australian national politics as recently as the early 1970s. But his critique does not rest on nostalgia alone, and he contemplates a future that would involve reassertion of the lifeworld and communicative action, and, more practically, elements of European-style social democracy. Some of his social scientific critics have suggested that Pusey has creatively overinterpreted his survey data. But the appropriate tests for a critical theory of Australian politics are to be found in the reflective reaction of the intended audience, rather than in the canons of statistical methods.

III. COMMUNICATIVE RATIONALITY AS AN EVALUATIVE PRINCIPLE

Beyond providing a frame for the interpretation of social phenomena, Habermas's ideas about communicative action can also be used in the evaluation of social practices. All such practices are going to be in violation of precepts of communicative rationality to greater or lesser degree. Conversely, glimmerings of communicative rationality should be apparent in almost all practices (save for the most abhorrent). Just like its precursor, the ideal speech situation, communicative rationality is not supposed to be an attainable ideal, but rather a critical principle. Moreover, it is best thought of as simply providing procedural criteria concerning how disputes might be resolved or the conditions under which consensus might be achieved, rather than any theory of human needs or principles for individual conduct and social arrangements.[20]

Such criteria can be applied to real-world cases ranging from the general to the specific. At a very general level, David Sciulli sketches a research program for comparative politics that would use a modified version of the principles of communicative rationality to assess and compare the degree of authoritarianism prevailing in political systems.[21] Such systems can be judged nonauthoritarian to the extent they respect what Talcott Parsons called the "collegial" form of social organization, which Sciulli interprets in Habermasian terms as the most politically significant real-world home of communicative rationality. Examples of the collegial form might include professions (in their internal dealings), communities, and informal networks. Sciulli wants to scrutinize and compare collegial formations using as a practical guide the principles of procedural legality enunciated by the legal theorist Lon Fuller. Sciulli claims (somewhat immodestly) that his approach "emancipates Habermas from the corner into which he has painted himself."[22] This approach would do so by specifying a procedural threshold for the recognition of a situation as truly collegial, rather than merely positing an abstract ideal speech situation which nothing can ever attain or approximate. One might question here the degree to which Fuller's principles really are consistent with Habermas's notions of communicative rationality. Putting such concerns aside, it remains the case that Sciulli has established the basis for a rich program of empirical and comparative social science research on an important set of questions. As yet, neither he nor anyone else has actually carried out such research.

At a somewhat less general and more empirical level of analysis,

Daniel Hallin conducts a broad-ranging analysis of the mass media in the United States.[23] From the perspective of communicative action, this kind of case is particularly important because the mass media is of course central to social and political communication in industrial societies and beyond. To Hallin, the American mass media systematically distorts public debate by narrowing the discussion of issues to the technical problem-solving level, and so denying the possibility of major conflicts in problem definition and social values. Thus the mass media undermines the very preconditions for communicatively rational collective will formation. There is simply no way in which implicit validity claims pertaining to the truth, appropriateness, and truthfulness (or sincerity) of utterances made in the mass media can be challenged, for communication goes almost entirely in one direction: from the screen or the printed page to the viewer or reader.

To Hallin, this dismal state of affairs has arisen not because the mass media is an arm of, or legitimating device for, the state or capitalists. Rather, it is due to the simple fact that private ownership means that the media is shaped by market forces (though not necessarily market ideology), in which advertisers demand "objective" or "nonpartisan" news coverage for fear of offending consumers identified with particular ideological groups. This situation is an example of what Habermas refers to as the colonization of society's lifeworld, which is the proper home of communicative rationality, by impersonal forces of money and power tied up with functional imperatives embedded in society's system. Substantively, Hallin's analysis brings to mind Habermas's own account of the decline of the early bourgeois public sphere, one aspect of which was the increasing commercialization of newspapers in the nineteenth century.[24]

A good example of the application of the precepts of communicative rationality to a very specific kind of case is made by Ray Kemp, whose topic is the 1977 public inquiry into the construction of a controversial thermal oxide reprocessing plant at Windscale in England.[25] Again, this is an interesting case from the point of view of communicative action because the implicit claim to legitimacy of such an inquiry lies precisely in its status as a forum for public debate open to submission from a wide variety of points of view. Kemp exposes the systematic distortions that characterized the Windscale Inquiry and guaranteed that it would find in favor of British Nuclear Fuels Ltd. (a government-owned corporation) and against environmentalists and other objectors. Though superficially impartial, the legalistic rules of the inquiry were congenial to the proponents, but not the objectors. The Official Secrets Act was invoked at key points. The objectors lacked the research resources of the proponents. And the rules of admissibility excluded economic evidence against the proposal. Perhaps one could criticize the Windscale Inquiry along such lines without the assistance of any theory of communicative action, but Kemp's critique is sharpened and guided by the validity claims elucidated by Habermas.

These studies of the mass media and public inquiries illustrate that relationships of power in society can be, and are, reproduced through the medium of communicative interaction. Thus one can use close analysis of this kind of interaction to uncover power, and, in particular, hegemonic power that may not be revealed in any overt social or political conflict. Along these lines, John Forester appropriates Habermas's analysis of communicative action for use as a guide for fieldwork in "critical ethnography."[26] In this ethnography, the analyst takes a close look at conversations or even just conversation fragments, scrutinizing them for the implicit validity claims (to truth, appropriateness, truthfulness or sincerity, and comprehensibility) invoked by speakers. For example, using just the claim to appropriateness or legitimacy as a guide, we can scrutinize every sentence for implicit propositions concerning what norms govern the participants, what kinds of strategic actions are allowable, what distributions of competence and responsibility exist among them (and in relation to other individuals or groups), and what kinds of judgments are to be respected. Repeating this scrutiny using each of the other three validity claims as guides reveals the rich and multilayered meanings embedded in every utterance in even seemingly banal conversation. For example, the "truthfulness" validity claim would reveal much about the practical identities of participants as projected by themselves and interpreted, accepted, or rejected by the others. Forester's worked example explores the issues of power relationships and identity revealed in a few lines of conversation in a meeting of a city's planning staff.

IV. CRITICAL THEORY AND APPLIED SOCIAL
SCIENCE

Forester's context for the illustration of critical ethnography hardly
arises by accident. Perhaps somewhat surprisingly, the general area
of planning and policy analysis is one of the most significant locations for the application of Habermas's critical theory in at least
U.S. social science. The reason here is that policy analysis is essentially an attempt to put social science to good practical use in resolving social problems. Following failed attempts and ruined hopes
that relied on more established social science models and methodol-
ogies, critical theory's combination of theory and practice has
proven attractive to an increasing number of policy analysts.[27] Let
me briefly trace the reasons for this development.

Policy analysis is a field without any methodological orthodoxy.
Positivism, Popperian critical rationalism, and various optimizing
techniques rooted in microeconomics and decision theory have all
made their mark, and all still have their adherents despite their histories of failure. To cut a long story short,[28] the causal generaliza-
tions upon which positivists might base policy interventions have
proven thoroughly elusive. The kind of controlled social experimentation favored by Popperians is more plausible. However, such piecemeal social engineering requires manipulation of social conditions
on the part of some elite of policy engineers, who must in turn operate in the context of a fixed normative grid. Such a grid provides
standards for the evaluation of experimental success and failure.
Popperian experiments should be open to criticism both before and
after the fact; but only criticism that relates to empirical questions
of cause and effect, not of the values guiding the experiment. Moreover, the subjects of experiments (for example, residents in a community development project) can only be the objects of policy, and
cannot be allowed to reconstitute their identities, reshape the experiment as it proceeds, or otherwise interfere with experimental ma-
nipulations and controls. Economistic policy analysis techniques
such as cost–benefit analysis simply ignore the fact of politics, regarding policy as a purely technical matter. Thus all three of these
established orientations to policy analysis are both antidemocratic
(critical rationalism somewhat less than the other two), and failures

in the context of real-world politics, where communicative interaction looms large.

Despite their differences, these three established orientations have a common root in a purely instrumental notion of policy rationality. Drawing upon Habermas's work, critical policy analysts can in contrast emphasize the communicative dimension of policy formation. Now, this dimension has been recognized too by some liberal democratic policy analysts,[29] who recognize that in a democratic system public policy is or at least should be arrived at through discussion leading to some kind of consensus or compromise. In this light, policy analysts should offer arguments related to policy, rather than propose (still less dictate) solutions to policy problems. But such liberal analysts cannot distinguish between authentic and distorted communication in policy debates, or effectively sort out strategic and communicative interaction. Thus their own interventions may simply buttress established power and hierarchy, or at best offer supportive arguments that serve the strategic positions of actors (be they politicians, bureaucrats, or interest groups). Such analysts are in no position to uncover interests systematically excluded from policy debates, and so their policy analysis finds itself all too easily in the service of established power.

Critical policy analysts are, in contrast, more attuned to the conditions under which consensus and compromise are reached. Thus their role is not simply to offer arguments to support positions within policy debates, but, more importantly, to scrutinize the conditions under which debate proceeds. John Forester offers them a set of communicative ethics under which it is the task of analysts to expose and challenge agenda manipulation, point to strategic exercises of power that foreclose debate, equalize the information available to participants, and uncover moves to distract attention from embarrassing issues.[30] Analysts might also elucidate socializing forces that distort participants' assumptions and perceptions, and stress unseen threats and possibilities in a situation (concerning, for example, threats of cooptation in community development projects, or opportunities for community-controlled development). They should avoid portraying themselves as professional experts, for professional mystique is itself a source of hierarchy and distortion in policy debate.[31]

Many of these tasks for the policy analyst involve attention to the conditions of political interaction, rather than the content of policy proposals, and this emphasis too distances critical policy analysis from more traditional approaches. Indeed, there is no need to shrink here from contemplation of the design of political institutions and processes. The term "design" often connotes instrumental manipulation of conditions in pursuit of some predefined end (such is, for example, the essence of engineering design). However, in the context of political institutions, design itself can be a participatory and discursive process. Thus institutional reconstruction can itself be one major concern of critical theory.

Such a clearly "applied" emphasis might also give us pause to think a bit more deeply about what exactly puts the critique in critical theory. I have noted elsewhere that at least four kinds of critique are possible: metatheoretical, pure, indirect, and constructive.[32] Metatheoretical critique addresses the epistemological nature and basic contours of critical theory – and a great deal of Habermas's own work and the secondary literature falls into this category. Pure critique involves using a standard such as the ideal speech situation or communicative rationality to assess real-world structures and processes – Kemp's work as discussed earlier is a good example. The critique is pure inasmuch as it criticizes real-world practices to the extent they fall short of the ideal. Indirect critique would involve using this same standard to reconstruct a particular situation and then to contrast this reconstruction with what actually happened.[33] Along these lines, Russell Hanson reconstructs the discourse of the New Left in the 1960s (along with other episodes in U.S. political history) as it might have been had available norms of equality concerning gender in particular been taken seriously.[34] Constructive critique goes further in intimating institutional and structural alternatives to some problematic status quo,[35] though such critique should still seek validation for such proposals in the reflective assent of its intended audience.

This kind of constructive critique might profitably contemplate the design of institutions oriented toward consensus or compromise under conditions of free discourse among equals. Habermas himself has recently begun to speak of the need for institutional design to help promote "communicative power" over "administrative power." Such a move does not imply that one is here trying to institutionalize the ideal speech situation or something similar, but simply a recognition that institutions and practices can indeed be constructed so as to promote communicative rationality and limit instrumental rationality to greater or lesser degree. Institutions merit approval here to the extent they rule out hierarchy, authority on the basis of anything other than a good argument, barriers to participation, or formalized constitutions. More positively, they might embody informal canons of communicative ethics, and decision on the basis of consensus (or at least compromise) rather than majority rule.[36] While it can be hard to find real-world exemplars here, it is worth noting that the last two decades or so have seen an increasing number of institutional innovations whose very claim to legitimacy rests on their achievement of informed participation and consent of all the parties to a dispute. Examples include public inquiries, environmental and social impact assessment, mediation, informal dispute resolution, problem-solving workshops, and various sorts of principled negotiation. Now, such exercises can and do involve substantial violation of principles of communicative rationality, sometimes even blatant manipulation on the part of established power. Yet they can also help to erode the functional imperatives of the "system" by eating away at administrative rationality, whose own claim to legitimacy is based upon supposedly neutral expertise. In short, such innovations have an ambiguous potential, which might prove positive to the extent critical theorists and others interested in participatory democratization engage them in constructive dialogue.

I have dwelt at some length upon critical theory's potential engagement with "applied" social science in both policy analysis and institutional design. This project is likely to meet resistance from both state officials on the one hand and some critical theorists (though probably not Habermas himself) on the other. State administrators are probably not going to be too keen on a style of analysis that thoroughly questions their own authority and competence, and this perhaps explains why critical policy analysis is mostly a project of academics, rather than policy analysts actually working in public bureaucracies. Some critical theorists, for their part, might be uncomfortable with the flirtation with the state and the dangers of cooptation that such constructive endeavors entail. However, there is no need to make an either/or decision here. Such state-related endeavors might easily proceed in parallel with more uncompromising critique rooted in public spheres (such as new social movements) whose very identity is constituted by opposition to the state. Constructive critique can encompass both reform of and continued confrontation with the state.

At first glance, it might also seem odd that Habermas's critical theory has connected more easily with such "applied" endeavors of policy analysis and institutional reconstruction than with "purer" social science concerned primarily with explanation of phenomena. But on reflection this situation should not seem odd at all. More traditional epistemological orientations may locate pure science squarely between abstract theory and applied science, such that to get from theory to application one has to pass through pure science. In contrast, critical theory sees practice ("applied science") as properly central to the social scientific task, to the extent that pure science may simply be dissolved into applied science. Indeed, it is far from obvious that distinguishing the categories "pure" and "applied" social science makes any sense at all in critical theory.

V. ASSIMILATING OTHER RESEARCH PROGRAMS

My discussion so far has emphasized the ways in which social science can be practiced if it takes Habermas's ideas to heart. However, there is also a great deal in the way of social scientific knowledge that has been produced without any reference to critical theory, yet which may be pressed into its service. Habermas has claimed that his critical theory is not intended to replace existing approaches to social science inquiry, but rather to provide a context for the assessment of their contributions and limitations.[37] Indeed, I would argue that critical theory can often be vital in making sense of such bodies of knowledge by liberating them from self-misunderstanding. I shall illustrate my case here through reference to rational choice or public choice analysis, which uses microeconomic assumptions (most notably, the assumption that all individuals are rational egoists) to analyze topics that were traditionally the preserve of political science, sociology, social psychology, anthropology, and moral philosophy. Rational choice has been the most visible and successful interdisciplinary research program in the last decade or two of Western social science, which makes it all the more important for critical theory to try to make sense of it.

At one level, public choice and critical theory may be treated as rival research programs. Stephen White compares the two programs along these lines, and concludes that critical theory offers superior explanations in both the long-running debate over community power and in understanding the dynamics of modernization.[38] Claus Offe in his essay on "Two Logics of Collective Action" points to the limited applicability of the public choice treatment of collective action in instrumental and individualistic terms.[39] This treatment may be adequate for actors whose ends are clear and stable, such as corporations as they organize into business associations. Offe points out that other actors, notably workers as they organize into unions, must attend continually to matters of identity and solidarity, which relate directly to the definition of ends. Thus organizing for collective action by workers has to be a more complex and difficult matter than the public choice account of collective action can recognize. Here, critical theory can both take note of the logic as presented by public choice and expose its limits.

Reasoned comparison across public choice and critical theory of the sort undertaken by White and Offe is a rarity; scornful dismissal of each side by the other is far more common. Yet there is every reason for more productive encounters, and some possibility for synthesis of the two traditions of analysis. For both programs aspire to, among other things, a wholesale critique of politics. And both have developed detailed accounts of what happens when instrumental rationality dominates social and political interaction. Their main point of difference lies in the public choice belief that rationality is synonymous with its instrumental variant (though, as I shall note, a few of its practitioners are coming to doubt this equation), whereas critical theory of course recognizes the parallel existence of communicative rationality. The stance taken by critical theory here can in fact rescue public choice from several impasses, and also make its political program less unsavory. And together, public choice and critical theory enable an account of social and political life more persuasive than either can muster in isolation.

To see why such productive interchange can occur, consider the public choice critique of politics, which has concluded that politics of any sort, democratic or otherwise, is an incoherent mess. Social choice theory has shown that different aggregation mechanisms produce different collective choices from identical distributions of citizen preferences, such that there are large elements of arbitrariness, ambiguity, and instability in collective choice.[40] More specific public choice accounts demonstrate that majority rule is both economically inefficient and repressive,[41] public bureaucracies inevitably grow too large as a result of bureaucrats maximizing their own budgets,[42] legislators create complex programs that do little for the public good while requiring their personal intercession to yield tangible rewards to constituents,[43] labor unions and other economic interests conspire with each other against the public interest[44] and with self-interested politicians and bureaucrats to the detriment of ordinary taxpayers,[45] and government itself is an increasingly parasitic and out-of-control leviathan.[46] Thus politics is an irresponsible game, where everyone seeks benefits for themselves while imposing costs on others.

What is the status of these dismal results? Public choice has a positivist self-image, and so regards them as statements that explain features of the social world as it is. However, as James Johnson notes for one important subset of rational choice analysis, game theory is not really a predictive science, and so empirical test is not crucial in assessing its veracity.[47] Instead, game theory tells us simply what strategic rationality *is* in particular situations, those that can be modeled as games such as prisoner's dilemma. In the terms established by Habermas,[48] game theory is therefore a reconstructive science in that it reconstructs one, but only one, human competence. The capacity to act instrumentally or strategically may be a universal human competence, but other competences can exist too: most notably, of course, communicative competence.

In this light, public choice analyses are contingent upon individuals acting in certain kinds of ways. There is no reason why they must inevitably act in this instrumental or strategic fashion, even though, as Max Weber, Max Horkheimer, Theodor Adorno, and Habermas himself have all noted, there are aspects of the modern industrial and capitalist world that increasingly force such behavior. There are many reasons why individuals should *not* act in purely strategic fashion, foremost among which are the dismal consequences of such action for both society and the individuals who so behave, as described in great detail by public-choice analysis itself.

Habermas himself has long insisted that strategic or instrumental rationality alone cannot account for social and political coordination, and public-choice analysis would seem inadvertently to bear him out. From the perspective of critical theory, the key here is bringing instrumental rationality under the control of communicative rationality. This is not just a matter of advocating communicative rationality as a normative principle, but also of empirical investigation to reveal how such control already occurs. For occur it does, as the very existence of coherent social and political life intimates. Public choice inadvertently demonstrates that this coherence cannot be achieved through strategic or instrumental action. The only alternative means for achieving social integration are therefore tradition and ideology, on the one hand, and communicative rationality on the other. Empirical studies of prisoner's dilemma experiments which show dramatic increases in strategically irrational (but mutually beneficial) cooperative behavior when the experimental subjects are allowed to converse prior to their choices[49] can be explained rather easily in terms of the invocation of communicative rationality. As Johnson argues, talk in such situations is not cheap, but rather essential in moving game theory beyond the indeterminacy and impasse of its own predictions.[50] Johnson deploys Habermas's ideas about the validity claims implicit in conversation to explain how and why binding and credible commitments can occur in the context of strategic interaction, such as prisoner's dilemma games, and so make these interactions less a matter of strategy, more a matter of communicative action.

Public choice may therefore be reinterpreted as a critical theory that tells us what happens when instrumental rationality runs wild.[51] The point then is to render public choice predictions less true by pointing to the contingent nature of instrumentally rational behavior, and to the communicative alternatives to it. Thus might public choice and critical theory be conjoined. Public choice would benefit from this conjunction by shedding its politically embarrassing hostility to democracy and gaining an understanding as to exactly why political order really does exist, despite public-choice predictions to the contrary. Moreover, normatively useful public choice would then become possible. As it stands, normative public choice is incoherent: It either postulates a public-spirited institutional dictator whose behavior violates assumptions about rational egoism, or it would see institutional design as a matter of social choice on the part of individuals with different preferences. If institutional design is a question for social choice then it will be confounded by all the arbitrariness and instability that social choice theory has itself highlighted. But if we interpret public choice as a critical theory, then the problem becomes one of designing institutions to curb strategic behavior and promoting communicative rationality. There is no incoherence or inconsistency here, for (as I noted earlier) such design can itself be undertaken discursively.

Critical theory benefits from its assimilation of public choice by gaining a bit more content for its sometimes rather abstract political and social critiques, and purchase on some practical questions of political and social life. And further insight is gained into the dialectics of modernization. Habermas argues that modernity brings increasing potential for communicative as well as instrumental rationalization. Public-choice analyses can be deployed to show exactly why increasing instrumental rationalization must be accompanied by communicative rationalization, for otherwise social and political life becomes increasingly hard to sustain. Moreover, there are signs that leading public-choice practitioners recognize this point. For example, Viktor Vanberg and James Buchanan argue that constitutional choice in a complex world is characterized by uncertainty as to how particular constitutional rules will affect individual interests.[52] Vanberg and Buchanan proceed to argue that rational discursive scrutiny of the sort Habermas describes can alleviate uncertainty and so facilitate constitutional choice. Though they argue in static terms, it is quite straightforward to extend their argument to conclude that as complexity increases, then the more is such discourse necessary.

Given its centrality in contemporary social science, rational choice theory is obviously an important focus for critical theory's attention. But there is no reason to stop here: Organization theory, "realist" analyses of international relations, voting studies, and any other research program in which instrumental rationality looms large can all benefit from similar treatment.

VI. CONCLUSION

Clearly, there can be more to critical theory than the aridity and abstraction with which empirically oriented social scientists often dismiss it. Indeed, critical theory points to a rich and important conjunction of social theory and empirical research. Yet there remains a shortfall between the programmatic statements of Habermas and other critical theorists on the one hand, and what has actually been accomplished in terms of putting critical theory into social science practice on the other. This situation can be corrected to the extent critical theorists come down from the metatheoretical heights to actually practice the critique they preach. The possibilities are as numerous as the sites of human interaction. There is no shortage of work for those interested in critical theory as a research program.

NOTES

1 See the discussion of the self-inflicted alienation of political theory from political science and political practice in John G. Gunnell, *Between Philosophy and Politics: The Alienation of Political Theory* (Amherst: University of Massachusetts Press, 1986).

2 Jürgen Habermas, *On the Logic of the Social Sciences* (Cambridge: Polity Press, 1988), which first appeared in 1967; Jürgen Habermas, *Knowledge and Human Interests* (Boston: Beacon Press, 1971).

3 Ibid., p. xiv.

4 Terence Ball, "Deadly Hermeneutics: Or, *Sinn* and the Social Scientist," in *Idioms of Inquiry: Critique and Renewal in Political Science,* ed. Terence Ball (Albany: State University of New York Press, 1987).

5 Habermas, *Knowledge and Human Interests,* p. 241.

6 Stephen T. Leonard, *Critical Theory in Political Practice* (Princeton, N.J.: Princeton University Press, 1990).

7 Ralph P. Hummel, *The Bureaucratic Experience,* 3d ed. (New York: St. Martin's Press, 1987).

8 Jürgen Habermas, *Autonomy and Solidarity,* interviews with Jürgen Habermas ed. Peter Dews (London: Verso, 1992), p. 56.

9 Jürgen Habermas, *The Theory of Communicative Action,* Vol. I, *Reason and the Rationalization of Society* (Boston: Beacon Press, 1984); *The Theory of Communicative Action,* Vol. II, *Lifeworld and System* (Boston: Beacon Press, 1987).

10 Shawn Rosenberg, *Reason, Ideology, and Politics* (Princeton, N.J.: Princeton University Press, 1988).

11 Rosenberg, *Reason, Ideology, and Politics,* pp. 209, 212.

12 Jürgen Habermas, *The Structural Transformation of the Public Sphere: An Inquiry into a Category of Bourgeois Society* (Cambridge, Mass.: MIT Press, 1989).

13 Jürgen Habermas, "New Social Movements," *Telos* 49 (1981): 33–37; Habermas, *Theory of Communicative Action*, Vol. II, pp. 393–96.

14 Claus Offe, "New Social Movements: Challenging the Boundaries of Institutional Politics," *Social Research* 52 (1985): 817–68.

15 Jean L. Cohen and Andrew Arato, *Civil Society and Political Theory* (Cambridge, Mass.: MIT Press, 1992).

16 Nancy Fraser, *Unruly Practices* (Minneapolis: University of Minnesota Press, 1989); Jane Braatan, *Habermas's Critical Theory of Society* (Albany: State University of New York Press, 1991), pp. 147–50.

17 Carol J. Hager, "Democratizing Technology: Citizen and State in West German Energy Politics, 1974–1990," *Polity* 25 (1992): 45–70.

18 Michael Pusey, *Economic Rationalism in Canberra: A Nation-Building State Changes Its Mind* (Cambridge: Cambridge University Press, 1991).

19 Ibid., p. 170.

20 Jürgen Habermas, *Communication and the Evolution of Society* (Boston: Beacon Press, 1979), p. 90; Stephen K. White, *The Recent Work of Jürgen Habermas* (Cambridge: Cambridge University Press, 1988), p. 70.

21 David Sciulli, *Theory of Societal Constitutionalism: Foundations of a Non-Marxist Critical Theory* (Cambridge: Cambridge University Press, 1992).

22 Ibid., p. 105.

23 Daniel Hallin, "Critical Theory and the Mass Media," in *Critical Theory and Public Life*, ed. John Forester (Cambridge, Mass.: MIT Press, 1985).

24 Habermas, *Structural Transformation of the Public Sphere*.

25 Ray Kemp, "Planning, Public Hearings, and the Politics of Discourse," in *Critical Theory and Public Life*, ed. John Forester (Cambridge, Mass.: MIT Press, 1985).

26 John Forester, "Critical Ethnography: On Fieldwork in a Habermasian Way," in *Critical Management Studies*, eds. Mats Alvesson and Hugh Wilmott (Newbury, Park, Calif.: Sage, 1992).

27 See, among others, Frank Fischer, *Politics, Values, and Public Policy: The Problem of Methodology* (Boulder, Colo.: Westview, 1980); John Forester, "Questioning and Organizing Attention: Toward a Critical Theory of Planning Practice," *Administration and Society* 13 (1981): 161–205; John Forester, *Planning in the Face of Power* (Berkeley: University of California Press, 1989); Douglas Torgerson, "Between Knowledge and Politics: Three Faces of Policy Analysis," *Policy Sciences* 19 (1986): 33–59; John S. Dryzek, *Discursive Democracy: Politics, Policy, and Political Science* (Cambridge: Cambridge University Press, 1990), chs. 6, 7.

28 For details, see Davis B. Bobrow and John S. Dryzek, *Policy Analysis by Design* (Pittsburgh: University of Pittsburgh Press, 1987).

29 See, for example, David C. Paris and James F. Reynolds, *The Logic of Policy Inquiry* (New York: Longman, 1983).

30 Forester, "Questioning and Organizing Attention."

31 See Douglas Torgerson, "Contextual Orientation in Policy Analysis: The Contribution of Harold D. Lasswell," *Policy Sciences* 18 (1985): 241–61, pp. 254–55.

32 Dryzek, *Discursive Democracy*, pp. 30–32.

33 Jürgen Habermas, *Legitimation Crisis* (Boston: Beacon Press, 1975), p. 113.

34 Russell J. Hanson, *The Democratic Imagination in America: Conversations with Our Past* (Princeton, N.J.: Princeton University Press, 1985).

35 See also Claus Offe, "Designing Institutions in East European Transitions," in *The Theory of Institutional Design*, eds. Robert E. Goodin and H. Geoffrey Brennan (Cambridge: Cambridge University Press, forthcoming).

36 For greater detail, see Dryzek, *Discursive Democracy*, pp. 40–43.

37 Habermas, *Theory of Communicative Action*, Vol. II p. 375.

38 Stephen K. White, "Toward a Critical Political Science," in *Idioms of Inquiry: Critique and Renewal in Political Science*, ed. Terence Ball (Albany: State University of New York Press, 1987).

39 Claus Offe, *Disorganized Capitalism* (Cambridge: Polity Press, 1985), pp. 170–220.

40 William H. Riker, *Liberalism against Populism: A Confrontation between the Theory of Democracy and the Theory of Social Choice* (San Francisco: W. H. Freeman, 1982).

41 James Buchanan and Gordon Tullock, *The Calculus of Consent* (Ann Arbor: University of Michigan Press, 1962).

42 William A. Niskanen, Jr., *Bureaucracy and Representative Government* (Chicago: Aldine-Atherton, 1971).

43 Morris P. Fiorina, *Congress: Keystone of the Washington Establishment* (New Haven, Conn.: Yale University Press, 1977).

44 Mancur Olson, *The Rise and Decline of Nations: Economic Growth, Stagflation, and Social Rigidities* (New Haven, Conn.: Yale University Press, 1983).

45 Milton Friedman and Rose Friedman, *Tyranny of the Status Quo* (New York: Harcourt, Brace, Jovanovich, 1984).

46 William C. Mitchell, *Government As It Is* (London: Institute of Economic Affairs, 1988).

47 James Johnson, "Rational Choice as a Reconstructive Theory," in *The Economic Approach to Politics*, ed. Kristin Monroe (New York: Harper Collins, 1991).

48 Habermas, *Communication and the Evolution of Society*.

49 See John M. Orbell, Alphons J. C. van de Kragt, and Robyn M. Dawes, "Explaining Discussion-Induced Cooperation," *Journal of Personality and Social Psychology* 54 (1988): 811–19.

50 James Johnson, "Is Talk Really Cheap? Promoting Conversation between Critical Theory and Rational Choice," *American Political Science Review* 87 (1993).

51 John S. Dryzek, "How Far Is It from Virginia and Rochester to Frankfurt? Public Choice as Critical Theory," *British Journal of Political Science* 22 (1992): 397–417.

52 Viktor Vanberg and James M. Buchanan, "Interests and Theories in Constitutional Choice," *Journal of Theoretical Politics* 1 (1989): 49–62.

6   Communicative rationality and cultural values

In elaborating his theory of communicative action, Habermas distinguishes the scope of rational agreement available to theoretical and practical discourse, on the one hand, from that available to aesthetic criticism, on the other. In doing so, he distinguishes moral norms from cultural values and questions of justice from questions of the good life. In this essay, I want to examine the grounds Habermas finds for this distinction and explore the conception of communicative reason on which it rests.

I. COMMUNICATIVELY ACHIEVED AGREEMENT

The general question with which Habermas's account of communicative rationality begins might be reconstructed as the question of how language has the ability to coordinate action in a consensual or cooperative way as opposed to a forced or manipulated one. In other words, how does the employment of language in contexts of interaction produce mutual agreement on a course of action, a fact in the world, an aesthetic evaluation, or an expression of intention, desire, need or the like? The presumption here is that there is a difference between consensual agreement and simple compliance and Habermas grounds this presumption in a reconstruction of the pretheoretical knowledge of competent speakers and actors. Competent speakers and actors can themselves distinguish the cases in which they are attempting to come to agreement with others from the cases in which they are using any means possible to bring about compliance, including deceit, manipulation, or outright coercion. Moreover, according to Habermas even this capacity to force compliance can be shown to rest on the possibility of acting communicatively. That is, the "communicative" use of language to reach agreement is the "original" mode of language use upon which its "strategic" use to bring about compliance "is parasitic."[1] In order to make this argument Habermas turns to Austin's distinction between illocutionary and perlocutionary effects.

Austin distinguishes the locutionary aspect of a speech act which designates its propositional content ("p" or "that p") from its illocutionary and perlocutionary aspects. By its illocutionary aspect he refers to the action a speaker performs in saying "p" or "that p," in other words, to such actions as promising, avowing, or commanding. By perlocutionary acts, Austin designates the effect the speaker produces on the hearer. For his part, Habermas distinguishes between two sorts of illocutionary effect – first, the understanding and, second the acceptance of a speech act offer – and three sorts of perlocutionary effects.[2] A perlocutionary effect$_1$ refers to that effect that the speech act produces on the hearer merely because of what follows from its meaning; this sort of perlocutionary effect thus counts as a grammatically regulated one. By a perlocutionary effect$_2$, Habermas refers to an effect on the hearer that is not grammatically legislated by the speech act itself but that could be revealed to the participants in the communication without affecting their understanding and acceptance of the speech act offer. Finally, perlocutionary effects$_3$ refer to those effects that are not grammatically legislated by the speech act and that could *not* be revealed to the participants in the communication *without* affecting their understanding and acceptance of the speech act offer.

Suppose, then, that a hearer understands and accepts a request that she give Y some money. Understanding and accepting the request, are its illocutionary effects. That the hearer actually gives Y some money is a perlocutionary effect$_1$. If the hearer thereby pleases her husband, this perlocutionary effect$_2$ could be a consequence of which she could be aware without changing the course of her action. But if the speaker is trying to convince her to give Y money so that Y can commit some sort of crime and her prior knowledge of this consequence must be prevented if the speech act offer is to succeed, then her giving Y the money is a perlocutionary effect$_3$. This third kind of perlocutionary effect is allied with strategic action insofar as it eschews consensual cooperation and depends on causal inducements, in this case deceit. But the example also shows that perlocutionary effects$_3$ depend upon the illocutionary effects in which hearers can understand and accept speech act offers. That is, only because a hearer assumes that the speech act offer is oriented toward mutual understanding and accepts it at face value can the offer have a hidden strategic influence. As Habermas writes, perlocutionary effects$_3$ are possible only "if the speaker pretends to pursue the illocutionary goal of his speech act unreservedly and thereby leaves the hearer unclear as to the actually present one-sided infraction of the presuppositions of action oriented towards understanding."[3]

But if communicative and strategic uses of language are distinct and if the communicative use is "original," how is it possible? How does a speech act offer issue in cooperative acceptance and agreement? Habermas argues, first, that accepting a speech act offer requires accepting all the grammatically regulated effects that follow from it. And he argues, second, that the possibility of accepting these effects rests on the guarantee that the speaker implicitly raises to redeem the validity claims contained in the speech act offer if challenged. If, for example, a speaker tells a hearer that rain will ruin a vacation the hearer has planned, the ability of the hearer to understand this claim, to accept it as a good prediction, and to act accordingly depends upon knowing the conditions under which the validity claim that it will rain could be accepted. But knowing the "acceptability conditions" of this claim, in turn, requires knowing the sorts of reasons or evidence that the hearer could point to in order to support it. Hence, the ability of the hearer to coordinate her action cooperatively depends on the sort of warranty that the speaker can offer for her claim. As Habermas writes, "A speaker owes the binding . . . force of his illocutionary act not to the validity of what is said but to the coordinating effect of the warranty that he offers: namely to redeem, if necessary, the validity claim raised with speech act."[4]

At issue in a prediction of rain is a claim to the truth of the statements contained in the speech act offer. But hearers can challenge validity claims in other dimensions as well. If a speaker says, "I am hereby ordering you to stop smoking," the hearer's ability to accept the order depends upon knowing the normative or institutional conditions under which the order would be legitimate. There is a difference here, Habermas insists, between backing this claim with power – for instance, with the threat of sanctions – and invoking legitimate authority for the order. If speaker and hearer are to arrive at a communicative agreement, then the speaker must be able to refer to existing norms and regulations concerning smoking and the hearer must be able to adopt what Habermas calls a "yes or no" attitude toward their legal or moral-practical validity. Again, the ability of the claim to lead to the coordination of action depends upon the speaker's implicit guarantee that she could point to evidence that would support the claim to the rightness or appropriateness of both the order and the norms or regulations backing it if the hearer challenged her to do so.

Just as the prediction that it will rain on someone's vacation raises a claim to truth, the order cited above raises a claim to normative rightness. Statements that Habermas refers to as expressive self-presentations raise validity claims to truthfulness or sincerity. If a speaker says that she intends to visit her grandmother, the condition of accepting this speech act offer is a hearer's satisfaction that the speaker really does intend to do as she says. To this extent, the conditions of acceptability of the speech act offer continue to depend upon the implicit guarantee the speaker offers with her speech act to redeem the validity claim if challenged.

But if the acceptability of speech act offers rests on the possibility of redeeming the validity claims they contain, then the acceptability of speech act offers is also tied to reason. Language has the ability to achieve mutual understanding and to coordinate action in a consensual or cooperative way because its original, communicative use involves raising validity claims and supporting them if challenged. Thus Habermas ends the statement I cited above by arguing that "In all cases in which the illocutionary role expresses not a power claim but a validity claim, the place of the empirically motivating force of sanctions . . . is taken by the rationally motivating force of accepting a speaker's guarantee for securing claims to validity."[5] And as he writes elsewhere, "Both ego, who raises a validity claim with his utterance, and alter, who recognizes or rejects it, base their decisions on potential grounds or reasons."[6]

But what concept of rationality is required here if we are to make sense out of the way reason grounds mutual understanding and the cooperative coordination of action? Since Habermas's answer to the question of how language makes understanding possible points to the "validity basis of speech," we now need to explore the concept of reason that is suitable to the function of redeeming validity. In order to do so, I shall return to the "preliminary specification" of rationality with which Habermas begins *The Theory of Communicative Action*.

II. "RATIONALITY – A PRELIMINARY SPECIFICATION"

Habermas's account of Western rationality begins with the assessment of teleological or goal-directed actions. To the question of what concept of reason supports claims to validity, the answer on a "cognitive-instrumental" view is simply that concept which assumes certain goals or life plans as given and focuses on the most effective means of achieving them. Habermas claims that this concept "has, through empiricism, deeply marked the self-understanding of the modern era."[7] But he also contends that crucial to it is its connection to criticizable knowledge. Teleological actions presuppose knowledge about the situation in which one wants to intervene as well as knowledge of what means are available and what the consequences of the action might be. In all these respects, however, we can be mistaken and we can be shown to be mistaken by others who can point to consequences, circumstances, or means that we have overlooked. But once we acknowledge the criticizability of our knowledge, we have already expanded the concept of rationality beyond narrow instrumental dimensions to include an assessment of the presuppositions or assertions in which we claim effectiveness for our means and truth for our knowledge of situations and consequences.

Goal-directed actions and assertions, Habermas claims, involve the same knowledge content employed in different ways. In the first case, propositional knowledge allows for a successful intervention in the world while in the second case, it allows for "an understanding among participants in communication." Both forms of knowledge are susceptible to criticism insofar as both contain knowledge that can be contested. We can be wrong about the situation in which we intervene to realize our goals and we can be equally wrong about the claims we assert as objectively true. Still this difference affects the concept of rationality. Whereas the rational adjudication of a teleological action involves the – potentially monological – assessment of its actual success, with regard to the expression of the propositional knowledge presupposed by the action rational adjudication involves the – necessarily dialogical – capacity to defend one's beliefs and assertions against challenges and hence to give reasons that others can accept.

But if this is the case, it becomes clear that reason has a still broader application than that pertaining either to the assessment of teleological actions or to the defense of the propositional knowledge embodied in assertions. If, in these cases the idea of rationality is connected ultimately to the willingness to defend criticizable validity claims, then this connection also applies to other sorts of expressions in which we also raise criticizable validity claims and also try to defend them. As Habermas writes:

In contexts of communicative action, we call someone rational not only if he is able to put forward an assertion and, when criticized, to provide grounds for it by pointing to appropriate evidence, but also if he is following an established norm and is able, when criticized, to justify his action by explicating the given situation in the light of legitimate expectations. We even call someone rational if he makes known a desire or an intention, expresses a feeling or a mood, shares a secret, confesses a deed etc., and is then able to reassure critics in regard to the revealed experience by drawing practical consequences from it and behaving consistently thereafter.[8]

Hence, only if we withdraw the concept of rationality entirely from intersubjective communication, can we restrict its province to the instrumental domain. But we cannot do this unless we also accept a naive realism according to which there is no need to ground our beliefs about the world in consensus because the world is immediately and identically accessible to all without intersubjective checking or collaborative interpretation. Once we move beyond "the ontological presupposition of an objective world," however, to an inquiry into the way in which "the world gains objectivity" by "*counting* as one and the same world *for* a community of speaking and acting subjects,"[9] we have moved to a communicative concept of reason that also must include the way in which norms, expressions, and evaluations count as valid.

We saw earlier that the power of language to coordinate cooperative action lay in the rational or validity basis of speech. We have now seen that the concept of rationality must extend beyond the question of the rationality of assertions or teleological actions to include a wider spectrum of contexts in which validity claims are raised and redeemed. Still, Habermas insists that the logic of rationally redeeming validity claims differs depending upon their structural or "formal-pragmatic" features. Claims to the truth of statements and rightness of actions or norms of action require a discursive justification to which claims to truthfulness or sincerity are not subject. Habermas also exempts from discursive justification "a type of expression that is not invested with a clear-cut validity claim, namely, evaluative expressions." [10] These are such preferences and desires as the "desire for a vacation," a "preference for autumn landscapes" or the "rejection of the military" and, in his view, stand midway between merely subjective self-presentations and normative regulations. In order to get clearer on the distinctions with which Habermas is concerned here and, particularly, on the distinction he asserts between normative questions and questions of the good life, I shall turn to his analysis of discourse, on the one hand, and aesthetic criticism, on the other.

III. DISCOURSE AND AESTHETIC CRITICISM

Habermas's argument for the discursive redemption of the validity claims of truth and rightness looks to the pragmatic structure of communication oriented to understanding in these cases. In considering or deliberating about disputed claims to truth or normative rightness what must the participants to the discussion presuppose? In the first place, if acceptance of the disputed claim is to be cooperative and based on reasons, then the communication must be one in which participants are free to raise and challenge claims without fear of coercion, intimidation, deceit, or the like and in which all have equal chances to speak, to make assertions, self-presentations, and normative claims and to challenge others. The point here is that we can only be said to have redeemed a disputed claim if all can assent to the reasons given in its support and hence if all have equal chances to raise challenges and assert claims. In the second place, if the communication is to secure the validity of a disputed claim it must follow certain rules: "Participants thematize a problematic validity claim and, relieved of the pressure of action and experience, in a hypothetical attitude, test with reasons, and only with reasons, whether the claim defended by the proponents rightfully stands or not."[11] Finally, following Toulmin, Habermas claims that the product of the communication must have a certain general structure; it must form a conclusion with a ground obtained by means of a rule (such as a rule of inference) and backed by certain forms of evidence.

Taken together, these "formal-pragmatic" aspects of validity securing communication constitute a theory of discourse. To the extent that speakers and hearers are concerned to reach agreement over a disputed claim to truth or rightness, they necessarily make certain assumptions about the structure of their argumentation. They assume that it prohibits all constraints that would exclude or diminish the equal voice of all concerned and hence that the agreement reached is the unconstrained agreement of a universal communication community. They also assume that all those involved ignore all motives other than the cooperative search for truth in a hypothetical attitude. And finally, they assume that only the force of the better argument may hold sway.

Habermas is not concerned with how arguments are actually conducted in the course of trying rationally to assess claims to truth or rightness. He is rather concerned with the pragmatic presuppositions that competent speakers and actors necessarily make in trying to reach agreements over disputed claims with others. And the consequence of denying these presuppositions is what, following Karl-Otto Apel, he terms a performative contradiction. Were we to raise the claim that argumentation does not have this pragmatic structure we would have to presuppose that it did in assuming that precisely this claim could be justified. In other words, we would have to suppose that the claim that argumentation does not have this pragmatic structure is true in the sense that it would be reached by a universal communication community of free and equal participants in a hypothetical attitude, engaged in a cooperative search for truth and motivated only by the force of the better argument.[12]

These conditions do not hold for either expressive self-presentations or evaluations. If a hearer challenges the truthfulness of a speaker's claim, the speaker cannot show her sincerity by arguing, because the truthfulness of her expressions, including her arguments, is precisely that which is at issue. Instead, she can show her sincerity only by acting in a manner consistent with her expressed intentions. The same holds for expressions in which a speaker reveals a feeling or mood, shares a secret, or confesses a deed. The capacity to redeem the claims raised here depends, as in the case of intentions, upon the speaker's capacity to draw "practical consequences" from her expressions and behave "consistently thereafter."[13]

Similar conditions anchor evaluative judgments, according to Habermas. Evaluations possess a rational basis insofar as a speaker can have good reasons for her desires and preferences. If, to use an example he takes from Richard Norman, I desire a saucer of mud, I make this desire intelligible to others by giving reasons for wanting it, by referring, for instance, to its "rich river smell." The enjoyment of a rich river smell, just as a desire for a vacation or the rejection of the military, reflects the substantive content of a particular form of life in which certain likes, attitudes, and ideas of work and life, if not shared, are at least intelligible. Thus, Habermas claims that we can "call a person rational who interprets the nature of his desires and feelings [Bedürfnisnatur] in the light of culturally established standards of value."

We call someone rational especially if she "can adopt a reflective attitude" to these standards, Habermas thinks,[14] and he terms this reflective attitude aesthetic criticism. Still, he insists that it does not have the same scope as discourse does, nor does the better argument in aesthetic criticism possess the same force as it is meant to in discourse. First, the cultural standards of value at issue do not include a claim to universality. As Habermas puts the point, "The circle of intersubjective recognition that forms around cultural values does not yet in any way imply a claim that they would meet with general assent within a culture, not to mention universal assent."[15] Habermas's position is not that the truth of an assertion or the validity of a norm can serve as the rational ground of action only after we have actually secured the assent of all under the specified conditions. Still, the regulative ideal in these cases remains one of universal agreement in which only the force of the better argument may hold sway. In neither the case of expressive self-presentations nor that of evaluative judgments, does universal agreement serve even as an ideal. I do not rest the validity of my evaluations on giving arguments to skeptics as to why they must accept them. Nor does their validity rest on all concerned being able to accept them. Rather it rests on their providing me with authentic motivations for action, in expressing my feelings in an undistorted way and in my being able to make myself at least intelligible to some others within the culture to which I belong.

But, second, in trying to make myself and my values intelligible to others, the force of reasons is only indirect. If someone does not understand my enjoyment of rich river smells, I can refer to other sorts of experiences, pleasures, and memories that I connect with the smell and I can try to connect these considerations up with her values. But these experiences, pleasures, and memories cannot force agreement in the way that argument can. Habermas puts the argument in terms of works of art:

> In this context reasons have the peculiar function of *bringing us to see* a work or performance in such a way that it can be perceived as an authentic expression of an exemplary experience, in general as the embodiment of a claim to authenticity. . . . In practical discourse reasons or grounds are meant to show that a norm recommended for acceptance expresses a generalizable interest; in aesthetic criticism grounds or reasons serve to guide perception and to make the authenticity of a work so evident that this aesthetic experience can itself become a rational motive for accepting the corresponding standards of value.[16]

Thus, whereas practical discourse secures the validity of norms for a universal audience through the direct force of reasons, aesthetic criticism secures the validity of values only for a circumscribed audience where reasons function merely to guide perception. This distinction, however, is not as rigorous as Habermas sometimes seems to suggest. He admits that rationally justified norms must be applied to concrete situations of action which are already interpreted in light of cultural values. Moreover, he insists that "any universalistic morality is dependent upon a form of life that *meets it halfway.*"[17] In the remainder of this essay, I want to look more closely at these claims since they seem to me to imply even more complex relations between normative principles and cultural values than the ones on which Habermas has thus far focused.

IV. APPLICATION AND FORMS OF LIFE

Participants in practical discourses take up what Habermas calls a hypothesis-testing attitude toward disputed norms. The norms they consider are those that have become problematic within the cultural context of an ongoing form of life. Discourse disconnects them from the unquestioned validity of this context and examines them in terms of the question of whether they would find the uncoerced assent of all those potentially affected under ideal conditions. This assent establishes the legitimacy of norms and principles, but it does not yet contain prescriptions for their application to concrete situations of action. Moreover, concrete situations of action may be already interpreted in terms of standards of value and conceptions of the good that express evaluative rather than normative claims. Examples of the sort of problem that might arise here are the controversies over abortion in the United States and the conflicts over immigration in Germany. These seem to be cases in which a consensus on normative principles such as liberty, equality, the sanctity of life, and human rights in general threatens to split apart as soon as the principles are applied to circumstances in which cultural values, religious beliefs, national identities, and the like still hold sway.

Hence, Habermas argues that the "decontextualization" of norms in practical discourse requires "an offsetting compensation"[18] that can make good on their application. Justificatory discourses must be supplemented by discourses of application that can determine "which of the norms already accepted as valid is appropriate in a given case in the light of all the relevant features of the situation conceived as exhaustively as possible."[19] Habermas rejects an Aristotelian approach to the sort of compensation needed here. In his view, we cannot rely upon our capacities for prudence or sensitive judgment because these capacities remained tied to "the parochial context of some hermeneutic starting point" and hence may involve values and prejudices on which we need more critical reflection. Instead, he looks to certain classical principles of application such as those requiring that "all relevant aspects of a case . . . be considered and that means . . . be proportionate to ends."[20] These principles can be rationally justified and thereby allow for some distance from hermeneutic starting points. Moreover, he claims that the history of basic human rights is a directed one, exhibiting "shall we cautiously say, a less and less selective reading and utilization of the universalistic meaning that fundamental-rights norms have."[21]

Habermas's point, then, is that while the procedural justification of disputed norms requires a hypothesis-testing abstraction from concrete forms of life and while rationally justified norms must be

applied to concrete situations of action, the impartial justification
of norms accomplished in practical discourses can be supplemented
by a learned capacity for impartial application. We need not simply
succumb to the cultural values and prejudices with which we initially understand specific situations of action. Rather, we can rely
upon discourses of application that can justify our judgments of the
appropriateness of applying specific normative principles to specific cases.[22]

But it is not clear that issues of application can be so neatly resolved. Take the question of the morality of abortion. We might
think of this question either as a question of the way we think justified principles of life, liberty, and equality are to be applied in a concrete instance or as a question of which justified principles, those
of life or those of liberty, are to be applied. Still, in the first case,
it remains unclear what standards determine the proper mode of
application. While we might be able to assent to the principle that
all relevant aspects of a case must be considered in its adjudication,
this principle seems itself to require some sort of "offsetting compensation." In other words, if we are to apply this principle, we must
be able to give some content to the notion of relevance. But the
content we give would seem both to depend upon and to differ with
our values. In particular it would seem to depend upon and to differ
with our religious traditions and heritage, so that from the point of
view of some religious perspectives all that will be considered relevant is the sanctity of life, while, from other more secular perspectives, considerations about the quality of a woman's or a child's life
might seem equally relevant.

We might also diverge in ways that depend upon cultural values
in our applications of the principle that the means must be proportionate to a given end. If we equate abortion with the ungodly killing
of innocent life, then any act that interrupts the work of abortion
clinics may seem proportionate to the end. If we oppose legal abor-
tions but place even higher importance on the rule of law and on
legislative or constitutional attempts to resolve the issue, then such
actions do not seem to count as legitimate means. It is not clear that
such disagreements on the way classical principles of application are
themselves to be understood or applied can be resolved in discourses
of application. Rather, these principles appear themselves to be tied
to a hermeneutic starting point from which forms of evaluative ori-

entation cannot be eradicated. We must apply justified norms to concrete situations of action that we already interpret in light of our cultural values but the influence of our cultural values seems to extend right through the way we understand principles of application and judgments of appropriateness themselves.

With regard to the second case, in which we view the debate over abortion as a debate about which justified principles we are to apply to it, again the hermeneutic dimensions of the problem seem to be neglected. That is, it does not seem adequate to limit the question of application to the question of which of the norms we already accept as valid is to be applied to the specific case. Rather, the question of application seems to extend to the meaning of norms, to the question of how we are to understand the norms we apply or, indeed, which principles of liberty or life are to be applied. We might say that both sides in the abortion debate take the same principles to be justified and that what divides them is the way these principles are understood. So-called pro-life proponents understand the principle of the sanctity of life in terms of the biological life of the fetus, while so-called pro-choice proponents understand it in terms of the quality of life of women and children. Pro-life proponents understand the principle of liberty in terms of the rights of fetuses to the opportunities and life chances due them as members of the human species; pro-choice proponents understand the same principle in terms of the right of women and families to choose when and under what circumstances it makes sense for them to have children.

Perhaps because of the possibility of interpretive conflicts of this kind, Habermas insists that a "universalistic morality is dependent upon a form of life that *meets it halfway.*" As long as the principles justified in practical discourses are to determine action within concrete forms of life, those forms of life as well as the orientations, sensibilities, and forms of understanding they permit must already be constructed in a certain way. As Habermas explains, there must be some congruence between moral norms and the socialization and educational practices of the society; the education system must help in the "requisite internalization of superego controls and the abstractness of ego identities";[23] and finally there must be sufficient fit between morality and sociopolitical institutions. This fit is not automatic. If Habermas is unwilling to leave questions of application up to Aristotelian capacities for prudence, he is also unwilling to leave the motivational and contextual embodiment of normative principles up to Hegelian spirit. "Rather," he writes, "it is chiefly a function of collective efforts and sacrifices made by sociopolitical movements." And, as he concludes, "Philosophy would do well to avoid haughtily dismissing these movements and the larger historical dimension from which they spring."[24]

Habermas's conception of the way a form of life meets universalistic morality halfway begins from top down, as it were, in terms of the question of how a form of life and the cultural values and orientations that compose it must be molded to meet the requirements for the application of rationally justified norms. But the question I would like to examine in the rest of this essay is whether we also have to think of the relation of normative justification and evaluative judgment from the bottom up, in terms of the question of how the meaning of such rationally justified principles as those we have explored in the debate over abortion must be molded to meet the requirements of forms of life, cultural values, and traditions through which people find their lives meaningful. This way of putting the issue is clearly indebted to Charles Taylor and I shall therefore turn to one of his recent essays in order to explore it.[25]

V. CULTURAL VALUES AND LIBERAL PRINCIPLES

The problem with which Taylor is concerned in "The Politics of Recognition" is whether liberal pluralistic societies can satisfy the demand for recognition of minority cultures or forms of life within them. According to one view of liberalism, liberal societies must base their legitimacy on the ability to guarantee fundamental rights for all citizens. Principles of justice are neutral with regard to different conceptions of the good and secure the equal treatment by the state of individuals without regard for race, sex, religion, or the like. Neutrality and equal treatment are themselves based on some version of the principle of universalization, which Habermas, for his part, grounds in the normative implications of communication oriented to understanding.

But suppose one's conception of the good requires more from the society than neutrality? Suppose the survival of one's culture requires a conception of a collective right to cultural survival as opposed to the individual rights secured by liberal principles? This is the challenge Quebec raises against the Canadian Charter of Rights, according to Taylor. While the Charter defines a set of individual rights guaranteeing equal treatment regardless of race, sex, or other irrelevant grounds, the Quebeckers maintain that the survival of their culture requires certain restrictions on precisely these rights. For example, French-speaking citizens are not to send their children to English-language schools, businesses of more than fifty employees are to be run in French, and no commercial signs are to be written in English. But such restrictions seem inherently discriminatory. Why should Francophones not be able to send their children to any school to which they want to send them provided they can afford it? Why should individuals in Quebec not run their businesses in English or write signs in the language they prefer?

Taylor suggests that in order to answer this question, we need to acknowledge another conception of liberalism to the one sketched above. If "Liberalism 1"[26] is committed to individual rights and remains adamantly neutral with regard to cultural identities and projects, "Liberalism 2" allows for a state that is "committed to the survival and flourishing of a particular nation, culture, or religion, or of a (limited) set of nations, cultures and religions – so long as the basic rights of citizens who have different commitments or no such commitments are protected."[27] The Quebeckers assume that the survival and flourishing of French culture in Quebec is a good. Moreover, they assume that this survival requires more than the simple tolerance of the French language. Rather, policies are required that can sustain the French language in Quebec, create new members of French culture and assure that future generations identify themselves as French. Liberalism 2 thus distinguishes between fundamental rights such as "rights to life, liberty, due process, free speech, free practice of religion and so on" from other "privileges and immunities that are important but that can be revoked or restricted for reasons of public policy."[28] As Taylor puts the point, this form of liberalism is "willing to weigh the importance of certain forms of uniform treatment against the importance of cultural survival, and opt sometimes in favor of the latter."[29]

This view thus conceives of the relation between universal principles and cultural values in the opposite way to Habermas's conception. On Taylor's view, it is not clear that the latter must always mold themselves to fit the former. Rather, the "politics of recognition," which Taylor also refers to as the politics of difference, seems to involve a demand by diverse cultures that liberal principles themselves be molded to allow for the value of particular cultures and their conceptions of the good. In cases in which the survival of a culture that is perceived as a good is at stake it may be necessary to reinterpret the meaning of principles so that they allow not just for individual rights such as the right to send one's child to the school of one's choice but for collective rights, such as the right of Quebec's French culture to survive. But, if this is the case, then cultural values and orientations must be acknowledged not just as elements of the concrete situations to which principles of justice apply but as codeterminers of their meaning. Taylor's conclusions seems to affirm at a more general level the conclusion we reached in exploring the debate over abortion. The normative principles that are justified in discourse can be interpreted differently and the politics of difference is just the demand that we recognize and respect these interpretive differences. Indeed, respect for the importance of and difference in the cultural values of different groups leads us to understand the meaning of liberal principles not in terms of Liberalism 1 but rather in terms of Liberalism 2.

We do not, then, require a rigorous neutrality or uniform treatment. In his comment on Taylor's essay, Michael Walzer insists that the official neutrality of the United States, for example, itself makes sense only as a consequence of Liberalism 2 rather than Liberalism 1. The United States is a country of immigrants who have chosen the risks to their cultural identity that emigrating to the United States involves. Moreover, it is a country of such multiple and diverse cultures that, in this case, official neutrality may simply constitute the best chance for any one culture's survival. But many liberal states, Walzer argues, are more similar to Quebec than to the United States. The governments of Norway, France, and the Netherlands do not claim to be neutral with regard to the language, history, literature, and "even the minor mores" of the majority culture. Rather, they actively support this culture while, at the same time, "tolerating and respecting ethnic and religious differences and allowing all minorities an equal freedom to organize their members, express their cultural values, and reproduce their way of life in civil society and in the family." In Walzer's view, as presumably Taylor's, this form of Liberalism 2 makes sense for them and for Quebec just as Liberalism 1 makes sense for the United States:

Liberalism 1 chosen from within Liberalism 2. *From within:* that means that the choice is not governed by an absolute commitment to state neutrality and individual rights – nor by the deep dislike of particularist identities (short of citizenship) that is common among liberals of the first sort. It is governed instead by the social condition and the actual life choices of *these* men and women.[30]

One might argue that the considerations that Taylor and Walzer raise pertain only to questions of scope. The problem is simply one of how different countries apply principles of individual rights that guarantee equal treatment to all citizens regardless of race, sex, religion, or other irrelevant grounds. In some liberal countries the sphere in which neutrality is appropriate will be wider than others, but in none will rights to life, liberty, due process, free speech, free practice of religion, and so on be curtailed. But the argument seems to go further than this objection allows. Taylor and Walzer are concerned not simply with the scope of liberal principles but with what liberalism means. And because of the good of cultural values and traditions, they think liberalism means Liberalism 2 as opposed to Liberalism 1. Hence, if forms of life have to be molded to meet liberal principles halfway, as Habermas stresses, we need to emphasize the opposite as well: that the meaning of consensually justified principles must be molded to meet cultural values and traditions halfway as well.

But a question seems to arise at this point. Must we allow for any way in which principles meet cultural values halfway or, indeed, for any cultural values that principles are to meet halfway? Taylor rejects a procedural model of liberalism for one grounded "on judgments about what makes a good life – judgments in which the integrity of cultures has an important place."[31] But are all judgments about what makes a good life of equal standing here? Must principles be modified to accommodate the integrity of any culture?

For his part, Taylor begins with a presumption in favor of an affirmative answer to this question or, in other words, with a presumption of the worth of diverse cultures. "As a presumption, the claim is that all human cultures that have animated whole societies over some considerable stretch of time have something important to say to all human beings." At the same time, this presumption has to be worked out and checked in the actual study of a particular culture. To this extent, Taylor thinks that the demand for recognition that the politics of difference raises is somewhat odd. Respect cannot be demanded as a right. Rather, it has to be gained in the assessment of others that the culture does indeed "have something important to say."[32]

Still, Taylor points to the transformative aspect of the study of alien cultures. If we approach a culture as one of even merely possible value, then we cannot simply impose our preexisting standards upon it. Instead, we must be open to the way in which the "something important" it has to say to us can involve precisely those standards:

To approach, say, a raga with the presumptions of value implicit in the well-tempered clavier would be forever to miss the point. What has to happen is what Gadamer has called a "fusion of horizons." We learn to move in a broader horizon, within which what we have formerly taken for granted as the background to valuation can be situated as one possibility alongside the different background of the formerly unfamiliar culture.[33]

At issue here is not only Gadamer's fusion of horizons but also what he calls a preconception of completeness or perfection.[34] We must provisionally assume that other cultures have something important to say to us, Gadamer thinks, in order both to understand them and to test our own prejudices about ourselves. If we assume that other cultures have nothing important to say to us, then we also have no way of checking the adequacy of our own initial prejudices about them. We will find, as Saul Bellow seems to have done, that the Zulus have no resource as valuable as a Tolstoy (or as he is said to have said "when the Zulus produce a Tolstoy we will read him"[35]), because we will be able only to maintain our initial parochial assumptions as to what is valuable. But these assumptions prevent us from discovering what the Zulus do have and how what they have might provide a productive mirror for viewing ourselves.

But this notion that we might learn to understand our own values and standards differently in our efforts to understand those of others seems to complicate the issue of whether principles must be shaped to accommodate preexisting cultural values. On the one hand, according to Taylor, we are not to accord respect to any culture simply because it is a culture. Rather, we are to accord it the provisional respect that allows us to study it seriously and assess it in terms of what of importance it has to say to us. On the other hand, we cannot simply impose our standards of value upon it but must be open to seeing ourselves through the standards it offers. But how are we to know, then, when we have learned to understand our values within a wider perspective and when we understand them within a worse one? How can we guarantee that the politics of recognition opens up for us the value of cultures that have a value and when this politics leads us simply to abandon standards of value altogether?

This question, of course, is at the heart of current debates not only over university curricula, Western values, and the Western literary canon but also over the value of Western democratic values. Is the effect of opening the canon up to women's diary writing or African oral traditions one of enriching the Western literary tradition or of debasing its standards? Is the effect of placing Western values within a wider perspective one of better understanding them or learning to tolerate fanatics, totalitarians, and the like? If we combine Habermas's conception of practical discourse with the emphasis Taylor and Walzer place on cultural values and forms of life, it seems to me, we might have a way of beginning to answer these questions.

The argument I have tried to pursue thus far is the following. In the course of developing a communicative conception of reason, Habermas distinguishes between the sorts of discourse in which we justify claims to truth and rightness and other less universalistic and less consensually inclined discussions in which we consider our evaluative assessments and cultural values. He also recognizes that the principles and norms of action justified in practical discourse must be applied to concrete situations of action and therefore calls for offsetting compensations and judgments of appropriateness in which the evaluative assessments and cultural values that comprise forms of life can be reshaped to fit rationally justified norms and principles. Considerations that Taylor and Walzer raise, however, suggest that rationally justified norms and principles must also be shaped to fit the evaluative assessments and cultural values that comprise forms of life. Still there is a limit here. In elaborating the contours of Liberalism 2, Taylor and Walzer rely upon a principle of tolerance. Liberalism 2 can encourage the survival of particular cultures by officially fostering their language, history, literature, and mores while remaining neutral with regard to the language, history, literature, and mores of others. But it cannot try to eradicate these others. Rather, Liberalism 2 distinguishes fundamental rights that cannot be violated for the survival of cultures from other privileges and immunities that can be "revoked or restricted for reasons of public policy."[36] Hence, although Liberalism 2 is not neutral with regard to official support for certain cultural conceptions of the good, it also cannot retreat behind a principle of tolerance.

But how is such a principle justified? Habermas refers to the conditions of discourse. Principles of tolerance are principles to which all concerned could assent in a communication unconstrained by overt coercion or relations of power in which all participants are free and equal and in which only the force of the better argument holds sway. To this extent and despite the revision Liberalism 2 exacts from Liberalism 1, its foundation would seem to be built on procedural grounds. Not every life choice of men and women, to use Walzer's language, would be admissible, but only those that comply with the conditions of tolerance or discourse.

But we might also find a hermeneutic ground or starting point for the principle of tolerance in the claims Taylor makes for the survival and flourishing of cultures and in the claims Gadamer makes for the fusion of horizons and the preconception of completeness or perfection. If we start, not from the side of principles, as Habermas does, but from the side of cultural values, then the question we might pose is what principles are necessary to the survival and flourishing of our own cultures? In my view the answer has to be the one Gadamer suggests, namely the possibility of discussions in which I can use the standards and evaluative orientations of other cultures to check and develop my own. Part of what the survival and flourishing of a culture would seem to mean is a capacity to reflect on and assure itself of its own worth and to be able to communicate that worth to a new generation. But this would seem to entail its capacity to show its worth in relation to the worth of other cultures, to be able to enrich itself with what it takes to be valuable in other cultures, to show its own members how its values stack up against those of others, where it fits in the panoply of cultures and so on. Cultures and traditions survive and flourish not by enforcing an endless and exact reproduction but by developing and enriching themselves and by remaining relevant to new generations.

But this consideration seems to mean that the survival and flourishing of one's own culture depends upon the survival and flourishing of others against which I can test my own, in terms of which I can see its value, and from which I can even borrow. Hence, I must maintain a principle of tolerance toward other cultural values as a condition of the health of my own. In contrast, if we extend Liberalism 2 to include not only the interest in "the survival and flourishing of a particular nation, culture, or religion, or of a (limited) set of nations, cultures, and religions" but also the interest in eradicating others with "different commitments or no such commitments," we also risk the ossification of our own. If cultures are to be living cultures, they must live with others, for a serious effort to understand the values and cultures of others is our only option for reflecting upon our own.

Although this argument begins with the good of the flourishing of distinct cultures, it is not antithetical to a modified principle of ideal speech. If our capacity to reflect on our cultural values depends upon interaction with those that differ, then we must encourage those differences, and such encouragement would seem to mean that we must question any evaluative orientation or set of cultural values that tries to restrict in advance the evaluative orientations or cultural values to which we can have access. In other words, the survival and flourishing of our own culture requires the survival and flourishing of those that differ as well as the possibility of nonexclusive and nondiscriminatory discussions in which we review our values against those of others. But these conditions are the idealized conditions of discourse. We need to assure the sort of universal participation in our discussions that is not impeded by power, wealth, race, or gender. Otherwise we deny just the conditions under which our own cultures can survive and flourish.

Still, universal participation does not necessitate universal assent to concrete meaning. Our discussions of both our principles and our values are to exclude direct or implicit force, the effects of relations of power, fear, or the threat of sanctions. Even so, the world might still contain as many legitimate interpretations of the meaning of its universal principles as Habermas's own notion of aesthetic criticism indicates it has of its art and literature. It follows that normative discourse and aesthetic criticism are perhaps closer or more complexly related than Habermas has yet explained.

NOTES

1. Jürgen Habermas, *The Theory of Communicative Action*, Vol. I, *Reason and the Rationalization of Society*, trans. Thomas McCarthy (Boston: Beacon Press, 1984), p. 288.
2. Jürgen Habermas, "Handlungen, Sprechakt, sprachlich vermittelte Interaktionen und Lebenswelt," in *Nachmetaphysischen Denken* (Frankfurt: Suhrkamp, 1988).
3. Ibid., p. 72.
4. *Theory of Communicative Action*, Vol. I, p. 302.
5. Ibid.
6. Ibid., p. 287.
7. Ibid., p. 10.
8. Ibid., p. 15.
9. Ibid., pp. 12–13.
10. Ibid., p. 16.
11. Ibid., p. 25.
12. Habermas, "Discourse Ethics: Notes on a Program of Philosophical Justification," in Habermas, *Moral Consciousness and Communicative Action* (Cambridge, Mass.: MIT Press, 1990), pp. 79–82.
13. *Theory of Communicative Action*, p. 15.
14. Ibid., p. 20.
15. Ibid.
16. Ibid.; emphasis in original.
17. Habermas, "Morality and Ethical Life," in *Moral Consciousness and Communicative Action*, p. 207.
18. "Discourse Ethics," p. 106.
19. Habermas, "On the Pragmatic, the Ethical and the Moral Employments of Practical Reason," in *Justification and Application: Remarks on Discourse Ethics*, trans. Ciaran P. Cronin (Cambridge, Mass.: MIT Press, 1993), p. 14.
20. "Morality and Ethical Life," p. 206.
21. Ibid., p. 208.
22. See Habermas, "Remarks on Discourse Ethics," in *Justification and Application*, pp. 35–38.
23. "Morality and Ethical Life," p. 207.
24. Ibid., p. 208.
25. See Charles Taylor, "The Politics of Recognition," in Amy Gutmann, ed., *Multiculturalism and "The Politics of Recognition"* (Princeton,

N.J.: Princeton University Press, 1992), pp. 25–73. My analysis of this essay and its relevance to the question of the relations of cultural values and normative principles was written too early to benefit from Habermas's own analysis of Taylor's essay in "Struggles for Recognition in Constitutional States," which appeared in the *European Journal of Philosophy* 1, no. 2 (Aug. 1993). Here, Habermas reemphasizes the necessity for democratic procedures in the application of universal principles and argues that these procedures guarantee respect for cultural values insofar as those who debate and apply universal principles do so both as citizens and as private persons. My concern in turning to Taylor's essay, however, is not only cultural values that must meet universal principles halfway but differences in these cultural values. How do we guarantee respect for differences in the interpretation of norms and principles, how do we distinguish legitimate from illegitimate interpretations and how should we conceive of continuing "legitimate" disagreement in interpretation that stems from differences in cultural value?

26. See Michael Walzer, "Comment," in Guttmann, *Multiculturalism and "The Politics of Recognition,"* pp. 99–103.
27. Ibid., p. 99.
28. Taylor, "Politics of Recognition," p. 59.
29. Ibid., p. 61.
30. Walzer, "Comment," p. 102.
31. Taylor, "Politics of Recognition," p. 59.
32. Ibid., p. 66.
33. Ibid., p. 67.
34. See *Truth and Method*, (New York: Seabury Press, 1974).
35. Taylor, "Politics of Recognition," p. 42. It should be noted that Taylor also says, "I have no idea whether this statement was actually made in this form by Saul Bellow or by anyone else."
36. Ibid., p. 59.

7   Practical discourse and communicative ethics

As the idea of an ultimate foundation for moral and political beliefs has become increasingly implausible, theorists have turned to "discourse" to provide a basis on which to defend the legitimacy of social and political practices. The turn to discourse, which includes but is not limited to communicative ethics, is in part a move from a substantive to a procedural conception of moral and political theory. Rather than providing values grounded in an account of human nature or reason, discourse-based approaches offer a set of procedures that, if followed, would yield principles legitimating social practices and institutions. The fundamental intuition underlying the move to discourse is the ideal of a moral community, one whose norms and practices are fully acceptable to those subject to them, a society based not on imposition, but on the agreement of free and equal persons.

Jürgen Habermas has presented one of the most powerful accounts of a discourse-based morality; it is grounded in an understanding of practical reason which explains how the validity of norms can be tested, thereby demonstrating their cognitive character. According to Habermas, valid norms can be freely accepted by all of the individuals who are affected by them. Thus, a society whose institutions and practices were governed by valid norms would instantiate the ideal of a moral community.

Habermas's account is rigorously procedural. Unlike theorists such as John Rawls, he does not advance specific norms or principles, nor does he project a vision of a just society. Nonetheless, his project raises the obvious question of what sorts of norms could be vindicated in the way he proposes, and whether they could adequately provide for the "just resolution of conflict."[1] I will argue

143

that there are good reasons to believe that moral community, in the sense suggested above, may not be possible in societies characterized by value pluralism – and these are the very societies in which discourse ethics is most applicable. My point in making this argument is not that we should abandon the project of a discourse-based ethics, but that we need to recognize what might be called an "agonistic" element or dimension of our moral and political lives. I will develop my argument in three steps. In the first, I will set out Habermas's theory, in part by contrasting it with Rawls's discourse-based approach, and use it to explore the possibility of discovering valid norms under conditions of moral pluralism. In the second, I will develop a brief account of the agonistic dimension of moral life. In the third, I will briefly present the implications of my argument for the issue of political legitimation, which will lead me to return to the contrast between Rawls and Habermas with which the essay begins. I will suggest how Rawls's original strategy might be reformulated in light of Habermas's criticism to provide a more satisfactory approach to this problem. The reformulation I propose is broadly compatible with Habermas's most recent thinking about how political life ought to be structured in contemporary societies.[2]

I. GROUNDING COMMUNICATIVE ETHICS

As early as 1958 Rawls put forward his well-known conception of "justice as fairness" in explicitly procedural terms.[3] Although Rawls's argument bears important similarities to classical social contract theories, his move to discourse differs from standard forms of contractarianism in that it is not based on "a general theory of human motivation" nor does it "establish any particular society or practice."[4] In making this proceduralist turn, Rawls had a specific purpose in mind: to put forward a particular theory of justice which, he argued, would be adopted by individuals who followed the procedures he established. His argument was not intended to provide a foundation for morality in general; indeed, it explicitly *presupposes* such moral conceptions as a "duty of fair play." This point is often misunderstood, as Rawls is frequently interpreted as offering an account of justice as a modus vivendi among amoral, purely self-interested agents. But even in his earliest formulations, he insisted that "The conception at which we have arrived . . . is that the principles of justice may be thought of as arising *once the constraints of having a morality* are imposed on mutually self-interested parties. . . ."[5]

Habermas's conception of communicative ethics is in one way a much more ambitious undertaking than Rawls's, for he seeks to use discourse to establish the moral constraints that Rawls takes for granted:

> It is incumbent on moral theory to explain and ground the moral point of view. What moral *theory* can do and should be trusted to do is to clarify the universal core of our moral intuitions and thereby to refute value skepticism.[6]

On the other hand, in another respect Habermas's program is more limited than Rawls's, for

> What [moral theory] cannot do is make any kind of substantive contribution. . . . Moral philosophy does not have privileged access to particular moral truths.[7]

Although their theories are often seen as competing, they might be seen as pursuing complementary projects. Where Rawls *assumes* "the moral point of view," using it to derive substantive principles of a just political and social order, Habermas aims to ground the moral point of view itself. Both accounts are broadly discourse-based and proceduralist, but are aimed at different ends.

There is obviously a certain priority to Habermas's project, since an adequate account of the "universal core of our moral intuitions" could significantly affect the substantive conclusions that we might reach. Habermas himself has criticized Rawls for misunderstanding the requirement of impartiality, which is an essential component of the moral point of view. Rawls conceives of impartiality in terms of the idea of an "original position" in which free and equal individuals, who are ignorant of their own particular identities, determine the principles of justice to govern a social order in which they will be assigned places in the future. Because they are ignorant of the interests that divide them from others, and because they do not know what positions they will hold in the social order, individuals so conceived could only choose principles that are impartial or fair to everyone. Lacking the information necessary to advance their own, partial interests, they could only decide on the basis of general interests.

Rawls's construction is obviously not intended to describe the steps people would actually go through in discussing and agreeing to principles of justice, for we could never literally forget who we are. Rather, it is intended to model the concept of impartiality that is an essential aspect of the moral point of view. Its inadequacy, according to Habermas, can be seen once we realize how morality is rooted in the structure of what he calls communicative action. In communicative action, we coordinate our plans with each other in a consensual way, by making or invoking claims that all concerned accept as valid or binding. Habermas distinguishes communicative action from strategic action, action that is rationally chosen in order to influence "the decisions of a rational opponent" in order simply to achieve the agent's own goals. In acting communicatively, I do not seek to manipulate you, that is, merely to cause or influence you to do something that I want you to do. Rather, I hope to harmonize my plans with yours on the basis of our having, or coming to have, a common understanding of the situation we are in.[8] When we are dining together and I say, "Please pass the salt," I hope that you will pass me the salt not because you fear what I might do to you if you don't, nor because you expect to get some advantage from me by obeying my request, but because you recognize the validity of the rules of etiquette and so recognize that passing the salt is the required or appropriate response to my request. By making this request I invoke a norm that I implicitly take to be valid. And in the case of moral norms, Habermas argues, I undertake an obligation to show its validity if it should be challenged.[9]

We could avoid this conclusion if we could imagine a successfully functioning form of life in which actors relate to one another only in strategic terms, but such a society is not possible. Elster (among others) has convincingly shown the limitations of the model of instrumental rationality in explaining social order, arguing that "social norms provide an important kind of motivation for action that is irreducible to rationality or indeed to any other form of optimizing mechanism."[10] Habermas has argued that the reproduction of the forms of culture, social integration, and individual personality systems takes place through communicative action.[11] These social functions can be performed only as long as there is at least a de facto acceptance of some set of social norms.

For many social interactions, de facto acceptance of norms is sufficient to ensure that the behaviors of different actors are coordinated. We commonly invoke norms in the expectation that they are accepted by those to whom our actions are directed, but we do not necessarily have to accept those norms ourselves. Indeed, we do not even have to assume that the others accept the norms in question as valid, but only that they will in fact respond according to them. I may not think that the social roles of waiter and customer are morally defensible, but – lacking any practical options – I may still eat at restaurants, at least on occasion. And my waiter may share my view, yet he or she will still take my order and bring me my food. And I will undoubtedly leave a tip, even if I think the practice of tipping is reprehensible. Although we implicitly invoke these norms, neither of us would seek to "redeem" them as valid. We simply use them in order to achieve our various ends, given that we live in the society we do.

Although these actions are obviously purposive, it would be misleading to suggest that they are examples of strategic action, since the type of interaction in question is "coordinated on the basis of mutual understanding."[12] Such interactions might be called "incomplete communicative action"; coordination is achieved because participants have mutually compatible expectations, even though they do not accept the same normative validity claims. A limiting case of coordination achieved communicatively occurs when parties successfully employ a set of symbols to regulate their interactions, but when the symbols do not have the same meaning for all participants. As Wallace has argued, "cognitive sharing is not necessary for stable interaction."[13] Indeed, "cognitive nonsharing" may even be essential for a social order as "it permits a more complex system to arise than most, or any, of its participants can comprehend," and "it liberates the participants in a system from the heavy burden of learning and knowing each other's motivations and cognitions."[14] What is critical is that the participants be able to predict each other's behavior, rather than that they possess the same "cognitive maps" of their society and culture.

Incomplete communicative action is common, but it is hard to imagine that it could be the only kind of communicative action in which social actors engage. Even if we do not always make normative validity claims that we are prepared to redeem, we must do so in some interactions. Unless some of the norms we invoked were norms that we accepted as valid, it is hard to see how any norms could have motivational force. In incomplete communicative action, normative validity claims are "bracketed," but the norms could always be called into question, thereby disrupting the interaction. If the participants wished to continue acting communicatively, they would have to raise validity claims explicitly, and negotiate rules that all could accept to govern their interaction.

Thus, our success in coordinating our behavior through communicative action does not depend on the actual validity of the norms we invoke, but on our having a common understanding of the situation. This common understanding must be based on "the speaker's guarantee that he will, if necessary, make efforts to redeem the claim that the hearer has accepted."[15] These validity claims can be redeemed only through "practical discourses" among the social actors involved.

Given this analysis of the concept of norms and their validation, we can see why Rawls's construction is problematic. When the validity of a norm is challenged, the coordination sought through communicative action is disturbed and so the parties must enter "into a process of moral argumentation" through which they "continue their communicative action in a reflexive attitude with the aim of restoring a consensus that has been disrupted."[16] When they are successful in reaching a consensus on the validity of the norms governing their interaction, their agreement "expresses a *common will*," an agreement that is reflexive in the sense that the parties know "that they have collectively become convinced of something."[17] Only an actual discourse among the affected parties can produce such an agreement. As a general account of normative validity, the Rawlsian model of a hypothetical agreement of parties in an original position is inadequate because it fails to provide scope for the reflexivity that is essential to the idea of morality.

Let us agree that Habermas has shown that the idea of normative validity is implicit in communicative action, and that challenges to the validity of a particular norm must be met through "a process of moral argumentation." But why, the skeptic might ask, should we expect such argumentation to yield results? Moral arguments obviously can't be deductive in form, for deductive arguments presuppose the (contestable) truth of their premises. Rather, we need a principle of argumentation for normative questions analogous to the principle of induction for empirical questions. According to Habermas, that need is met by the principle of universalization. Every valid norm, he argues, must fulfill the condition that

All affected can accept the consequences and the side effects its *general* observance can be anticipated to have for the satisfaction of everyone's interests (and these consequences are preferred to those of known alternative possibilities for regulation).[18]

The principle of universalization is implicit in the idea of moral argumentation itself. Any "process of argumentation must, among other things, make presuppositions"[19] such as:

> Every subject with the competence to speak and act is allowed to take part in a discourse.
> Everyone is allowed to question any assertion whatever.
> Everyone is allowed to introduce any assertion whatever into the discourse.
> Everyone is allowed to express his attitudes, desires, and needs.
> No speaker may be prevented, by internal or external coercion, from exercising his rights as laid down [above].[20]

Understanding "what it means to discuss hypothetically whether norms of action ought to be adopted"[21] amounts to "implicitly acknowledging" the principle of universalization.[22] If interlocutors follow these "rules of discourse," then "a contested norm cannot meet with the consent of the participants in a practical discourse unless" the principle of universalization is satisfied.[23]

This argument rests on the idea of a "performative contradiction": People engaging in communicative action at least implicitly invoke and so presuppose the validity of certain norms, whose validity could only be tested through argumentation. If they were to reject the cognitive status of judgments of normative validity, they would have to engage in forms of argumentation that implicitly support the principle of universalization itself.

This account effectively brings out the ways in which communicative action involves validity claims that are subject to criticism.

Whenever I invoke a norm to influence your behavior, I implicitly recognize you as a partner in a dialogue in which that norm could be justified. We are able to coordinate our interactions consensually because we have or are able to achieve a common understanding of our situation. What is critical here is that "a speaker can *rationally motivate* a hearer to accept his speech act offer because . . . he can assume the *warranty* for providing, if necessary, convincing reasons that would stand up to a hearer's criticism of the validity claim."[24] In communicative action, one undertakes "to redeem, if necessary, the validity claim raised with [one's] speech act,"[25] rather than seeking to manipulate or coerce the other. Thus, communicative action can be said to "presuppose those very relationships of reciprocity and mutual recognition around which *all* moral ideas revolve in everyday life."[26]

But if the principle of universalization provides a cognitive status to moral judgments, the significance of this status is not entirely clear. For one could accept the principle of universalization without necessarily believing that there are any norms that could pass the test of universal acceptance. Habermas argues that "moral-practical issues can be decided on the basis of reasons"[27] since "anyone who takes part in argumentation of any sort is in principle able to reach the same judgments on the acceptability of norms of action."[28] But this is true only if those affected by an action or norm have values, emotions, affections, and preferences that are more or less compatible, for only in that case could they "reach consensus on generalizable maxims."[29]

The possibility that participants might fail to reach consensus follows from Habermas's understanding of the nature of practical discourse. In Habermas's account, moral discourse is limited to determining the acceptability of *norms* or the rules that we have a duty to observe, as opposed to the *values* or ends that we pursue. While the former involve questions of justice, the latter reflect views of what constitutes a good life and are based on our conceptions of ourselves and our basic identities, which are rooted in the culture in which we live and to which we are socialized. "Moral-practical discourses" about the validity of norms "require a break with all of the unquestioned truths of an established, concrete ethical life, in addition to distancing oneself from the contexts of life with which one's identity is inextricably interwoven."[30]

Part of becoming a mature adult is learning to distinguish rules that are merely conventional from those that are valid, and so genuinely binding. But one cannot distance oneself in a similar manner from the ends or values one pursues, because to do so would be to abstract oneself from "the fabric of the communicative practices of everyday life through which the individual's life is shaped and his identity is secured," and to question "the forms of life in which his identity has been shaped [is to question] his very existence."[31] Thus, we do not have the capacity to call our values into question in the way that we can interrogate the norms to which we are subject. We are faced with an irresolvable plurality of value configurations in modern, pluralist societies, and at the international level in relations among different societies. But because of this plurality, it may be impossible to find norms that are "equally in the interests of all," and which could therefore pass Habermas's universalization test.

Habermas rejects this suggestion, arguing that the "need-interpretations" that individuals bring to discourse can be challenged and may be revised in such a way as to discover common interests.[32] In the process of moral argumentation, individuals do not simply confront each other, divided by the conflicting interests and values they hold prior to discourse. Rather, "the principle of universalization requires each participant to project himself into the perspectives of all others" and to be open to "reciprocal criticism of the appropriateness of interpretive perspectives and need interpretations." Discourse is a process of "ideal role taking" in which participants are engaged in "checking and reciprocally reversing interpretive perspectives," thereby enabling them to alter their own need-interpretations and to discover common or generalizable interests.[33]

Although Habermas separates questions of justice from questions of the good, he does not make this a radical separation. Both justice and the good, he argues, are rooted in "the specific vulnerability of the human species, which individuates itself through sociation. Morality . . . cannot protect the rights of the individual without also protecting the well-being of the community to which he belongs."[34] Because we exist as individuals only through our membership in concrete forms of life, justice cannot be conceived without some form of solidarity. Thus, the norms that could be reached through discourse must enable individuals to realize certain common values that are central to their way of life.

Because discourse ethics conceives of a universal "communication community that includes all subjects capable of speech and action," solidarity in some form must extend to include all humans.[35] But since people vary a great deal in the particular values and identities they hold, discourse ethics must include, according to Habermas, "those structural aspects of the good life that can be distinguished from the concrete totality of specific forms of life."[36] Because the forms of the good are plural and because all humans are subject to common vulnerabilities, the solidarity projected by a discourse ethics must be based largely on a vision of "the damaged life" rather than an affirmative view of the "good life."[37]

To the extent that all humans are vulnerable in similar ways, it is plausible to suppose that there are "generalizable interests" that could provide the basis for norms that would command universal assent.[38] Obvious examples include a right to life and bodily integrity, but even these examples are problematic, inasmuch as a consensus on such norms is likely to mask deep conflicts over their application and the conditions under which they may be overridden.[39] Moreover, it would appear that norms could be valid without being acceptable to *everyone* who is capable of participating in discourse. The principle of universalization requires only that those *affected* by a norm accept it. Many of the norms invoked in communicative action are limited in their application to particular forms of life because they make use of culturally specific concepts such as particular role definitions. If there is a universal moral community, it is constituted by a relatively narrow set of norms. But we are all members of a number of different, overlapping moral communities, which are constituted by a richer set of norms that are binding on their members; the range of behaviors that are normatively regulated and that could constitute occasions for resentment are greater in such communities, but these behavioral expectations apply to fewer people.

There are, then, reasons to believe that some norms could be validated through discourse, but it is far from obvious that they would be sufficient to settle the conflicts that arise in a pluralist world. We might be able to avoid this conclusion, and to guarantee universally acceptable norms, if "all other goals and purposes are subordinated to that of reaching agreement."[40] There are points where Habermas seems to flirt with this idea, as when he writes that communicative actions are those in which participants "coordinate their individual plans *unreservedly* on the basis of communicatively achieved agreement,"[41] but it is hard to see how this strong model of communicative action could be vindicated. The power of Habermas's argument is that it brings out the way in which redeemable normative validity claims are rooted in "communicative action," a form of action that is essential to social life. But, it is only a "weak" model of communicative action that is essential to the constitution of a social lifeworld; it is only the weak model that is implicated in the "performative contradiction" committed by one who would reject the idea of normative validity altogether. Unfortunately, the weak model cannot guarantee the existence of universal norms.

II. PLURALISM AND AGONISTIC CONFLICT

One possible response to this dilemma is to reject the distinction between normative and evaluative discourses, or between questions of justice and questions of the good life. In this vein, Benhabib criticizes Habermas's (qualified) restriction of moral-practical discourse to questions of justice, arguing that, "there is no privileged subject matter of moral disputation." She insists that "the language of rights can . . . be challenged in light of our need interpretations, and that the object domain of moral theory [be] so enlarged that not only issues of justice but questions of the good life as well are moved to the center of discourse."[42] Benhabib concludes that we must "reconsider, revise and perhaps reject the dichotomies between justice versus the good life, interests versus needs, norms versus values upon which the discourse model, upon Habermas's interpretation of it, rests."[43]

In making this argument Benhabib deepens the critiques of traditional ethical theory articulated from a feminist perspective. In her interpretation, "universalistic moral theories from the social contract tradition down to Rawls's and Kohlberg's work" enshrine an "ideal of autonomy" that presupposes an understanding of "the 'personal,' in the sense of the intimate, domestic sphere, as ahistorical, immutable and unchanging," and so "removed from discussion and reflexion."[44] This conception, she argues, is implicitly gendered and so fails adequately to account for the experience of women.

In place of Habermas's model of a discourse ethics, Benhabib substitutes what she calls "interactive universalism." In contrast to the thought of both Rawls and Habermas, this model conceives of moral relationships as holding between concrete or particular selves, rather than merely "abstract" individuals. Traditional universalism is oriented to the "generalized" other, in which "each individual is a moral person endowed with the same rights as ourselves," and is capable of respecting others' rights while pursuing his or her own "vision of the good." Interactive universalism accepts this ideal, but also insists upon the "standpoint of the concrete other," which "enjoins us to view every moral person as a unique individual, with a certain life history, disposition and endowment, as well as needs and limitations."[45] When we look upon other people only from the standpoint of the "generalized other," we replace the concrete plurality of acting subjects with a "definitional identity" among persons. For interactive universalism, the moral point of view involves the individual's ability to take up the perspective of the other[46] and to develop an "enlarged mentality," a sensitivity to, and appreciation of, the wide range of moral considerations that are relevant in particular settings.[47] Because traditional universalism annuls or abstracts from differences among people, it "leads to *incomplete reversibility*, for the primary requisite of reversibility, namely, a coherent distinction between me and you, the self and the other, cannot be sustained under these circumstances."[48]

Not surprisingly, Benhabib rejects Habermas's core idea that for a norm to be valid "all affected can *freely* accept the consequences and the side effects that the *general* observance of a controversial norm can be expected to have for the satisfaction of the interests of *each individual*."[49] If moral discourse must include questions of the good life as well as questions of justice, and if it must acknowledge others in their concrete particularity, then the ideal of a universal consensus must elude us. Rather, our goal should be to sustain moral dialogue and "the relationships through which we practice the reversibility of perspectives implicit in adult human relationships."[50] Similarly, in our political lives, we should act to ensure that "collective decisions be reached through procedures which are radically open and fair to all."[51]

There is no denying the force of these concerns, but it must be recognized that extending moral discourse to include questions of the good life would make agreement on norms more difficult, and therefore make Habermas's "just resolution of conflict"[52] less likely. However, it might be possible to overcome or at least to ameliorate these difficulties if we were to explicitly recognize what might be called an "agonistic" dimension to communicative ethics. Without abandoning the demand for impartiality, we must also acknowledge that there may be deep conflicts of values which preclude agreement on norms that all could accept. In such cases, justice may be impossible, since there may be no way of resolving conflicts that all could accept.

The idea that the moral point of view involves the "reversibility of perspectives," an idea that is central to all formulations of a discourse ethics, is often presented in a one-sided manner, to the neglect of the claims that each individual can make for his or her own aspirations and ideals. The overriding commitment to the idea of the reversibility of perspectives is particularly problematic when it is extended to include the viewpoint of the concrete other. In many of our relationships with concrete others (most especially in the family and among friends, but not only in such intimate contexts), reciprocity typically involves creating patterns of mutual affirmation and reciprocal recognition.[53] But reciprocal recognition in such settings is only the beginning of mature human relationships. Even or especially when recognition is genuinely reciprocal, when both parties to a relationship practice the reversibility of perspectives and view issues from the point of view of the concrete other, each often comes to depend on the other's response for an affirmation of his or her own sense of worth or value: I value myself because you recognize me, and vice-versa. Each thus becomes vulnerable to the other and, in a world where our hopes and expectations are inevitably disappointed from time to time, each develops a motive to protect oneself by limiting the ways in which one exposes oneself to the other. Fear of disapproval, of the withdrawal of recognition, can lead one to repress some aspects of oneself. Thus, there is an important limit to the ways in which either party can develop – and to the intimacy they can achieve – in their relationship. As long as a relationship is rooted in the idea of reciprocal recognition, it can become self-limiting in this way.

To go beyond reciprocal recognition requires that one value oneself enough that one can act more self-affirmatively. Rather than responding to the expectations or needs of others in order to receive approbation, one must sometimes act on one's own aspirations, even at the risk of conflict and disapproval. That does not mean that one no longer recognizes or tries to understand and respond to another's needs; on the contrary, it may free one to be more open to others and to offer them more, because the desire for their recognition and approval is no longer a basic motive for one's action. It also makes greater intimacy possible, as self-disclosure need no longer be limited by the fear of rejection. In acting in this way an agent goes beyond the idea of mutual recognition as the source of his or her activity.

I do not offer these reflections as criticisms of Habermas's or Benhabib's views, which are not necessarily inconsistent with this line of reflection. It might be said that the kind of relationship I am describing is a pathological form of reciprocal recognition, and in many ways it is. But it is also very common. More important, we don't have the concepts to understand and overcome it as long as we take our departure principally from the idea of the "reversibility of perspectives." Mature forms of reciprocal recognition involve other elements as well, including an internal sense of self-worth, that may involve an agent's acting in a way that frustrates or disappoints another.

The one-sidedness of "reciprocal recognition" in private life has a political analogue in the politics of resentment and victimization. Both are characterized by the centrality of resentment, as aggrieved parties feel outrage at groups or conditions that are felt to deny their dignity (thereby feeding whatever self-doubts they may have).[54] There are of course any number of occasions when resentment is an appropriate response to a "breach of a generalized norm or behavioral expectations.[55] Even in such cases, though, it is a dangerous emotion, sometimes blinding us to the humanity of those who perpetrated the wrong.[56] Moreover, and perhaps more important, it is often the case that the norm or expectation that was violated was not one that could survive discursive testing, and in yet other cases there may be countervailing considerations that at least mitigate (if they do not excuse or even justify) the violation. We cannot expect that everyone who is affected by our actions will accept what we do, at least not in a world where goods are scarce, where self-esteem and identities are vulnerable, and where what we desire or need is often that others respond to us in ways that may or may not meet or reflect their needs. Hurt feelings, anger, disappointment, conflict, struggle – all are essential parts of our moral and political lives. All of these (and related) feelings are often experienced and expressed as resentment and indignation. An adequate morality must recognize the place of agonistic struggle in moral and political experience, even commending the integrity displayed by those who advance their purposes while refraining from the insult of insisting that others acknowledge that they are "right."

In principle, there is no reason why a discourse ethic could not accommodate this concern. Indeed, to the extent that it incorporates a strong principle of universalization, there are likely to be relatively few areas of social interaction governed by moral norms, and so there would be significant scope within which people must work out the issues that divide them as best they can. At least this would be true for a communicative ethics based on a "weak" model of communicative action, in which (at least some) of one's purposes are not subordinated to achieving understanding. But when a discourse ethic puts too much emphasis on "reciprocal recognition," it can contribute to the pervasiveness of inappropriate resentment in both politics and personal life. We must have "the will and the readiness to seek understanding with the other and to reach some reasonable agreement,"[57] but we must also recognize that agreement may elude us. At times we must act without agreement or approval, and so acting is not always a reason for self-condemnation or for resentment toward others.

III. LEGITIMATION AND THE BRACKETING OF DIFFERENCES

I would now like to return to Habermas's criticism of Rawls, that Rawls's conception of a hypothetical agreement of parties in an "original position" fails to provide scope for the reflexivity that is essential to the idea of morality. Moral norms, Habermas argues, must be tested in actual argumentation among the affected parties. Rawls's construction of a practical discourse, by contrast, is essentially "monological" in that it allows every individual "to justify basic norms on his own." Rather than viewing his work as the "contribution of a participant in argumentation to a process of discursive will formation," Rawls mistakenly sees it "as the outcome of a 'theory of justice,' which he as an expert is qualified to construct."[58]

In one sense this criticism is well taken. If we follow Habermas in seeing the moral point of view as rooted in the structure of communicative action, then moral norms can be vindicated only through the affirmations of social actors as they reach mutual understanding through processes of argumentation, broadly conceived. But we might view Rawls's theory not as an "expert" construction to which citizens should defer, but as a proposed *strategy* for the discovery of norms that all can accept under conditions of moral pluralism. Critical to this strategy is that it enjoins what we might call the "bracketing of difference." Argumentation at the level of defining fundamental principles of justice, Rawls proposes, should be based on the interests that are broadly shared, rather than on identities and interests that differentiate us, making us specific, concrete persons.[59] By bracketing our differences behind a veil of ignorance, we can discover norms that all can accept because they would be impartial, protecting widely shared interests and incorporating a genuinely common good.

Rawls's specific formulation of the "bracketing strategy," however, is not sufficiently inclusive. Some participants in actual discourses would not be willing to bracket their differences in the way the Rawlsian strategy requires because doing so would prevent them from articulating their needs and aspirations.[60] In Rawls's theory, the principles of justice determine the appropriate distribution of "primary goods," goods that are necessary or instrumental to the realization of our basic interests. In Rawls's view, we have "two highest-order interests," to realize and exercise our capacity for justice and our capacity to form and pursue a conception of the good. In addition, Rawls's persons have an interest in advancing their "determinate conceptions of the good," but this is subordinate to the first two interests.[61] It is crucial to note that "what are to count as primary goods is not decided by asking what general means are essential for achieving the final ends which a comprehensive empirical or historical survey might show that people usually or normally have in common." Whatever ends people actually adopt, and whatever means may be required for those ends, the primary goods are determined "in the light of a conception of the person given in advance."[62]

This restriction on the concept of the "original position" means that the scope of conflict is limited by the conception of the person on the basis of which Rawls constructs his theory of justice. Certain kinds of issues and claims will not be given a hearing, certain voices will be excluded on the grounds that they do not express legitimate claims. Excluded are people for whom the "capacity to form and pursue a conception of the good" is not subordinate to their "determinate conceptions of the good," that is, those for whom the capacity for agency may be overridden by their particular moral beliefs or religious views. This exclusion does not reflect a rational consensus of citizens, but is a *presupposition* of the processes through which a rational consensus is formed, delimiting the range of political choice prior to public discourse and debate. This will not pose a problem if moral pluralism is sufficiently limited that such voices do not exist. But if Rawls's concept of the person is not universally shared in a society, then his theory of justice cannot serve as the basis for a moral community. Those whose voices are excluded will experience this as an imposition and thus as unjust.

Habermas and Benhabib insist on the open-ended character of discourse, and the need to include all voices and perspectives, requirements that Rawls's theory fails to meet. But Rawls's work suggests that it is only by reducing the scope of issues that must be authoritatively decided that we can have hope of finding norms that are broadly acceptable in a society characterized by value pluralism.

In this context we might follow some hints Habermas offers in his discussion of justice and solidarity. Although there may be a plurality of forms of human flourishing, there may be much less diversity in the forms of suffering and vulnerability to which we are subject. In particular, the very idea of a society whose practices are vindicated through discourse rests on a conception of human agency, in which we see ourselves as beings who are at least sometimes "doers," who control and direct some of our actions according to our purposes and beliefs. A notion of agency is inherent in the idea of giving or withholding assent to a particular proposition, not to mention the idea that we can be bound, and bind ourselves, to norms that regulate our interactions. The impairment of one's capacity for agency results in a "damaged life," a judgment that can be accepted by people who have widely divergent notions of what constitutes a good life. Bracketing questions of the good life and focusing on a common interest in protecting our capacity for agency, therefore, could provide a suitable basis for achieving the agreement necessary to a discourse-based view of political legitimacy.

Norms protecting the capacity for agency include a basic set of rights protecting the privacy and integrity of individuals, and rights to speak and communicate.[63] They would also include a set of welfare rights, providing the resources necessary for participation in the political community and the institutions of political democracy.[64] But they would allow significant scope for individual liberty, a significant sphere of private – in the sense of nonpolitical – life, within which individuals and groups would be free to pursue their distinct, and often conflicting, ideals and purposes. Employing a "bracketing strategy" of the sort originally suggested by Rawls holds out the hope of discovering a sufficient level of commonality to make a discourse ethics determinate, and so suitable to the task of creating a political community that can accommodate moral pluralism.[65]

Such a society would be one where deep conflicts would still occur, including conflicts over the specification of the rights and responsibilities necessary for agency. In some cases, as Habermas observes, there may be problems such as abortion "that cannot be resolved from the moral point of view" because they are so "inextricably interwoven with individual self-descriptions of persons and groups, and thus with their identities and life projects."[66] Many of these disputes can be managed by discovering "how the integrity and the coexistence of [different] ways of life and worldviews . . . can be secured,"[67] but we might also find that the differences are so great that citizens will not be able to find reasonable compromises that all can accept. Some will therefore experience whatever decision is reached as an imposition. But we can hope that such occasions will be sufficiently rare so that the ideal of a social order whose norms are fully acceptable to its members can be a reasonable goal for us to pursue.

NOTES

1 Jürgen Habermas, *Justification and Application* (Cambridge, Mass.: MIT Press, 1993), p. 9.
2 See, for example, Jürgen Habermas, "Three Normative Models of Democracy," presented at the 1993 meeting of the Conference for the

Study of Political Thought, "Democracy and Difference," Yale University, New Haven, Conn., April 1993.

3 John Rawls, "Justice as Fairness," *Philosophical Review* 67 (1958), reprinted in a somewhat revised form in *Philosophy, Politics, and Society,* ed. Peter Laslett and W. G. Runciman, 2d series (Oxford: Blackwell, 1962), from which all quotations have been taken. See the discussion in sec. 3–5 (pp. 136–49 in Laslett), where the procedural character of Rawls's construction is brought out clearly.

4 Ibid., pp. 141, 142.

5 Ibid., p. 148, my emphasis.

6 Jürgen Habermas, *Moral Consciousness and Communicative Action,* trans. Christian Lenhardt and Shierry Weber Nicholsen (Cambridge, Mass.: MIT Press, 1990), p. 211. Hereafter cited as MCCA.

7 Ibid., p. 211.

8 Jürgen Habermas, *The Theory of Communicative Action,* Vol. I, (Boston: Beacon Press, 1984), pp. 285, 287.

9 Ibid., p. 302. Rules of etiquette should not be confused with moral norms. Habermas describes them as "customary rules that are followed for the most part without needing, or being amenable to, rational justification," *Justification and Application,* p. 161.

10 Jon Elster, *The Cement of Society* (Cambridge: Cambridge University Press, 1989), p. 15. See ch. 3 of that text for a full statement of his argument, and his *Solomonic Judgments* (Cambridge: Cambridge University Press, 1989), chs. 1 and 4, for an analysis of the limitations of the model of instrumental rationality.

11 See *Theory of Communicative Action,* Vol. II, *Lifeworld and System* (Boston: Beacon Press, 1987), pp. 119–52.

12 Kenneth Baynes, *Normative Grounds of Social Criticism* (Albany: State University of New York Press, 1982). Habermas would exclude "latently strategic action, in which the speaker *inconspicuously* employs illocutionary results for perlocutionary purposes," from the category of communicative action. Although my action is obviously purposive, it is not "latently strategic"; I am not "pursuing undeclared ends" nor seeking to influence another through power or sanctions.

13 Anthony F. C. Wallace, *Culture and Personality,* 2d ed. (New York: Random House, 1970), p. 32.

14 Ibid., p. 35.

15 MCCA, p. 58. Habermas discusses several types of communicative action and the validity claims they involve, but I will focus my discussion on the problem of normative validity.

16 MCCA, p. 67.

17 Ibid.

18 Ibid., p. 65.

19 Ibid., p. 92.

20 Ibid., p. 89. In developing this argument, Habermas draws on the work of Robert Alexy. See Alexy's "A Theory of Practical Discourse," in *The Communicative Ethics Controversy*, ed. Seyla Benhabib and Fred Dallmayr (Cambridge, Mass.: MIT Press, 1990). Alexy discusses the rules of argumentation cited in the text on pp. 209–10.

21 MCCA, p. 92.

22 Kenneth Baynes, in his *Normative Grounds of Social Criticism*, stresses that the derivation of "a distinctively *moral* principle of universalizability" requires not only the acceptance of rules of argumentation but also "the idea of what it means to justify a norm of action" (p. 114).

23 MCCA, p. 93.

24 *Theory of Communicative Action*, Vol. I, p. 302.

25 Ibid.

26 MCCA, p. 130.

27 Ibid., p. 120.

28 Ibid., p. 121.

29 Ibid., p. 120.

30 *Justification and Application*, p. 12.

31 MCCA, pp. 177–78.

32 For an excellent discussion of this aspect of Habermas's account, see Stephen K. White, *The Recent Work of Jürgen Habermas* (Cambridge: Cambridge University Press, 1988), esp. ch. 4.

33 *Justification and Application*, p. 52. As Rehg puts it, "the individual's needs, values, or interests become *normative* only if they find the assent of others" (William Rehg, "Discourse and the Moral Point of View," *Inquiry* 34 (March 1991, p. 44).

34 MCCA, p. 200.

35 Jürgen Habermas, "Justice and Solidarity," *Philosophical Forum* 21 (1989–90), pp. 48–49.

36 MCCA, p. 203.

37 Ibid., p. 205.

38 Habermas often speaks of valid norms as being "equally in the interest of all" (e.g., *Justification and Application*, p. 29), or "equally good for all" (e.g., p. 151). This appears to be an unnecessarily strong requirement; in a pluralist world, it is not obvious that there could be a metric that could be used to measure the extent to which a norm served the interest or the good of people whose values differ significantly.

39 Habermas argues that "discourses of application" must be separated from "discourses of justification." In discourses of application, we must decide which norm(s) are most appropriate to apply to a particular situa-

tion. In discourses of justification, we attempt to anticipate the kinds of situations to which a norm would apply, but it is obviously impossible to anticipate every eventuality. See *Justification and Application*, pp. 35–39.

40 Baynes, *Normative Grounds of Social Criticism*, p. 84.

41 *Theory of Communicative Action*, Vol. I, p. 305, my emphasis. Similarly, Habermas writes that in communicative action participants carry out their plans "only on condition that consent has been reached," which suggests that only a strong model of communicative action is adequate ["Remarks on the Concept of Communicative Action," in *Social Action*, ed. Gottfried Seebass and Raimo Tuomela (Dordrecht: D. Reidel, 1985), p. 154].

42 Seyla Benhabib, *Situating the Self* (New York: Routledge, 1992), p. 169.

43 Ibid., p. 170.

44 Ibid.; see also pp. 185–87.

45 Ibid., p. 10.

46 Ibid., p. 29ff.

47 · Ibid., pp. 53, 165.

48 Ibid., p. 162,

49 Habermas, MCCA, p. 93.

50 Benhabib, *Situating the Self*, p. 52.

51 Ibid., p. 9.

52 Habermas, *Justification and Application*, p. 9.

53 Benhabib, *Situating the Self*, p. 52.

54 Following Stawson, Habermas argues that it is the feeling of resentment, and the way it is tied to the belief that a perpetrator has "violated something impersonal or at least suprapersonal, namely a generalized expectation that both parties hold," which provides the phenomenological grounding for morality, an experience that noncognitivist and prescriptivist views of morality are incapable of capturing (MCCA, pp. 45–50).

55 Ibid., pp. 48–49.

56 While working on this essay I watched a program on MTV with my thirteen-year-old daughter on racist, skinhead groups and their music. Part of the program involved informal interviews with skinheads as they talked and joked with the interviewer and each other. She found the episode confusing, seeing them acting in ways that were recognizably "like us." "It would be so much easier just to hate them if they weren't like us at all," she observed.

57 Benhabib, *Situating the Self*, p. 9.

58 Habermas, MCCA, p. 66.

59 There are other conditions defining the original position, of course, such as reciprocity and freedom: we must see ourselves as free and equal per-

sons and society as a system of mutual advantage. I focus on the idea of the veil or ignorance and the related notion that deriving principles of justice requires a model of hypothetical rather than actual discourse.

60 The following discussion draws on my *Constructing Community* (Princeton, N.J.: Princeton University Press, 1994), pp. 56–57.

61 John Rawls, "Social Unity and Primary Goods," in *Utilitarianism and Beyond*, ed. A. Sen and B. Williams (Cambridge: Cambridge University Press, 1982), p. 165.

62 Ibid., pp. 166–67.

63 See Jean Cohen's development of this theme in her "Discourse Ethics and Civil Society," in *Universalism vs. Communitarianism*, ed. David Rasmussen (Cambridge, Mass.: MIT Press, 1990), pp. 88ff.

64 See Habermas's defense of positive rights in *Justification and Application*, pp. 68–69.

65 I have developed the ideas hinted at in this concluding section at much greater length in my *Constructing Community*.

66 *Justification and Application*, p. 59.

67 Ibid.

Part IV

DISCURSIVE DEMOCRACY

8 The self in discursive democracy

The tradition of radical democracy includes, in different ways, figures such as Jefferson and Emerson, Marx and Gramsci, John Stuart Mill and Dewey. What unites these otherwise diverse thinkers – what makes them "radical" democrats – is the view that democratic participation is an important means of self-development and self-realization. They also hold that more participation will produce individuals with more democratic dispositions – individuals who are more tolerant of difference, more sensitive to reciprocity, better able to engage in moral discourse and judgment, and more prone to examine their own preferences – all qualities conducive to the success of democracy as a way of making decisions. For the radical democrat, democracy is always more than a means of checking power and distributing values, as it is for most liberal democrats. Radical democrats hold, in the well-known reversal of Lord Acton's phrase, that powerlessness corrupts, and absolute powerlessness corrupts absolutely. Democracy is a way of life, a mode of decision making that generates its own ethics and values – expectations I have referred to elsewhere as the *self-transformation thesis* in democratic theory.[1]

Habermas's work has been central to rejuvenating radically democratic expectations such as these, in large part because he has rethought radical democracy within a broad and uniquely comprehensive theory of communicative action. From Habermas's perspective, radically democratic ideals reside in the close relationship between the discursive nature of political judgment and democratic institu-

This chapter is an expanded version of "Can Participatory Democracy Produce Better Selves? Psychological Dimensions of Habermas's Discursive Model of Democracy," *Political Psychology* 14 (June 1993):209–34.

167

tions.[2] His *discursive theory of democracy* places discourse at the center of democratic theory, conceived both as a means of resolving disputes and enabling collective actions, and as a measure and justification of democratic institutions.[3]

My aim in this chapter is to recount and sometimes reconstruct Habermas's discursive theory of democracy in light of the radically democratic view that (a) politics ought to relate closely to individuals' opportunities for self-development, self-realization, and control over everyday life, and (b) democratic participation leads to desirable transformations of individual capacities. Viewing Habermas's approach from this perspective, I suggest, highlights the originality of his contributions to radical democratic theory. But it also reveals issues that remain to be addressed.

I. ARE RADICALLY DEMOCRATIC IDEALS OBSOLETE?

Not the least of Habermas's contributions is that his account of modern societies suggests why it is worth attending to radically democratic ideals at all. Conventional wisdom holds that such ideals – especially those related to self-transformation – are obsolete in advance industrial societies. High levels of complexity, large scale, and extensive divisions of labor radically diminish both the possibilities for democratic participation and the quality of democratic judgments. On this view, the best possible democracy is one in which groups and coalitions can check (but not guide) experts and political elites through the formal powers of voting and lobbying.[4]

In contrast, Habermas views democratic possibilities in light of a countertendency in modern societies: As traditional "lifeworld" horizons disintegrate, individuals find themselves burdened with new demands, choices, and freedoms.[5] And as societies become more complex, individuals find themselves inhabiting multiple and pluralistic roles for which traditional identities are unsuited. Under these circumstances, new identities must be generated by individuals themselves. Moreover, the performance of complex institutions increasingly requires that identities be discursively negotiated, which in turn requires appropriate institutional spaces. In political language, this means that democratic empowerment – a condition of discursively formed identities – is increasingly necessary for modern societies to function. In Habermas's view, radical democracy, especially within institutions of civil society, is rapidly becoming the only means of restoring solidarity, authority, and capacities for collective action in posttraditional societies.[6]

Habermas's view that democratic empowerment is a functional possibility (and perhaps a functional requirement) of complex, posttraditional societies gives us a new reason to attend to the self-transformation thesis in democratic theory – the view that democratic experience produces better people. While the thesis has seemed overly optimistic under any circumstances,[7] perhaps most damaging is its apparent irrelevance to democracy in modern societies. Habermas's perspective revitalizes questions of democratic transformations because he views them in light of developmental conflicts within modern societies. Earlier participatory democrats assumed that people would be attracted to political participation if only they had the opportunity, time, and resources. In the terms of Habermas's developmental sociology, however, self-making via democracy is a functional pressure built into differentiation and complexity as such. Moreover, as Habermas conceives the issue, political self-transformations are not something we can choose (as we mistakenly assume in debating the merits of the current politicization of the "private" realm). Instead, they will occur as societies develop, because structural developments throw individuals back onto their own resources to create their identities. The relevant questions are not whether this will happen, but how, and whether democratic designs can encourage desirable results.

As Habermas constructs the issue, democracy is a generic means of resolving conflict and negotiating collective actions rather than a process with a specific institutional locus. This approach fits nicely with the fact that contemporary states are involved with virtually every facet of civil society – through economic regulation, fiscal and monetary policy, industrial and technological development, welfare entitlements, civil rights, education, affirmative action, and so on.[8] These developments undercut the distinction between civil society and state, a distinction upon which democratic theories traditionally have depended in conceiving notions of representation and popular control of government. As institutions of civil society are politicized, so questions of political democracy become appropriate to these institutions. Indeed, they become necessary: The pattern of increased politicization means that other means of coordinating actions – tradition, markets, coercion – lose their legitimacy. Democracy increasingly appears as a means of reestablishing authorities, precisely because it is the only means of coordinating collective actions that attends to, and is part of, individuals' negotiating their identities in posttraditional contexts.[9]

These points add up to a counterintuitive insight: Even as societies become more complex and decision making seems more remote, democratization may proceed within and between the institutions of civil society, which in turn alters and fragments the boundaries of the state. Radically democratic expectations are not necessarily utopian; rather, they are one concrete possibility enabled by the modernization process itself. This insight is not visible from the perspective of more traditional democratic theory, even in its radical variants: In taking for granted that democracy is primarily a matter of the people controlling the state, it relies on an obsolete location of politics.

In addition, because Habermas detaches the notion of democracy from its civil society/state institutional locus, he can put the question of the authority of democratic judgment in generic terms. The question: "Why should I obey?" conceived within much liberal democratic theory as a question of why individuals should give up self-rule, is redefined by Habermas in terms of the "force" exercised by validity claims within discursive processes. Political authority is something that can be generated by discourse, just because "discursive will formation" produces institutional locations for individuals at the same time that it engages and forms their capacities for self-direction.

These authority-generating properties of speech can develop, however, only within settings that hold other forms of power and authority at bay. Indeed, Habermas uses the term *discourse* to refer *only* to communication that occurs in such settings. Discourse, he writes,

can be understood as that form of communication that is removed from contexts of experience and action and whose structure assures us: that the bracketed validity claims of assertions, recommendations, or warnings are the exclusive object of discussion; that participants, themes, and contributions are not restricted except with reference to the goal of testing the validity claims in question; that no force except that of the better argument is exercised; and that, as a result, all motives except that of the cooperative search for truth are excluded.[10]

Thus, to participate in the process of discursive will formation is already to have assented to rational authority – namely, to the authority inherent in discourse, or to the force of validity claims.

Habermas is not arguing that discourse can be an organizing principle of institutions. Rather, it is an organizing principle of democratic judgment and legitimacy. Institutions cannot conduct all of their affairs through discourse, any more than individuals would wish to devote their lives to discourse. Most speech (itself just one mode of communication) is not discourse, even if any particular speech act – such as a command, assertion, demonstration, expression, strategic use of language, or lie – could be raised to the level of discourse through questioning. We usually avoid discourse because it is cumbersome and consumes much time and effort. We appropriately resent people who "make an issue of everything" even if we inappropriately resent people who make issues of injustices we had thought were settled. So, ideally, since discourse is a matter of creating understandings (as opposed to coordinating actions, expressing feelings, and so on), we resort to discourse only when there is a disruption of everyday understandings that orient actions in common directions, a disruption serious enough to require that common understandings be developed or restored. But this is also why discourse is central to democratic politics: What sets "political" relationships apart from social relations more generally is that they involve disruptions and conflicts that require explicit negotiation.

We can see, then, why for Habermas the definitive institution of democracy is what he calls a "public sphere." The institutional concerns common to most democratic theorists – rights, representation, voting, and balances of power – are important for Habermas primarily as means of enabling public spheres.[11] A public sphere is an arena in which individuals participate in discussions about matters of common concern, in an atmosphere free of coercion or dependencies (inequalities) that would incline individuals toward acquiescence or silence. Habermas's institutional concerns center on empowering voice, and on disenabling other means of collective judgment within democratic arenas – coercion, markets, and tradition. At the same time, Habermas emphasizes that public spheres cannot be organizers of collective action, and must be protected from imperatives of collective action. In any collective action, it is virtually impossible to have symmetrical relations of power, even if relations are fluid and voice is formally equal. Thus, whatever else democratic institutions entail, they must distinguish arenas of decision and organizations of action, with arenas of decision serving to guide and justify collective actions.[12]

II. AUTONOMY

Habermas's thoughts on where radically democratic ideals might be located in complex, posttraditional societies suggest that it is worthwhile taking a closer look at how the self-transformation thesis fares in his thinking. Habermas's version of the self-transformation thesis can be reconstructed from his view that democracy and discursive reasoning are contingent upon one another, and developmentally linked. When viewed from the perspective of the self, we might say that democratic discourse develops the *autonomy* of participants – that is, their capacities to engage in critical examination of self and others, engage in reasoning processes, and arrive at judgments they can defend in argument.[13] Thus a Habermasian version of the self-transformation thesis is more specific than is typical of radical democratic theories.[14] Habermas does not argue that participation makes people more socially inclined, virtuous, or attentive to others, but rather – because of the discursive context – that participation develops individuals' capacities for practical reasoning, as well as the kind of mutual respect that is entailed in the very possibility of discourse. And it is precisely these capacities and dispositions that discursive democracy needs to work well. Habermas clearly hopes that autonomous participants would also discover common interests of which they had not been previously aware, but this is an entirely contingent matter.[15]

Autonomy is a normative ideal. It is important, however, that Habermas does not treat autonomy as something given to individuals by nature, or as a logical "presupposition" or as an empirical precondition of democracy. Rather, he conceptualizes autonomy in such a way that it is one developmental possibility embedded within social relations as such, when these relations are viewed in light of human potentials for self-reflection.

Here is how he constructs the concept. First, an autonomous self is self-identical, not in the trivial sense of being a distinct physical object (physical identity is an inappropriate metaphor for self-identity), but in the reflexive sense that one can identify oneself as an individual who maintains a certain continuity in time and who is distinguished by a unique life history.[16] One maintains identity in this sense by projecting goals into the future, and organizing one's present in terms of these goals.[17] That is, if one is autonomous, one can locate oneself in terms of biographical projections ("projects") and retrospections. These provide, according to Habermas, a content to the self. The continuous core of the self resides in the reflexive traces of relations with the world that have been desired, projected, maintained, or broken.[18]

Second, autonomy implies capacities of agency, the ability to initiate projects, to bring new ideas, things, and relations into being. And agency implies some amount of control over one's life history – not apart from one's biography and context, but because these serve as resources of agency that neither impose absolute limits nor allow for arbitrary creativity. Autonomy thus involves the capacities for origination that we often think of as uniquely human, but which also underwrite the future-oriented nature of political judgment.[19]

To the extent one can act as an originator, one is not merely determined by circumstance, whether internal or external. A third quality of autonomy, then, is the capacity to distance self-identity from circumstances at the same time that one locates the self in terms of these circumstances. Autonomy is a kind of freedom. Internally, autonomy implies that one can adopt a reflexive attitude toward one's own internal impulses, interpreting, transforming, censoring, and providing names for needs, impulses, and desires, as well as expressing them to others as interests. Ideally, says Habermas, ego identity "makes freedom possible without demanding for it the price of unhappiness, violation of one's inner nature."[20] With regard to the social world, autonomy implies that one can distance oneself from traditions, prevailing opinions, and pressures to conform by subjecting elements of one's social context to criticism.

Autonomy includes, then, the capacity for critical judgment. In the Kantian tradition upon which Habermas draws, this implies an ability to project universal reasons against heteronomous particulars, as a means of gaining autonomy with respect to particulars. "Universalistic action orientations reach beyond all existing conventions and make it possible to gain some distance from the social roles that shape one's background and character. . . ."[21] Such orientations develop in part through the imagination – the ability to think of alternatives – and in part through expressing these alternatives to others through reason giving. In this sense, autonomy depends on public representations of imagination, and these require certain kinds of internal disciplines, namely, imposing consistency on one's thoughts and actions so that they produce a public representation of the self that is reducible to neither internal nor external circumstance. Thus the identity of the autonomous self develops within an intersubjective fabric of reason giving through which selves are represented to others. But it does so in a way that, through the consistency of reason giving, the self also develops a reflexive relationship to the traditions, habits, customs, and attributions upon which identity draws. Although it is unnecessary to accept the Kantian identity between autonomy and transcendental reason, it is easy to see that autonomy requires reason giving in the form of public representations.

When related to the social world, then, autonomy implies a capacity for reason giving or discourse. Thus, fourth, the autonomy of the self depends on an individual's capacity to participate in intersubjective processes of reason giving and response. Autonomy, in other words, implies "communicative competencies" that cannot exist as individual properties, but only as a part of a shared fabric of communicative understandings.[22] Indeed, the linguistic subject "I," recognized by others, is a condition of self-identification.[23] For this reason, discursive relations are central to demarcating and developing autonomy.

Fifth, and following from this point, because autonomy requires participation in linguistic interaction, it also implies reciprocal recognitions of the identities of speakers, if only as a condition of language which depends on the intelligibility of linguistic subjects such as "I" and "you." Without some degree of reciprocity individuals would lose the intersubjective resources of their autonomy. Autonomy thus implies and requires *equality* in the sense of a reciprocal recognition of speaking subjects.[24]

Finally, autonomy implies some measure of responsibility, simply because autonomy means that one has the capacity to relate intention and behavior, and thus to give reasons for behaviors to others. This is a key capacity for a discursive democracy since this kind of democracy lacks other means of aligning individual and collective judgments.

III. HOW DOES AUTONOMY DEVELOP?

Habermas's view that autonomy develops through language use in social interactions is an important, although not entirely remarkable linkage: What he has done (and says he is doing) is to translate ideas that are well established in developmental and social psychology into the terms of philosophical discourse. Habermas's translations would be quite remarkable, however, if they pointed toward the more specific and problematic link between the development of autonomy and specifically *political* contexts. Political contexts differ from social contexts more generally because they are marked by more conflict and less solidarity. Part of what defines a context as "political" is that many of the social coordinating mechanisms that we usually take for granted we can no longer count on because of significant disagreements, challenges to entrenched power or social structures, or other kinds of disruptions that throw individuals back onto their own resources. These are the circumstances that call for more or less formalized procedures for making collective decisions in the absence of other means. Politics can emerge in any sphere of social life, but when it does so, it indicates that other kinds of relationships – intimacy, friendship, care, reciprocity, solidarity – are not available as means of psychological development and support, at least with regard to the politicized issues. This is why autonomy is, above all, a dimension of the person suited to political situations, and describes the capacities individuals would need were they to respond in discursively democratic ways. So it would be significant if Habermas could show that there is a developmental link between democratic politics and the development of autonomy, since the case is not obvious, even if we accept the terms of developmental and social psychology.

Habermas's analysis does indeed point toward this more specific link, a link he pursues in three interrelated ways. The first has to do with identifying the potentials within social relations for the development of autonomy. The second has to do with the specific moral competencies required by situations of political conflict. The third concerns the motivational force of speech in the direction of autonomy.

Social development of autonomy

At the most general level, Habermas seeks to identify autonomy as one normatively desirable possibility within general structures of social interaction. Borrowing from Piaget and Kohlberg as well as ego psychologists in the psychoanalytic tradition, Habermas projects a logic of ego development, combining it with theories of interactive and communicative competence, such as Mead's. One of his purposes is to show that as general interactive competencies develop, they also produce capacities for autonomy. Habermas points out that there is already much support for this thesis in a general way, although specifics remain debatable: Analytic ego psychology, cognitive developmental psychology, and symbolic interactionism agree that development proceeds in stages, and that each stage is characterized by increasing autonomy.[25]

It is important, Habermas notes, that none of these schools views cognitive capacities as attributes of the mind as such (as do many philosophers and political theorists), but rather as one dimension of the development of social competence. As long as attributes of the self are viewed as epistemic preconditions rather than as pragmatically developed capacities, it is impossible to show any developmental linkage between self and social interactions. Ego identity, Habermas notes in summarizing conclusions common to psychologists, "is not a determination of the epistemic ego. It consists rather in a competence that is formed in social interaction. Identity is produced through *socialization*, that is, through the fact that the growing child first of all integrates itself into a specific social system by appropriating symbolic generalities; it is later secured and developed through *individuation*, that is, precisely through a growing independence in relation to social systems."[26]

These conclusions are promising in a general way for the self-transformation thesis: They suggest that social interactions generally will produce the competencies valued by democracy, and that democracy – as one kind of social interaction – will do so as well. But the problem remains underspecified at this level of analysis because we cannot assume that what holds in a general way for social interactions also holds for politics. In political contexts social relations are strained, including those that develop autonomy. Latent conflicts become explicit, interests are threatened, and identities dislocated. We need to ask, then, whether the parallel development of social relations and autonomy can carry over into politics.

Moral development

Because political conflicts resist being resolved through reference to widely shared rules or norms, the authority of particular moral rules cannot be taken for granted in politics. Rather, whatever authority they come to have must be developed within the political medium of discourse. And if discourse succeeds in establishing the authority of a rule or norm, then the resolved issue moves, as it were, from politics to the background of "lifeworld" understandings that we share and take for granted. This is why politics has the peculiar quality of demanding moral competencies of individuals – one dimension of autonomy – without having moral foundations.[27]

Such capacities of autonomy, in Habermas's view, are implied in situations of moral conflict generally. We might then understand discursive democracy as one arena that draws on these competencies, while also further developing them. Habermas illustrates this possibility by recasting Kohlberg's well-known six-stage theory of moral development to suggest how a progression toward increasing moral competency is embedded in a more general development of social and communicative competencies.[28] The capacities of autonomy required by participatory democracy, in other words, are "always already" embedded in social and communicative relations; they are latent in general structures of interaction. The self develops out of reciprocal recognitions through which individuals define their identities. Such recognitions, although they may be conventional and role-bound at certain states of development, are necessary for any social interaction whatsoever. When combined with social developments that differentiate roles and require individuals to distance themselves from any particular role in order to maintain an identity, reciprocity – recognition of persons as such – is immanent to general interactive competence.[29] "Moral consciousness" in turn "signifies the ability to make use of interactive competence for *consciously* processing morally relevant conflicts of action."[30] The logic of social development is also a logic of moral development because it embodies the "point of view" of reciprocity upon which more specific moral claims can build. Humans understand and are motivated by reciprocity, Habermas claims, "independently of accidental commonalities of social origin, tradition, basic attitude, and so on" because it "arises from the very structures of possible interaction. . . . Thus the point of view of reciprocity belongs *eo ipso* to the interactive knowledge of speaking and acting subjects."[31] The capacities of judgment and ethic of reciprocity necessary for discursive democracy, then, are always already a developmental potential of social interaction.

At the same time, only in a discursive context can moral capacities develop fully. This is a key point: For Habermas, the moral dimension of autonomy in politics depends upon discursive democracy.[32] Thus, whereas Kohlberg defines the highest form of judgment (his stage 6) as a formal (Kantian) ethics of universal principle, Habermas would add a seventh stage, what he calls "discourse ethics." In so doing, Habermas follows a long line of critics of formal ethics who – from Hegel to Carol Gilligan – argue that general principles of judgment abstracted from social relations cannot be sufficiently attuned to the particulars that are always part of our conceptions of right and wrong.[33] What distinguishes Habermas's discursive ethics is the mode of attunement he proposes: Only discursive interaction is both aligned with reason and attentive to the particularity of conflicts. Habermas proposes, then, a strong link between democratically empowered discourse and the moral dimension of autonomy, a link absent in both Kant and Kohlberg. Kantian ethics is "monological" in that one makes moral choices by having a hypothetical conversation with oneself about what would universalize maxims of conduct.[34] Discourse ethics is "dialogical": Individuals can develop principles of judgment only by conversing with those affected. Only in this way can maxims of conduct relate to individual needs, interests, and situated commitments. And only in this way can individuals challenge the need interpretations of others and be motivated to challenge their own. It is here, where individuals are empowered to converse in the face of conflict, that one might expect democracy to induce a developmental effect on the self.

In contrast, formal ethics provides principles of universalization only at the cost of separating moral judgments from examinations and justifications of needs and interests. It understands individuals – their needs and interests – as given, and in this way leaves individuals to be determined by prevailing cultural interpretations combined with the inner desires these interpretations exclude. In political theory, formal ethics is aligned with those liberal-democratic theories that view needs and interests as prepolitically determined, and politics as a matter of conflict and compromise without self-transformation. It is important for the self-transformation thesis that prevailing interpretations of needs and interests be conceived as open to challenge. Because individuals are unlikely to be able to challenge their own interpretations of needs and interests, however, they must be challenged by other individuals. When one must explain oneself to others, Habermas holds, individuals come to understand why they feel as they do in justifying their needs and interests to others. In doing so, they may alter their need interpretations, finding that their previous need interpretations, often absorbed uncritically from their culture, were inappropriate and perhaps even a source of unhappiness to themselves. Or they may become more convinced of the rightness of their claims. In either case, however, discursive argument increases individual autonomy.

The motivational force of speech

It is a different question, however, as to why individuals might be motivated to resolve conflicts by means of democratic discourse. After all, discourse is difficult and by no means psychologically cost free. It is not hard to imagine that even if individuals were presented with real possibilities for discursive democracy, they might still choose a comfortable dependence or unexamined consensus, unwilling or unable to engage in reflexive self-examinations that are, after all, stressful.

Habermas's answer involves a theory of cognitive motivation that maps the general structure of social interaction onto the pragmatics of communication. Speech has a motivational force toward resolutions of conflict because of the general importance of shared understandings in social life. These motivations, Habermas suggests, are likely to become overriding under democratic circumstances – that is, when nondiscursive means of decision making are foreclosed.

The theory is interesting not only because it further elaborates the idea of discursive democracy, but also because it bridges a common divide in social psychology between theories of motivation and theories of cognition,[35] while raising some important difficulties for the discursive ideal, or so I shall argue in later sections. Habermas holds that speech simultaneously frames cognitive capabilities and relates these to the relationships (natural, intersubjective, and reflexive) that pragmatically situate individuals within their worlds. To the extent that we deal cognitively with the relations that situate us in the world, we do so through the medium of language. But since language is not private, since it is learned and sustained intersubjectively, we are also motivated to come to understandings with others about the validity of our claims about these relations. Habermas's important proposition is that *cognitive veracity depends on intersubjective validity.*

Thus, in Habermas's view, we are always motivated toward consensus in speech (about facts, norms, aesthetic judgments, and the like) simply because validity claims in language are pragmatically embodied in the relations to the world through which we reproduce ourselves.[36] The meaning of "consensus" here is not immediately political or practical but cognitive. Habermas does not argue (as his critics often assume) that we are necessarily motivated toward political consensus. His claim is more modest and plausible: We aim at understanding one another as a condition for arguing about this or that fact or norm or procedure; otherwise we would have no cognitive basis for arguing at all. Nor does Habermas mean that every speech act is overtly motivated by cognitive commitments and their corresponding interests, but only that, should the topic of discussion become problematic (and this is the relevance to conflict resolution in democratic theory), then, as the discussion moves toward discourse, the motivation toward consensus is manifested in participants' desires for their validity claims to have an impact. This is the kind of motivation that one experiences when, for example, one has nothing but argumentative means to press a point, and one feels compelled to make oneself understood. Habermas's point is that the logic of all speech manifests such motivation toward consensus: The effectiveness of lying or strategic manipulation depends on both speaker and audience assuming that individuals normally intend to be understood truthfully.

Under ideal speech conditions, it would be the motivation toward (cognitive) consensus, always embedded in the very possibility of speech, that would become determinant. This does not mean that people will agree, but rather that they are motivated to resolve conflicts by argument rather than by other means – and this is all discursive democracy requires. This point emerges from Habermas's model because the motive toward understanding and consensus is not *given* by the conflict under discussion (which is usually foremost in one's consciousness), but only *occasioned* by it, and remains even when individuals discover that their interests are genuinely conflicting. The effect of Habermas's formulations is not, then, to project a consensual politics (as his critics believe), but rather to project the possibility of discursive responses to, and negotiation of, conflicts. His point is that there can be no prediscursive propositional authority in politics, and therefore no rational politics that is not also discursively structured. Because of this, discursive democracy also cultivates the autonomy of its participants.

IV. IS DISCURSIVE DEMOCRACY VIABLE FROM A PSYCHOLOGICAL PERSPECTIVE?

In the remaining sections I shall examine several difficulties with Habermas's ideal of discursive democracy from a psychological perspective and suggest reconstructions. The difficulties stem from the fact that Habermas's ideal relies heavily on the cognitive rather than affective dimensions of the self, resulting in what may be an overly optimistic account of the motivational powers of reason, even under ideal circumstances.

Discursive democracy requires individuals who are autonomous in the sense that they can question elements of their lives and lifestyles without drawing into question their own identity and value. They must be so little threatened that they will remain rational, even when they could turn to other means of resolving conflict – fighting, praying, trading insults – that might work better than argument to maintain the psychodynamics of their identity. And even within language use itself, individuals must be motivated to separate the cognitive uses of language from its other (noncognitive) identity-securing functions in symbolizing, interpreting, demonstrating, and controlling internal balances of desires and impulses.[37]

The point of discursively democratic institutions is, of course, to structure situations so that individuals are drawn to cognitive uses of language – if only because they lack other means of resolving conflicts. The question remains, however, as to how autonomous individuals must be – that is, how competent at negotiating conflict and identity by discursive means – if they are to respond to discursively structured politics.

Habermas's assumption that the cognitive uses of language can be institutionally separated from noncognitive uses poses a challenge to the ideal of discursive democracy. The assumption implies a particular kind of personality as a condition of discursive resolutions of conflict, namely, an autonomous individual who is capable of cognitive motivation and reflection, who can distinguish discursive from other uses of languages, and who is motivated to ascend to a discursive level in the face of conflict. And yet if a key idea of discursive democracy is that democratization also produces the kinds of individuals that enables discursive politics, then we will need to look much more closely at the relationship between politics and self-transformation to produce an account that does not presuppose the kinds of individuals it needs to function.

Habermas is, of course, acutely aware that autonomy cannot be taken for granted. In *Knowledge and Human Interests*, for example, he interprets neurosis as blocked autonomy, expressed in distorted communication.[38] A neurotic reacts to certain expressions, symbols, or statements because they serve unconscious functions in stabilizing a self-identity. This in turn means that he will be incapable of discursive responses: Expressions gain their motivating status from their roles in stabilizing personal identity rather than from their overt meanings or "validity claims." Their unconscious functions will dominate their conscious meanings so that maintaining a neurotic self-identity virtually requires category mistakes. These are not mistakes that can be altered through discourse because subjecting them to challenge threatens the identity of the self as such, a threat that is met by unconscious resistances. In politics, ideologies may come to serve identity functions in ways that systematically undermine discourse.[39] In *Knowledge and Human Interests*, Habermas notes that the "dogmatic limitation of false consciousness consists not only in the lack of specific information but in its specific inaccessibility. *It is not only a cognitive deficiency; for the deficiency is fixated by habitualized standards on the basis of affective attitudes."* [40]

Habermas's aim in this work, however, is not to relate internal blockages to democratic theory, but to demonstrate that psychoanalysis has the structure of a critical theory rather than a natural science. Nor does he come back to these psychodynamic issues with discursive democracy in mind except in passing. [41]

Habermas does, however, return to the relationship between cognitive motivation and identity in a recent discussion of George Herbert Mead. He is concerned here with how self-identity can be secured in a postmetaphysical world, without dogmatic reassurance, and within pragmatic structures of social interaction. [42] In principle, Habermas argues, all that is available for securing identity is the reciprocity of recognition. Since the actual structure of interaction rarely approximates this reciprocity, however, what provides for the security of self-identity is the *anticipation* of recognition that is embedded logically in language use. "The individuation effected by the linguistically mediated process of socialization is explained by the linguistic medium itself. It belongs to the logic of the use of the personal pronouns, and especially to the perspective of a speaker who orients himself to a second person, that this speaker cannot *in actu* rid himself of his irreplaceability, cannot take refuge in the anonymity of a third person, but must lay claim to being an individuated being." [43] Recognitions, however, occur not in the substance of what is said, but in the attributions that enable communication as such. Thus, the

self of the practical relation-to-self reassures itself about itself through the recognition that its claims receive from an alter ego. But these identity claims aiming at intersubjective recognition must not be confused with the validity claims that the actor raises with his speech acts. For the "no" with which the addressee rejects a speech-act offer concerns the validity of a particular utterance, not the identity of the speaker. The speaker certainly could not count on the acceptance of his speech acts if he did not already *presuppose* that the addressee took him seriously as someone who could orient his action with validity claims. The one must have recognized the other as an accountable actor whenever he expects him to take a position with "yes" or "no" to his speech-acts offers. In communicative action everyone thus recognizes the other in his own autonomy. [44]

Habermas's distinction between the substance of validity claims and the logic of identity is well-taken. The distinction is, however, an analytic one, following from the pragmatics of language use. So even here the question remains as to whether the analytic distinction carries over into psychology. The distinction does highlight the fact that the logic of language use suggests a normatively desirable kind of person (a mature, autonomous person who is not threatened by argument, and can therefore respond to argument with argument). But it also highlights the fact that a presupposition of *political* discourse (which is, perhaps, uniquely threatening to identity) is a type of person who can separate psychologically argumentative conflict and self-identity.

We are thus left with a hiatus between Habermas's earlier concerns with depth psychology and epistemology, and his later concerns with cognitive motivation and democracy. The hiatus is important, since the concerns of depth psychology are, at least in principle, disruptive of the ideals of discursive democracy.

V. THERAPY AND COMMUNICATION

In the remainder of this chapter I shall argue that we need not abandon Habermas's ideal of discursive democracy, but that psychodynamic considerations will affect how we conceive its institutional possibilities. Habermas's own thinking about psychoanalytic theory is not without resources, and I shall draw on them in the reconstruction that follows. What I shall suggest is that communication and character structure are indeed closely linked, but the linkage is captured by therapeutic rather than discursive models of communication. With regard to democratic theory, the issue is the extent to which discursive democracy can, and ought to, involve a therapeutic dimension oriented toward developing autonomy.

Habermas's original interest in psychoanalysis came from the fact that it relates questions about cognitive competencies to affective motivations by viewing the ego as the part of the self that develops in a pragmatic context, by mediating internal desires and external possibilities for satisfaction. Thus the motivational basis of cognitive development is that satisfactions are more achievable when one relates to the world in a cognitive way. This point links affective motivations to language and social interaction, since these are the

media that enable cognitive capacities. Habermas notes that the relationship between ego and communication subjects desires to the
"possibility conditions" of communication, namely, the several
kinds of validity claims immanent to any ego assessment that can
be expressed in language. This is why Habermas can view neurosis
as a case of "distorted" communication: For the neurotic the mediating relationship between internal impulses and desires, cognition,
and communication – relationships that should allow for ego-
directed satisfactions – have failed to develop or have broken down.
"Because the symbols that interpret suppressed needs are excluded
from public communication, *the speaking and acting subject's
communication with himself is disrupted.* . . . What happens is that
the neurotic, even under conditions of repression, takes care to
maintain the intersubjectivity of mutual understandings in everyday life and accords with sanctioned expectations. But for this un-
disturbed communication under conditions of denial, he pays the
price of *communicative disturbance within himself.* . . . Thus *the
privatized portion of excommunicated language,* along with the un-
desired motives of action, are silenced in the neurotic and made in-
accessible to him."[45]

On the one hand, autonomy is limited by the neurotic's inability
to subject to questioning his own needs and interests without at
the same time threatening his self-identity. On the other hand, the
neurotic's incapacities show that the rationality associated with ego
autonomy has its motivational basis in concerns with maintaining
the kinds of connections to the world that allow for happiness. Or,
as Habermas generalizes the point in *Knowledge and Human Interests,* "If we comprehend the cognitive capacity and critical power of
reason as deriving from the self-constitution of the human species
under contingent natural conditions, then it is *reason that inheres
in interest.*"[46]

But Habermas also means these considerations to suggest how it
is possible to enlist the powers of communication to transform character structures. And this is how he interprets the therapeutic situation. By challenging the patient's own accounts of his or her feelings
and biography, the therapist attempts to restore consistency between past events, memories, desires, and behavior. This occurs by
restoring the patient's communication with himself so that repressed symbolizations of desires no longer assert their unconscious

influence, but do so consciously in ways that the patient can deal with desires at a cognitive level. In this way the therapist enlists affective interests to restore cognitive capabilities.

VI. DOES THE THERAPEUTIC MODEL HAVE A PLACE IN DEMOCRATIC THEORY?

Any conceivable discursive democracy will include individuals who must develop autonomy if they are to participate in the discursive resolution of conflicts. It is an open question, however, as to whether the therapeutic model of self-transformation – even one following from a theory of communicative action – is compatible with discursive designs. On the face of it, the problem is that therapy is not discourse, and so lacks the (democratic) symmetry of discourse. Therapy is what Habermas calls *critique:* It is a means of clarifying "systematic self-deception" in order to develop the "presuppositions of discourse."[47] The lack of symmetry between participants is part of the technique: The therapist often responds to an assertion as if it were a sign of unconscious thought processes rather than to its manifest validity claims. This lack of symmetry holds even if the therapist intends his or her strategies to make a discursive relationship possible.[48]

To be sure, Habermas does not draw a direct analogy between therapeutic critique and political enlightenment. But he does, in Thomas McCarthy's words, intend the model to "highlight the normative goals of enlightenment – self-emancipation through self-understanding, the overcoming of systematically distorted communication, and the strengthening of the capacity for self-determination through rational discourse. . . ."[49] Still, it is not clear how therapy might relate to the model of political enlightenment that discursive democracy presupposes. As McCarthy points out, therapy and democratic politics are not analogous, even if we could understand them as complementary. For example, the success of a psychoanalytic cure depends on the therapist not permitting the patient's suffering to come to a premature end.[50] But clearly no democratic organization could be structured in this way.

And another problem: Therapy very often involves transferences in which the therapist becomes the object of the patient's desires. Left unsettled, transferences can work against further improvement because they usually involve infantile desires that can be indulged only at the expense of those (cognitive) parts of the self attuned to reality. Part of the therapist's job is to keep these transferences from settling into new patterns of self-defeat. In politics, transferences probably are involved in basic mechanisms of ideology. But without a therapist to dissuade, why should someone give up their "love affair" with a charismatic leader who will "take care of them" when the realities are much less pleasing? Certainly the tendency in political life is not to seek out "therapists" to unsettle illusory hopes based on projections of infantile desires. The motive is absent, since political transferences often lack the direct associations with misery that cause a neurotic to seek help. To the contrary, in politics we are more likely to seek out those who reassure us about the transferences to which we are already subject. Public personalities often become the symbolic reservoirs of infantile desires, while whole classes of people become symbolic reservoirs of narcissistic rage.[51]

In addition, a therapeutic situation usually involves a convergence of interest between patient and therapist that may not exist in political settings, so there is a much greater danger that communication will be manipulative rather than therapeutic. In criticizing Habermas, Hans Gadamer argues that because "therapy" in political groups is not constrained by professional knowledge and codes of conduct, "the generalization of the physician-patient model to the political practice of large groups . . . runs the risk of encouraging an uncontrolled exercise of force on the part of self-appointed elites who dogmatically claim a privileged insight into the truth."[52]

And finally, many existing models of therapeutic community leadership are not to be recommended for their democratic qualities. Hierarchically organized churches come to mind. These are not, of course, organizations that intend their members to gain autonomy, leaving them with infantile transferences that simply bind them to the organization.

VII. INCORPORATING THE THERAPEUTIC MODEL INTO DEMOCRATIC THEORY

For all these reasons, the therapeutic model does not lend itself to direct incorporation into democratic theory. But it is also clear that discursive democracy, if it is not simply to assume autonomy, requires some kind of therapeutic dimension. So the question becomes the following: If the therapeutic model does not lend itself to direct incorporation into the democratic model, can it somehow be incorporated indirectly? Can we conceive of functional equivalents in politics? Politics cannot, of course, become a realm of therapy: No political group can deal with deep dislocations of the self. These will remain matters for the intensely intimate and sheltered spheres. The question is slightly different: Can persons who have relatively functional selves but who are nonetheless subject to internal blockages that disrupt group decision-making processes – insecurities, anxieties, overconfidence, and so on – become more autonomous if these groups are subject to democratization?

Habermas suggests that we find a positive model of political therapeutic critique in new social movements, such as the feminist and Green movements.[53] The reason he locates a therapeutic potential in social movements rather than in, say, the institutions of government proper, is that the institutional requirements of therapeutic critique are parallel to those of discourse. Like discourse, therapeutic critique requires a situation protected from everyday constraints. In therapy proper, the patient must be free to say anything he or she wants, motivated by the concerns of expression and sheltered from the consequences he or she would ordinarily expect. Critique in political institutions would require similar protections, specifically those that enable public spheres. This is why Habermas suggests that if therapeutic critique has a place in politics, it will be institutions that are "close to the base" and which rely on communication for coordinating collective actions, institutions that because of their size have a high potential for "self-reflection" but are limited in their powers of collective action.

Yet not all such institutions are conducive to therapeutic critique, even if they have the formal protections of public spheres. Although Habermas's account of democratization specifies the organizational level where we might locate transformative expectations, the key questions raised above – questions about the limits to the therapeutic model in politics – remain unanswered as regard to the institutional structures of discursive democracy.

Self-organized groups

We can begin to answer these questions, however, by looking at how the interests, identities, and functions that define the group's existence structure motivations for critique and discourse. Considered from this perspective, the democratically "self-organized groups" typified by the new social movements to which Habermas refers are not unambiguously promising as models of self-transformative institutions. These groups form around common identities, causes, and problems: People come together because they share life-styles, have common images of the future, wish to press a common cause, or have common problems. But because they are based on common interests and identities, most will lack internal imperatives for critique and discourse.[54] The voluntary character of these groups and the ease of exit will mean that they will be relatively homogeneous, self-selecting for values and life-styles. In these cases, dogmatic ideological or religious identities may reinforce one another, and attempts at critique and discourse may be regarded as unwelcome challenges to the solidarity of the group. And in the case of many political interest and pressure groups, the likelihood of critique and discourse is low not only for this reason, but also because goals are action-oriented. This will tend to steer communication away from critique and discourse, and toward strategic concerns.

The important exception among self-organized groups (and these are certainly the ones Habermas has in mind) are *counterhegemonic* and oriented toward *self-help*. These include some women's and men's consciousness-raising groups, some ethnic self-help groups, groups composed of individuals disillusioned with corporate ethics of performance, and the like. What distinguishes these groups is that their reason for being is to criticize prevailing cultural identities as they relate to the self. To the extent that these kinds of groups aim to restore autonomy to individuals against prevailing norms and expectations that deprive them of autonomy, they involve a therapeutic dimension, and they understand themselves in this way. The shared interest that defines these groups *is* in developing autonomy, so that we might indeed expect them to cultivate autonomy in ways intrinsic to their political activities.

Functionally organized groups: Workplaces

With the exception of counterhegemonic self-help groups, however, we would do better to look for models of self-transformative democratization in groups that are functionally organized rather than self-organized. The reason is that external functions can impose imperatives for critique and discourse, a point that is not obvious if we try to apply the model of the therapeutic group (which requires protections from external demands) directly to politics. But in situations that are not constructed with therapy in mind, external demands for performance can alter the membership criteria (away from self-selection on the basis of identity), while placing a value on cognitive interaction (thus unsettling and checking transferences).[55] Democratic workplaces provide good examples of why this might be so. In workplaces individuals are likely to be thrown together out of need, selected by their skills, and related to one another through divisions of labor. Here individuals are not necessarily drawn together by common identities or causes, so that a single organization might be quite diverse in terms of life-style, gender, race, ethnicity, religious orientation, and class, or at least more so than in a self-selected group. In principle, the structural imperatives for critique and discourse stem from the ways workplaces bring individuals with different identities and interests together to pursue a goal: The need to perform makes it costly for the group to ignore conflicts and failed communication. These costs can, under many conditions, induce persons with different identities and interests to work together, to motivate one another, to appreciate or at least to tolerate differences, and to produce a working group in spite of the fact that most would not choose this *particular* group had they chosen on the basis of identity alone. Ideally, a functionally organized group will value the development of cognitive capacities as well as consensus, simply because a solidarity of mature people enables the group to discuss, decide, and organize collective actions.[56]

It is important to the self-transformation thesis that transformative processes increase with democratization. In the case of workplaces, we would indeed expect this to be the case. In nondemocratic workplaces, performances can often be maintained by imposing rules and reinforcing traditional work ethics. When workplaces democratize, however, they can no longer depend on imposed rules, roles, and identities for their performances. Often, the kind of agreement necessary for an organization to perform will require it to resort to therapeutic critique and discourse. And when differences of interest and identity in such organizations are empowered, they can serve as a check on premature consensus, a premature consensus being one not based on the autonomy of participants. Finally, we might also expect democratization of workplaces to provide a check against identities that undermine cognitive competence. This is because democratic decision making increases the cognitive demands on individuals, not only because they are involved in self-government, but also because a democratic organization is likely to have a less rigid division of labor, increasing individuals' arenas of competence.

This is not, of course, to say that workplaces today incorporate the discursive ideal, although there are a few that do so. But it is to suggest that typical pathologies of the workplace (alienation, anxiety, lack of motivation and boredom, alcoholism and drug use, failures of communication, sluggish productivity and innovation, absenteeism, etc.) are in part a result of power relations that do not allow for therapeutically and discursively generated identities, a point increasingly recognized in the business literature.[57]

Leadership as critique

Even if structural imperatives for critique and discourse exist within a group, it remains unclear as to how a therapeutic dimension might be incorporated without giving rise to the inherently undemocratic qualities of therapeutic situations to which I referred above. The issue has to do with the kind of authority that is inherent in therapy. Again, Habermas's interpretation of Freud is not without resources. Freud was ambiguous as to the source of the therapist's authority: Although he viewed a patient's "trust" (an intersubjective source of authority) as important, his attempt to view psychoanalysis as a natural science suggested that the therapist's authority is technical in nature. Authority flowing from technical knowledge is undemocratic since the patient lacks the expertise to question the therapist's judgment and "cure."

Habermas argues that the scientific model fails to describe the kind of authority that the therapist establishes within the process of therapy itself.[58] On Habermas's reading of Freud, the therapist cannot depend on professional certification for authority, but establishes it through his or her skill in helping the patient to reformulate expressions until they align with feelings, sources of anxiety, and bodily messages.[59] The aim of the therapist is to encourage the patient to have a conversation with himself, not to prescribe a cure. Although the knowledge of the therapist is crucial, it manifests itself as authority by keeping the process of self-interpretation going: A good therapist reformulates expressions and asks questions with the aim of producing an increased sense of certainty in the patient that he has formulated cognitively what other parts of the self already "knew." The conversational model of authority relies to a large extent upon self-knowledge that only the patient can have, and which has therapeutic value only insofar as the patient brings this knowledge into the domain of language. The authority of the therapist depends on increasing the autonomy of the patient, which the patient experiences as an effect of the dialogue itself. That is, therapeutic authority is ultimately discursive in structure, and has "force" only insofar as dialogue moves from critique to discourse. Such authority is intrinsically democratic.

Habermas's redescription of the communicative bases of authority in therapy suggests an analogous kind of authority in public spheres, an authority compatible with democracy, *assuming that the structure of the organization imposes a solidarity of interests in cognitive performance*, as I have suggested that functionally organized groups do. In such groups, there are often individuals whose personalities and skills of communication dispose them to act as mediators and facilitators, and who gain (discursive) authority within the group because they are very good at listening, probing, drawing out opinions, interpreting, offering options, and restating them. Such persons often sense when positions have become polarized, say, as a result of threats to self-esteem, and can recommend delaying decisions, allowing time to disentangle motives. This is the kind of authority possessed by a chairperson who serves at the pleasure of the meeting, or for a specified period within an organization. Because formal powers of the chair are limited, authority rests on discursive means, and success often depends on his or her ability to play a quasi-therapeutic role.

This is, of course, an ideal transformational model, based on organizational structures that are not now widespread. Such structures would have to be based on relations of power that are not so unequal that critique and discourse can be short-circuited in favor of coercive means of organization. In workplaces, this would presumably require some form of worker ownership and self-management in order to provide internal pressure toward discursive means of problem solving. Moreover, such organizations would have to find ways of setting aside within themselves "public spheres" that are sheltered from immediate constraints of action. A variety of devices might be used to address different kinds and levels of problems in different settings with different numbers of people. The form of critique and discourse might be quite fluid, determined in part by the kind of problem to be addressed – from appropriate divisions of labor and reward, to investment decisions, to day-to-day operations problems, or to subtle forms of racism or sexism. The structure of worker self-management would have to be such that the internal rules governing distributions of rewards will naturally, as it were, become a topic, so that individuals are put in the position of having to engage in moral discourse about distributive justice. In addition, democratic workplaces would have to divide labors in such a way that even outside its "public spheres" all members engage in cognitively demanding tasks so that they are better equipped for the more difficult demands of critique and discourse.

Experiences of work are one of the most extensive of everyday life, suggesting that if democracy can be developed here, then not only will this make the most difference for most people, but it should also produce capacities that would spill over into political arenas where transformational potential are limited by size or structure.

VIII. THE PUBLIC TRANSPARENCY OF THE SELF

Let me conclude by pointing to a danger that follows from the way Habermas constructs the relationship between discourse and the self: His constructions tend to assimilate the self to its public dimensions – that is, to those aspects of the self that can be formulated within the medium of language. Habermas's reconstruction of Freud in terms of his communication model, for example, interprets inner drives and experiences as prelinguistic, consisting in symbols and signs that are not yet formulated in publicly accessible forms.

This has the effect, as one critic puts it, "of blunting the categorical distinction between the linguistic and the nonlinguistic within humans," and tends to "deny the existence of the unconscious as a 'nonlinguistic substratum.' "[60]

The danger is that because the body's nonlinguistic "talk" cannot be conveyed in linguistic form, it will come to seem illegitimate, something that falls outside of the interests and needs of the self. This possibility is evident in Seyla Benhabib's account of discursive democracy, one that draws heavily on Habermas. She writes that the "communicative concept of autonomy implies that what resists articulation, even to oneself, originates in the dark recesses of the psyche and has not lost its 'paleosymbolic linguisticality.' Epistemically, we cannot say that *all* needs that permit linguistic articulation are true, but only that those which do *not* permit linguistic articulation cannot be true. It is ultimately the *process* of discourse, what I have named the moral-transformative experience, that establishes the truth and falsehood of our needs."[61]

These implications have not been lost on Habermas's critics, who sometimes suggest that his focus on the rationality of language threatens a tyranny of discourse over the necessary and desirable ambiguity of inner experience.[62] The point is not a romantic one, but rather a recognition of the manifest inadequacy of language to inner experience. Inner experience, though it may not be formulated in discourse, anchors parts of the self that not only "disturb" language, but also account for happiness, uniqueness, and difference. Taken as a theory of the self, Habermas's approach threatens to sever autonomy and happiness, and produce a tyranny of discourse over needs, something he does not intend.

How important is this criticism for discursive democracy? It is important only if we confuse a theory of discursive transformation of the self with a theory of the self as such. Unlike Freud, Habermas does not start with the demands of the self against society, but rather with *political* problems. The importance of Habermas's initial problematic cannot be overemphasized. His question is: What must we demand of the self *if* we wish our political life to be governed by talk rather than coercion, autonomous structures, or blind consensus? It is from this perspective that Habermas reaches into the self, but it is *only a reaching*, only an interest in those competencies that might best fit the demands of the self with the demands of political life, which we have no a priori way of knowing to be the same. To the contrary, we must suspect that the fit cannot be perfect; that, because of their inherent demands for universality, public expressions can never exhaust the self. Public life stops where the inarticulate begins; a complete self, a healthy self, will always go beyond language.[63]

The only way we have of dealing with this problem at present is, I think, to be aware of the limits and dangers of political theories of the self. They ought not to aim at comprehensive theories of the self (assuming there could be such a thing), even though they must draw on alternative accounts of the self – in literature, drama, and psychology, for example – to situate political accounts, as well as to illuminate the permeability and ambiguity of political arenas. Likewise, alternative accounts of the self remind us that the value of autonomy follows from the *political* dimensions of the human condition. Not all that we value can be achieved politically, and different descriptions of the self will illuminate differently situated values. If we understand this, we will also be suspicious of any theory that is not bounded explicitly by a problematic it seeks to illuminate. Habermas's theory, I think, provides promising new approaches to democratic theory because it problematizes commonalities implicit in discourse, the only means we know of conducting political life in a way consistent with respect for individuals. But his theory does not problematize intimacy, irony, or silence, and will appear clumsy and tyrannical when we understand it as doing so.

NOTES

1 See Mark Warren, "Democratic Theory and Self-Transformation," *American Political Science Review* 86 (March 1992): 8–23 for a review and criticism of this literature.

2 Two of Habermas's works are explicitly framed by questions of democratic theory: *The Structural Transformation of the Public Sphere*, trans. Thomas Burger (Cambridge, Mass.: MIT Press, 1989; first published in 1961), and *Faktizität und Geltung* (Frankfurt: Suhrkamp, 1992), forthcoming in English as *Between Facts and Norms: Contributions to a Discourse Theory of Law and Democracy*, trans. William Rehg (Cambridge, Mass.: MIT Press). For commentary on *Facticity and Validity*, see Kenneth Baynes's "Democracy and the *Rechtsstaat*: Remarks on Habermas's *Faktizität und Geltung*," the next essay in this

volume. A number of commentators have contributed to a Habermasian democratic theory. The most extensive to date is Jean Cohen and Andrew Arato, *Civil Society and Political Theory* (Cambridge, Mass.: MIT Press, 1992). See also Seyla Benhabib, *Critique, Norm, and Utopia* (New York: Columbia University Press, 1986); James Bohman, "Communication, Ideology, and Democratic Theory," *American Political Science Review* 84 (March 1990): 93–109; John Dryzek, *Discursive Democracy: Politics, Policy, and Political Science* (Cambridge: Cambridge University Press, 1990); David Ingram, "The Limits and Possibilities of Communicative Ethics for Democratic Theory," *Political Theory* 21 (May 1993): 294–321.

3 I borrow the term from John Dryzek, *Discursive Democracy*.

4 See Danilo Zolo, *Democracy and Complexity*, trans. David McKie (University Park: Pennsylvania State University Press, 1992) for an especially bleak assessment. Zolo follows Niklas Luhmann, *Political Theory in the Welfare State*, trans. John Bednarz, Jr. (New York: Walter de Gruyter, 1990).

5 See esp. Jürgen Habermas, *Postmetaphysical Thinking*, trans. William Mark Hohengarten (Cambridge, Mass.: MIT Press, 1992), ch. 7.

6 Jürgen Habermas, "What Does Socialism Mean Today? The Rectifying Revolution and the Need for New Thinking on the Left," *New Left Review* 183 (1990): 3–21.

7 See recent criticisms by those disposed toward radical democracy: Edward Greenberg, *Workplace Democracy: The Political Effects of Participation* (Ithaca, N.Y.: Cornell University Press, 1986); Jack Crittenden, *Beyond Individualism: Reconstituting the Liberal Self* (Oxford: Oxford University Press, 1992); Robert Dahl, *Democracy and Its Critics* (New Haven, Conn.: Yale University Press, 1989), pp. 92–93; David Held, *Models of Democracy* (Stanford, Calif.: Stanford University Press, 1987), p. 263; Jane Mansbridge, "Measuring the Effects of Direct Democracy," unpublished manuscript, Northwestern University, 1986.

8 See, e.g., Claus Offe, *Contradictions of the Welfare State*, trans. John Keane (Cambridge, Mass.: MIT Press, 1984); Cohen and Arato, *Civil Society and Political Theory*, part I.

9 This does not mean, of course, that democracies will not make use of coercion, markets, and traditional identities, but only that these means of coordination do not provide democratic legitimacy. For pragmatic reasons, a people might decide (democratically) to organize certain of its activities through markets. They might decide that some kinds of traditional identities ought not fall under the regime of politics, democratic or otherwise. And any polity makes use of some degree of coercion, as when collecting taxes for democratically decided projects.

10 Jürgen Habermas, *Legitimation Crisis*, trans. Thomas McCarthy (Boston: Beacon Press, 1975), pp. 107–8.

11 See esp. Habermas, *Faktizität und Geltung; Structural Transformation of the Public Sphere;* and "Further Reflections on the Public Sphere," in *Habermas and the Public Sphere*, ed. Craig Calhoun (Cambridge, Mass.: MIT Press, 1992), pp. 447–50; and Kenneth Baynes, "Democracy and the *Rechtsstaat*." For institutional implications, see Dryzek, *Discursive Democracy*, part II; Cohen and Arato, *Civil Society and Political Theory*, chs. 8, 9.

12 Jürgen Habermas, *Jürgen Habermas on Politics and Society*, ed. Steven Seidman (Boston: Beacon Press, 1989), pp. 231–32; "What Does Socialism Mean Today?" pp. 17–20.

13 I use the term "autonomy" to signify individuals in terms of their cognitive capacities of judgment. Habermas often uses the term "ego-identity," which I take to be equivalent for present purposes. These terms are related to, but narrower than, the terms "individuation" (distinction, uniqueness), "self-realization" and "self-development." These attributes of the self may or may not be developed by democratic engagement, but in any case they describe the self in ways that are not attuned specifically to discursive resolutions of political conflicts, and which would be valuable whether or not they contributed to democracy.

14 Warren, "Democratic Theory and Self-Transformation," pp. 11–15.

15 Habermas, *Legitimation Crisis*, p. 108.

16 Jürgen Habermas, *The Theory of Communicative Action*, Vol. II, trans. Thomas McCarthy (Boston: Beacon Press, 1987), pp. 98–99.

17 Habermas, *Theory of Communicative Action*, Vol. II, pp. 102–5; cf. Charles Taylor, *Sources of the Self* (Cambridge, Mass.: Harvard University Press, 1989), pp. 25–52.

18 Habermas, *Postmetaphysical Thinking*, p. 182.

19 Habermas, *Theory of Communicative Action*, Vol. II, pp. 98–99; cf. Hannah Arendt, *The Human Condition* (Chicago: University of Chicago Press, 1958), part V.

20 Habermas, *Communication and the Evolution of Society*, p. 73.

21 Habermas, *Theory of Communicative Action*, Vol. II, p. 97.

22 Jürgen Habermas, *Moral Consciousness and Communicative Action*, trans. Christian Lenhardt and Shierry Weber Nicholsen (Cambridge, Mass.: MIT Press, 1990), p. 199.

23 Habermas, *Postmetaphysical Thinking*, pp. 190–91; cf. Rom Harré, "The Social Construction of Selves," in *Self and Identity: Psychosocial Perspectives*, ed. Krysia Yardley and Terry Honess (Chichester: John Wiley and Sons, 1987).

24 Habermas, *Postmetaphysical Thinking*, pp. 1989–91.

25 Habermas, *Communication and the Evolution of Society*, pp. 73–74.

26 Ibid., p. 74.

27 See my "Nonfoundationalism and Democratic Judgment," *Current Perspectives in Social Theory* 14 (1994); cf. Habermas, *Communication and the Evolution of Society*, pp. 78, 92.

28 Habermas, *Communication and the Evolution of Society*, pp. 69–94.

29 Habermas, *Theory of Communicative Action*, Vol. 2, sec. V.1.

30 Habermas, *Communication and the Evolution of Society*, p. 88.

31 Ibid.

32 Cf. Habermas, *Moral Consciousness and Communicative Action*, pp. 70–76.

33 Habermas, *Theory of Communicative Action*, Vol. II, pp. 108–10; *Moral Consciousness and Communicative Action*, pp. 195–215; Carol Gilligan, *In a Different Voice* (Cambridge, Mass.: Harvard University Press, 1982).

34 Habermas, *Communication and the Evolution of Society*, p. 93.

35 Cf. Viktor Gecas, "The Self-Concept as a Basis for a Theory of Motivation," in *The Self-Society Dynamic: Cognition, Emotion, and Action*, ed. Judith A. Howard and Peter L. Callero (Cambridge: Cambridge University Press, 1991): 171–87.

36 Habermas, *Communication and the Evolution of Society*, pp. 1–68.

37 This point parallels William Connolly's criticism of Habermas in *Identity/Difference: Democratic Negotiations of Political Paradox* (Ithaca, N.Y.: Cornell University Press, 1991), pp. 162–63. However, whereas Connolly argues that Habermas hopes to keep problems of identity out of politics, it seems to me that Habermas wishes to find ways of politically negotiating piecemeal changes in identity by holding the relationship between language and self-transformation to a cognitive level.

38 Jürgen Habermas, *Knowledge and Human Interests*, trans. Jeremy Shapiro (Boston: Beacon Press, 1971), chs. 10, 11.

39 Cf. Alvin Gouldner, *The Dialectic of Ideology and Technology* (Oxford: Oxford University Press, 1976), p. 47; Mark Warren, "Ideology and the Self," *Theory and Society* 19 (1990): 599–634.

40 Habermas, *Knowledge and Human Interests*, p. 229; emphasis added.

41 Habermas, *Communication and the Evolution of Society*, p. 91.

42 Habermas, *Postmetaphysical Thinking*, ch. 7.

43 Ibid., pp. 190–191.

44 Ibid., pp. 189–190.

45 Habermas, *Knowledge and Human Interests*, p. 228.

46 Ibid., p. 287.

47 Jürgen Habermas, *The Theory of Communicative Action*, Vol. I, trans. Thomas McCarthy (Boston: Beacon Press, 1984), p. 21.

48 Thomas McCarthy, *The Critical Theory of Jürgen Habermas* (Cambridge, Mass.: MIT Press, 1978), p. 208.

49 McCarthy, *Critical Theory of Jürgen Habermas*, p. 213.

50 Ibid., pp. 211–12.

51 Cf. C. Fred Alford, *The Self in Social Theory: A Psychoanalytic Account of Its Construction in Plato, Hobbes, Locke, Rawls, and Rousseau* (New Haven, Conn.: Yale University Press, 1991).

52 Quoted in McCarthy, *Critical Theory of Jürgen Habermas*, p. 206.

53 Habermas, *Jürgen Habermas on Politics and Society*, pp. 297–98; Jürgen Habermas, "On Social Identity," *Telos* 19 (Spring 1974): 91–103, esp. pp. 99–100; cf. Offe, *Contradictions of the Welfare State*, ch. 11; Cohen and Arato, *Civil Society and Political Theory*, ch. 11.

54 Cf. Dennis Thompson, *The Democratic Citizen* (Cambridge: Cambridge University Press, 1970), pp. 89–90.

55 In *Civil Society and Political Theory*, Cohen and Arato follow Habermas in assuming that democratic transformations of the self are most likely to take place within social movements located in civil society because the external imperatives of markets do not interfere with self-reflective processes. See pp. 416–17, 560–62. In contrast, while granting that some kinds of social movements aim to produce these transformations, I am suggesting that the dynamic of self-selection that operates in the relative freedom of civil society may also produce structural pressures against discourse, while the structural pressures of markets or administration may impose limitations on organizations that require discourse.

56 Michael Schwalbe, *The Psychosocial Consequences of Natural and Alienated Labor* (Albany: State University of New York Press, 1986).

57 John Kotter and James Heskette, *Corporate Culture and Performance* (New York: Free Press, 1992).

58 Habermas, *Knowledge and Human Interests*, ch. 11.

59 Eugene Gendlin, "A Philosophical Critique of the Concept of Narcissism," *Pathologies of the Modern Self: Postmodern Studies on Narcissism, Schizophrenia, and Depression*, ed. David M. Levin (New York: New York University Press, 1987).

60 Joel Whitebook, "Reason and Happiness: Some Psychoanalytic Themes in Critical Theory," in *Habermas and Modernity*, ed. Richard J. Bernstein (Cambridge, Mass.: MIT Press, 1985), p. 156.

61 Benhabib, *Critique, Norm, and Utopia*, p. 338.

62 Cf. William Connolly, *Identity/Difference*, pp. 161–63; Donald Moon, "Constrained Discourse and Public Life," *Political Theory* 19 (1991): 202–29, esp. pp. 219–22.

63 Richard Rorty captures something of this point in *Contingency, Solidar-*

ity, and Irony (Cambridge: Cambridge University Press, 1989) in which he argues that political life demands universals, while creative individuality demands ironies that are intolerable to public life. Although Rorty inadequately assimilates his distinction to the contemporary political landscape, his point could be salvaged by looking at tensions between language and silence, between universal and situated meanings. The possibility is developed extensively in William Connolly's *Identity/Difference*.

9 Democracy and the *Rechtsstaat:* Habermas's *Faktizität und Geltung*

One version of the project of radical democracy, which has roots in Rousseau and Marx, has been expressed in the vision of a rational self-organization of society or a "rational collective identity." Jürgen Habermas has aligned himself with this version in the past and, with some important qualifications, he continues to do so in his new book, *Faktizität und Geltung.*[1] Two departures from his earlier position, however, particularly stand out: First, Habermas takes great pains to distance himself from the holistic or totalistic conception that often accompanies this version of democracy and in which society is regarded as a kind of macrosubject integrated via a central agency (the state) or organizing principle (labor).[2] Second, the new book assigns to law and the legal community generally a more positive and prominent role in the legitimation process.[3] The first shift results from Habermas's long engagement with Niklas Luhmann's systems theory; the second reflects an increased appreciation for Talcott Parson's identification of the "societal community" (and particularly law) as the primary institutional complex responsible for social integration in highly differentiated and pluralist societies.[4] Consequently, it is no longer society as a whole – not even all governmental bodies – but rather the "association of free and equal consociates under law *(Rechtsgenossen)*" that becomes simultaneously the primary subject and object – source and target – of democratization. Radical democracy, in short, must practice an art of "intelligent self-restraint" that acknowledges the systemic divisions of modern and highly complex societies by realigning itself in a more creative manner with the liberal *Rechtsstaat.*[5]

In addition to this reassessment of the significance of systems theory for legal and political thought, *Faktizität und Geltung* also takes

201

up current debates in "Anglo-American" political theory – especially concerning the nature and limits of liberal democracy. It
should thus be possible to form an initial judgment about how Habermas's "discourse theory of law" and model of "procedural democracy" might fare when confronted by some of the more pressing
issues in liberal democratic theory. In these discussions three issues
stand out: First, there is a longstanding debate about the relation
between democracy and other political ideals (such as political
equality, the rule of law, and the guarantee of basic rights and liberties). Are these political values in conflict with the ideal of democracy, or can they be made compatible with one another?[6] Second,
there has been a lengthy discussion about the ideal of liberal neutrality.[7] Is the claim that the liberal state should not act in ways
intended to promote a particular conception of the good defensible
when, on the one hand, the diversity of distinct cultures and life-
forms is increasingly threatened by global markets and, on the
other, the ethical foundations of liberal society are being called into
question by nonliberal regimes? Third, as an extension of the critique of neutrality, the "dilemma of difference" (Minow) poses a distinct challenge to liberal ideology: Must any attempt to address "difference" under the liberal ideals of equality, impartiality, and
toleration necessarily perpetuate injustices and do violence to those
categories and classes not traditionally recognized as within the
norm? This issue has been raised particularly (though not exclusively) in recent feminist jurisprudence.[8]

In what follows, I will first indicate the ways in which *Faktizität
und Geltung* continues some basic themes introduced in *The Theory of Communicative Action* (Section I). Without some acquain-
tance with the central claims of Habermas's major work it will not
be possible to appreciate the current project. I will then outline
some of the main elements of the new book, especially his reinter-
pretation of Kant's "system of rights" in a way that indicates how
the private and public autonomy of citizens mutually presuppose
each other (Section II), and his proposal for a procedural democracy
centered around a two-track conception of deliberative politics (Section III). In the concluding section, I will return to the three challenges to liberal democracy just mentioned in order to see how they
might be addressed from within Habermas's theoretical perspective
(Section IV).

I. COMMUNICATIVE REASON AND THE TENSION BETWEEN FACTICITY AND VALIDITY

A central thesis of *The Theory of Communicative Action* is that the conceptions of reason or rationality used in most social theory do not provide a basis for answering the Hobbesian problem of social order or, beyond that, for adequately describing the processes of modernization. Neither the model of instrumental rationality (familiar in rational choice theory) nor the model of functional rationality (found, for example, in Marxism and systems theory) can account for the contribution of the normative self-understanding of social actors (which are subsequently embodied in social institutions) to processes of social reproduction and integration.[9] These self-interpretations employ idealizations (or "fictions") that cannot be regarded by the participants as "mere" fictions without undermining their social efficacy. Habermas traces these idealizations back to those suppositions actors must make whenever they seek to communicate with one another – suppositions regarding an objective world, the identity of linguistic meaning, the mutual accountability of actors, and the context-transcending validity of claims to truth and rightness (18).[10]

Communication is not reducible to getting someone to believe something. For Habermas, it consists (paradigmatically) in reaching an understanding with someone about something, where "reaching an understanding" draws upon (unavoidable) suppositions constitutive for a weak and fragile (but nonetheless socially effective) form of mutual recognition: To reach an understanding with someone about something implies that one is also prepared to provide warrants for the claims raised with one's utterances should they be contested and that one recognizes the other as someone who is free to take a Yes/No position with respect to those claims. Communicative reason refers, then, to this rationally binding/bonding illocutionary force present in all communicative action, and "communicative freedom" refers to the fundamental "right" or capacity to take a Yes/No position with respect to any speech-act offer (152).

A second theme taken over from *The Theory of Communicative Action* is that processes of cultural reproduction, social integration, and socialization unavoidably depend on these idealizations implicit in communicative action and reason. The transmission of knowledge and values, the maintenance of social orders, and the formation of individual identities and life-plans cannot proceed without reference to the common suppositions of an objective world, identical meaning, accountable actors, and the validity of claims to truth and rightness. Although such idealizations invariably involve counterfactual assumptions, they are nevertheless effective in actual processes of social integration and reproduction.

The ideal moment of unconditionality is deeply bound up in factual processes of reaching understanding because validity claims display a Janus-face: as claims they overshoot every context; at the same time, they must be both raised and accepted here and now if they are to support an agreement effective for coordination – for in this case there is no null-context. The universality of asserted rational acceptability bursts all contexts, but only the local, binding act of acceptance enables validity claims to bear the load of a context-bound everyday practice. (37)

This reference to counterfactual idealizations effective for social coordination – to a context-transcending reason existing *in* society – is the origin of the tension between "facticity and validity" that structures Habermas's new book. In a more sociological vein, Habermas analyzes various ways in which societies have reckoned with this tension through reliance on shared background assumptions in everyday interactions or through the creation of "strong institutions" (such as religion) that fuse the moments of validity and facticity together (39f). The claim Habermas pursues in the new work is that, in the wake of secularization and disenchantment, highly differentiated and pluralist societies are compelled to rely less on traditions and "strong institutions" to bridge the tension between facticity and validity and thus must look elsewhere to fulfill the tasks of social reproduction and integration. In this situation law presents its own means for dealing with the tension between facticity and validity:

In the dimension of legal validity, facticity and validity interlock once more, but this time the two moments do not bond together – as they do in life-world certainties or in the overpowering authority of strong institutions withdrawn from any discussion – in an indissoluble amalgam. In the legal mode of validity the facticity of the state's enforcement of the law is interlocked with the validity-grounding force of a lawmaking process that claims to be rational because it guarantees liberty. The tension between these two distinct moments is both intensified and behaviorally operationalized. (46)

When the tension between facticity and validity moves into the legal medium itself – in what Habermas calls the "internal" tension – it is reflected in the law's claim to reach judgments that are both rational and certain (or predictable) as well as in its claim to issue legitimate orders that can be coercively enforced. At the same time the legal system itself becomes the principal means by which modern societies are able to address the "external" tension between a political order's claim to be legitimate and its reliance on the de facto recognition of its members. To summarize Habermas's thesis: In highly differentiated and pluralist societies the task of social coordination and integration falls to institutionalized procedures of legitimate lawmaking that transform into binding decisions the more diffuse public opinions initially produced via the anonymous communication network of a loosely organized and largely autonomous public sphere.

It might be useful to illustrate this "external" tension between facticity and validity by reference to Rawls's recent account of public reason as the core of a liberal principle of legitimacy. Rawls claims that the justification of principles for regulating the basic social structure must be "political, not metaphysical" – that is, it cannot appeal to anything "outside" the practice of public justification among free and equal citizens – yet it must not be "political in the wrong way" – that is, it cannot be a mere modus vivendi or stand-off between competing interest positions or incompatible conceptions of the good.[11] In this connection he introduces a "liberal principle of legitimacy" which reads: "Our exercise of political power is fully proper only when it is exercised in accordance with a constitution the essentials of which all citizens as free and equal may reasonably be expected to endorse in the light of principles and ideals acceptable to their common human reason" or, as he also puts it, "acceptable to them as reasonable and rational."[12] Yet if institutions satisfying this criterion are also to be stable, the ideals implicit in this "common human reason" (or conception of the "reasonable and rational") cannot exist only at the level of ideal theory, but must be the focus of an "overlapping consensus" within the public political culture.[13] The moment of validity present in the idea of public justification requires the stabilizing "facticity" of a wide overlapping consensus.[14] However, to the extent that Rawls acknowledges a certain tension between facticity and validity – between the question of stability and the conditions of justification or acceptability – he tends to assume that it is sufficiently overcome within a liberal political culture, or at least that we must proceed *as if* it were. Habermas, by contrast, makes the tension explicit in order to consider how, in modern societies, it might be bridged by law as the means by which communicative reasons generated in a process of discursive opinion formation and will formation are transformed into collectively binding decisions.

Despite this and other important differences, there is nonetheless a deeper affinity between the respective appeals to "public reason" (Rawls) and "communicative reason" (Habermas) as a response to the question of legitimacy. Both conceptions invoke a basic notion of autonomy as a capacity for reason giving whether it be grounded in a conception of the fundamental moral powers of citizens (Rawls) or the mutual supposition made by those who act communicatively (Habermas).[15]

II. DISCOURSE THEORY, THE PRINCIPLE OF DEMOCRACY, AND THE SYSTEM OF RIGHTS

Habermas next turns to the centrally important question of the legitimacy of law: What makes legal authority legitimate? In effect, Habermas advocates a sophisticated version of consent theory (one that depends not on actual or hypothetical consent, but one in which the legal-political order retains roots in processes of communicative sociation). He rejects the legal positivist position, advocated as well by Luhmann, that law is legitimate if it has been enacted in accordance with established legal procedures. At the same time, however, appeal to natural law theory is precluded on the basis of his own commitment to radical democracy. As Habermas puts it, "Nothing is given prior to the citizen's practice of self-determination other than the discourse principle, which is built in the conditions of communicative sociation in general, and the legal medium as such" (161–62). Thus, just as he earlier argued that "modernity must generate its own normativity out of itself," he now claims that legality must account for its own legitimacy. In brief, Habermas's strategy is to show that the legitimacy of law is based on a rationality immanent to law, even though that rationality is dependent on and open to dimensions of (communicative) reason that reach beyond the legal medium. "In modern societies, too, the law can fulfill the function of stabilizing expectations only if it preserves an internal connection with the socially integrative force of communicative action" (111).

Habermas approaches the question of the legitimacy of legality through a central difficulty in Kant's political thought frequently discussed in the secondary literature. The difficulty is reflected in the question whether Kant is best understood as a natural rights theorist or a social contract theorist. Habermas concurs with those who argue that Kant is closer to the natural right tradition in that his "Universal Principle of Right (*Recht*)" is generally regarded as a "subsidiary formula" (Nell) of the categorical imperative and hence derived from and subordinate to the moral law. This implies, however, that the Universal Principle of Right, as well as the system of public and private law (*Recht*) Kant generates from it, do not ultimately depend on the consent (actual or hypothetical) of the parties to the social contract.[16]

In a provocative and original reading, Habermas suggests that the tension between a social contract and a natural rights reading arises from an ambiguity in Kant's concept of autonomy or self-rule. As Kant took over this notion from Rousseau, it suggests the idea of both individual *and* collective self-legislation: "A person is subject to no laws other than those that he (either alone or at least jointly with others) gives to himself."[17] For Kant, the concept of individual autonomy is almost synonymous with morality, while the notion of collective self-determination is identified with the idea of the social contract. However, insofar as Kant's argument for the establishment of civil society (or the state) relies solely on the Universal Principle of Right, which guarantees equal subjective liberty for all, the notion of collective self-determination is subordinated to a moral principle (or natural right). As Habermas argues, this sets off a dialectic in the tradition of legal dogmatics between positivism (objective law as command of the sovereign) and natural law (which stresses subjective liberties) in which the notion of collective self-determination is gradually effaced. However, so doing fails to account for the legitimacy of law, for it ultimately removes law from the process of demo-

cratic lawmaking and/or deprives the right to subjective liberty of
any relation to a conception of public autonomy.[18] It fails, in other
words, to reconcile the public and private autonomy of citizens in a
manner that could in turn secure the legitimacy of legality.[19]

Of course, Habermas is not interested in Kant's system of rights
only for historical reasons. He uses the problematic in Kant to clarify the basic structure of his own discourse theory and to respond
to some earlier criticisms of it.[20] He now insists, for instance, on a
sharper delineation between the principle of discourse – "Only
those action norms are valid to which all those possibly affected
could agree as participants in rational discourses" (138) – and its
specification as a rule of *moral* argumentation, that is, as a principle
of universalizability (or Principle U).[21] The principle of discourse is
now conceived as a more general principle that applies to all action
norms prior to any distinction between moral and legal norms. Principal U is then introduced *simultaneously* with the principle of democracy – roughly equivalent to Kant's idea of the social contract –
which specifies a general procedure for legitimate lawmaking (see
141). The principle of democracy states: "Only those juridical stat-
utes may claim legitimate validity that can meet with the
agreement of all legal consociates in a discursive law-making process that in turn has been legally constituted" (141). Though distinct, the two principles are not hierarchically ordered as in Kant;
rather, they are complementary and, in important ways, the principle of democracy (as a principle of legitimation for positive law)
supplements various "deficits" that necessarily accompany a postconventional rational morality. These include, for example, the cognitive indeterminacy that arises with a moral principle requiring
that all relevant features of a situation be taken into consideration
as well as the motivational uncertainty that results from the fact
that moral insight does not guarantee compliance. In both cases
legal norms are thus able to complement moral norms even though
the former must also remain open in various ways to processes of
moral argumentation.[22]

Even more important than this complementary relation between
the basic moral principle and a principle for legitimate lawmaking
is Habermas's parallel claim that the principle of democracy is not
subordinate to a system of rights. On the contrary, Habermas claims
that they are "equiprimordial" or "co-original" (*gleichursprünglich*)

(155) and "reciprocally explain each other" (123). The system of rights is the "reverse side" (123) of the principle of democracy, and "the principle of democracy can only appear as the heart of a system of rights" (155). These remarks indicate Habermas's commitment to a reconciliation of democracy with other political values, especially a system of basic rights and liberties. Since, according to Habermas, earlier efforts to achieve such a reconciliation have not been successful (111), I will summarize what I take to be the main steps in his own attempt.

Habermas's general strategy is to recall attention to "the intersubjective sense" of legally granted subjective liberties (118). Echoing Hegel as well as Kant, he emphasizes the fact that rights are not primarily things individuals possess but relations that have their basis in a form of mutual recognition – however circumscribed and artificial.[23]

> *At a conceptual level*, rights do not immediately refer to atomistic and estranged individuals who are possessively set against one another. On the contrary, as elements of the legal order they presuppose collaboration among subjects who recognize one another, in their reciprocally related rights and duties, as free and equal consociates under law. This mutual recognition is constitutive for a legal order from which actionable rights are derived. In this sense 'subjective' rights emerge equiprimordially with 'objective' law. (117)

Basic rights do not exist in a determinate form in a prior state of nature. They are something individuals mutually confer on one another insofar as they undertake to regulate their common life via positive law and thus to regard one another as free and equal consociates under law.

More specifically, Habermas's claim is that the system of rights (along with the principle of democracy) can be developed from the "interpenetration" (*Verschränkung*) of the discourse principle and the legal form (154). As I understand it, this "derivation" – Habermas speaks of a "logical genesis" (*logische Genese*) – of a system of rights occurs in two stages: First, the notion of law cannot be limited to the semantic features of general and abstract norms. Rather, bourgeois formal law has always been identified with the guarantee of an equal right to subjective liberty.[24] This is reflected in Kant's Universal Principle of Right (*Recht*) as well as Rawls's First

Principle, both of which guarantee the greatest amount of liberty compatible with a like liberty for all. For Habermas this link between positive law and individual liberty means that insofar as individuals undertake to regulate their common life through the legal form they must do so in a way that grants to each member an equal right to liberty.

However – and this is the second step – although the legal form is conceptually linked to the idea of subjective rights, it alone cannot ground any specific right (162). A system of rights can be developed only if and when the legal form is made use of by the political sovereign in an exercise of the citizens' public autonomy. This public autonomy in the last analysis refers back to the discourse principle, which implies the "right" to submit only to those norms one could agree to in a discourse. Of course, in connection with the principle of discourse this "right" has only the "quasi-transcendental" status of a communicative act and does not carry with it any coercive authorization. It can acquire a coercive authorization only when, as the principle of democracy, it is realized in the legal medium together with a system of rights.

The principle of discourse can assume through the medium of law the shape of a principle of democracy only insofar as the discourse principle and the legal medium interpenetrate and *develop* into a system of rights bringing private and public autonomy into a relation of mutual presupposition. Conversely, every exercise of political autonomy signifies both an interpretation and concrete shaping of these fundamentally 'unsaturated' rights by a historical law-giver. (162)

Habermas hopes in this way to have reconciled democracy and individual rights in a manner that does not subordinate either one to the other. "The system of rights can be reduced neither to a moral reading of human rights [as in Kant and the tradition of natural rights] nor to an ethical reading of popular sovereignty [as in Rousseau and some communitarians] because the private autonomy of citizens must neither be set above nor made subordinate to their political autonomy" (134). Rather, the co-originality or "equiprimordiality" of the system of rights and the principle of democracy, which also reflects the mutual presupposition of citizens' public and private autonomy, is derived from this "interpenetration" of the legal form and the "quasi-transcendental" discourse principle that "must" occur if citizens are to regulate their living together by means of positive law.

In connection with the strategy outlined above, Habermas introduces five basic categories of rights (155–56):

(1) Basic rights that result from the politically autonomous development of the *right to equal subjective liberties*

(2) Basic rights that result from the politically autonomous development of the *status of a member* in a voluntary association of consociates under law

(3) Basic rights that result immediately from the *actionability* of rights and from the politically autonomous development of *legal measures*

(4) Basic rights to equal chances at participation in the processes of opinion- and will-formation in which citizens exercise their *political autonomy* and through which they make legitimate law

(5) Basic rights that secure the conditions of life, including social, technical and environmental protection, that are necessary under given circumstances for an equal chance to use the civil rights listed in (1) through (4).

The first three categories cover those rights traditionally identified with the "subjective liberties" that secure the private autonomy of citizens and are constitutive of the legal medium in which citizens confront one another as *legal addressees* – freedom of speech, conscience, and the person under category (1); rights to association under (2); and rights to legal protection, due process, and so forth under (3). These are, however, "enabling" rights and thus, according to Habermas, cannot properly be construed as a limitation upon the legislator's sovereignty (162).[25] The fourth category, by contrast, points to the role of legal subjects as *authors* of law and thus secures their public autonomy in the form of rights to political participation. Finally, the last category, to which Habermas assigns a more derivative status, includes various rights to welfare and the conditions necessary for an effective opportunity to exercise the first four categories of rights.

Two final observations on this system of rights are worth noting: First, Habermas claims that the system of rights is universal not in the sense that it specifies a pregiven set of natural rights, but in the sense that it presents a general schema or "unsaturated placeholder" (160) that legal subjects must presuppose if they want to regulate their living together by positive law. It is thus constitutive for the legal medium, yet at the same time it is not fixed or determinate. The system of rights must be "developed in a politically autonomous manner" by citizens in the context of their own particular traditions and history.[26]

Second, in response to Albrecht Wellmer's claim that citizens have a "right *not* to be rational," Habermas acknowledges that there is a paradox involved in the "juridification of communicative liberty" (165).[27] The rights guaranteeing public autonomy, like those guaranteeing private autonomy, must assume the form of subjective liberties. This means that it is left up to citizens themselves to choose to exercise their communicative liberty. "Subjective liberties entitle one to *step out of* communicative action, to refuse illocutionary obligations; they ground a private realm freed from the burden of a reciprocally acknowledged and expected communicative liberty" (153). At the same time, however, this juridification of communicative liberty also reveals the fact that the legitimacy of legality is not guaranteed by the legal form alone but depends on sources beyond its control, namely the realization of a rational public opinion and will formation in an autonomous public sphere (165).

With this derivation of the system of rights securing the private and public autonomy of citizens, Habermas believes he has accounted for the legitimacy of legality. It is based neither on the legal form alone (as maintained by positivists) nor on its conformity to an extralegal set of natural rights or natural law. Rather, the legitimacy of law derives from the fact that it has a rationality of its own, secured in the mutual guarantee of the private and public autonomy of citizens, that ultimately refers back to the bonding/binding illocutionary force inherent in communicative reason and action.

III. THE *RECHTSSTAAT*, PROCEDURAL DEMOCRACY, AND "WEAK" AND "STRONG" PUBLICS

If the legitimacy of law depends on the fact that it preserves "an internal connection with the socially integrative force of communicative action" (111), then the system of rights (including the rights of public autonomy) must be institutionalized, and the communicative power that comes about whenever, in Arendt's phrase, people act in concert must be mobilized and effectively secured within the legal medium itself. This requirement reveals still another aspect of the internal tension between facticity and validity: To become socially effective law requires a centralized political power with the capacity to enforce collectively binding decisions; at the same time, however, law is the sole medium through which the communicative power of citizens can be transformed into administrative power.

Habermas first introduces a set of "principles of the constitutional state" (*Rechtsstaat*) that specify general institutional guidelines for both the *generation* of communicative power (through the institutionalization of the system of rights) and the *exercise* of power (by insuring a connection between communicative power and administrative power).[28] These include the principle of popular sovereignty, the guarantee of legal protection, the legality of administration, and the separation of state and society (208ff). Habermas's discussion attempts to locate these classical doctrines within the framework of his own discourse theory. Taken together, the principles should explain the idea of the constitutional state by showing how "legitimate law is generated from communicative power and the latter in turn is converted into administrative power via legitimately enacted law" (209).

Although his discussion cannot be summarized here, it is clear Habermas wishes to establish two general points. First, in contrast to Hannah Arendt, the notion of communicative power should not be understood too substantively as the (more or less spontaneous) expression of a common will but rather as the product of an overlapping and intermeshing of a variety of (more and less institutionalized) pragmatic, ethical-political, and moral discourses (207). Communicative power neither presupposes a shared ethical-political self-understanding nor orients itself to the ideal of a rational consensus in the manner constitutive (for Habermas) of moral argumentation. Rather, it is identified with the realization of a rational public opinion formation and will formation in a process of lawmaking that comprises a complex network of processes of reaching understanding *and* bargaining (221). This interpretation of communicative power should also warn against an overly hasty and too direct identification of moral argumentation (which aims at consensus) with political discourse.

Second, the legitimate *exercise* of power can only occur through the medium of law but in a way that nonetheless remains tied to communicative sociation: Rule by the people must be a rule of law, but the rule of law must be joined to rule by the people or, as Frank Michelman has expressed it, rooted in a "jurisgenerative politics."[29] A discourse theoretical approach offers a way of understanding this connection between the rule of law and popular sovereignty without appealing to a "transcendent" notion of reason or overburdening citizens' capacities for public virtue. It also provides for a less concretistic interpretation of the classical principle of the separation of powers in that the functions of the legislature, judiciary, and administration can now be differentiated according to various forms of communication and a corresponding potential for reasons:

Laws regulate the transformation of communicative power into administrative in that they come about according to a democratic procedure, ground a legal protection guaranteed by impartially judging courts, and withhold from the implementing administration the sorts of reasons that support legislative resolutions and court decisions. These normative reasons belong to a universe within which legislature and judiciary share the work of justifying and applying norms. An administration limited to pragmatic discourse must not disturb anything in this universe by its contributions; at the same time, it draws therefrom the normative premises that have to underlie its own empirically informed, purposive-rational decision-making. (235)

This analysis of the principles of the constitutional state and their justification – which I have only been able roughly to indicate – is nevertheless one-sided unless it is accompanied by an account of the *process* by which citizens are to govern themselves or engage in a "jurisgenerative politics." It is at this point that the model of a "procedural democracy" is introduced. Within the context of North American discussions, however, this label could be misleading since the term "procedure" is not used in contrast to a "substantive" conception of democracy (as it is, for example, in Ely's influential account).[30] Rather, as Habermas uses the term, it designates the attempt to realize the rights of public and private autonomy through an institutional design that incorporates various practical discourses. Procedural democracy is thus closer to what has recently been called a "public reasons" approach.[31]

Habermas introduces his model of procedural democracy by way of a contrast between two highly stylized alternatives: liberal and republican (or communitarian). These have become familiar reference points in recent discussions. Cass Sunstein, for example, has recently summarized the liberal model well: "Self-interest, not virtue, is understood to be the usual motivating force of political behavior. Politics is typically, if not always, an effort to aggregate private interests. It is surrounded by checks, in the form of rights, protecting private liberty and private property from public intrusion."[32] By contrast, republicanism characteristically places more emphasis on the value of citizens' public virtues and active political participation. Politics is regarded more as a deliberative process in which citizens seek to reach agreement about the common good, and law is not seen as a means for protecting individual rights but as the expression of the common praxis of the political community.

Habermas's procedural democracy attempts to incorporate the best features of both models while avoiding the shortcomings of each. In particular, with the republican model, it rejects the vision of the political process as primarily the competition between, and aggregation of, private preferences. However, more in keeping with the liberal model, it regards the republican vision of a citizenry united and actively motivated by a shared conception of the good life as unrealistic in modern, pluralist societies.[33] Since, as we have seen, political discourses involve bargaining and negotiation as well as moral argumentation, the republican or communitarian notion of a shared ethical-political dialogue also seems too limited (347). "Discourse theory has the success of deliberative politics depend not on a collectively acting citizenry but on the institutionalization of the corresponding procedures and conditions of communication, as well as on the interplay of institutionalized deliberative processes with informally constituted public opinions" (361–62). What is central is not a shared ethos, but institutionalized discourses for the formation of rational political opinion.

The idea of a suitably interpreted "deliberative politics" thus lies at the center of Habermas's procedural democracy. In a deliberative politics attention shifts away from the final act of voting and the problems of social choice that accompany it.[34] The model attempts to take seriously the fact that often enough preferences are not exogenous to the political system, but "are instead adaptive to a wide range of factors – including the context in which the preference is expressed, the existing legal rules, past consumption choices, and culture in general."[35] The aim of a deliberative politics is to provide for the transformation of preferences in response to the considered views of others and the "laundering" or filtering of irrational and/or morally repugnant preferences in ways that are not excessively paternalistic.[36] For example, by designing institutions of political will formation so that they reflect the more complex preference structure of individuals rather than simply register the actual preferences individuals have at any given time, the conditions for a more rational politics (that is, a political process in which the outcomes are more informed, future oriented, and other regarding) can be improved.[37] One could even speak of an extension of democracy to preferences themselves since the question is whether the reasons offered in support of them are ones that could meet the requirements of public justification.[38] What is important for this notion of deliberation, however, is less that everyone participate – or even that voting be made public – than that there be a warranted presumption that public opinion be formed on the basis of adequate information and relevant reasons and that those whose interests are involved have an equal and effective opportunity to make their own interests (and the reasons for them) known.

Two further features serve to distinguish Habermas's model of procedural democracy and deliberative politics from other recent versions. First, this version of deliberative politics extends beyond the formally organized political system to the vast and complex communication network that Habermas calls "the public sphere."

[Deliberative politics] is bound to the demanding communicative presuppositions of political arenas that do not coincide with the institutionalized will-formation in parliamentary bodies but extend equally to the political public sphere and to its cultural context and social basis. A deliberative practice of self-determination can develop only in the interplay between, on the one hand, the parliamentary will-formation institutionalized in legal procedures and programmed to reach decisions and, on the other, political opinion-building in informal circles of political communication. (334)

The model suggests a "two-track" process in which there is a division of labor between "weak publics" – the informally organized public sphere ranging from private associations to the mass media located in "civil society" – and "strong publics" – parliamentary bodies and other formally organized institutions of the political system.[39] In this division of labor, "weak publics" assume a central responsibility for identifying and interpreting social problems: "For a good part of the normative expectations connected with deliberative politics now falls on the peripheral structures of opinion formation. The expectations are directed at the capacity to perceive, interpret, and present encompassing social problems in a way both attention-catching and innovative" (434). However, decision-making responsibility, as well as the further "filtering" of reasons via more formal parliamentary procedures, remains the task of a strong public (e.g., the formally organized political system).

Second, along with this division of labor between strong and weak publics and as a consequence of his increased acknowledgment of the "decentered" character of modern societies, Habermas argues that radical-democratic practice must assume a "self-limiting" form. Democratization is now focused not on society as a whole, but on the legal system broadly conceived (370). In particular, he maintains, it must respect the boundaries of the political-administrative and economic subsystems that have become relatively freed from the integrative force of communicative action and are in this sense "autonomous." Failure to do so, he believes, at least partially explains the failure of state socialism.[40] The goal of radical democracy thus becomes not the democratic organization of these subsystems, but rather a type of indirect steering of them through the medium of law. In this connection, he also describes the task of an opinion-forming public sphere as that of laying siege to the formally organized political system by encircling it with reasons without, however, attempting to overthrow or replace it.[41]

This raises a number of difficult questions about the scope and limits of democratization. Given the frequent metaphorical character of his discussion (see, e.g., the references to colonization, sieges, and sluices), it is not clear what specific proposals for mediating between weak and strong publics would follow from his model.[42] Some have questioned, for example, whether he has not conceded too much to systems theory, and Nancy Fraser, in an instructive discussion of Habermas's conception of the public sphere, raises the question whether there might not be other possible "divisions of labor" between strong and weak publics.[43] Habermas's response, I think, would be that an answer to these questions will not be found at the level of normative theory, but depends upon the empirical findings of complex comparative studies. However, a more general question that arises in connection with this model of democracy is whether Habermas's confidence in the rationalizing effect of procedures alone is well founded. In view of his own description of "weak publics" as "wild," "anarchic," and "unrestricted" (374), the suspicion can at least be raised whether discursive procedures will suffice to bring about a rational public opinion. To be sure, he states that a deliberative politics depends on a "rationalized lifeworld" (including a "liberal political culture") "that meets it halfway."[44] But without more attention to the particular "liberal virtues" that make up that political culture and give rise to some notion of shared purposes, it is difficult not to empathize with Sheldon Wolin's observation concerning the recent politics of difference. Describing the situation of someone who wants to have his claim to cultural exclusiveness recognized while at the same time resisting anything more than minimal inclusion in the political community, Wolin exposes a disturbing paradox within it:

I want to be bound only by a weak and attenuated bond of inclusion, yet my demands presuppose a strong State, one capable of protecting me in an increasingly racist and violent society and assisting me amidst increasingly uncertain economic prospects. A society with a multitude of organized, vigorous, and self-conscious differences produces not a strong State but an erratic one that is capable of reckless military adventures abroad and partisan, arbitrary actions at home . . . yet is reduced to impotence when attempting to remedy structural injustices or to engage in long-range planning in matters such as education, environmental protection, racial relations, and economic strategies.[45]

Habermas no doubt shares some of these same concerns about the conditions necessary for maintaining a liberal political culture, and his own focus on the abstract form of mutual recognition at the basis of a legal community may make the requirements for inclusion less demanding than Wolin suggests. The question nevertheless remains whether Habermas's almost exclusive attention to questions of institutional design and discursive procedures offers an adequate basis for dealing with this paradox or whether he must not supplement his model with a more specific account of the "liberal virtues" or "ethical foundations" that must "meet these halfway."[46]

IV. THREE CHALLENGES TO LIBERAL DEMOCRACY

I would now like to consider how Habermas's theory fares with respect to the three issues noted in the introduction: the project of reconciliation, the question of liberal neutrality, and the dilemma of difference.

1. From the discussion in Section II of this essay it is clear that Habermas's book represents a major effort to reconcile democracy with other political ideals. Since he claims that no one has yet succeeded in this project, it is worth considering how his view differs from some other recent attempts.

In *Democracy and Its Critics* Robert Dahl acknowledges the potential conflict between a "procedural" democracy and a "substantive" set of basic rights and attempts to resolve it by arguing that the right to self-government through the democratic process is basic and that other political rights can be derived from this fundamental right.[47]

> These specific rights – let me call them *primary political rights* – are integral to the democratic process. They aren't ontologically separate from – or prior to, or superior to – the democratic process. To the extent that the democratic process exists in a political system, all the primary political rights must also exist. To the extent that primary political rights are absent from a system, the democratic process does not exist.[48]

This strategy faces two serious objections. First, it is not clear whether other "nonpolitical" rights can be accounted for in a similar manner and, even if so, whether this would not amount to an instrumentalization of private autonomy for the sake of public autonomy. Second, although it is a "substantive" not "procedural" account, Dahl's strategy suffers from a reliance on an "aggregative" conception of democracy that is in the end similar to Ely's procedural conception referred to previously. This is suggested, for example, in his endorsement of a fairly utilitarian reading of the "principle of equal consideration of interests" in contrast to the autonomy-based conception implicit in Habermas's account.[49]

In a recent essay, Ronald Dworkin has also attempted to reconcile democracy and basic rights.[50] He begins with Ely's observation that many of the "disabling provisions" of the U.S. Constitution (roughly the Bill of Rights) may be seen as "functionally structural" to the democratic process and thus not in conflict with it. The right to freedom of expression is an example: "Since democratic elections demonstrate the will of the people only when the public is fully informed, preventing officials from censoring speech protects rather than subverts democracy. . . . So a constitutional right of free speech counts as functionally structural as well as disabling in our catalogue." [51] However, as Ely concedes, this strategy will not work for all the "disabling provisions" – for example, the Establishment Clause of the First Amendment or rights that regulate the criminal process – and so, Dworkin concludes, "Ely's rescue of democracy from the Constitution is only a partial success." [52]

Dworkin's own response to the "supposed conflict between democracy and a constitution" (330) begins by distinguishing between a "statistical reading of democracy" (i.e., the aggregative conception referred to previously) and a "communal reading of democracy" (e.g., Rousseau's general will). [53] He then argues for a specific version of the latter which he calls "democracy as integration." This model is specified in connection with three principles: the principle of participation, requiring that each citizen have an equal and effective opportunity to make a difference in the political process; the principle of stake, requiring that each person be recognized or shown equal concern; and the principle of independence, specifying that individuals be responsible for their own judgments. Dworkin then concludes that on this model many of the disabling provisions Ely rejected may be regarded as functionally structural and, hence, not antidemocratic: "On the communal conception, democracy and constitutional constraint are not antagonists but partners in principle." [54]

Dworkin's model is clearly preferable to aggregative conceptions. The three principles appeal directly to the ideals of autonomy and mutual recognition, and the analysis of democracy (as well as law) in connection with the integrity of a community's practices and attitudes points away from a metaphysical or substantialist conception of community. On the other hand, as he recognizes, his "principle of stake" threatens to become a "black hole into which all other political virtues collapse." [55] His response, however, which is to claim that the principle requires not that each citizen be shown equal concern but that there exist a "good faith effort," seems to undervalue the public autonomy of citizens.

Habermas's proposal, as we have seen, reconciles popular sovereignty and human rights in the sense that public and private autonomy are said mutually to presuppose one another. A virtue of the model is that it relates these ideals at an abstract level: Public and private autonomy are two dimensions of the fundamental "right" to communicative liberty as this is expressed in the legal form. If one begins with this notion of communicative liberty, it is possible to regard the constitution as a sort of "public charter" and the system of rights as a form of "precommitment" that citizens make in undertaking to regulate their common lives by public law.[56] As such, the proposed reconciliation of democracy and rights neither undervalues public autonomy nor overtaxes private autonomy. It is not based on a shared conception of the good, but on a more abstract form of recognition contained in the idea of free and equal consociates under law.

At the same time, the principal strength of this approach may also prove to be its greatest weakness. Given the abstract character of the reconciliation of public and private autonomy, it is difficult to determine how it might contribute to more specific constitutional debates, for example, regarding the interpretation of the Establishment Clause of the First Amendment, or the more specific scope and content of the right to privacy. Habermas would most likely claim that the system of rights is "unsaturated" and must be filled in with reference to a political community's particular tradition and history and in response to ongoing deliberations within the public sphere. This may be so, but it also seems reasonable to expect that the general proposal for a reconciliation of democracy and basic rights should provide some guidance to more specific debates about rights (e.g., would it support a constitutional right to abortion as a condition for securing the public autonomy of women?). I suspect, in fact, that the theory will be able to provide such guidance, but much more work needs to be done in this middle range between general conceptions and the enumeration of specific rights and liberties.

2. Despite his emphasis on "weak publics" and pluralist civil society Habermas's model of procedural democracy and deliberative politics endorses a "nonrestrictive" or "tolerant" version of the principle of liberal neutrality (374ff). This principle has been criticized

by communitarians and others who argue that it is excessively individualistic or atomistic in its conception of the citizen or that it presupposes its own conception of the good and thus is inherently self-defeating (since it cannot allow for the promotion of values required for a liberal society).[57] In particular, it has been argued that the principle of liberal neutrality is not compatible with the state's pursuit of measures intended to promote or maintain a diverse civil society and robust public sphere.[58] Is Habermas's endorsement of a principle of neutrality consistent with his affirmation of the value of a robust public sphere?

It is important that the meaning of liberal neutrality, at least on its best interpretation, not be misunderstood. First, the principle of neutrality is not itself a neutral or nonmoral principle. It does not imply a merely procedural neutrality with respect to whatever conceptions of the good life citizens may happen to have. Rather, it is an ideal introduced in conjunction with a principle of right (for example, Kant's Universal Principle of Right or Rawls's Principle of Equal Liberty) and thus one that is biased against conceptions of the good that are incompatible with the basic rights and liberties specified by that principle.[59] Second, the principle of neutrality does not even require that the state treat equally any permissible conception of the good citizens may have or that the policies pursued by the state must have the same effect upon any and all (permissible) conceptions of the good life. This form of neutrality, which has been called neutrality of effect or consequential neutrality, is both impractical and undesirable. Rather, what liberal neutrality entails is "neutrality of aim" or "neutrality of grounds" in the sense that arguments and considerations introduced in support of specific principles or policies should not appeal to particular conceptions of the good life but should regard all citizens and their (permissible) conceptions with equal concern and respect.[60]

Even on this interpretation the principle can be contested. Can policies be neutral in their justification in this way, or must not such claims to neutrality inevitably appeal to some (permissible) conceptions of the good over others? One version of neutrality, suggested by Ackerman's notion of "constrained conversation" and Rawls's "method of avoidance," is susceptible to this challenge since by unduly restricting the issues that can be placed on the political agenda or raised in public discussion there is the danger of reinforcing the status quo and inhibiting mutual understanding.[61] This strategy also suggests that there is a relatively fixed and clear distinction between those matters appropriate for public discussion and those that are not.

An alternative interpretation of liberal neutrality is able to avoid this objection. On this interpretation, the principle of neutrality is not understood as part of a general strategy of avoidance, but as part of what is required in showing equal concern and respect in a stronger sense: The state should not act in ways intended to promote a particular conception of the good life since that would constitute a failure to show each citizen equal concern and respect. Unlike the method of avoidance, this interpretation of neutrality does not require keeping controversial issues off the political agenda in order to avoid moral conflict. Rather, it is quite consistent with the view that the state act in ways intended to promote rational discussion in order to help resolve potentially divisive social and moral conflicts.[62] On this interpretation neutrality is compatible with the attempt to secure a form of mutual respect or "militant toleration" in which difference is not only tolerated, but in which individuals seek to understand one another in their differences and arrive at a solution to the matter at hand in view of a common recognition of one another as free and equal citizens.

It will perhaps be objected that this view leads beyond liberal neutrality to a liberal or "modest" perfectionism. In fact, a similar argument for a more robust and pluralist public sphere has recently been made by Michael Walzer.[63] As paradoxical as it may seem, in view of the tremendous "normalizing" effects of the market economy and bureaucratic state there is little reason to assume that either a robust and pluralist public sphere or the other general social conditions for a more deliberative politics can be secured without the (self-reflective) intervention and assistance of the state. However, while I have argued that the state may be justified in acting in ways to secure such forums, I do not see that this requires embracing a perfectionist account of liberalism rather than the alternative principle of neutrality outlined here. For, on this interpretation, the actions of the state are justified not because of their contribution to a particular way of life or conception of the good, but because robust and pluralist deliberative forums are necessary conditions for the effective exercise of basic rights of public and private autonomy derived, for Habermas, in the manner outlined in Section II. The state may at times be justified in acting in ways aimed at promoting or securing the conditions for a pluralist civil society not because it regards a pluralist society as a good for its citizens, but because it regards such conditions as requirements of practical reason in the sense that informed and reasonable deliberation could not be achieved without them.

3. Finally, issues raised in the critique of liberal neutrality re-emerge in a heightened form in the "dilemma of difference." For the claim is now that the pursuit of "justice" through the bourgeois legal form (e.g., general law aimed at guarantee of equal rights) nec-essarily devalues difference and does violence to individuals, groups, and practices that deviate from the established norm.[64] The di-lemma of difference, which has been most extensively discussed in recent feminist jurisprudence, is inextricably entwined with the fundamental principle of legal equality. "Treat equals equally" re-quires a judgment about the respects in which two things are equal and what it means to treat them equally. But this gives rise to the following dilemma:

> By taking another person's difference into account in awarding goods or dis-tributing burdens, you risk reiterating the significance of that difference and, potentially, its stigma and stereotyping consequences. But if you do not take another person's difference into account – in a world that has made that difference matter – you may also recreate and reestablish both the dif-ference and its negative implications. If you draft or enforce laws you may worry that the effects of the laws will not be neutral whether you take difference into account or you ignore it.[65]

Attempts to secure legal equality have generally pursued either an "assimilationist model" (which emphasizes the extent to which we are all alike) or an "accommodation model" (which seeks to create "special rights" on the basis of "real" differences). As some femi-nists point out, however, both models founder upon the same prob-lem. In attempting to determine which differences deserve legal remedies and which should be ignored, the background norms that establish terms of relevance and in light of which judgments of simi-larity and difference are made frequently go unchallenged.[66]

One response has been to resist making judgments of sameness and difference altogether.[67] However, once the problem is framed in the manner described, that is, not as a problem of judgments of sameness and difference per se, but as a critique of the underlying norms and criteria guiding them, attention shifts to the process through which those norms have been defined. And here, I think, the strength of Habermas's approach emerges: The efforts to secure equal rights and the protection of law for each citizen must go hand in hand with efforts to secure the exercise of the public autonomy of all citizens. Public and private autonomy mutually suppose one another and must be jointly realized to secure processes of legitimate lawmaking. With this model in view, one could then take up the suggestion of some feminists that the point is not for the law to be "blind" to difference, nor to fix particular differences through the introduction of "special rights," but "to make difference costless."[68]

With respect to these three challenges to liberal democracy, I conclude that the abstract and highly procedural character of Habermas's version of the project of radical democracy is its primary strength and weakness. Its strength is that, in connection with his theory of communicative reason and action, Habermas generates a unique and powerful argument for a model of democracy in which the public and private autonomy of citizens are given equal consideration. It generates an intersubjective account of basic rights and a procedural democracy more attractive than any of the liberal or republican accounts currently available. It also offers a strong argument for the design of institutions that will facilitate discussion based on mutual respect. On the other hand, the highly abstract character of the proposal suggests that more work still needs to be done if it is to contribute *directly* to more specific debates about basic rights, the "dilemmas of difference," or what counts as the appropriate correspondence (or "meeting halfway") of liberal virtue and institutional design that, as Habermas concedes, is required if the notions of a procedural democracy and deliberative politics are to be effectively realized in the contemporary world.

NOTES

1 *Faktizität und Geltung* (Frankfurt: Suhrkamp, 1992). I have made use of a draft translation by William Rehg, forthcoming from MIT Press; all pagination cited in the text is to the German edition.

2 Habermas has recently suggested that traces of this holistic conception can be found, for example, in his *Structural Transformation of the Public Sphere*; see his "Further Reflections on the Public Sphere," in *Habermas and the Public Sphere*, ed. Craig Calhoun (Cambridge, Mass.: MIT Press, 1992), p. 433f.

3 This assessment of law reflects a change even from *The Theory of Communicative Action*, which held a more ambivalent view of law as both an "institution" responsible for integration and a "medium" through which the lifeworld could be colonized (see Vol. II, p. 365).

4 For a discussion of the implications of this rejection of holistic conceptions of society for political theory, see N. Luhmann, *Political Theory in the Welfare State* (New York: de Gruyter, 1990); for Parson's discussion of the societal community, see "Equality and Inequality in Modern Society, or Social Stratification Revisited," in *Social Systems and the Evolution of Action Theory* (New York: Free Press, 1977).

5 For earlier brief statements of this "reconstructed" version of radical democracy, see "The New Obscurity," in *The New Conservatism* (Cambridge, Mass.: MIT Press, 1990), and "What Does Socialism Mean Today? The Rectifying Revolution and the Need for New Thinking on the Left," *New Left Review* 183 (1990): 3–21; see also the discussion in Jean Cohen and Andrew Arato, *Civil Society and Political Theory* (Cambridge, Mass.: MIT Press, 1992), esp. ch. 9. It would also be instructive to compare (and contrast) Habermas's attempt to reconcile the project of radical democracy with constitutionalism with the radical democratic proposals of Roberto Unger, Cornelius Castoriadis, and Sheldon Wolin.

6 Two recent attempts at a reconciliation can be found in John Ely, *Democracy and Distrust* (Cambridge, Mass.: Harvard University Press, 1980), and Robert Dahl, *Democracy and Its Critics* (New Haven, Conn.: Yale University Press, 1989).

7 See, for example, the criticisms of communitarians (such as Charles Taylor) or "critical legal studies," e.g., Mark Tushnet, *Red, White, and Blue* (Cambridge, Mass.: Harvard University Press, 1988).

8 See, for example, the essays collected in *Feminist Jurisprudence*, ed. Patricia Smith (Oxford: Oxford University Press, 1992); more generally, see Iris Young, *Justice and the Politics of Difference* (Princeton, N.J.: Princeton University Press, 1990), and William Connolly, *Identity/Difference* (Ithaca, N.Y.: Cornell University Press, 1991).

9 For a critique of rational choice theory see A. Sen, "Rational Fools" and other essays in *Beyond Self-Interest*, ed. Jane Mansbridge (Chicago: University of Chicago Press, 1990).

10 For a discussion of these idealizations and their treatment in social theory, see Thomas McCarthy, *Ideals and Illusions* (Cambridge, Mass.: MIT

Press, 1991) and Jürgen Habermas, *Justification and Application: Remarks on Discourse Ethics* (Cambridge, Mass.: MIT Press, 1993), pp. 54–55.

11 See John Rawls, "The Domain of the Political and Overlapping Consensus," *New York University Law Review* 64 (1989): 234.

12 *Political Liberalism* (New York: Columbia University Press, 1993), pp. 137 and 217.

13 Ibid., Lecture IV.

14 For a discussion of the complex relation between justification and stability in Rawls's work, see Joshua Cohen, "Moral Pluralism and Political Consensus," in *The Idea of Democracy*, ed. David Copp (Cambridge: Cambridge University Press, 1993); compare also Habermas's remarks on the two stages in Rawls's project, *Faktizität und Geltung*, pp. 79ff.

15 In this respect both Rawls and Habermas are engaged in analogous attempts to "de-transcendentalize" Kant's conception of practical reason in order to apply it to the problem of legitimacy – compare, for example, Rawls's remarks on Kant's linking of reason and freedom in *Political Liberalism*, p. 222 n. 9 and Habermas's remark in *Faktizität und Geltung* (p. 537), where he states that the idea of autonomy is the one "dogmatic" (though unavoidable) element in his theory; see also my own "Constructivism and Practical Reason in Rawls," *Analyse und Kritik* 14 (1992): 18–32.

16 See J. W. Gough, *The Social Contract* (Oxford: Oxford University Press, 1936), p. 173; Patrick Riley, *Will and Political Legitimacy* (Cambridge, Mass.: Harvard University Press, 1982); and, most recently, Mullholland, *Kant's System of Rights* (New York: Columbia University Press, 1990), p. 293.

17 Kant, *Metaphysik der Sitten* (Hamburg: Meiner, 1966), p. 223.

18 *Faktizität und Geltung*, p. 117; see also the comprehensive study of Ingeborg Maus, *Zur Aufklärung der Demokratietheorie* (Frankfurt: Suhrkamp, 1992).

19 For a comparable reading of Rousseau's primary political concern as an attempt to incorporate two distinct notions of freedom (social autonomy and civic freedom) into a coherent system, see Frederick Neuhouser, "Freedom, Dependence and the General Will," *Philosophical Review* 102 (1993): 363–95.

20 Many have commented on the ambiguity in Habermas's discourse ethics as to whether U is a moral principle or princip of political justice – see, for example, Albrecht Wellmer, *The Persistence of Modernity* (Cambridge, Mass.: MIT Press, 1991), p. 148.

21 For Habermas's earlier formulation of the relation between the discourse principle and the principle of universalizability, see "Discourse Ethics"

in *Moral Consciousness and Communicative Action* (Cambridge, Mass.: MIT Press, 1990), p. 65–66. His new position still leaves open the question about the precise "derivation" of D from the "pragmatic presuppositions of argument" since, in the earlier work, D was dependent on the derivation of U.

22 See *Faktizität und Geltung*, pp. 144f. for further discussion of the distinct, though complementary, character of legal and moral norms.

23 Recent communitarian criticism of "rights-talk" was already anticipated by Hegel, who nevertheless stressed their social importance as *one* form of recognition: "If someone is interested only in his formal right, this may be pure stubbornness, such as is often encountered in emotionally limited people; for uncultured people insist most strongly on their rights, whereas those of nobler mind seek to discover what other aspects there are to the matter in question" (*Elements of the Philosophy of Right*, par. 37A). For a balanced defense of rights-talk against the communitarian critique, see Jeremy Waldron, "When Justice Replaces Affection: The Need for Rights," *Harvard Journal of Law and Public Policy* 11 (1988).

24 Some support for this claim can already be found in the fact that the German '*Recht*', like the French '*droit*', means "subjective right" as well as "objective law."

25 Here Habermas pursues a strategy similar to Ely and Dworkin, though one that for him begins with the concepts of communicative reason and liberty and the "abstract" conception of autonomy implicit in them; see Section IV of the present essay.

26 See pp. 163–64; compare also Rawls's discussion of the specification of the basic liberties in a coherent scheme in *Political Liberalism*, Lecture VIII. For some of the problems involved, see my own discussion in *The Normative Grounds of Social Criticism: Kant, Rawls, and Habermas* (Albany: State University of New York Press, 1992), p. 154f.

27 Albrecht Wellmer, "Models of Freedom in the Modern World," in *Hermeneutics and Critical Theory in Ethics and Politics*, ed. Michael Kelly (Cambridge, Mass.: MIT Press, 1990), p. 245.

28 Habermas already noted this important distinction between the generation and the exercise of power in his essay on Arendt; see "Hannah Arendt's Communications Concept of Power," in *Power*, ed. S. Lukes (New York: New York University Press, 1986), p. 84.

29 Frank Michelman, "Law's Republic," *Yale Law Journal* 97 (1988): 1502.

30 See John Ely, *Democracy and Distrust* and Brian Barry's procedural conception in "Is Democracy Special?": "I follow . . . those who insist that 'democracy' is to be understood in procedural terms. That is to say, I reject the notion that one should build into 'democracy' any constraints

on the content of outcomes produced, such as substantive equality, respect for human rights, concern for the general welfare, personal liberty
and the rule of law" [*Philosophy, Politics, and Society*, ed. Peter Laslett
(Oxford: Blackwell, 1979), pp. 155–56]. Habermas's model is not procedural in this sense since it draws upon the notion of communicative
liberty, articulated in the public and private autonomy of citizens, implicit in the notion of communicative reason.

31 For examples of this "public reasons" approach, which is influenced by
the work of Rawls and Scanlon, see esp., Joshua Cohen, "Deliberation
and Democratic Legitimacy," in *The Good Polity*, ed. Alan Hamlin and
Philip Pettit (Oxford: Blackwell, 1989), pp. 17–34 and several essays by
Samuel Freeman: "Constitutional Democracy and the Legitimacy of Ju-
dicial Review," *Law and Philosophy* 9 (1990–91): 327–70; "Original
Meaning, Democratic Interpretation, and the Constitution," *Philosophy
and Public Affairs* 21 (1992): 3–42; and "Reason and Agreement in Social Contract Views," *Philosophy and Public Affairs* 19 (1990): 122–57.
For a discussion of some difficulties with it, see Bruce Brower, "The
Limits of Public Reason," *Journal of Philosophy* 91 (1994): 5–26.

32 "Preferences and Politics," *Philosophy and Public Affairs* 20 (1991): 4.

33 Habermas cites Frank Michelman's "Law's Republic" as an example of
this sort of republicanism; he might also have referred to some of the
writings of Charles Taylor. Habermas's own position seems closest, however, to the "Madisonian" republicanism of Cass Sunstein; see "Beyond
the Republican Revival," *Yale Law Journal* 97 (1988): 1539–90.

34 See also B. Manin, "On Legitimacy and Political Deliberation," *Political
Theory* 15 (1987): 338–68 and David Miller, "Deliberative Democracy
and Social Choice," *Political Studies* 40 (1992): Special Issue, pp. 54–67.

35 Sunstein, "Preferences and Politics," p. 5; see also Jon Elster, *Sour
Grapes* (Cambridge: Cambridge University Press, 1983).

36 See Robert Goodin, "Laundering Preferences," in *Foundations of Rational Choice Theory* ed. Jon Elster (Cambridge: Cambridge University
Press, 1985), pp. 75–101.

37 Specific proposals for realizing the ideals of a deliberative politics could
range from something like James Fishkin's idea of a "deliberative opinion poll" to alternative procedures of voting and modes of representation; see Fishkin, *Democracy and Deliberation* (New Haven, Conn.:
Yale University Press, 1990); Ian McLean, "Forms of Representation and
Systems of Voting," in *Political Theory Today*, ed. David Held (Stanford,
Calif.: Stanford University Press, 1991), pp. 172–96; and Iris Young, "Polity and Group Difference," *Ethics* 99 (1989): 250–74 (which discusses
the question of special or group representation).

38 Although I think Donald Moon overestimates the dangers of "uncon-

strained conversation," esp. for individual privacy rights, he points to the difficult question concerning the kinds of institutional design that are appropriate to help ensure that the deliberations conducted in an "unconstrained conversation" influence the process of decision making. Should there, for example, be a system of public voting? See "Constrained Discourse and Public Life," *Political Theory* 19 (1991): 202–29.

39 Habermas takes these terms from Nancy Fraser, who used them to describe Habermas's two-track conception of the public sphere; see "Rethinking the Public Sphere: A contribution to the Critique of Actually Existing Democracy," in *Habermas and the Public Sphere.*

40 See "What Does Socialism Mean Today?" *New Left Review* 183 (1990): 3–21.

41 See "Die nachholende Revolution," in *Die Nachholende Revolution* (Frankfurt: Suhrkamp, 1990), p. 199, and "Volkssouveraentitaet als Verfahren," in *Faktizität und Geltung*, p. 628.

42 It is not clear, for example, how receptive Habermas's model would be to proposals concerning different modes of interest representation both within and without the formal governmental arena, the use of voucher systems to support secondary associations as semipublic institutions, or the introduction of special group rights for persistent minorities – all of which challenge more traditional forms of territorial representation.

43 Specific proposals for a shared "division of labor" can be found in recent discussions concerning "neocorporatist" and "associative" democracies, see esp., Joshua Cohen and Joel Rogers, "Secondary Associations and Democratic Governance," *Politics and Society* 20 (1992): 393–422 and the discussions that follow.

44 *Faktizität und Geltung*, p. 366; compare also Habermas's corresponding remark that a postconventional morality "is dependent upon a form of life that meets it halfway. . . . There must be a modicum of fit between morality and socio-political institutions" [*Moral Consciousness and Communicative Action* (Cambridge, Mass.: MIT Press, 1990), pp. 207–8], and the interesting essay on this topic by Claus Offe, "Binding, Shackles, Brakes: On Self-Limitation Strategies," in *Cultural-Political Interventions in the Unfinished Project of Enlightenment*, ed. Axel Honneth, Thomas McCarthy, Claus Offe, and Albrecht Wellmer (Cambridge, Mass.: MIT Press, 1992).

45 Sheldon Wolin, "Democracy, Difference and Re-cognition," *Political Theory* 21 (1993): 480.

46 I have in mind something like Dworkin's recent remarks on the "ethical foundations" of liberalism in "The Foundations of Liberal Equality," *The Tanner Lectures* (University of Utah Press, 1990), vol. 11 and Stephen Macedo's discussion in *Liberal Virtues* (Oxford: Clarendon, 1990);

see also the related criticism of Habermas's "constitutional patriotism" from a Hegelian perspective, Andrew Buchwalter, "Hegel's Concept of Virtue," *Political Theory* 20 (1992): 576.

47 *Democracy and Its Critics*, pp. 169–70.

48 Ibid., p. 170.

49 For the principle of equal consideration of interests, see Dahl, p. 85; for a similar criticism (to which I am indebted) see Joshua Cohen's Review of *Democracy and Its Critics*, in *Journal of Politics* 53 (1991): 221–25.

50 "Equality, Democracy and Constitution: We the People in Court," *Alberta Law Review* 28 (1990): 324–46.

51 Ibid., p. 328.

52 Ibid.

53 Ibid., p. 330.

54 Ibid., p. 346.

55 Ibid., p. 339.

56 For this use of the notion of "precommitment" and the Constitution as a "public charter," see Samuel Freeman, "Original Meaning, Democratic Interpretation, and the Constitution," *Philosophy and Public Affairs* 21 (1992): 3–42.

57 See, for example, Charles Taylor, "Cross-Purposes: The Liberal-Communitarian Debate" in *Liberalism and the Moral Life*, ed. Nancy Rosenblum (Cambridge, Mass.: Harvard University Press, 1989); Joseph Raz, "Facing Diversity," *Philosophy and Public Affairs* 19 (1990): 3–46; and Michael Walzer, "The Communitarian Critique of Liberalism," *Political Theory* 18 (1990): 6–23. In the following section I draw at points on my "Liberal Neutrality, Pluralism, and Deliberative Politics," *Praxis International* 12 (1992): 50–69.

58 Walzer, "Communitarian Critique of Liberalism."

59 See "The Idea of an Overlapping Consensus," *Oxford Journal of Legal Studies* 7 (1987): p. 9.

60 Rawls, "The Priority of the Right and the Ideas of the Good," *Philosophy and Public Affairs* 17 (1988): 260–68; Peter de Marneffe, "Liberalism, Liberty, and Neutrality," *Philosophy and Public Affairs* 19 (1990): 253–74; and Will Kymlicka, "Liberal Individualism and Liberal Neutrality," *Ethics* 99 (1989): 883–84.

61 See Bruce Ackerman, "Why Dialogue?" *Journal of Philosophy* 86 (1989): 5–22, and the discussion in Seyla Benhabib, "Liberal Dialogue versus a Critical Theory of Discursive Legitimation," in *Liberalism and the Moral Life*, pp. 143–56.

62 Amy Guttman and Dennis Thompson, "Moral Conflict and Political Consensus," in *Liberalism and the Good*, ed. G. Mara, B. Douglass, and H. Richardson (New York: Routledge, 1990), pp. 125–47.

63 "Communitarian Critique of Liberalism," p. 19.

64 See Iris Young, *Justice and the Politics of Difference* and Martha Minow, *Making All the Difference* (Ithaca, N.Y.: Cornell University Press, 1990).

65 Martha Minow, "Justice Engendered," in Smith, *Feminist Jurisprudence*, p. 232.

66 See Christine Littleton, "Reconstructing Sexual Equality," in Smith, *Feminist Jurisprudence*; Deborah Rhode, *Justice and Gender* (Cambridge, Mass.: Harvard University Press, 1989); and Habermas's discussion in *Faktizität und Geltung*, p. 509ff.

67 See Catharine MacKinnon, "Difference and Dominance," in her *Feminism Unmodified* (Cambridge, Mass.: Harvard University Press, 1987).

68 This position, which she calls the "acceptance model," is proposed by Christine Littleton in "Reconstructing Sexual Equality." I do not mean to suggest (nor does Littleton) that this is an easy task for, as Charles Taylor points out in a related discussion, there can arise conflicts between the "politics of equal dignity" and "the politics of difference" – conflicts, for example, between equal opportunity and cultural membership – that cannot easily be resolved (see *Multiculturalism and 'The Politics of Recognition'*, Princeton, N.J.: Princeton University Press, 1992, p. 37).

10 Discourse and democratic practices

Habermas has always implied that discourse ethics contains or leads to a theory of democratic legitimation.[1] Only recently, however, has he begun a systematic investigation of the political potential of discourse.[2] He and much of the wider critical debate have focused in the past on discourse ethics as a moral philosophy – a cognitive ethics in the neo-Kantian tradition that sets out to articulate the modern moral point of view of impartiality. As a contribution to moral philosophy, Habermas often stresses that discourse ethics is more descriptive than normative, for it represents "a reconstruction of everyday intuitions underlying the impartial judgment of moral conflicts of action."[3]

Drawing on language philosophy and an analysis of what we mean when we say such and such is morally right, Habermas concludes that what we mean is that we could redeem this claim in an ideal conversation. To put this another way, to believe something is right is to believe that we have good reasons to hold this position. To believe that we have good reasons entails the idea that given enough time, given interlocutors of goodwill, and given a constraint-free environment, everyone would come to the same conclusion as we have. Thus, impartial judgments are judgments that would gain universal agreement in an ideal communication community.

The ideal conversation replaces the monological universalization test of the categorical imperative with a dialogical universalization test. Morality is still about universalizing the maxim of one's action. But now the test of successful universalization is no longer found in the question: Is a world regulated by my maxim logically consistent? From the discursive perspective, the question we ask ourselves is: Would everyone agree to be regulated by my maxim?

233

The discursive universalization test has come under a certain amount of criticism.[4] One problem appears to be that there can never be a determinate outcome to such a test. Habermas proposes to replace the monological test of the categorical imperative with a dialogical test. But, for this test to be genuinely dialogical it cannot be undertaken as a counterfactual thought experiment. The test fails to be truly dialogical if it amounts to me imagining a universal conversation in my head. Thus Habermas insists that discourse must be undertaken in fact by real social agents.[5] But, by insisting that the test must be undertaken in fact, we ensure that we will never arrive at a fully justified moral judgment. The conditions of the ideal conversation can never be fully met in the real and less than ideal world. Every actual consensus is always a finite consensus and so never a universal consensus.

The stipulation that discourse must be undertaken in fact has led a number of theorists to conclude that it is more appropriate as a model of democratic legitimation than moral validity.[6] Moral validity by definition should transcend concrete communities, but democratic legitimacy is situated within concrete communities. If we understand democratic legitimacy to mean that institutions and norms are legitimate if citizens would freely consent to them, then discourse can serve as a test for such free consent. This consent need not encompass an ideal communication community but only those people who will have to live under the laws.

I want to suggest that the problems raised by the ideal communication community do not disappear when we move to politics. Not just any conversation is a discourse. Conversations are more or less discursive to the extent that they approximate the *ideal* conditions of discourse. This is just as true for political discourse as for moral discourses. These conditions can no more be fully met by citizens discussing what is in their concrete general interests than persons discussing what is the abstract universal interest. A discursive theory of political legitimation begins with an ideal picture of discourse and one of the tasks of such a theory is to explain what it would mean for real people living real lives to engage in discourse as a face-to-face practice.

Always keeping the ideal as a backdrop, this paper investigates four questions: (1) What is discourse as a face-to-face practice supposed to accomplish? (2) Why is it important that we engage in such a practice? (3) What is required of us if we do engage in such a practice? And (4), what place can such a practice realistically have within democratic politics? Very briefly, the answers to these questions are as follows: (1) Discourse as a face-to-face practice is supposed to accomplish a rationalization of public opinion and will formation. (2) It is important that we engage in such a practice because only through rationalizing the process through which we come to believe something to be legitimate can we reconcile justice and stability. (3) To engage in discourse requires that we strive to be discursive rather than strategic actors. Finally, (4), discourse, short of the ideal communication community, has no mechanism through which we can bring about closure. This means that it has a limited, but nevertheless essential, role to play in democratic *decision* making.

I. "TO BE CONVINCED BY REASON"

One way to understand the shift from moral theory to political theory is to say that rather than a reformulated version of the categorical imperative, discourse ethics represents a reformulated version of Kant's principle of publicity.[7] "Publicity" (*Publizität*) reconciles the requirements of right (justice/general interest) with the requirements of politics (obedience/stability).[8] The idea of public right finds expression in the following principle: "All actions affecting the rights of other human beings are wrong if their maxim is not compatible with their being made public."[9] The idea is that the sovereign is the guardian of the general interest and therefore should have no reason to fear public debate on the legitimacy of his actions. Indeed, a sovereign who fears public debate is a sovereign who fears that his actions are not in the general interest: "(a maxim) which cannot be publicly acknowledged without thereby inevitably arousing the resistance of everyone to my plans, can only have stirred up this necessary and general (hence, a priori foreseeable) opposition against me because it is itself unjust and thus constitutes a threat to everyone."[10]

In addition to serving as a negative test for the justness of laws, publicity also serves as a means of gaining obedience while respecting each citizen as an autonomous moral agent capable of making rational judgments: "There must be a *spirit of freedom*, for in all

matters concerning universal human rights, each individual requires to be convinced by reason that the coercion which prevails is
lawful, otherwise he would be in contradiction with himself."[11]
Thus, by making public the grounds for state action and subjecting
these grounds to the critical force of "independent and public
thought"[12] one can ensure that the state has just reasons for its actions as well as that citizens believe that these reasons are just.

Kant, as we know, was no democrat in our modern sense. The
sovereign's mandate to rule could be explained through the idea of a
contract and therefore through consent, but there was no question
of actual, universal, and renewable consent. Furthermore, while citizens should not be discouraged from judging the actions of the sovereign, citizens should definitely be discouraged from actively opposing the sovereign.[13] Thus, although the principle of publicity sets
out the rudiments of a theory of political legitimacy, it is limited by
the fact that Kant did not tie it to a theory of popular sovereignty.
Kant was still preoccupied with the problem that consumed seven-
teenth-century English political thought: Who will judge between
the people and the sovereign when they make opposing claims to
right?[14] The adjudication of such competing claims presupposes that
"there would have to be another head above the head of state to
mediate between the latter and the people, which is self-contra-
dictory."[15]

When we join Kant's idea of publicity with modern notions of democracy, we arrive at a deliberative theory of democratic legitimacy.
Rather than pure consent, this theory stresses the deliberative processes that lead to consent and the reasons that underpin consent.
The central idea is that citizens should be "convinced by reason"
that the institutions and norms of their community are in the general interest. Conversely, the institutions and norms of the community are not in the public interest when citizens cannot be convinced by reason that they are such.

But what does it mean to be "convinced by reason"? In answering
this question, Kant appealed to the distinction between the public
and the private use of reason.[16] Reason is used privately when it is
put into the service of one's private interests or when one thinks in
terms of one's particular post or office: as a police officer, as a lawyer,
as a businessperson. Reason is used publicly when it is put into the
service of the common good or general interest. Here we must try

to rise above our particular places in society and assess public issues and policies from a more general perspective. To be "convinced by reason" for Kant meant to be convinced by public reason. But how do we know whether or not citizens are really convinced by public reason or simply acquiesce to the rules imposed upon them? Kant does not suggest a test. Furthermore, Kant tended to think that only the highly educated, particularly philosophers who are accustomed to viewing questions from an impersonal point of view, were capable of using reason publicly.[17] The general public, in forming their opinions, should take their cue from these "men of learning."

Discourse ethics both democratizes this idea of public reason and suggests procedural guidelines to secure the public use of reason. The structure of discourse sets out what is entailed and presupposed by the idea of being convinced by reason or rational opinion and will formation. When this is tied to the idea of democratic legitimacy, we have a picture of what is entailed in rational *public* opinion and will formation.

Discourse is an idealized and formalized version of communicative action. In communicative action participants search for mutual understanding by offering arguments that could command assent. As opposed to strategic action, where participants are primarily interested in bringing about a desired behavioral response, in communicative action, participants are interested in bringing about a genuine understanding. For example, in strategic action participants often attempt to sway each other by introducing influences unrelated to the merits of an argument, for example, threats, bribes, or coercion. Such inducements can bring about the desired behavior even in situations where the other player is not convinced that there are any inherently good reasons to act that way.

When external inducements are brought to bear in order to force participants to accept a claim, understanding the claim can become irrelevant. John might understand that if he does not do X, Susan will bash him over the head, thus, he has understood the meaning of the threat. But John has not (necessarily) come to see why Susan wants him to do X in the first place so he does not have a full understanding of Susan's claim. Nor has he (necessarily) come to see why he, independent of Susan's threat, has any good reason to do X. This does not mean that questions of, say, material benefit or risk have no place within communicative action. People have legitimate economic interests, the satisfaction of which can stand as an inherently good reason.

Communicative actors are primarily interested in mutual understanding as opposed to external behavior. Therefore, they attempt to convince each other that there are inherently good reasons to pursue one course of action over another. Only the "force of the better argument" should have the power to sway participants. Discourse, as an idealization of this kind of activity, must set conditions such that only rational, that is, argumentative convincing, is allowed to take place. It must be a structure that is immunized in a special way against repression and inequality.[18]

The immunization is gained through a set of rules designed to guarantee discursive equality, freedom, and fair play: No one with the competency to speak and act may be excluded from discourse; everyone is allowed to question and/or introduce any assertion whatever as well as express her attitudes, desires, and needs; no one may be prevented, by internal or external coercion, from exercising these rights.[19]

Whereas in his earlier writings these rules were associated with practical or moral discourse, Habermas now adds two more types of discourse: pragmatic and ethical.[20] Pragmatic discourse concentrates on means/ends issues, ethical discourse on the self-understanding of individuals and groups, and moral discourse on generally valid moral principles. All are governed by the rules of equality, freedom, and fair play. All are directed at mutual understanding through the power of reasoned argument. However, only moral discourse sets itself the high standard of rational consensus.

Democratic deliberation entails all three types of discourse.[21] The more the issue under public discussion involves deep foundational issues of justice the more important consensus becomes. However, the rationality of public opinion and will formation in general does not depend on citizens reaching a rational consensus on all issues. A discursively formed public opinion can represent a process of *Bildung* or education in which citizens build better foundations to their opinions through discursive interaction. Through discursive interaction on various issues from who are we? to the best means of securing deficit reduction, citizens become more informed about the issues; they become aware of what others think and feel; they reevaluate their positions in light of criticism and argument; in short, by defending their opinions with reason their opinions become more reasoned. The result of such interaction is that public opinion and the exercise of democratic responsibility are embedded in reasoned convictions, although reasoned convictions do not always need to reflect a consensus on an issue. Questions of legitimacy, on the other hand, are also questions of justice and on these issues consensus is still to be aimed at.

Even if we understand discourse as not always aimed at rational consensus, a discursively formed public opinion requires more than guaranteeing that no one is excluded from discourse, that everyone may speak his or her piece, and that no one may be coerced. Discourse under the aforementioned conditions will be successful only if participants adopt attitudes of equal respect and impartiality. The rules of discourse stipulate that we must treat one another as equal partners in the process of deliberating about principles that will govern our collective interaction, who we are, and what we want, and the means to achieve a collective good. This means that each individual must be given the opportunity to speak her piece and stand up and say yes or no to a proposal. But, in addition to the negative requirement that individuals be given the space and opportunity to speak, productive discourses contain the positive requirement that individuals listen to one another, respond to one another, and justify their positions to one another. To treat one another as equal dialogue partners means that we must start from the assumption that each participant has something potentially worthwhile to contribute to the discourse; that each participant deserves to have his or her claims considered. This embodies the Kantian idea that respect involves treating people as ends in themselves and not merely as means. Strategic actors view their dialogue partners as means: as either limiting or enabling them in the pursuit of their ends. Communicative actors view their dialogue partners as ends in themselves: as autonomous agents whose capacity for rational judgment must be respected. Most day-to-day interaction is a combination of these two orientations. Discourse, as an idealization of communicative action, asks participants to exclude all strategic and instrumental attitudes toward interlocutors from the conversation.[22]

Impartiality is achieved by putting oneself in the position of the other and trying to see the situation from her perspective. Only in trying to understand how the world looks to other people will participants be flexible and open enough to undertake a genuine evaluation of their opinions. Discourse is directed at mutual understanding. At a minimum, this means understanding the real issues that divide you from your interlocutor. At a maximum, this means coming to a shared understanding. Even the minimum case calls for impartiality. Deep disagreement is not always or even primarily a case of misunderstanding. Deep disagreement is often a case of understanding too well the gulf that separates you from others. But disagreement, like agreement, can be more or less rational depending on the reasons one has. Rational disagreement requires that you understand the claim that you are rejecting, and this calls for putting yourself in the other's place. If participants are unwilling to make a sincere effort to assess their motives, ends, and needs in light of the motives, ends, and needs of their interlocutors the discursive process, no matter how structurally equal, will go nowhere.

Equal respect and impartiality are implied by the structure of rational argumentation. If (and this is, of course, a big if) we are interested in convincing with reason then we should deal with our interlocutor as someone who *could be* convinced with reason, that is, as a rational autonomous agent. If we hold out any hope of success in this endeavor, then we must also be willing to make our arguments appeal to the other's point of view. Although these requirements contain substantive moral assumptions about how we should be talking to each other, they are still formal in that they do not determine how the conversation will turn out, or even what we should be talking about.

The theory of democratic legitimacy that emerges from this analysis is one in which citizens are called upon to collectively and critically evaluate the institutions and norms of their society through the procedures of discourse. These procedures ensure that the process of evaluation is fair and that deliberation is rational. But what would it mean to undertake such a conversation? How do we translate this into real-world practices? When we try to envision discourse as something concrete that citizens undertake, two points emerge. The first is that the internal attitudes of equal respect and impartiality become central. Rules of inclusion, equality, and noncoercion do not guarantee that discursive opinion and will formation take place. Only when citizens approach disputes as discursive rather than strategic actors do we have a discursive *practice*. Second, the more public debate conforms to the ideal of discourse the less useful it is as a tool of democratic decision making. Discourse involves a trade-off between efficiency and the goal of mutual understanding. The more our conversations are directed at mutual understanding, the less efficient they are in producing a determinate outcome that can be acted upon. This does not, however, marginalize discourse as an essential component of democratic legitimacy.

II. SETTING UP A DISCOURSE

Although discourse ethics points to a general principle of democratic will formation, it does not point to a particular way of organizing that formation. It is not only that we cannot determine a priori what will be said in discourse; we also cannot determine a priori how, when, where, or even if anything will be said. The institutional form of democratic will formation must itself meet with standards of discursive validity.[23] This appears to lead to a circle: The institutional arrangements that make discourse possible must be justified by a discourse. If the mandate to set up a discourse can only be conferred in a discourse, we are left with no means of justifying the initial establishment of discourse.

The issue of an original mandate to justify the establishment of discourse only comes up if we assume that discourse represents a revolutionary practice that must be established de novo. But a political discourse is not set up the way a constituted assembly is set up. The political ideal contained in discourse ethics centers on a more reflective and widespread undertaking of an activity that already has a place in our lives.

As Habermas has said, communication does not have to be established as an ought.[24] Communication is the way we transmit and reproduce our lifeworld. More particularly, we can identify three activities that function as transmitters of the lifeworld: cultural reproduction, through which traditions and cultural meanings are passed down; social integration, through which we recognize norms of cooperation and interaction; and finally, socialization, through which we acquire identities both as collectives and as individuals.[25] These three functions are symbolically mediated. We pass on cultural understandings, learn to live together under certain rules, and form our identities, by talking and communicating with one another.

Following Durkheim and Weber, Habermas argues that social and political institutions cannot be maintained solely through force or strategic manipulation.[26] Although the threat of sanctions or the prospect of rewards are often part of what motivates citizens to play by the rules, by themselves such inducements cannot guarantee mass loyalty and thus stability. Stability requires that "reasons for obedience can be mobilized" which "at least appear to be justified in the eyes of those concerned."[27]

Laws need to be inter-subjectively recognized by citizens; they have to be legitimated as right and proper. This leaves culture with the task of supplying reasons why an existing political order deserves to be recognized.[28]

When the reasons culture supplies are no longer convincing, then the fragile maintenance system of a norm falls apart. At this point a process must be undertaken whereby mobilization is either regenerated or shifted to an alternative norm. And mobilizing reasons for obedience is achieved through the communicative practice of convincing one another that there really are (or are not) good grounds to recognize a norm. Without such a regenerating process, not simply at our disposal but constantly in use, the shared background to our social world would fall apart.

According to Habermas this process often takes place unreflectively, in what he calls the "negotiation of a new situation definition." The negotiation is informal and partial, and is characterized by a "diffuse, fragile, continuously revised and only momentarily successful communication in which participants rely on problematic and unclarified presuppositions and feel their way from one occasional commonality to the next."[29] Thus, the image is one of a world where we continually renegotiate, in small and sometimes big ways, the normative backdrop to our actions. The decisive force in these renegotiations is communication: We reach partial understandings through symbolic interaction in which we justify, convince, defend, criticize, explain, argue, express our inner feelings and desires while interpreting those of others. Without partial understandings between members of a community, normative regulation cannot be said to take place.

But partial understandings are, after all, only partial. These understandings are neither fully reflective, nor are they fully rational. What this means is that they often do not go very deep into the background presuppositions that maintain a way of life, what Habermas calls the lifeworld context. Further, they are not fully rational in the sense that within everyday communication other influences filter into the process such that the outcomes are not exclusively the result of the "force of the better argument." We also cajole, threaten, subtly persuade (*uberreden*), bribe, exploit, manipulate, and lie our way into new situation definitions. Our conversations are rarely exhaustive, inclusive, or "convincing" (*uberzeugend*). Voices are often silenced and unilateral closure imposed. Sometimes we hear only what we want to hear.

The "negotiation of new situation definitions" is the process through which the social validity of a norm is reproduced. But a socially valid norm, that is, a norm that is recognized by a certain group of people, cannot claim to be right simply on the grounds that it is in fact recognized. The task of a theory of discursive legitimacy is to formalize, clarify, and universalize the unavoidable presupposition that behind every legitimate norm stands a good reason, and in doing so to rationalize the "diffused, fragile, continually revised, only momentarily successful communication" by which we unreflectively renew social norms. In this way we arrive at a fair, rational, and impartial method to reflectively test the legitimacy of a norm. This procedure serves the dual function of producing norms that *are* in the general interests as well as norms that are *recognized* to be in the general interest.

There are two aspects to a discursive theory. First, there is the recognition and analysis of the real-world processes through which a citizen body generates the recognition necessary to sustain a stable system of justice. Culture and communication underpin this process. This analysis brings out the consensual foundation to all stable systems of rules and norms. Overlaid upon this social analysis is the theoretical/ethical analysis, which points to the optimal conditions under which this process ought to take place if the outcomes are to represent what is in the common interest. Thus rationalism is introduced not as a rational plan for society but as a process of rationalizing the consensual foundations to society. Like Kant's publicity requirement, discourse ethics joins the requirements of stability (that people actually believe that institutions are in their interest) with the requirements of justice (that institutions actually are in the interests of everyone). This is what Habermas means by bringing together the moment of facticity (*Faktizität*) with that of validity (*Geltung*).

It is not controversial to hold that stable political systems require some underlying belief in the legitimacy of the system. What is more controversial is to hold that this legitimacy must be rationally constructed through a democratic public debate. One need only think of Madison's remark that frequent appeals to the public would destroy "that veneration which time bestows on everything, and without which perhaps the wisest and freest governments would not possess the requisite stability."[30] Madison is echoing the conservative view that stability is maintained through noncognitive, affective motivations such as reverence, respect, and patriotism. But the rise of pluralism in the modern world has made reliance on such shared community feelings increasingly implausible. Pluralism does not necessarily undermine the substance of traditional ways; rather it undermines "the *sanctity* . . . of a politics attached to traditional ways."[31] Pluralism challenges the authority of tradition more than its content. When this authority is challenged then reverence and respect must be earned; it cannot simply be assumed to be the natural by-product of the passage of time.

The historical circumstances in which we, in modern liberal democracies, find ourselves, point to the conclusion that we can no longer depend on unquestioned veneration for our stability. We no longer share a common religious view nor a comprehensive moral outlook. The authority of tradition has been greatly weakened in a world where "nontraditional" perspectives are gaining an ever stronger voice. We have very little homogeneity to fall back on to do the work of keeping our world together when a normative dispute arises. Thus, we must construct a consensus; we can no longer appeal to one that is ready-made.[32]

The conditions for producing, reproducing, or maintaining a consensus in the modern political world point to the necessity of rationalizing and democratizing our public debates. In addition, without a rationalized foundation to generally recognized norms, there is always a risk of distortion. Which is to say, citizens claim to revere institutions that they not only do not understand but that their day-to-day attitudes and actions belie. And this can undermine those very institutions in the long run.

Let us say, for the sake of argument, that liberal democratic societies presupposed a norm of noncoercion: We should try to resolve our disputes through peaceful means whenever possible. This norm has force only so long as enough people share the understanding (even if vague and submerged) that force is an illegitimate means in resolving our normative disputes.

Shared understandings are fluid and change over time. They have a tendency to erode, subtly shift, and mutate. Why shouldn't a commitment to noncoercion erode as, for example, the commitment to religious intolerance did in the sixteenth century? The answer cannot be simply that the principle of noncoercion is right and religious intolerance is wrong. The continuity of an understanding over time does not depend on there *being* good grounds for such an understanding, but on those good grounds and that understanding being reproduced within a culture. If we reject, as I think we must, any claims regarding the necessary course of history, then there is no reason why historically specific understandings must continue. That historically specific understandings can be justified on non-contingent ahistorical grounds (natural rights theory, neo-Kantianism, and so on) is not a reason why they *will* continue; it is only a reason why they perhaps *ought* to continue. And if these understandings are to continue, the reasons why they ought to must be kept alive within the cultural belief system of the community. A discursive rationalization of the process through which modern values are reproduced is the way to do this.

Even Herbert McClosky, who argued in his famous essay "Consensus and Ideology in American Politics" that "a democratic society can survive despite widespread popular misunderstanding and disagreement about basic democratic and constitutional values" worried about how long such a society could survive.

I do not mean to suggest, of course, that a nation runs no risks when a large number of its citizens fail to grasp the essential principles on which its constitution is founded. Among Americans, however, the principal danger is not that they will reject democratic ideals in favor of some hostile ideology, but that they will fail to understand the very institutions they believe themselves defending and may end up undermining rather than safeguarding them.[33]

McClosky adds that agreement, even pseudo-agreement, can play an important role maintaining a stable system:

Not only can this keep conflicts from erupting, but it also permits men who disagree to continue to communicate and thus perhaps to convert their pseudo-consensus on democratic values into a genuine consensus.[34]

The conversion of a pseudo, and potentially undermining, consensus into a genuine consensus requires a rationalized public debate motivated by an interest in mutual understanding. Rationalization involves a reflective and critical approach to opinion formation; it involves reasons for and against norms being given and publicly assessed; it involves public participation in which communication is raised to a discursive level. A rationalization of the process through which culture, social integration, and socialization is reproduced allows citizens to reflectively reproduce or change those aspects of their shared lifeworld for which they think there are or are not good reasons.

All this points to the conclusion that there is no need for a special mandate to set up discourse. As a rationalized version of the processes through which culture and social integration are reproduced, discourse does not take place in any specially designated institutions. It can take place wherever public opinion is formed, and this means at all levels of society – from one-on-one debates in informal settings to debates in Parliament.[35] What this means is that the defining characteristic of discourse cannot be found in any one set of institutional rules. Certain institutional rules can be *necessary* conditions for discourse but not sufficient conditions. For example, at the most general level institutionalized rights are part of the context that can enable us to pursue discursive solutions. The legal protection of free speech is part of such an enabling context. But the First Amendment does not enforce the reciprocal requirements of practical discourse. It does not require us to *listen* to what others have to say; it does not require us to attempt to *understand* the other's point of view; it does not require us to *refrain* from manipulating or deceiving others; it does not require us to be *swayed* by the force of the better argument.

In distinguishing discursive democracy from republican or communitarian ideals of democracy, Habermas points out that discourse does not depend on a shared community ethos or the creation of a collective subject that acts as one.[36] These are unrealistic ideals in a modern pluralist context. Instead, discursive democracy depends, on the one hand, on institutionalizing the necessary (but not sufficient) procedures and conditions of communication and, on the other, the interplay between institutionalized decision making and informally yet rationally shaped public opinion.[37] However, in avoiding the pitfalls of communitarianism and the need for a high level of civic virtue, he overstresses the purely procedural requirements of discursive democracy. Discourse does depend on institutionalizing the necessary procedures and conditions of communication. But discourse also depends on citizens participating in institutionalized as well as informal discourse as discursive actors. If citizens do not possess this willingness, then no matter how well designed institutional arrangements are for the purposes of discourse, discourse will not take place. Everyone might have the opportunity to speak, but if no one is listening you have the equivalent of a tower of Babel. Habermas does not deny that discourse requires an interest in mutual understanding, but he never deals fully with the possibility that citizens might generally lack such an interest or not possess the competencies to pursue such an interest. In a world where negotiation, instrumental trade-offs, and strategic bargaining are the most common routes to reaching collective "agreement," and resolving disputes, it is plausible that the most serious barrier to discourse can be found in the conversational habits that citizens have become used to.

Discourse ethics replaces the image of public debate as a marketplace of ideas between elites in which interests and understandings compete with each other for domination with the idea of public debate as a democratized forum in which we cooperatively construct common understandings and work through our differences. Part of this transformation can take place by opening up opportunities to participate, by including excluded voices, by democratizing media access, by setting up "town meetings," by politicizing the depoliticized, by empowering the powerless, by decentralizing decision making, by funding public commissions to canvas public opinion, and so on. But all such initiatives will fail to produce a discursively formed public opinion if citizens are unwilling to or uninterested in acting discursively.

III. THE PROBLEM OF EFFICIENCY

Anyone who has ever participated in a group whose decision rule was consensus knows how difficult and drawn out such deliberations can be. Discourse is constraint free. This means that no one may force closure. The conversation continues until (ideally) every single participant is in full agreement. The larger and more diverse the group, the more difficult and drawn out the process. Clearly this is not a realistic model for all of the decisions we associate with democratic government. The question then becomes which decisions should be made discursively and which by more efficient means? One answer is that the more the issue is a foundational one dealing with the legitimacy of the rules, the more we are under an obligation to include all citizens.

But in what sense is a face-to-face conversation between all citizens a feasible model of democratic legitimation? Do we imagine a series of participatory face-to-face constituent assemblies? In large modern democracies this is impossible. The problem here is that we are imagining practical discourse as a decision procedure with a determinate outcome. Thinking of discourse in this way will always bring us back to small, manageable groups. A decision procedure implies a set of rules that govern closure. These rules tell us when the process is over – what counts as a fair decision that can be acted upon. Now, as a decision rule, discourse stipulates that full, rational agreement under the ideal conditions of discourse of all affected by a norm constitutes the point of closure. However, when translated into the real world of politics it turns out that this point can never be definitively reached. Because real agreements can never be perfectly universal, they never settle a question once and for all. Through the idea of an ideal communication community we can imagine the conditions of a perfectly rational consensus and therefore the criterion of ideal legitimacy. But, as we can never attain the ideal in the real world, the question becomes the degree to which we can and should try to approximate that ideal under real conditions. Discourse is not a contract where there is a privileged moment of promising which is then binding on all parties for perpetuity. Discourses must be understood as open ended and fallible. This means that discourse is ongoing and conclusions and agreements reached by means of discourse are always open to revision.

The notion of consensual will formation cannot be understood as the outcome of one constituent conversation, but must be seen as the cumulative product of many criss-crossing conversations over time and often a long time. The single conversation, as it is represented in moral philosophy, helps explicate the complicated web of conversations that we undertake in the real world. But understood too literally, the model of the single conversation can be misleading. The argumentative dynamic of a web of conversations is somewhat different from that of the single conversation.

Some critics have suggested that the more open and constraint-free our debates, the less likely we are to reach agreement.[38] This is true if we look only at the single conversation. We often require chairpersons, mediators, judges, or time limits to *force* closure. We do not like to admit that we are wrong even in the face of evidence; we are very attached to our own views; we often enter conversations with set opinions and leave with the same set opinions. Furthermore, there are and will always be real differences of opinion: questions upon which agreement is unlikely.[39]

That a single "unconstrained" conversation, especially on a highly charged subject, appears much more likely to end in disagreement than agreement is not strong evidence against the power of rational argumentation. It is, however, an argument for why discourse is not appropriate for all political decisions. If we step back from the model of the single conversation, we see that people do in fact change their minds; they do find new arguments, positions, and perspectives more convincing than old ones; they are swayed by argumentation. This process goes on over time, however; it does not happen as it happened to Polemarchus in the *Republic*. One often reevaluates one's position between conversations rather than within them. One is sometimes not even aware that that position has subtly shifted in response to and reflection upon a criticism or challenge. Not only is the process gradual, but it is fragmentary and partial. One reevaluates fragments of one's world-view by bringing them into line with cogent argument; one does not reassess one's entire view of life, or at least very rarely.

Thinking of the argumentative dynamic of a web of conversations in this way alters what we mean by agreement. Although consensus represents a general agreement, it is not an agreement in the sense that we can point to one particular time or place at which the agreement occurred. A general agreement can emerge as the product of many single conversations even when no single conversation ends in agreement. Consensual agreement, if and when it does emerge, emerges gradually and is fragmentary and partial.

The point here is simply to highlight the diffuse nature a real discourse would have to have if its outcome is to be a consensus that underwrites a legitimate social norm. On this reading, then, discourse is a long-term consensus-forming process and not a decision procedure. The democratic element of discourse ethics should not be identified too closely with the day-to-day procedures of democratic decision and policy making. Discourses potentially underpin and justify institutional democratic arrangements; they are not an alternative to such arrangements.

Unconstrained discourse is highly inefficient. The closer our conversations come to embodying the ideal, the more inefficient they are. The more general the norm under discussion, the more diffuse, fragmented, and complicated will be the web of discourse, not to mention the longer the process is likely to take. With this in mind, it becomes difficult even to talk about a decision being taken in discourse; instead we must visualize discourse as the place where collective interpretations are constructed. Indeed, the more parties to a discourse are constrained by the need to take a decision, the less motivated they will be to act discursively and the more motivated to act strategically. To illustrate this point I wish to conclude with a real world example. The Canadian constitutional debate illustrates both why rational public opinion and will formation are so important but also how difficult it is to achieve the interplay Habermas talks about between informally constructed public opinion and institutionalized decision making.

IV. DISCOURSE AND BARGAINING IN THE CANADIAN CONSTITUTIONAL DEBATE

Because of some very complex historical circumstances, Canada lacked, until 1982, a written constitution as an act of the Canadian Parliament. In 1982 nine provinces and the federal government agreed to repatriate an amended constitution.[40] French-speaking Quebec, representing about one-quarter of the population, abstained from endorsing the document because it did not provide Quebec with additional powers to protect French language and culture. The 1982 constitution is legally binding because, prior to 1982, the conventional amending formula did not require the unanimous support of all provinces. However, the 1982 document sets out unanimity as the standard of all future structural amendments. In short, the constitution itself stipulates unanimity as the standard of legitimacy, yet it lacks the support of the largest minority in the country. Thus Canada is in the position of having a legal constitution the legitimacy of which is not universally accepted. Since 1982 there has been a continuous political dialogue about how to achieve unanimity and why it is important to do so.

Canada, like all Western democracies, is a pluralist society. Despite this pluralism, or more accurately because of it, there is one point on which all Canadians seem to agree: A legitimate constitution should rest on a general agreement. This is often cited as an impossible standard to fulfill. It has kept Canadians in constitutional limbo for years. But the drawn-out nature of the debate does not point to the impossibility of agreement but rather to the more demanding standard of agreement that is necessary in modern, post-conventional, societies.

But what counts as actual agreement? Who agrees? The 1989 attempt to get unanimous endorsement by the ten provincial legislatures and the federal government, known as the Meech Lake accord, failed. The Manitoba legislature was stymied by Native Canadian opposition, and the Newfoundland legislature was unwilling to endorse an accord which it felt it had no part in forging. Despite the fact that eight of the ten provinces did agree to the accord, the failure produced a general, coast-to-coast, reevaluation of the constitutional situation.

Many people argued that it was not the document per se that was flawed but the process through which the document was brought before Canadians.[41] The process was dominated by elite bargaining, trade-offs, and pressure tactics on the part of the federal government. And the discussion of what exactly is wrong with elite bargaining, trade-offs, and pressure tactics placed the conditions of democratic legitimacy on the discursive agenda. For example, in the aftermath of Meech Lake, the federal government was forced to see that a constitutional agreement worked out among elites, but not firmly anchored in the beliefs, attitudes, and convictions of the citizens, would fall short of being a real constitution. In a document outlining proposals for reviving the constitutional debate after Meech Lake, the government acknowledged that it had failed to deal seriously enough with this aspect of constitutional politics.

A constitution has two key purposes: one legal, one symbolic. It sets the rules by which a people govern themselves. But it should also convey a sense of why the rules are drafted as they are, what values shape them, what purposes and characteristics identify the people to whom they apply. All Canadians should be able to relate to the description of the qualities that define the country to which they are bound by birth or choice. As our Constitution stands, that second symbolic component is particularly weak.[42]

In an effort to bring more Canadians into the process, a number of new constitutional initiatives were launched. One such initiative was the Citizens Forum on Canada's Future. This forum, created by the federal government, was not only intended to give ordinary Canadians the opportunity and the public space to articulate their views on the future of Canada, it was also designed to foster discussion among diverse groups across the country.[43] In addition to the Citizens Forum, a traveling task force, the Beaudoin–Edwards Commission, was set up to canvas national opinion on the specific question of an appropriate amending formula. Also worth noting were five regional theme conferences held across the country.[44] Participants included representatives from cultural communities, visible minority groups, the disabled, women, native Canadians, academics, and numerous other interested parties. Any Canadian who wished to participate in these conferences could put his or her name in a pool from which 10 percent of the places at each conference were drawn.

These initiatives indicate that one of the lessons learned from the Meech Lake breakdown was that discourse must be inclusive to be fair and that agreement means more than getting the ten premiers at one time and one place to sign on the dotted line. What was important about these initiatives was that their aim was not to reach a negotiated settlement, but rather to create public spaces for the articulation and exchange of ideas, grievances, and claims.

When the search for agreement through negotiation and bargaining became derailed, a more discursive enterprise geared toward understanding took its place. This enterprise was aimed at bringing about a better understanding of the issues, principles, and values at stake in the debate as well as a better understanding of the various interests, needs, and claims of the parties involved. From one perspective this was a setback, for the possibility of a hard-and-fast settlement of the constitutional question receded. From another perspective, the widening of the constitutional debate was a move toward building the kind of consensus necessary to underwrite any future "settlements." Consensus formation is possible only when the focus of the debate shifts away from fixed deadlines, bargaining between entrenched major powers, and the coveted eleven signatures on a constitutional document. When these kinds of constraints on discourse are lifted, there is freedom to rationalize and democratize the debate in the sense of dealing with issues and reasons in a more substantive and inclusive way.

Consensus is not brought about by negotiation; consensus is brought about by sustained argumentation and discussion in which people contemplate, analyze, and articulate the fundamental principles that are to govern their interaction. As another government document stated: "The Constitution must be a framework that reflects our values, our aspirations, and the best of what Canadians really are." [45] The long-term stability of the Canadian constitution depends on the recognized accuracy of this reflection. This, in turn, can only come about through a conversation in which Canadians come to understand what values and aspirations they do share. "Cutting a deal" today might give short-term relief to the Canadian constitutional crisis, but without a deeper and popular moral agreement on principles, Canadians will lack the commitment and allegiance necessary to sustain a constitution over time.

However, when all is said and done, a decision has to be made. And democratic decisions are made by counting votes, not by assessing the rationality of the deliberation that precedes the vote. In the Canadian context this meant a referendum on what is called the Charlottetown agreement. On October 26, 1992, 55 percent of Canadians rejected the agreement that had been reached in August in Charlottetown, Prince Edward Island, by elites. What interplay existed between the discursive process outlined earlier and the decision taken by Canadians on October 26? At a minimum, we can say that certain things got on the agenda which had not been on previously. Most notable, of course, was the principle of aboriginal self-government. Although a majority of native voters as well as many Canadians rejected the agreement because it was too vague on the issue of aboriginal self-government, the *principle* of aboriginal self-government is now widely accepted. This is the result of the inclusion of aboriginal peoples into the mainstream public debate on constitutional issues.

Alain Noel has put forward an even more optimistic interpretation of the interplay between deliberation and decision. Against those who claim that the No vote was "based more on emotion and hyperbole than on reason" and that it represented the victory of prejudice, racism, and self-interest over the community's good, Noel argues that "democratic deliberation played an important role in helping Canadians make up their mind about the Charlottetown agreement."[46] A prominent Canadian journalist echoes this interpretation by noting that "Canadians took their civic duty as decisions-makers extremely seriously, poring over documents, questioning the details and voting in mass numbers."[47]

Noel argues that a new era of deliberative politics was inaugurated in the 1980s and came to fruition after the Meech Lake failure. "Genuine democratic deliberation," he argues, "can be signalled by meaningful opinion movements, by explicit references to conceptions of justice, and by the emergence of a clear and limited set of alternatives." In contrast, "the 'rational' politics of self-interest displays stable preferences, motivations that are primarily economic, and amorphous conceptions of the polity."[48] I cannot detail all his evidence here, but Noel, using public opinion research, an analysis of public statements and issues, as well as building on the work of such leading Canadian political analysts as Alan Cairns and Charles Taylor, plausibly defends the claim that much of the debate leading up to the referendum can be characterized as deliberative in the sense defined. According to this view, the majority had good reasons to reject the Charlottetown agreement and Canadians came to a rationally motivated disagreement.

Despite this optimistic reading, Noel also concedes that as the referendum deadline approached, the discursive process gave way to a tough bargaining process.[49] Elites played on fears in the final advertising campaigns and used pressure tactics to get the desired outcome. To some extent this backfired as the No vote also reflected a widespread dissatisfaction on the part of many Canadians with elites and their handling of constitutional issues. But I am not interested in the particular reasons for the No vote. I am more interested in the structural issue of how deadlines and decisions affect the deliberative process.

The more general point here is that the taking of a decision, that is, the prospect of closure, will always place a constraint on the discursive process. The closer and more final is that point of closure, the more participants will be motivated to act strategically rather than discursively. Habermas is certainly right to say that bargaining has a place in democratic politics. But how to keep it in its place is the real issue. On fundamental questions, such as constitutional principles, it is important that citizens are given the opportunity to discuss and deliberate in a constraint-free forum. This in turn means that the institutional forums in which we visualize discursive practices taking place must, on the one hand, be insulated from the pressures involved in decision making but, on the other hand, they must inform the decisions we do take. The period between the Meech Lake failure and the final referendum campaign represented such a breathing space for Canadians.[50] Many people complained that these discussions were amorphous and unfocused because participants did not have a clear decision schedule before their eyes. My argument is that it was precisely because participants had no clear decision schedule that they were able to free themselves from constraint and discuss issues at the level of public reason. This does not mean, of course, that discursive democracy implies indecision. It implies that a very careful balance must be struck between deliberation and decision making. Discourse is essentially open ended. Decision making is essentially closed ended. A realistic model of deliberative democracy must concede that decision rules in large democracies will always place constraints on constraint-free dialogue. This means that the potential for a more rational politics is found in fostering and promoting dialogues in which the goal is mutual understanding and not necessarily a binding decision.

NOTES

1 Jürgen Habermas, *Legitimation Crisis*, trans. Thomas McCarthy (Boston: Beacon Press, 1975).
2 Jürgen Habermas, *Faktizität und Geltung: Beitrage zur Diskurstheorie*

des Rechts und des demokratischen Rechtsstaats (Frankfurt: Suhr-kamp, 1992).

3 Jürgen Habermas, *Moral Consciousness and Communicative Action*, trans. by Christian Lenhardt and Shierry Weber Nicholsen (Cambridge, Mass.: MIT Press, 1990), p. 116.

4 For the most systematic and comprehensive discussion of the problems with a dialogical universalization test, see Albrecht Wellmer, "Ethic and Dialogue: Elements of Moral Judgment in Kant and Discourse Ethics," in *The Persistence of Modernity*, trans. David Midgley (Cambridge, Mass.: MIT Press, 1991), pp. 113–231.

5 Jürgen Habermas, *The Theory of Communicative Action*, Vol. II, trans. Thomas McCarthy, (Boston: Beacon Press, 1987), p. 95. See also Habermas, *Moral Consciousness and Communicative Action*, p. 67.

6 Wellmer, "Ethics and Dialogue", pp. 145–88. Jean Cohen and Andrew Arato, *Civil Society and Political Theory* (Cambridge, Mass.: MIT Press, 1992), pp. 350–51

7 Seyla Benhabib makes this suggestion in "Liberal Dialogue versus a Critical Theory of Discursive Legitimation" in *Liberalism and the Moral Life*, ed. Nancy Rosenblum (Cambridge, Mass.: Harvard University Press, 1989), p. 144. For a comparison of Kant, Rawls, and Habermas on the question of publicity, see Kenneth Baynes, *The Normative Grounds of Social Criticism: Kant, Rawls, Habermas* (Albany: State University of New York Press, 1992), pp. 4–5. For a discussion of Kant's understanding of publicity, see Howard Williams, *Kant's Political Philosophy* (New York: St. Martin's Press, 1983), pp. 149–61.

8 Immanuel Kant, "Perpetual Peace," in *Kant's Political Writings*, ed. Hans Reiss (Cambridge: Cambridge University Press, 1970), p. 130.

9 Ibid., p. 126.

10 Ibid.

11 Immanuel Kant, "On the Common Saying: 'This May be True in Theory, but It Does Not Apply in Practice,'" in *Kant's Political Writings*, p. 85 (henceforth, "Theory and Practice").

12 Ibid., p. 85.

13 Ibid., p. 81.

14 Julian Franklin, *John Locke and the Theory of Sovereignty* (Cambridge: Cambridge University Press, 1978).

15 Kant, "Theory and Practice," p. 81.

16 Immanuel Kant, "An Answer to the Question: 'What Is Enlightenment?'" in *Kant's Political Writings*, p. 55.

17 Kant, "What Is Enlightment?" p. 55. Williams, *Kant's Political Philosophy*, pp. 155–57.

18 Habermas, *Moral Consciousness and Communicative Action*, p. 88.

19 Ibid., p. 89. External coercion are things like threats and bribes; internal coercion are things like psychological pressure, rhetorical manipulation, and deception.

20 Jürgen Habermas, *Erläuterungen zur Diskursethik* (Frankfurt: Suhrkamp, 1991), pp. 100–18. Habermas, *Faktizität und Geltung*, pp. 138–43.

21 Habermas, *Faktizität und Geltung*, pp. 349–98.

22 It is not entirely correct to say that discourse does not contain any instrumental calculation. Discourse is goal oriented in the sense that participants are looking for the best means of attaining the goal of mutual understanding. Thus it is not means–ends rationality that is excluded from discourse but only viewing one's dialogue partner as the means to attaining one's own ends. Furthermore, despite my exaggerated example of strategic action, the distinction between communicative action and strategic or instrumental action is not intended to imply that strategic action is always or necessarily bad. If the goal is mutual understanding then strategic action has no place. But there are many very legitimate goals that require that we calculate strategically. Indeed Habermas now accepts that bargaining is a legitimate part of the democratic process (*Faktizität und Geltung*, pp. 204–6).

23 Jürgen Habermas, *Communicative Action and the Evolution of Society*, trans. Thomas McCarthy (Boston: Beacon Press, 1979), pp. 185–86.

24 Jürgen Habermas, "A Reply to My Critics," in *Habermas Critical Debates*, ed. John Thompson and David Held (Cambridge, Mass.: MIT Press, 1982), p. 227.

25 Habermas, *Theory of Communicative Action*, Vol. II, p. 63.

26 Habermas, *Communicative Action and the Evolution of Society*, pp. 178ff.

27 Habermas, *Moral Consciousness and Communicative Action*, p. 62.

28 Habermas, *Theory of Communicative Action*, Vol. II, p. 188.

29 Habermas, *Theory of Communicative Action*, Vol. I, pp. 100–1.

30 Alexander Hamilton, James Madison, and John Jay, *The Federalist Papers* (New York: Penguin, 1987), no. 49.

31 Michael Oakeshott, "Rationalism in Politics," in Oakeshott, *Rationalism in Politics and Other Essays* (London: Methuen, 1962) p. 22; my emphasis.

32 Habermas, *Theory of Communicative Action*, Vol. II, pp. 342–43.

33 Herbert McClosky, "Consensus and Ideology in American Politics," *American Political Science Review*, no. 58 (1964): 376–77.

34 McClosky, "Consensus and Ideology," p. 376.

35 Habermas, *Faktizität und Geltung*, pp. 361–66.

36 Ibid.

37 Ibid., p. 362.

38 Michael Walzer, "A Critique of Philosophical Conversation," *Philosophical Forum*, no. 21 (1989), pp. 182–96.

39 As Rawls has pointed out, pluralism is simply a fact about us, and pluralism is characterized by irreconcilable disputes and differences of opinion on a plethora of deep issues. However, it is important to remember that "irreconcilable" does not necessarily describe each particular dispute but a general state of affairs: there will always be things that people disagree about; they will not always be the same things. What is disputed and contested today may not be disputed and contested tomorrow. And what is uncontroversial today may tomorrow give rise to bitter dispute.

40 The constitution was "repatriated" because, prior to 1982, the Canadian constitution was an act of the British Parliament.

41 Much of the blame for this was placed on the prime minister, Brian Mulroney. As one journalist put it, "Mulroney's failed attempt (to secure agreement) has been widely criticized because the deal was cooked up behind closed doors by him and the premiers" (*The Gazette*, Montreal, Nov. 2, 1990, A1).

42 *Shaping Canada's Future Together: Proposals* (Government of Canada, 1991), p. 9.

43 The initiative included, among other things, a satellite hook-up between different communities, a citizens' "hot-line," and small-scale town and community meetings all across the country. In inaugurating the initiative, the prime minister stated, "Every Canadian who wants to, will have a say" (*The Gazette*, Montreal, Nov. 2, 1990, A1).

44 These conferences were a response to the initial and not entirely successful efforts of the Castonguay–Dobbie Commission (later the Beaudoin–Dobbie Commission). Because of poor advance planning and an unclear vision of what was involved in large-scale consultation, the Castonguay–Dobbie Commission had a number of false and highly criticized starts. Nevertheless, their final report was very helpful in identifying and articulating interests and values that Canadians share (*Renewal of Canada Conferences*, Government of Canada, 1992).

45 *Shared Values: The Canadian Identity* (Government of Canada, 1991), p. 2.

46 Alain Noel, "Deliberating a Constitution: The Meaning of the Canadian Referendum of 1992," in *Constitutional Predicament: Canada after the 1992 Referendum*, ed. Curtis Cook, (Montreal: McGill-Queen's University Press, forthcoming) MS p. 3.

47 Graham Fraser, "What Does It Mean for Government? How to Decide What to Do Next?" *Globe and Mail*, Oct. 27, 1992, A1, quoted in Noel "Deliberating a Constitution," p. 3.

48 Noel, "Deliberating a Constitution," p. 12.
49 Ibid., p. 22.
50 Noel argues that rekindling deliberation would involve recapturing "the spirit of the 1992 conferences," ibid., p. 21. These were the conferences that brought Canadians together to discuss issues and grievances, not to bring about a decision.

Part V

THE DEFENSE OF MODERNITY

11 Habermas's significant other

In the profane understanding, anyone who is also interested in the latest German writing is a Kantian. In the scholarly understanding, a Kantian is only he who believes that Kant is the truth and that, if the mail coach from Königsberg were ever to have an accident one might well find oneself without the truth for some weeks.

F. Schlegel, *Athenaeum*, Fragment 104

We have to stand by our traditions ... if we do not want to disavow ourselves.

Jürgen Habermas, "On the Public Use of History"

If in what follows we appear critical, it is not because we are unappreciative of the real achievement of the work of Jürgen Habermas. The theory of communicative action makes the case that rationality is a relevant moral *social* concept. That humans speak with and to each other places them, he shows, in a moral relationship, simply by the actuality of the fact of that speech. Habermas develops this position into a critical defense of modernity around a vision of the "formation of autonomous public spheres, which ... enter into communication with one another as soon as the potential for self-organization and the self-organized employment of communication media is made use of."[1] This is a democratic picture based upon the potential egalitarianism of uncoerced participation in discourse.

The refreshing claim in Habermas is that the intellectual resources for this ethicopolitical democratic project lie in the Anglo-American and European tradition. No reader of Habermas can fail to be impressed by the range of his sources, and even more by the constant assimilation of new material. Like the participants in the great eighteenth-century *Encyclopédie*, Habermas seeks to bring all

263

human activity under one project. But his ambitions go beyond those of Diderot, d'Alembert, and the others. Almost every thinker since roughly Rousseau has a place to take and a contribution to make to the great and ongoing enterprise of Western civilization. In Habermas's early work, this modality was almost, we might say, Hegelian. There appeared to be little that was not of use in the history of nineteenth- and twentieth-century thought.

Whatever Habermas's intentions, one of the effects of his work, at least until the 1980s, was to relegitimate the tradition of Western philosophy that one associates with the Enlightenment. He did not, it should be noted, seek to rehabilitate Western thought as *Western* thought but on a universalistic basis. The Enlightenment project, as it appears in Habermas, revolves around the fact or the claim that the ability to communicate rationally separates humans from non-humans. It is clearly to the defense of this claim that he has directed his intelligence and his writing, both philosophical and topical. Why though, might we ask, does the Enlightenment project *need* preservation and continuation? Some considerable portion of the answer must derive from the awful politics that this century has seen. Whatever one makes of the nature and origins of National Socialism and attendant ideologies, one cannot find those politics consonant with the spirit of the Enlightenment.

Over the course of Habermas's work, the question of protecting the Enlightenment project has changed somewhat. In his earlier work – that of the "Hegelian" sweep – Habermas was to our knowledge only slightly explicitly concerned with the problems associated with what Lukács had called "The Destruction of Reason." It was sufficient for the critical project to "follow immanently the movement of thought."[2] Nietzsche, for instance, is addressed in *Knowledge and Human Interests* (1968; English 1971) as an important link between Comte and Max Weber with ideas interestingly cognate to those of Freud. But Nietzsche is not in that book a threat.

In recent years, however, the sweeping diachronic synthesis that characterized a book like *Knowledge and Human Interests* has discovered a resistance to its claim to universalizability. This comes in the group that Habermas refers to as the "neoconservatives." Now Nietzsche *is* a threat; and thinkers who return to him via "Derrida and Heidegger" are politically dangerous. It is clear that some considerable portion of Habermas's concern here is politically motivated, most especially by developments in his native Germany. The rebirth of neofascist groups and, more important, their unwitting legitimation by a group of revisionist German historians threatens all that has been achieved since the Second World War. Habermas writes in 1982:

The political culture of the Federal Republic would be in worse condition than it is today if it had not adopted and assimilated ideas from American political culture during the first decades after the war. For the first time, the Federal Republic opened itself without reservation to the West; at that time we adopted the political theory of the Enlightenment, we came to understand the power to shape attitudes of a pluralism borne initially by religious sects, and we came to know the radical democratic spirit of American pragmatism, from Pierce to Mead and Dewey.[3]

There is a great deal of anxiety in this paragraph. Consider these implicit claims: (1) Being "Western" involves adopting the "political theory of the Enlightenment." (2) Germany was not unreservedly "Western" until after the Second World War. (3) This transformation was to some degree an act of will or choice. (4) What was missing from Germany – what kept it from being Western – was the acceptance of the possibility of a society founded on rationality, a rationality importantly modified by democratic pragmatism imported from across the Atlantic. Overall, the sense of the fragility of contemporary German political culture is extraordinary as is the sense that it needs to be protected.[4]

Habermas sees postmodernism and European neoconservatism as in the service of a "New Paganism," by which he means a *Weltanschauung* in which different value frameworks compete to see which will be stronger. Habermas's critique of "postmodernist" thinkers as well as of the revisionist historians is that they try to say "farewell to modernity." If the essence of modernity is the maintenance of a critical stance toward one's foundations,[5] then the neoconservative postmodernists are conservative in that they deny that a critical stance toward one's foundations can be an available stance. That is, they deny that our embeddedness in history can be part of a universal moral consciousness that is our own.

What does it then mean in practice to say farewell to modernity? The answer has, we think, two parts. Most generally, it means turning one's back to history. It is history, Habermas is quite clear, that has given us "moral universalism." Indeed, such universalism is the result of human struggle and action, and philosophy would "do well to avoid haughtily dismissing these [sociopolitical] movements and the larger historical dimension from which they spring."[6] The second, more specific, aspect of saying "farewell to modernity" is close to home. It means denying the fact of Nazism. Nazism, says Habermas, was a "moral catastrophe [that] brought with it . . . opportunities." It made and makes it not only possible but necessary to think in universalist terms. He continues:

First . . . having been torn out of continuities, we are subject to the constraint of being able to relate to the past only with a reflexive attitude. . . . Second, we can now appropriate traditions only in terms of precisely those universalist value orientations that were violated in such an unprecedented way at that time.[7]

This says that "we" (we will raise the question of this "we" subsequently) *must* think in universalistic ethicopolitical terms as long as we remember the fact of Nazism. If this history of the past two hundred years was not sufficient to settle the question of the necessary universalism of ethics, then the fact of National Socialism is. The danger of the revisionist historians is that they seek to render the experience of Auschwitz unexceptional in recent human history (with the sole exception of the technical achievement of gassing). In a similar fashion, a postmodernist thinker like Jacques Derrida, Habermas argues, is only saved from the "political-moral insensitivity and aesthetic tastelessness of a New Paganism" by the unselfconscious presence in his thought of a cabalistic Jewish mysticism that takes him back to "the context of monotheism" and "the historical locale where mysticism turned into Enlightenment."[8] By implication, Habermas is arguing that the natural development of Derrida's thought from his critique of phonocentrism would be at best only to initiate a more or less pointless retracing of the Enlightenment project as it was begun in the late eighteenth century. Religion is no longer a modern alternative, for when God is dead the religious mode becomes monstrous.

For Habermas, the experience of National Socialism has consequences that cannot be avoided. There is no longer, he appears to be saying, any project that is a human project that is not universalist, democratic, egalitarian. That project can be avoided, but not in favor of an alternative one: It can be avoided only at the cost of denying humanity altogether. But there is an ambiguity here, and it comes in Habermas's use of the first person plural pronoun. We have given some examples. Here is another:

> *Our* own life is linked to the life context in which Auschwitz was possible not by contingent circumstances but intrinsically. *Our* form of life is connected with that of our parents and grandparents through a web of. . . . None of *us* can escape this milieu. . . . [9]

Who is "we"? Is the "we" universal, or does it mean "we Germans." Or does it even mean that because of their historical experience Germans now carry the world historical burden of the universal. If so, Habermas would be in perhaps uncomfortably close proximity to Heidegger's claim that "when [others] want to philosophize they speak German." [10] We should note that whoever is meant by the "we" here, it is at least "we Europeans." At the end of his book on modernity we find: "Who else but Europe could draw from its own traditions the insight, the energy, the courage of vision – everything that would be necessary to strip from the . . . premises of a blind compulsion to system maintenance and system expansion their power to shape our mentality." [11]

We should like to explore the relationship between Habermas's invocation of German experience and his claims to universalism. We want to suggest that the ferocity and comprehensiveness with which he attacks postmodernist and neoconservative, while perhaps merited, is in the end not successful and that the reasons for this misfire have to do with unresolved complexities in his relation to Kant, or more precisely to ambiguities in Kant's thought. Habermas, like Kant, wants a comprehensiveness in his account of reason. The consequences of this demand are what interest us here.

Habermas's official position on Kant is fairly straightforward and in keeping with the systematic structure of the theory of communicative action: Kant provides the original moment of modernity's self-critique but fatefully chooses to interpret reason from a "subject-centered" rather than "intersubjective" or "communicative" perspective. [12] The contribution of Kant's critical philosophy to the project of modernity, Habermas acknowledges, is enormous; but Kant's misleading emphasis on the "principle of subjectivity" in his critique of reason forces him unwittingly to affirm many of the negative qualities of modernity that Nietzsche, Heidegger, Foucault and the rest of the "neoconservatives" have so thoroughly disparaged. In this way Habermas is able to identify Kant with Descartes, the Utilitarians, and even Max Weber as equal participants in the philosophy of subjective consciousness, the mode of philosophy that initiated the full-flowering of the Enlightenment period.[13]

The difference between the "subjective" orientation of reason he attributes to Kant (and the like) and the "intersubjective" position of the theory of communicative action is essential to Habermas's system. The very affirmation of modernity itself is predicated on this distinction: "The critique of subjective idealism is at the same time a critique of modernity; only in this way can the latter secure its concept and assure its own stability."[14] Habermas, then, needs an interpretation of Kant – or even more strongly: Modernity itself needs such an interpretation. But Habermas only offers the most general outline of what this interpretation might look like. He argues that the principal problem with the subjective version of reason is its unwarranted reliance on an exhausted principle of "speculative self-reflection." This principle takes reason out of context, removing it from its inherent social embeddedness. In this way Habermas claims that Kant's rational agent places it- (him/her-) self at a distance from the world, applying reason in an abstract, disembodied, and disengaged fashion. Reason here is pure, and yet it is also paradoxically "distorted."[15] The net effect of this is a politics of exclusion, the same politics that has been the focal point of so much postmodern criticism of the Enlightenment. "Reason," remarks Habermas, "as reduced to the subjective faculty of understanding and purposive activity corresponds to the image of an exclusive reason."[16]

For Habermas, the critique of modernity points to the deep problems associated with this (too limited, Kantian) vision of reason. Taking the position of the neoconservative, he sees the "tyrannical" and "totalizing" quality of a reason alienated from concrete social practices.[17] The theory of communicative action recognizes and rectifies the philosophy of "subjective reason" by replacing it with a reason embedded in language and the shared practices of communicative actors. In this way Habermas claims to be initiating a new period in the philosophical discourse of enlightenment, one that throws out the subjective bath water while retaining the reasonable baby. He promises, not insignificantly, "a *new orientation* for the critique of instrumental reason." [18]

But this manner of distinguishing himself from Kant (on which much of his "new orientation" depends) is perhaps not as clear as Habermas would like it to be. In fact, it is notable that to our knowledge nowhere in Habermas's work does there appear an extended critical analysis of Kant of the kind to which he subjects Hegel, Mead, Freud, and many others. [19] Consider for a moment Kant's views on reason, subjectivity, and communication. Kant thought the *Critique of Pure Reason* to bring a new *orientation* to the world of philosophy and the world of politics. Kant's "Copernican revolution" was in fact a "change in point of view," one that would provide the "universal voice" of reason a "secure foundation" by inaugurating a "lasting and peaceful reign of reason over [the] understanding and the senses." [20] The new orientation was called for in light of the antinomial conflict that pitted reason against itself, fragmenting the rational public, and eliminating the possibility of a comprehensive reason and a coherent discourse. Before the critical revolution, Kant argues, the warring metaphysical schools were unable even to hear each other, simply because reason itself lacked a common ground. There could be no reconciliation of reason, not any consensus, until reason itself was straightened out. And this is what Kant, not unlike Habermas, set himself about doing. Establishing the possibility of fair communication and a comprehensive reason was already at the heart of Kant's new point of view.

An exploration of the parallel between Kant's enterprise and that of Habermas can be instructive in revealing some of the limitations inherent in Habermas's own project. For Kant, we shall argue, ran into questions about the solution to which he was ambivalent. Habermas, we shall try to show, by not engaging in a critique of Kant, has avoided the confrontation of problems in his own thought. And, finally, the avoidance of these problems means that his critique of so-called postmodernists is, we think, ineffective and possibly even harmful to his own thought. The strength of Habermas's thought should require that he retain the postmodernists as other and not seek to eliminate them as enemies.

Let us turn now to a consideration of Kant. The ostensible work of the first *Critique* was to extirpate the possibility of skepticism in any form, albeit without denying the persistence of the claim of the skeptic. Skepticism, as Kant saw it, amounts to the claim that what we take as the self-evident "public world" is in fact composed merely of endless fragmentation and localisms. For the skeptical stance, any expression of unity or comprehensiveness is always contingent, never final, often nothing more than a happenstance "heap" of unrelated fragments, as Hume once put it. The skeptic doubts the rational validity of existing "transcendental principles" of unity in any form, especially those that make normative claims on our behavior. Reason is no exemption to the skeptical position: It denies that the giving of a reason tears oneself out of the fabric of a limited solipsistic existence. With the denial of any legitimate principles of a broader discourse community, reason will never get us beyond the local into the general. If reason is truly "subjectivist" as the skeptic claims, if reason is irreconcilable to itself and paradoxical at its core, then for Kant it is dead. The skeptical position is the "euthanasia" of making sense to each other. If we are to doubt the possibility of transcendental principles, then we are to doubt reason itself. The threat of the skeptic is thus for Kant a threat to *communication*.

Kant thus argues that "in the absence of this critique reason is, as it were, in the state of nature, and can establish and secure its assertions and claims only through war. The critique, on the other hand, arriving at all of its decisions in light of fundamental principles of its own institution, the authority of which no one can question, secures the peace of a legal order."[21] Kant had searched for this solution for some time. "Everything goes by in a flux," he muses in a frequently cited reflection from the precritical period, "and the varying tastes and different shapes of men make the whole game uncertain and delusive. Where do I find the fixed points of nature that man cannot displace and can give him marking signs concerning the bank to which he should adhere?" The fixed points were articulated with the first *Critique*. The "system" of the critical philosophy is designed to establish a *comprehensive* framework for *communication*; the critique of *pure* reason furnishes us with the perspective that is not subjective, the perspective of reason itself. Reason is made tame – desubjectivized, if you will – through the constraint of dialectic, which provides the foundation for certainty in all the flux. Kant makes this clear in the section of the first *Critique* entitled the "Discipline of Pure Reason." He argues:

The opposing party we must always look for in ourselves. For speculative reason in its transcendental employment is *in itself* dialectical; the objections which we have to fear lie in ourselves. We must seek them out, just as we would do in the case of claims that, while old, never become superannuated, in order that by annulling them we establish a more permanent peace. External quiescence is merely specious.[22]

The recognition of the "other" – the opposing party – is an essential moment in Kant's vision, a first step in setting reason upon more secure foundations and in that kin to Hobbes's legislative *Leviathan*.[23] The dialectical quality of reason is in fact both its virtue and its vice. Its viciousness lies in the fact that it leads us to necessary illusions about our most pressing questions. Its virtue is that it also provides the tools with which we can arrive at intersubjective truth, foundations for collective action. Only a nondiscursive intelligence, complete in its understanding, would have no need of the "other" – for it, there could be no other.

All of the moral, political, and epistemological arguments that follow from the Copernican revolution revolve around Kant's *fear of rational subjectivism*. In the first *Critique* he states his case plainly: "The touchstone whereby we decide whether our holding a thing to be true is conviction or mere persuasion is therefore external, namely the possibility of communicating it and finding it to be valid for all human reason."[24] By communicating our experience to others, we are able to assure ourselves that our claims are not the "play of my fancy," a "mere dream," or even, as the skeptic would have it, "the blind play of representations."[25] The certainty of experience, which the *Critique of Pure Reason* is meant to ensure, is intimately linked to an intersubjective application of reason.

What experience teaches me under certain circumstances it must always teach me and everybody; it and its validity are not limited to the subject nor its state at a particular time. . . . Therefore objective validity and necessary universality (for everybody) are equivalent terms. . . . [26]

The moral philosophy functions in precisely the same fashion. The threat of subjectivity is overcome by demonstrating that if there is to be something we can call morality, it cannot be private, but rather necessarily carries with it a universal and necessary command to all rational individuals. Kant's perspective on reason is inescapably intersubjective; erecting the foundation for communication and communicative action is the most essential objective of the whole critical enterprise, the objective that comes to light only after the experience of skepticism.

The critical project etches this vision of communication in transcendental stone. With intersubjective reason in mind, Kant can argue that all human speech acts must be directed toward communication in order to avoid any kind of subjective "distortion." In this, it addresses itself to skepticism, for skepticism claims that all speech is in some sense a distortion simply because there is no ideal of pure speech. The "telos of language," which is the highest principle of Habermas's new orientation of reason, is thus already central in Kant's revolutionary point of view. Intersubjective communication is the aim of all language, and any use of it to the contrary represents the deepest violation of our human nature. For this reason, lying, insincerity, and rhetorical manipulation are supreme vices for Kant, as is the use of power to restrict the freedom of speech. He argues in the "Doctrine of Virtue" in the *Metaphysics of Morals*:

Communication of one's thoughts to someone through words that yet (intentionally) contain the contrary of what the speaker thinks on a subject is an end that is directly opposed to the natural purposiveness of the speaker's capacity to communicate his thoughts, and is thus a renunciation by the speaker of his personality, and such a speaker is a mere deceptive appearance of a man, not a man himself. . . . Man as a moral being cannot use himself as a natural being as a mere means (a speaking machine), as if his natural being were not bound to the inner end (of communicating thoughts). . . . [27]

The obligation to make sense is derivative of our character as human beings – rational human beings. Language is predicated on a teleological commitment to be comprehensible to others, to strive for comprehensiveness. We are not speaking machines; we are communicative agents.

Kant's actual position on reason is thus difficult to reconcile to Habermas's interpretation of it. The concept of comprehensibility – of making oneself and one's position available to others – is the backbone of Kant's whole critical turn. Kant's politics are in turn clearly tied to this vision: Witness the endless arguments of "popular essays" on the paramount importance of the freedom of reason in the public realm. His supposedly "subjective reason" needs a speaking public as much as Habermas, and Kant's politics are truly a politics of dialectical reason and comprehensibility. But the point here is not merely to indicate the seemingly endless parallels that exist between Kant and Habermas. So much is old news, as Lyotard has shown, and is in itself not very interesting.[28] What is important to note, though, is that in Kant there is a lesson about the politics of reason and comprehensibility, a lesson that is valuable in understanding Habermas's position on his "other,' the so-called "neoconservatives."

If we turn back to the philosophical discourse of modernity, the implications of the politics of comprehensibility become clear. Habermas argues that the history of the counter-Enlightenment is in fact the history of romanticism.[29] We can, he claims, make sense of the radical critique of postmodernism by considering it as a moment of a general attack on the subject-centered reason of Kant and others, a reason that he holds to be open to such attacks. The "other" of reason has many voices – Schlegel's feeling, Heidegger's being, Derrida's writing, Foucault's power – but only one antagonist: the rational subject. Each of these themes, seen as a species of the romantic, is taken up in the *Philosophical Discourse of Modernity* with a great deal of depth and skill.

Habermas's story, though, is only partially persuasive. The question of the "other," which is at the heart of both Kant and Habermas's vision of intersubjective reason, is more precisely taken up by counter-Enlightenment thought in the form of a *tension between the comprehensible and the incomprehensible*. Nowhere is this tension clearer than in Kant's only formal treatise on comprehensibility, the *Critique of Judgment*. The third *Critique* must be understood as Kant's contribution to the discourse of a "metacritique of pure reason" that necessarily followed out of the publication of the *Critique of Pure Reason*. The project of a metacritique was, as Habermas points out, designed to account for the problematic assumptions that Kant was forced to make in his refutation of skepticism.[30] The foremost of these assumptions was the "fact of reason" – the fact of our comprehensibility to ourselves and to others, our character as rational beings capable of being persuaded by Kant's argument.[31] The central paradox of the *Critique of Pure Reason* rests in the fact that the systematic exhaustiveness of the critical project was a revolution, a transformed point of view, one without any association to the systems of the past. Kant's new *orientation* was fundamentally original and yet completely comprehensive. Kant needed to account for himself: How could he be original and comprehensive at the same time?

Against this, the "metacritique of pure reason," as developed by Hamann (who invented the term) and Herder, was designed to demonstrate that reason is necessarily embedded in concrete contexts of social life. Some of their critique of course sounds like Habermas. As he sums it up: "There is no pure reason that might don linguistic clothing only in the second place. Reason is by its very nature incarnated in contexts of communicative action and structures of the life world."[32] However, for Herder and Hamann, the pioneers of the metacritique, the claim of "incarnation" amounted to an account of the "aesthetic" origins of reason. What the aesthetic interpretation offered was a way of understanding how it is possible to make sense in completely novel fashions. The metacritique was a discussion of the conditions of comprehensibility and as such a discourse on reason's "other."

The insight of the metacritique of pure reason is that the comprehensiveness of a system of reason cannot be predicated on comprehensiveness itself, and that a certain amount of *incomprehensibility* is necessary to make "systematic" or "complete" comprehension possible. The "other of reason," understood as that which stands outside of, or is precluded by, an existing system of reason, is the *ground* of reason in that in order to make sense, individuals must be oriented such that they can in fact understand each other. The orientation itself cannot come from within the system since the system itself is predicated on it. For Herder, whose *Ideas for a Philosophy for the History of Mankind* represent the first metacritical endeavor,[33] this meant that they must share a common history and concrete tradition that gives substance to their rational claims. But also, and more important, it provides a background from which new revolutionary points of view can be understood.

It is precisely these themes that Kant took up in the *Critique of Judgment*. The purpose of the third *Critique* is to demonstrate that in the contemplation of the incomprehensible we in effect broaden our perspective, change our point of view. Aesthetic judgments, Kant argues, have the effect of taking us from our limited understanding of the world around us, opening us up to think from "the standpoint of the other." Along with "thinking for oneself" and "thinking consistently," *thinking from the standpoint of others* is the essential moment of the critical revolution, the new "enlarged" or "broadened" position of the "universal voice," that is of Kant's point of view, what one might call the full perspective of *Enlightenment.*

It seems that we usually call someone limited (of a *narrow* mind as opposed to a *broad* mind) if his talents are insufficient for a use of any magnitude (above all for intensive use). But we are not talking here of a power of cognition, but about a *way of thinking* [that involves] putting this power to a purposive use; and this, no matter how slight may be the range and degree of a person's natural endowments, if he overrides the private subjective conditions of judgment, into which so many others are locked, as it were, and reflects on his own judgment from a universal standpoint (which he can determine by transferring himself to the standpoint of others).[34]

In the *Anthropology,* Kant identifies this as the principle of the "Liberals who accommodate themselves to the concepts of others."[35]

The "orientation of reason" which the critical turn promises in order to ward off the threat of skepticism and set reason on its secure foundations is identical to this "liberality" of mind. How, though, do we arrive at it? The answer lies in the contemplation of the beautiful. Kant argues that in making an aesthetic judgment we are actually judging the degree to which an incomprehensible object can, through the transformation of our point of view, come to make sense to us. "To judge an object by taste," Kant argues, "is to judge whether freedom in the play of the imagination harmonizes or clashes with the understanding."[36] All incomprehensible experiences start off clashing with our limited understandings, our limited points of view; only after reflection, which produces new rules for understanding, will we potentially arrive at harmony. In this way, Kant argues that the judgment of beautiful objects is a prior moment in the cognition of the foreign, and depends in turn on a prior orientation of the mind.[37] Judgments of beauty concern the configuration of the cognitive faculties that make communication possible through understanding.

Contained within reflective judgments of taste, then, is a *tension*

between the stimulus presented through something that appears in-
communicable to us, and the satisfaction that comes from constructing a principle or rule that will make sense of it. The *Critique
of Judgment* is a participant in the metacritical debate, then, in that
it seeks to understand the relationship between comprehensibility
and incomprehensibility that *necessarily* figures into any system of
communication. This tension is most evident in Kant's theory of
genius, which, unlike Herder's and the later romantics, is deeply
ambivalent. The incomprehensibility that is necessary to broaden
the mind and take the standpoint of others is, more than anything
else, the aesthetic work of the genius.[38] What makes the genius
unique is that in principle he or she has complete freedom of incomprehensibility in the creation of works of art. The genius, Kant argues, cannot be restricted by rule or limit to the understanding. Indeed, the genius is defined by *originality*, which, for Kant, merely
means that the work cannot be captured within the confines of any
systematic understanding.[39]

The work of the genius, then, is to transport the understanding in
all of its limitation to a position where it can become more comprehensive, make a greater amount of sense to more individuals. It
achieves this through the use of "aesthetic ideas." Kant argues that
genius "sets the power of intellectual ideas in motion" and in effect
"makes reason think more."[40] What results from this aesthetic employment is the new perspective, a new vision of a now comprehensible nature: "The imagination (as a productive cognitive power) is
very mighty when it creates, as it were, another nature out of the
material nature actually gives it."[41] In this way the genius is in fact
analogous to Kant's understanding of the lunatic who refuses to acknowledge the restriction that reason places on him.

Such a patient fancies that he comprehends the incomprehensible. . . .
There is in this type of mental disturbance not merely disorder and departure from the laws which govern reason, but also a positive unreason, that
is, *a different rule, a totally different standpoint to which the soul is transported,* so to speak. From such a perspective the soul *looks at objects in
another way,* and . . . it finds itself transported to a faraway place.[42]

The point is that genial creativity always transcends the system, always appears extraordinary. The genius requires the system in order
to be a genius. The system exists, one might say, because of its limits

on all sides and in turn requires those limits for its actuality. This point will become significant in just a moment.

A number of important consequences follow from Kant's understanding of genius and its relationship to the problem of the "broadening of mind" that grounds the point of view of the critical vision of reason. Foremost of these is the fact that the incomprehensibility of the genius cannot itself be accounted for. "The man of genius," Kant writes in the *Anthropology*, "cannot explain to himself its outburst or how he arrived at a skill which he never tried to learn."[43] The very extraordinary nature of genial work places it outside of the horizon of understanding available to reason as it stands. This is why the genius is incomprehensible, *but also it explains the role that the incomprehensible and extraordinary necessarily plays in the creation of a system of reason.* If the originality of the other can be made sense of under the reason of one system, then its transformative effects, its new point of view, cannot be established. For this reason, Kant argues, the genius appears as something akin to the *fanatic:* "Originality of the imagination is called genius when it harmonizes with notions. If originality does not harmonize with notions, then it is called fanaticism."[44] But the question is: With whose notions must the genius harmonize? The individuals who encounter him or her as incomprehensible? This would suggest that the genius is always interpreted as a fanatic. Or those who, broadening their perspective, share her point of view? This fundamental paradox – that the appearance of an attempt to communicate depends on one's point of view, one's reason – is the same that confronts Habermas in his effort to make sense of the extraordinary quality of the counter-Enlightenment. Clearly, however, there *should be no answer* to this question, no resolution to the paradox.

But, it must be said, Kant is by no means happily settled on the question of genius and incomprehensibility. The problem with genius for Kant is precisely located in the fact that genius always presents a *threat* to the established order of reason. We cannot be certain that the genius is sincere in his or her effort to communicate, simply because we have no idea of what communication might look like – *from that point of view.*[45] The presence of genius, of radical incomprehensibility, is like the skeptical threat in that both reject the validity (one might say "finality") of established practices and points of view. In both cases, the fear is that an authentic *sensus*

communis – a legitimate point of view of reason – will be sup-
planted by something merely private, merely subjective, the *sensus
privatus*, a personal point of view.[46] Kant's response to this threat is
to place the free incomprehensibility of genius under the restraint
of the rules of accepted discourse, the rules of taste – taste understood as aesthetic tradition. Ever since Rousseau, the conservative
power of taste has been acknowledged. Now Kant employs taste, not
as a means of liberalizing our orientation, but of restricting it.

Taste, like the power of judgment in general, consists in disciplining (or
training) genius. It severely clips its wings, and makes it civilized, or pol-
ished; but at the same time it gives it guidance as to how far and over what
it may spread. . . . It introduces clarity and order into a wealth of thought,
and hence makes it durable, fit for approval that is both lasting and universal, and fit for being followed by others and fit for every advancing culture.[47]

Kant's inherent and self-conscious conservatism is evident in his
well-known views on art. He argues, presaging Hegel, that the creative "art [of the genius] stops at some point, because a boundary is
set for it which probably *has long since been reached and cannot
be extended further.*"[48] For this reason all new works of art, and
new expressions of the tension between the comprehensible and the
incomprehensible,

must be composed in a language both scholarly and dead; dead, so that it
will not have to undergo the changes that inevitably affect living ones,
whereby expression becomes flat, familiar ones archaic, and newly created
ones enter into circulation only for a short while; scholarly, so that it will
have a grammar that is not subject to the whims of fashion, but has its own
inalterable rule.[49]

Kant is trying, in other words, to allow for the possibility of genius
and to tame it at the same time. His effort to restrict the freedom
of the genius to the confines of taste is actually an effort to eliminate the tension between comprehensibility and incomprehensibility that necessarily grounds all systems of reason. The threat of the
genius, like that of the skeptic, is a necessary threat, the prod that
forces us toward increasing liberality, toward increasingly broad
points of view. The systematic structure of the critical edifice is ultimately its demise; Kant takes his theory of genius to a conservative
vision of politics.

However, there is also evident in Kant's theory of genius a resistance to the requirements of his own theory of comprehensibility. As we saw, the maintenance of the tension between the comprehensible and the incomprehensible was necessary for comprehensibility to be humanly and intersubjectively available. Kant's theory of genius in the *Critique of Judgment* is thus informative for Habermas's account of neoconservatism. Kant, like Habermas, is confronted with the upholders of the possibility of incomprehensibility – for Kant Schlegel, Herder, and the others; for Habermas the postmodernists. The question is what to do with them and, here, with Habermas's analysis.

One could approach Habermas's analysis of these interlocutors by showing that he gets a number of his targets wrong, or at least that the conclusions that he draws do not counter other readings. The material on Nietzsche, for instance, seems to us simply incorrect in its accusation of Nietzsche of romantic aesthetic nostalgia. For Habermas, Nietzsche "takes leave of modernity" in favor of a stance (associated by Habermas with postmodernism as well as with archaism) that abandons the possibility of building a reasoned intersubjective consensus.[50] Insofar as the association of Nietzsche with postmodernism holds – and to some degree it must – Nietzsche and the postmodernists appear to make political action impossible or pointless or without standards. This is the gist of the Habermasian critique. Yet Nietzsche explicitly denies that he wants to return to the Greeks[51] and spends a good deal of time in the 1886 "Self-Critique" countering readings that he might have unintentionally enabled sixteen years before when the *Birth of Tragedy* was published.

When Habermas examines various "postmodernists," most especially in *The Philosophical Discourse of Modernity*, his rhetorical mode becomes quite distinctive. There is a touch of disdain, an intimation of naiveté, as if his subjects did not know that they were playing with something dangerous. The presumption is that there is a dark violence to humankind to which these writers – Nietzsche, Bataille, Heidegger, Derrida – are *apprentis sorciers*. And it is not Mickey Mouse for we have the historical evidence that what they are doing can be dangerous.

We do not think, however, that one can read the essays on postmodernity without the feeling that one has not learned very much about Bataille, Castoriadis, and the others from Habermas's critique. If Habermas is right, these writers have only constructed very interesting houses of cards on obviously untenable foundations. Generally speaking, and with the partial exception of his essays on Foucault, what Habermas has to say about "postmodernists" does not seem to us to be very engaging. We do not even mean that it is wrong; but it produces only resistance in those who do not already agree, for his opponents are given only the opportunity to admit their errors – hardly the stuff of dialogue. We are not interested here in trying to show that Habermas misunderstands his opponents.

There is something else going on. Let us approach this question from a different direction. Habermas feels compelled to attack the various postmodernists by reasserting elementary principles of formal logic.

> These discourses can and want to give no account of their own position. . . . These "theories" . . . raise validity claims only to renounce them. . . . There always emerges a symbiosis of incompatibles, an amalgam that resists "normal" scientific analysis at its core. . . .[52]

We take Habermas's arguments here to be philosophical (e.g., how can one have a valid critique of reason that proceeds with "reckless disregard for its own foundations"[53]) *and* political, that is, to be directed against the possible real-life consequences that such thought may have or legitimate. Habermas thinks that the postmodernists claim special, nonintersubjectively groundable, status for their efforts. They withdraw to a "special status of extraordinary discourse."

The postmodernists deny, in other words, that a "we" that is universal is at the basis of any objective moral discourse. Intersubjectivity does not, for Habermas, appear to require a tension with that of which I cannot speak. Now, it makes no real sense to see such a tension as between a single self and that of which the self cannot speak. The tension would have to be between a collectivity (with a language, with traditions, with a grammar – it could be a people or the discourse of morality) and that which cannot be said in that language. It is exemplified, for instance, by Wittgenstein's typical phrase, "When we speak, we say . . ." which invokes the *limits* of the "we" in order to actualize the "we." The we of universalizability is thus dependent on that availability of the nonuniversal – not just the particular, but that which cannot be comprehended in the terms of that world.

Here Habermas takes the highway that Kant in fact took, but without going by the paths that led him to it. Kant, in his theory of the genius, tried, or appeared to try, not to refute skepticism, but rather to maintain its appeal as a necessary part of the possibility of making sense. But none of this appears along the way that Habermas arrives at his notion of discourse ethics. He does feel the need to go through Kant, but he does so in the simplest of manners.

For Habermas, Kant chooses "a narrow concept of morality," focusing only on "how conflicts of action can be settled on the basis of rationally motivated action." The main tool is the categorical imperative, which although it has the "grammatical form of an imperative," is in fact a "principle of justification."[54] Habermas finds problematic in Kant the following points. First is the "unbridgeable" gap in the distinction Kant seems to make between the intelligible and phenomenal realms. Second is Kant's supposed assumption that the "individual tests the maxims of his action in . . . the loneliness of his soul" and the concomitant assumption that all transcendentally established consciousnesses will agree. Last is Kant's location of the effectiveness of the moral "ought" in autonomy, rather than in, as with discourse ethics, the intersubjectivity of discourse.[55]

Against all of these problems, Habermas makes moves that are fundamentally Hegelian: They consist in bringing moral questions and their answers into the world and making them part of practical life. The difference between practical and pure reason is in effect overcome. We are left with the establishing of the moral point of view inherent in discourse. *But if this is so, what is left then for philosophy?* It is (and Habermas as a philosopher is) to be the "guardian of rationality."[56] "What moral theory can do and should be trusted to do," he writes, "is to clarify the universal core of our moral intuitions and thereby *refute* value skepticism."[57] The philosopher is not privileged to know answers; he (or she) has only a responsibility to maintain the understanding that answers must have the quality of rationality and that rationality is available. Rationality is in this vision something that humans need to have kept for them.

"Value skepticism" is what bothers Habermas – the claim against all claim of reason that there are no reasonable claims to be made.

And, as we have seen, it bothers him philosophically and politically. And it bothers him because he thinks that it is a protean cousin to what Kant calls *Schwärmerei* – enthusiasm, fanaticism.[58] Habermas is distressed that value skepticism has been reborn in recent years and his mode is to stamp it out. But Kant had, already in the *First Critique*, posed the possibility of the fact that skepticism (and fanaticism) were built into the human condition, that this possibility was a condition of our knowledge itself. Famously:

Human reason has this peculiar fate that in one species of its knowledge it is burdened by questions which, as prescribed by the very nature of reason itself, it is not able to ignore, but which transcending all its powers, it is also not able to answer.[59]

We take the insistence to answer the question that humans are unable to ignore but cannot answer to be the foundation of skepticism and the refusal to entertain this question to be the foundation of fanaticism.[60] From this reading, one would say that the task of the *First Critique* (and that of genius) was not to establish rationality at the *expense* of sense with its doubt and certainties, but to establish rationality as a *balance* between the subjective and the objective, without denying either of them. The existence of two worlds that so distresses Habermas is for Kant the formulation of *ambivalence* as a necessary quality of knowledge that is human knowledge.[61]

One of the consequences of this way of approaching Kant is to change the focus of skepticism, including value skepticism. It follows, I think, from the preceding that skepticism has reference not to that which cannot be known but to that which can. It is precisely that which is rational which is also the realm of skepticism. From this it follows, we think, that if we try to eradicate skepticism (as Habermas enjoins us to in relation to values), that we also give up knowledge. And if this is so, then for all their exaggerations and all the sillinesses of some of their epigones, we owe a debt, we should think, to those whom Habermas attacks in *The Philosophical Discourse of Modernity*. They may just have found us on a road in knowledge.

Why does Habermas not want to think this about Kant? Or, one might ask, why is it that Habermas thinks that Kant is unproblematic? The answer comes, we think, in his understanding of language. He indicates that any "meaningful expression . . . can be identified from a double perspective, both as an observable event and as an understandable objectification of meaning. We can describe, explain, or predict a noise equivalent to the sounds of a spoken sentence without having the slightest idea of what this utterance means."[62] There is thus for Habermas a "purely cognitive, noncommunicative use of language" which is "*about* the world" (his italics). This use or kind of language does not involve us in a community of discourse. Getting language that is about the world right is a matter of epistemology; getting the language of community right is a matter of hermeneutics. Habermas goes on to show that hermeneutics involves us in a rational (and not merely interpretive) process.[63]

We are back with this to the classical distinction of the *Natur-* and *Geisteswissenschaften,* with the difference that objective rationality can be found also in the latter, which must therefore be clearly distinguished from "literary criticism, literature [or] religion."[64] Habermas's development of his position is ingenious and complex. But it implies, we think, only a codification of the most standard positivistic conclusions about the relation between knowledge and literature (or religion,[65] but that is another matter).[66] The dismissal – for it is that – of literature as in no important relation to philosophy reveals much. Poetry does not appear as part of knowledge for Habermas. We do not pretend to resolve this question here, but we do claim that it cannot be resolved as obvious.

One way to think of postmodernism – a way Habermas must deny himself because of this residual positivism – is that it seeks to maintain the necessity of the tension between the comprehensible and the uncomprehended. This has always been the miracle of literature. Postmodernism is not literature because it seeks to create that tension, rather than exemplify it. But it understands its relation to literature and constantly seeks to work on it. During his discussion of Foucault's essay on Kant's "What Is Enlightenment?" Habermas expresses surprise that Foucault presents himself as the heir of the Enlightenment.[67] He need not have. Foucault knew, we think, what Schlegel had realized 150 years earlier: "It is equally fatal to the mind to have system and to have none. It will simply have to combine the two."[68]

One point more. When Habermas attacks the revisionist historians, he does so in the name and from the stance of what he calls "the better traditions in our history."[69] Shortly before that passage he is explicit about the intrinsic link between the form of life in which Auschwitz was possible and "our form of life," by which he can only mean the German. It is hard to escape the conclusion that it is Auschwitz that requires of all Germans that they speak in terms that are universal. Fine – but where does that leave the rest of us? It cannot be that Habermas thinks (as one might surmise that Rawls does[70]) it is sufficient to say that non-German Westerners have completely assimilated the spirit of the Enlightenment. For such a conclusion there would be two problems. First, the evidence is not at all convincing – in twenty-five years Rawls has identified only slavery and religious toleration as evidence. There is a fascism in us all, we suspect, or, rather, we deny that there is at the peril of succumbing to it. Second, the romantic critique of the Enlightenment forces on us the need not to deny that the Enlightenment requires its critique. *No one can be guardian of rationality* – which means that the role that Habermas reserves to the philosopher needs to be approached with great caution.

These reflections in no way deny the real achievements of Habermas's project. They do, however, account in some small way, we think, for the fact that many of those who admire Habermas (and who are identified, if not by themselves, as "Habermasians") spend a great deal of their time trying to make minor adjustments to his work and trying to attach yet more theorists to it. Perhaps that is a sign of the openness of his work to others; perhaps it is a sign of a need to get everyone who can be on our side in the fort before the barbarians arrive.

NOTES

1 Jürgen Habermas, "Die Moderne: ein unvollendetes Projekt," in *Kleine Politische Schriften*, I–IV (Frankfurt: Suhrkamp, 1981), p. 462. Translation in Richard Wolin's "Introduction" to Habermas's *The New Conservatism* (Cambridge, Mass.: MIT Press, 1989), p. xxvi.
2 Jürgen Habermas, *Knowledge and Human Interests* (Boston: Beacon Press, 1971), p. vii. Note that this book originally appeared in German in 1968 and is in the context of European thought at that time somewhat conservative; whereas in the United States, just rediscovering the Continental tradition, it is on the progressive Left.

3 Habermas, *New Conservatism*, p. 42

4 Ibid., pp. 44–45.

5 Jürgen Habermas, *The Philosophical Discourse of Modernity* (Cambridge, Mass.: MIT Press, 1987), pp. 336–37.

6 Jürgen Habermas, *Moral Consciousness and Communicative Action* (Cambridge, Mass.: MIT Press, 1990), p. 208 (henceforth MCCA).

7 *New Conservatism*, p. 210; see p. 233.

8 *Philosophical Discourse of Modernity*, pp. 167, 184. A more sympathetic but similar set of moves as those Habermas makes about Derrida have been made about Freud by David Bakan, *Sigmund Freud and the Jewish Mystical Tradition* (Princeton, N.J.: Van Nostrand, 1958).

9 *New Conservatism*, p. 233, our emphasis.

10 Cited by Jacques Derrida, *De l'esprit* (Paris: Galilée, 1987), p. 111.

11 *Philosophical Discourse of Modernity*, p. 367.

12 Ibid., p. 18. Historically, Habermas indicates, the principle of subjectivity was established by "the Reformation, the Enlightenment, and the French Revolution" (p. 17).

13 Ibid., p. 18 and *The Theory of Communicative Action*, Vol. II: *Lifeworld and System* (Boston: Beacon Press, 1987), p. 95.

14 *Philosophical Discourse of Modernity*, p. 201.

15 Ibid., p. 311.

16 Ibid., p. 305.

17 Ibid., pp. 315 and 341.

18 Ibid., p. 312; emphasis added.

19 Habermas's lack of extended (published) interest in Kant derives, I believe, from his insistence on viewing Kant through the perspective of Hegel, who, for Habermas, is the "first philosopher to develop a clear concept of modernity." Indeed there is almost a resistance to Kant, and Habermas spends considerable time differentiating his "discourse ethics" from Kantian ethics. (See MCCA, pp. 195–211.)

20 I. Kant, *Critique of Pure Reason* (New York: St. Martin's Press, 1969), Bxxii, fn; A463/B491 (p. 422 in N. K. Smith translation); and A465/B493 (p. 423).

21 Ibid., A751–52/B779–80 (pp. 601–2).

22 Ibid., A778/B806 (pp. 617–18).

23 Kant writes: "The endless disputes of a merely dogmatic reason thus finally constrain us to seek relief in some critique of reason itself, and in legislation based on such criticism. As Hobbes maintains, the state of nature is a state of injustice and violence, and we have no option save to abandon it and submit ourselves to the constraint of law. . . ." [Ibid., A778/B806 (pp. 617–18)].

24 Ibid., A820/B848 (p. 645).

25 The first two quotes are from A202/B247 (p. 227). The third is from A112 (p. 139).

26 *Prolegomena*, pp. 46–47.

27 *Metaphysics of Morals*, trans. Mary Gregor (Cambridge: Cambridge University Press, 1991), p. 226 (pp. 429–30 in the Ak. edition).

28 J. F. Lyotard, *Post-Modernism Explained* (Minneapolis: University of Minnesota Press, 1993), pp. 2–4.

29 *Philosophical Discourse of Modernity*, p. 309.

30 Ibid., p. 322.

31 See Frederick C. Beiser, Introduction to *The Fate of Reason* (Cambridge, Mass.: Harvard University Press, 1987), 6, 37–43; and Lewis White Beck, "The Meta-Critique of Pure Reason," in *Essays on Kant and Hume* (New Haven, Conn.: Yale University Press, 1978), pp. 20–37.

32 *Philosophical Discourse of Modernity*, p. 322.

33 See Luanne Frank, "Herder and the Maturation of Hamann's Metacritical Thought: A Chapter in the Pre-History of the Metakritik," in *Johann Gottlieb Herder: Innovator through the Ages*, ed. Wulf Koepke (Bonn: Verlag Herbert Grundmann, 1982), pp. 157–89.

34 I. Kant, *Critique of Judgment*, Pluhar Translation §40 295 (161 in Pluhar).

35 I. Kant, *Anthropology* §59, p. 228 (p. 128).

36 Ibid., Ak. p. 241.

37 *Critique of Judgment*, "Introduction" §VI p. 187 (p. 27). He writes: "It is only because the commonest experience would be impossible that we have come to mix [the pleasure in the beautiful] with mere cognition and no longer take any special notice of it."

38 Kant's theory of genius is often given short shrift in the critical system because Kant himself often disparages genius and works of art in general in favor of natural beauty. The distinction, though, is actually illegitimate, since it is nature that ultimately stands behind both genial and natural art. See *Critique of Judgment* §46 p. 307 (p. 174).

39 Ibid., §47 p. 308 (p. 176).

40 Ibid., §49 p. 315 (p. 183).

41 Ibid.

42 *Anthropology* §52 p. 216 (p. 113).

43 Ibid., §58 p. 225 (p. 125); see also *Critique of Judgment* §46 p. 308 (p. 175).

44 *Anthropology* §30 p. 172 (p. 62).

45 Although we cannot develop it here, the lineal descendant of this understanding can be found in Søren Kierkegaard, "On the Difference between a Genius and an Apostle," *The Present Age* (New York: Harper and Row,

1962), pp. 89 ff and *On Authority and Revelation* (Princeton, N.J.: Princeton University Press, 1966), pp. 92–139.

46 *Anthropology*, §53 p. 219 (p. 117).

47 *Critique of Judgment*, § 50 p. 319 (p. 188).

48 Ibid., §47 p. 309 (p. 177), our emphasis.

49 Ibid., § 17 p. 232fn (p. 79).

50 An extended critique of Habermas's position has been accomplished by David Wellbury, "Nietzsche – Art – Postmodernism: A Reply to Jürgen Habermas," in *Nietzsche in Italy*, ed. Thomas Harrison (Stanford: Stanford University Press, 1988), pp. 77–100.

51 See Tracy B. Strong, *Friedrich Nietzsche and the Politics of Transfiguration* (Berkeley and Los Angeles: University of California Press expanded ed., 1988) pp. 135–85 and "Aesthetic Authority and Tradition: Nietzsche and the Greeks," *History of European Ideas*, 11, (1989): 989–1007. Cf. Nietzsche: "We must overcome even the Greeks" ("Die fröhliche Wissenschaft" [Gay Science]) in *Nietzsche Werke*, ed. Giorgio Colli and Mazzino Montinori (Berlin: de Gruyter, 1973), Abteilung 5, Band 2, para 340; see also the problem of Socrates in "Götzen – Dämmerung" [The Twilight of the Gods], in *Nietzsche Werke*, Abteilung 6, Band 3, para. 9).

52 *Philosophical Discourse of Modernity*, p. 336

53 Ibid., p. 337

54 MCCA, pp. 197–98

55 Ibid., pp. 202–4

56 Ibid., p. 20

57 Ibid., p. 211, our emphasis.

58 I. Kant, *Critique of Pure Reason*, B 128, p. 128.

59 Ibid., A vii, p. 7.

60 It is the problem of Oedipus and Othello, among others.

61 We are informed here centrally by Stanley Cavell, *In Quest of the Ordinary* (Chicago: University of Chicago Press, 1988) pp. 30–32.

62 MCCA, p. 23

63 Ibid., pp. 24–26

64 Ibid., p. 28

65 For some ideas as to why this positivistic attitude toward religion may not be tenable, see Tracy B. Strong, "How to Write Scripture: Words and Authority in Thomas Hobbes," *Critical Inquiry* (Autumn 1993)

66 This has been noticed in a somewhat different context by Richard Rorty in *Objectivity, Relativism, and Truth*. Vol. I. *Philosophical Papers* (Cambridge: Cambridge University Press, 1991), p. 168.

67 *New Conservatism*, p. 178

68 F. Schlegel, *Athenaeum*, Fragment No. 53

69 *New Conservatism*, p. 234

70 John Rawls, "Justice as Fairness: Political Not Metaphysical," *Philosophy and Public Affairs* 14, no. 3 (Fall 1985): pp. 223–51, reprinted in ed. Tracy B. Strong, *The Self and the Political Order* (Oxford: Blackwell, 1992)

12   The other of justice: Habermas and the ethical challenge of postmodernism

Injustice is the medium of real justice.

Theodor W. Adorno

If the philosophical movement of postmodernism was, in its beginnings, apparently strictly directed against every kind of normative theory, then this initial reticence has since given way to a dramatically changed attitude. Writers like Derrida and Lyotard, at first primarily concerned with a radical perpetuation of the critique of reason, turn today to questions of ethics and justice to such a degree that commentators are already speaking of an ethical turn.[1] The field of moral theory, which until recently had constituted for all representatives of poststructuralism a particularly salient example of modernity's compulsive universalism, has now become the true medium for the further development of postmodern theories. The change of attitude accompanying such a reorientation can be understood in part as a reaction to a critique that had been harbored for some time among philosophers and political theorists. Quite early in its development, not only critics but also partisans of postmodernism raised the objection that if the program of philosophical critique is exhausted in the language-theoretic subversion of metaphysics, this will necessarily lead to an indeterminacy in respect of ethical-political matters; for it is both with an interest in the expansion of human freedom and with the objective of simply destroying established systems that it is possible to direct criticism and protest against the uniform ideas of the European intellectual tradition.

I am grateful to Rainer Forst, John Farrell, and Stephen White for criticisms and suggestions. Translated from German by John Farrell.

289

Thus, in order to avoid the danger of ethical indifference, what is needed is the additional specification of the normative-political orientations according to which the critique of metaphysics is to be guided. But it is probably not just the attempt to invalidate objections of this kind that has recently occasioned the recurrence of ethical considerations in the philosophical movement of postmodernism. The very intention of criticizing metaphysics also carries with it certain normative-political consequences, as the example of Adorno's philosophy shows: Whoever attempts to uncover the separated and the excluded in the thought systems of the philosophical tradition is driven finally with a certain necessity to ethical conclusions, at least when, with regard to these "others," it is a matter not of cognitive alternatives but of human subjects. In such cases it appears justified to comprehend the element sacrificed to uniform thinking, that is, the unmistakable particularity of concrete persons or social groups, as the essential core of every theory of morality or justice. For this reason, the ethics of postmodernism today also proceeds theoretically from the idea of morally considering the particular, the heterogeneous. Not unlike Adorno's unwritten theory of morality, this ethics revolves around the idea that it is only in dealing appropriately with the nonidentical that the claim to human justice can be redeemed.

Of course, nothing very much has been stated by merely referring to this central motif, since various forms of ethics can be developed from it. Everything depends upon how one determines both the meaning of the particular worthy of protection and the kind of moral protection to be provided. There immediately arises a whole spectrum of possible alternatives, each of which constitutes a different version of a postmodern ethics. The threatened element of particularity can be seen in the singularity of a social language game, in the irrevocable difference of all human beings, or in the individual human being's constitutive need of help; and the kind of consideration, which is to protect that element morally, can be comprehended as an extended form of socially equal treatment, as an intensification of ethical sensitivity, or as an asymmetrical obligation between people. My reconstruction of the various approaches will amount to the thesis that only the last of these three alternatives leads to a form of postmodern ethics that represents a real challenge for modern theories of morality in the Kantian tradition. While the ethical concerns of the first two alternatives can be justified more appropriately within the framework constituted by Habermasian discourse ethics, the third approach remains conceptually intractable for such an ethics. Here, as I would like to demonstrate, particularity is introduced as a moral reference point in such a way that its consideration is guaranteed not by an expansion of the justice perspective but by its other, human care. The moral point of view of equal treatment – as we shall see – requires continuous correction and supplementation by a viewpoint indebted to our concrete obligation to individual subjects in need of help. I would like to proceed by first (I) presenting the reflections advanced by Jean-Francois Lyotard for justifying a postmodern ethics. One can show not only that this conception is compatible with discourse ethics but also that it can be articulated better within that framework, since its normative core is nothing but a radicalized idea of equal treatment. In a second step (II) I would like to turn to the novel reflections of Stephen K. White, who goes back to ideas of the later Heidegger in order to outline the basic features of a postmodern ethics. In comparison to conventional Kantianism, his contribution does indeed give effect to new perspectives; but they are constituted in such a way that they can be explicated productively within the framework of discourse ethics. Only in the reflections recently engaged in by Jacques Derrida, relying on the work of Emmanuel Levinas, do moral points of view emerge which go beyond the conceptual horizons of discourse ethics. His contribution to a postmodern ethics, which I shall deal with in the third part (III), ties to moral responsibility for the concrete other a perspective that is not congruent with the idea of equal treatment, but rather conflicts with this idea. From this perspective, care or help can be elaborated – in a final step (IV) and in critique of Habermas's ideas – as the moral point of view that forms as necessary a counterpoint to the justice perspective as the viewpoint of solidarity does on the other side.

I

Already at the end of his study on the "postmodern condition" Lyotard made the first reference to a concept of justice that, in contrast to the tradition of moral universalism, is to guarantee the protection of the heterogeneous. These somewhat casual remarks were then followed – in a work whose title alludes to Kant: *The Differend: Phrases in Dispute* – by an argument that, though still cryptic, is, on the whole, easier to reconstruct.[2] The departure point of the reflections forming the moral-philosophical core of both books is a specific version of the thesis that we are living under the conditions of postmetaphysical thinking today – and indeed, irreversibly so. Under the pressure of the historical experiences that have markedly shaped our century, any possibility of narratively legitimating the course of human history by referring to a supraindividual subject has vanished once and for all. For Lyotard, the end of the "grand narratives," as exemplarily represented by the philosophies of history of Marxism and liberalism, is also accompanied by the dissolution of the universal claim to reason which the sciences could hitherto unassailably assert for themselves; for their precedence over other forms of knowledge was secure against objection only as long as they could parasitically utilize the circumstance that they were constantly ascribed the role of an emancipatory force in all reconstructions guided by a philosophy of history. If, therefore, with the overcoming of metaphysical thinking, the legitimating source of the sciences has also dried up, then it becomes evident for the first time that no form of knowledge is, by nature, equipped with a superior epistemological competence; rather, numerous linguistically articulated forms of knowledge confront one another in social reality, and it is not possible on the basis of reason to decide which of them can raise a legitimate claim to validity. Thus, like Rorty, Lyotard starts off with the premise that the truth of a linguistically articulated validity claim is measured by the degree to which it has attained social predominance.

From this first thesis, which of course has not gone uncontested,[3] Lyotard proceeds in a second step to a detailed analysis of the characteristics that the field of linguistic utterances possesses. In his short study on the "postmodern condition," an idea dominates that reminds us of Foucault's "orders of discourse," even though it is introduced with reference to Wittgenstein. According to this idea, human language provides a potential for aesthetic possibilities of expression, and social groups compete permanently with one another for the appropriation of these possibilities. In *The Differend*, by contrast, a somewhat different model appears, one that is again explained by referring to Wittgenstein, although it now displays a certain proximity to cybernetics. Reaching understanding (*Verständigung*) in language is presented here as an anonymous process in which sentences are interlinked according to certain rules, enabling thereby an exchange between the sender and recipient.[4] Now, in Lyotard's view, this process is characterized by the circumstance that a principle of strict incommensurability prevails between the various rule systems according to which the specific possibility of linking sentences is measured: Every rule system or, as *The Differend* states, every genre of discourse follows a logic of argumentation that, in a strict sense, is incompatible with that of every other genre of discourse. For this reason, there can be no rationally verifiable transitions between the various language games whose employment obeys such a particular genre of discourse; rather, the collision of two sentences belonging to different genres of discourse means a "dispute" (*Widerstreit*)[5] in the sense that a comparison (of whatever kind) between them is no longer possible. Lyotard now only needs to draw the conclusions from this argumentation to arrive at the striking thesis that every sentence can conjure away the preceding utterance without a trace; for if the two sentences belong to different genres of discourse, the validity claim of the first sentence is fully obliterated by the validity claim of the second one, since the former can be neither perceived nor articulated in the latter's logic.

Lyotard uses this last thesis as an argumentative bridge to the moral-philosophical conclusions of his reflections; however, the basic idea behind these conclusions is not as obscure as the theory of language sketched here could lead one to believe. First, Lyotard translates what he has hitherto described as a purely linguistic event into one with moral character: The morally neutral fact that the validity claim of a linguistic utterance is not met by an appropriate rejoinder now becomes the fact of an "injustice" that the succeeding sentence perpetrates on the preceding one.[6] Because the scarcely plausible assumption that linguistic entities enjoy rights (of whatever kind) would have to be associated with such a claim, Lyotard's next step consists in reimporting human subjects into his theoretical system of concepts. While they were first totally ostracized from the linguistic event (*Sprachgeschehen*) because of an objectivistic approach, they now unexpectedly reappear in it as the agents of linguistic utterances. This becomes apparent, for instance, in the examples introduced to prove historically the injustice of the untranslatability of one language game into another: the survivors of Nazi concentration camps, whose moral grievances are gradually being silenced, because they do not find an appropriate medium of articulation in the genre of discourse constituted by formal law; and the workers, whose protest against unacceptable working conditions ultimately ends in silent indignation, because it cannot find expression in the language of economic efficiency. If examples of this kind are systematically generalized, we come to the intuition that probably represents the moral-philosophical core of Lyotard's reflections: Because in our society certain genres of discourse, particularly those of positive law and economic rationality, have achieved an institutionally secured predominance, certain language games with a different kind of validity remain almost permanently excluded from societal articulation. To rescue this "silent" dispute from the danger of being forgotten, a political-ethical orientation is necessary, one that can help the socially repressed, anomalous side find articulation.

At this point, Lyotard could choose between two alternatives in order to develop a model for philosophical ethics from his moral intuitions. He could reconcile himself to the social dominance of certain language games and assign to ethics the resigned task of again and again bearing "witness" to the existence of inarticulate interests and needs. Moral protection of the particular would then mean the ceaseless, but practically ineffective attempt to preserve in memory, and in the medium of another language, societally repressed experiences of suffering. Or else Lyotard could envision a critique of the predominance of certain language games and turn to the justification of a philosophical ethics whose normative goal is to open societal communication to hitherto ostracized language games. Moral protection of the particular would then mean the politically effective attempt to provide all subjects with the equal chance to publicly articulate their interests and needs. So far, Lyotard has not really decided between these two models – if I read him correctly. Sufficient evidence can be found in his writings both for the idea of ethics merely bearing witness and for the notion of envisioning a new form of justice with the help of this ethics. The first model, which displays a faint resemblance to Adorno's thoughts, can hardly be satisfactory for Lyotard, because it would mean forgoing every practical implementation of justice. As long as he retains the intention of bringing about a new form of justice[7] with his conception of "postmodernism," he will have to choose the second model. However, working this out would require of Lyotard an argumentation that would point in the direction he has so far emphatically and consistently opposed; after all, Habermasian discourse ethics is also based on the idea – as its morally propelling motif – that every subject must get an equal chance to articulate his or her interests and needs.

When viewing our present world, Habermas, like Lyotard, assumes a constitutive pluralism of competing ideals of life and value orientations; and just like the latter, he reckons with a society in which institutional and language barriers are responsible for the fact that only some of these dispositions reach a level of public articulation. In contrast to Lyotard, however, Habermas has been convinced from the outset that a critique of these circumstances necessitates the development of a moral theory that must have normative character: For him, there is no doubt that restrictions on societal communication are to be described as "injustice" only if they can be proven to be violations of justified claims raised by human beings. Habermas has attempted to provide such a moral justification with his draft of a discourse ethics. This ethics contains at its core that stock of universalist principles which Lyotard cannot completely forgo either, if he wishes to further develop his conception in the direction of a critique of the given relations of communication.

Habermas arrived at the basic assumptions of discourse ethics by taking as his starting point a premise that he shares with the entire Kantian tradition of moral theory:[8] Under modern conditions, individual ideals of life diverge to such an extent that, in view of moral-practical conflicts, ethics cannot normatively recommend particular values anymore, but can only provide a specific procedure of conflict resolution; and in order for it in turn to be able to satisfy moral claims, this procedure must give expression to the substantive conviction that all human beings have to respect one another as free and equal persons. In contrast to tradition, however, Habermas defends the thesis that Kant draws false conclusions from his correct initial thesis when he goes on to determine the appropriate procedure. The formulation of the categorical imperative evokes the misleading impression that every subject has to fend for him- or herself in moral conflicts and is separated from all the others affected by an abyss of speechlessness. That is why Habermas, in cooperation with Karl-Otto Apel, gives Kant's proposed procedure a formulation that attempts to take the linguistic intersubjectivity of the subject into consideration; accordingly, the universalization test (with whose help Kant has the individual subject check whether moral validity can be ascribed to the practical norms of his or her action) must now be conceived of as a procedure that can find appropriate application only in a discussion among all those potentially affected. Therefore, a subject must now explore whether a disputed norm can redeem the claim to universal validity not just in the light of his or her own particular arguments, but also against the background of the arguments of all those also affected. But Habermas sees an additional argument connected to this reformulation of the categorical imperative, one that can already be understood as an indirect reference to the normative standard of a conception of justice: If a moral norm may be regarded as justified only on the condition that all those potentially affected have agreed to it, then we must be able to assume – in principle always – that each of them has equally had the chance to take (free of constraint) a position (*Stellungnahme*) for or against it; for without such an assumption we would not be in a position to regard the agreement reached as an expression of the interests of all those involved. To that extent, however, the possibility of making the validity of norms dependent on a procedure of discursive will formation is tied to the transcendental idea of a discourse free from domination.

Of the many consequences accompanying this fundamental moral-theoretic idea, only those that can clarify the normative problems associated with the conception of dispute are of interest here. At various levels of his argumentation Lyotard is forced, against his own intentions, to employ moral ideas of the kind present in discourse ethics. Even the departure point of his analysis cannot be described at all appropriately without having recourse to the normative principle of discursive will formation. Only if we make the assumption that all those involved in a practical conflict have in fact been able to articulate their interests and views, can we establish in the first place whether there is a "dispute" between different genres of discourse. If, on the other hand, it is the case that some of those involved have not been able to express their convictions unconstrainedly because they were prevented from doing so by institutional or language barriers, then discourse ethics intercedes at a second level. Now we can infer from it what normative standards we must presuppose in the critique of those communication blocks that are operative; for instance, in certain ostracizing mechanisms, in the political regulation of language, or in the psychological exercise of violence.[9] When these two theoretical levels have been reached and a case of discursive will formation is on hand, then, finally, the possibility can arise that the parties involved might diverge from one another in their value convictions or interests so much so that a moral-practical consensus cannot be reached. Because discourse ethics does not assume any force (of whatever kind) necessary to reach an agreement, under such empirically infrequent conditions it accomplishes its task by describing the procedural rules according to which fair compromises can be reached in a "dispute."[10] Taken together, all three levels show unambiguously that Lyotard simply cannot accept what he, with Rorty, seems to claim in some places: that only that language game or that belief system which has successfully asserted itself socially may raise a claim to truth. Instead, he ought to be convinced, and not without good reason, that the socially repressed, ostracized language games contain a truth claim that, unjustly, has not yet obtained recognition within societal communication. To be able to defend this conviction, Lyotard is dependent upon discourse ethics' idea that every subject must equally get the chance to articulate his or her interests unconstrainedly – and that means: free from domination. Without moral universalism, which is present here in Kant's sense, one cannot at all understand what having to defend the particularity of the suppressed language game against the dominant agreement is supposed to mean.

But in the aforementioned writings of Lyotard, there is another line of argumentation that touches upon not the question of protection but that of the affective exploration of ostracized language games. What is in the foreground is the idea that a high level of moral sensitivity is always needed in order to grasp the injustice done to the suppressed in a society. It is precisely this thought that is the departure point of Stephen K. White's reflections in which he attempts to sketch the outlines of a postmodern ethics.

II

If for Lyotard the real mistake of modernity, which a postmodern ethics has to correct, is the repression of the existence of dispute, for White it is ignorance of the particularity of the other. His reflections proceed from the thesis that the moral universalism of the Kantian tradition is dependent upon an ontological premise that necessarily leads to a selective perception of reality. A social ontology has attained predominance in modern thought, an ontology that binds societal life solely to those processes possessing the characteristic of actively intervening in the world. In contrast to that, all actions (*Handlungsvollzüge*) or dispositions showing a merely passive character have to recede categorically into the background. Within modern ethics, this ontological bias takes effect in the tendency to regard as the reference point of moral judgment only human action that leads to empirically perceptible changes. On the other hand, all actions that do not trigger a practical effect in the world remain excluded from the horizons of moral reflection. That is why, for White, modernity's ethical thinking is molded by a principle that he terms the "responsibility to act."[11] By this he means that determining the morally right or good is always oriented by the question of what moral norms ought to guide us in practical action. Now, it is not difficult to recognize what theoretical issue White has in mind at this point, but the term he employs to characterize it is not well chosen: The concept of responsibility to act can scarcely be applied to Kantian ethics because, of course, here the moral quality of an action is to be measured not according to practical consequences but in terms of individual intentions. To avoid misunderstandings of the kind arising from the distinction (not intended by White) between an ethics of intention (*Gesinnungsethik*) and an ethics of responsibility, it would probably be, in his sense, more appropriate to speak of an activity orientation on the part of modern ethics. The latter regards as the subject matter and goal of moral judgments only actions that possess an active character, insofar as they have already led to, or ought to contribute to, a practical change of the world. What White is aiming at with his initial thesis does not, however, become completely clear until we examine the basic features of the ethical viewpoint that he sees as currently competing with modernity's moral theory.

For White, it is in the philosophical approaches of Nietzsche, Heidegger, and Adorno where, for the first time, there emerge the outlines of an ethics that places itself at a distance to the activity orientation of modern morality.[12] What brought this ethical countermovement to fruition was the insight that fixation on human action is necessarily accompanied by a categorical narrowing of the field of perception: Under the pressure to act morally in an appropriate and "responsible" manner, neither the other person nor the world in toto can be perceived in their inner diversity. To that extent, the tendency to repress the particularity of the other is latently tied to the action fixation of modern moral theory. However universal norms may be grasped specifically, they always contain a call for dynamic action, one that emphatically prevents the possibility of the other person being acknowledged in his or her particularity. To counter this repressive tendency, the philosophical pioneers of a new ethics normatively distinguished attitudes and modes of conduct in which the compulsion to act is, as it were, intercepted: what Heidegger wanted to express by the concept of *Gelassenheit*, "letting be";[13] in Adorno it is "mimetic reaction." For White, in these two concepts there is the same reference to a form of individual attitude taking that is characterized by a curbing of activity and a corresponding heightening of attention for the particularity of the other: In the demeanor characterized by *Gelassenheit* or in the "mimetic" attitude, we no longer perceive the other as a mere object on which we perform our moral duty, rather we disclose him or her in the complete differentiae of his or her person. It is now only a small step from this insight to the reflections that White believes must form the core of a postmodern ethics today.

White sees in postmodernism the culmination of that philosophical movement which recognized that modern thinking leads to a narrow, schematized perception of the social other. Accordingly, an ethics attempting to rectify this central mistake of modernity must assume the form of a moral doctrine through which a sense of the particularity of the other can be reawakened. However, that can happen only if those modes of conduct that contribute to sensitizing our perception of individual particularities are declared to be virtues, as it were. Thus, it is not really surprising that White develops his idea of a postmodern ethics in the form of working out a doctrine of virtue. What is normatively distinguished here are the atti-

tudes and demeanors that share the feature of enriching our perception of other persons and thereby of heightening our moral
sensitivity as a whole. The virtues that should achieve this follow,
for White, from a systematic generalization of the attitude Heidegger wanted to isolate in the concept of *Gelassenheit*. Thus, it is a
matter of demeanors or modes of orientation in which the tendency
to actively intervene in the world is blocked to such an extent that
there is sufficient time and attention for registering individual nu-
ances and differences. As examples of these virtues of sensitivity,
White mentions the ability to listen, the willingness to be emotionally involved, and, finally, the capacity to accept – indeed, encourage – personal particularities; in short, all those modes of conduct
that are summarized in the concept of "care" (*Fürsorge*) today.[14]

Now, White ascribes to these virtues not only the moral function
of regaining an appreciation for that dimension of the particular in
other persons which was repressed under the influence of a false
ontology in modernity. Like Lyotard, he too regards his own proposal
for a postmodern ethics first and foremost as a means for according
moral protection to the hitherto ignored element of the heterogeneous and unique. Thus, the "mimetic" and *gelassen* modes of conduct should, in the future, ensure that the individual person's specific particularity be accorded greater attention and recognition than
was the case in the formalism of traditional moral theory. Furthermore, however, White assigns the previously outlined virtues the
task of contributing to the exploration of the practical manner in
which the universalist idea of equal treatment should be imple-
mented in social reality. The thesis allowing him to accomplish this
second specification of function follows from generalizing a reflection developed by Richard Rorty. What plays a central part in his
understanding of liberalism is the idea that the moral progress of
a society transpires not directly in the form of making normative
improvements, but negatively in the manner of gradually eliminating social injustice. But because exploring such injustice always requires the ability of the artist to creatively familiarize us with the
possible suffering of the other person, it is, for Rorty, aesthetic sensitivity that constitutes the true motor of moral progress.[15] White, for
the purposes of his own ethics, can now conclude from this that the
moral idea of equal treatment can be realized socially only if the
virtues enabling the perception of individual particularities are al-

ready socially given; for what injustice is done to the individual, that is, how he or she is treated unequally, can be explored only to the extent to which we have been able to familiarize ourselves – by virtue of a heightened sensitivity – with his or her personal attributes. What Rorty can thus confidently expect solely of the artist's imagination, namely a greater ability to perceive individual variations and differences, White would like to understand basically as an ethical (*sittlich*) faculty anchored in each subject: Moral everyday culture as a whole should be permeated by those virtues that allow possible suffering of the other to be visualized imaginatively. But now it is not difficult to see from this perspective that the ethics outlined by White does not really oppose, but rather supplements, that moral theory which attempts to advance, on the premises of a theory of intersubjectivity, Kant's intentions.

For discourse ethics, as is generally known, a series of problems ensues from the circumstance that the universalization test is carried out not in the form of a monological self-examination, but in the manner of real dialogues, actually conducted. Of course, the advantage of such a proposal consists in merely imagined reactions being replaced by the factual taking of a position by all those potentially affected by a contested norm. In this way the test, in which we are to check whether a norm can find universal agreement, avoids the danger of being an egocentric projection and becomes a public procedure in which all those affected can actually have a voice. However, a central problem of this proposal is connected with the much debated question of what attributes and attitudes the subjects – for their part – have to be able to bring to a discussion for it to be truly regarded as a moral discourse. Here, the reflections White engages in regarding a postmodern ethics come into contact with a series of ideas that have meanwhile been developed in the context of discourse ethics. A certain congruence between the two models does of course follow from the fact that the approach taken by Apel and Habermas proceeds from a critique of Kantian moral theory similar to the one on which White also bases his theoretical program: From the outset, discourse ethics' proposal to leave the test of universalizability to a real process of common discussion was directed against the tendency present in Kant not to leave any room, in the formal procedures of norm justification, for an exploration of the factual interests of all persons. The whole idea of a moral discourse presents, first of all, nothing other than a means through which everyone affected by a norm should get the chance to articulate publicly his or her own view and thereby become visible as an unrepresentable (*unvertretbar*) individual.[16] Thus, as with White, it was the urge to take a stand against the ignorance of the other predominant in Kant and his successors which originally called discourse ethics into existence. But the congruence between the two models goes even further as soon as it has become clear that Habermas describes discourse as a type of intersubjective argumentation that is to be disburdened of all immediate pressure to act. The reason he puts forward for this condition is comparable to the objection White levels against the activity orientation of modern moral theory. In both cases the argument is that it is only under the presupposition of a temporary distancing from the compulsion to act that the possibility exists of acknowledging the arguments or views of every other person in his or her individual particularity. Therefore, Habermas and White both see the chance of taking the particularity of the single individual normatively into consideration as dependent upon the extent to which forming a moral judgment is free from the direct pressure of coping with problems of action.

However, this last formulation gives rise to the question as to how White would actually like to have his viewpoint of responsibility for the other understood with respect to forming moral judgments. Depending on whether it is a matter of an independent moral principle or of a merely corrective supplementing of the Kantian universalization principle, the relationship to discourse ethics varies. The reflections White engages in within the context of his theoretical borrowings from Rorty do indeed suggest that in view of the two alternatives he has decided on the second interpretative possibility. That would mean that the virtues he gives prominence to should constitute not the content of a new moral principle but only the quintessence of the attitude we have to adopt when we try to apply the idea of equal treatment with the necessary sensitivity. If that is the case, there still remains, as an unsolved problem in the determination of the relationship between the two models, the question of whether the virtues mentioned do not correspond to the sociocognitive attitudes that Habermas has to be able to presuppose when he describes moral discourse as a process of intersubjectively reaching agreement. What is at issue here is a problem that has already been touched upon briefly: Discourse ethics must also face the question of the extent to which it has to distinguish normatively those modes of conduct that, taken together, can guarantee the success of a moral discourse.

A particular difficulty in answering this question follows from the fact that there are basically two problems contained in it. In the first place, it is unclear whether the model of moral discourse is at all designed in such a way that it presupposes particular modes of conduct or attitudes on the part of the persons involved. Thus the question is what sociocognitive or habitual requirements are connected with discourse ethics' main idea of entrusting the resolution of all moral conflicts of action to a procedure of intersubjective consultation. If this question is answered positively in the sense that the necessity of these attitudes is affirmed, then it is still open whether, with respect to their status, they should be distinguished normatively, if not as virtues, then at least as specific patterns of conduct. We would thereby touch upon the explosive question of whether discourse ethics is so internally bound up with the privileging of a particular form of life that it could not be completely neutral ethically. The question concerning those patterns of conduct that, in the first place, enable participation in a moral discourse is logically independent of the question concerning their normative status; but it is only after answering both questions that we can determine whether White's postmodern ethics may be understood as a spelling out of an implication of discourse ethics.

In understanding what attitudes and modes of conduct moral discourse has to presuppose, the model of ideal role taking has served as the paradigm from the beginning. The idea, which goes back to George Herbert Mead, implies that subjects can reach communicative understanding only if they can put themselves in the role of the other. Yet this model admits of various interpretations, whose differences are measured above all according to whether the process of role taking should be grasped as a cognitive or as an affective one. If the first alternative strongly accentuates the argumentative character that moral discourses have to possess, since the universalizability of norms is to be tested rationally in them, the second alternative, by contrast, emphasizes that such an intersubjective test procedure cannot be successful without a certain degree of reciprocal empathy. For Habermas, who has always resolutely defended the cognitivist interpretation, the emotivist reading is inevitably accompanied by the danger of an affectively shielded particularism: If it is supposed to be primarily empathy and intuitive understanding that subjects have to show for one another, then moral discourse quickly becomes dependent upon chance emotional ties and loses the function of being a cooperative search for truth that relates only to reasons.[17] That is why Habermas adopts for his discourse ethics only those features of the model of ideal role taking that refer to the cognitive dimension of reciprocally reaching understanding. The capabilities necessarily presupposed here are reduced to the mere ability to understand the linguistically articulated claims of all those also affected. Against this position, it is of course not difficult to raise the objection that the normative claims of other subjects can be appraised in terms of their moral weight only if at the same time the particular views – from which these claims follow – are also understood. I can acquire an understanding of the value a particular interest has for a concrete person only to the extent that I also attempt to comprehend his or her individual life ideals and modes of orientation.[18] Such an interpretation should not be confused with the thesis advanced by Seyla Benhabib that in every moral discourse a level is necessarily reached at which the persons involved have to perceive one another as concrete others;[19] for that would indeed lead to the consequence that rational discussion would be pushed so far into the background – and affectively charged care into the foreground – that it would no longer be a matter of communicatively testing the universalizability of moral norms. The aforementioned proposal, on the other hand, should only imply that this joint undertaking of the subjects involved requires more than mere cognitive capabilities, even though an agreement mediated by reasons alone is regarded as its goal. This is the case because the normative claims of individual persons can be evaluated at all only to the degree to which we, with the appropriate empathy, can also detect what part they play in their unique, particular life histories. To that extent, the success of a moral discourse also depends on the presupposition that the persons affected share many (as many as possible) of those attitudes and modes of conduct White described in his model as capabilities of passive concern (Anteilnahme). The more characteristics of this kind the discussants possess, the more likely they will all be in a position to put

themselves in the role of the other in order to come to a real understanding of each others' interests. It is, however, a different question
whether these various conduct attributes ought to be also distinguished normatively as "virtues" simply because they are regarded
as desirable.

Two different positions on this question are also becoming apparent in the theoretical setting of discourse ethics today. Here, the
particular differences are measured according to whether an empirical or a normative approach is chosen to describe the dependence of
moral discourse on certain patterns of conduct. In the case of the
first alternative, for which Habermas's contributions vouch, the relevant attitudes and modes of orientation that enable participation
in moral argumentation are seen as the result of a historical learning
process. They are thus now socially available to a high degree. That
is why discourse ethics can, for empirical reasons, bank upon meeting halfway (*Entgegenkommen*) the forms of life to which it is appropriate, but it may not, for its part, will that they be distinguished
normatively as exemplary, even virtuous modes of action.[20] In contrast to that, the second alternative defends the thesis that the position adopted by Habermas is in a certain sense inconsistent. Whoever assumes that only practical discourses represent a justified
manner of resolving moral conflicts of action, but at the same time
grants that certain capabilities, even merely cognitive ones, constitute the presupposition for this, he or she must ultimately draw the
further conclusion that the acquisition of corresponding personality
attributes be regarded as something normatively worth striving for.
From the perspective of this second position, it is thus simply a misleading way of speaking on Habermas's part when he says in a functionalist sense that a universalist morality "needs" (*bedarf*) to be in
"congruence" with postconventional forms of consciousness;[21] for
what "need" means here has much more the normative sense of
referring to something that we should all aim at as soon as we are
convinced of the validity of a universalist morality. The latter's basic
principle, the idea of equal treatment, does require a few (if only
very formally determined) personality attributes. Their pervasiveness cannot be something for which we hope, but rather something for which we normatively strive. Viewed in this way, discourse
ethics is indirectly connected to the sketch of a doctrine of virtue
in which the attitudes and patterns of conduct enabling participa-

tion in moral argumentation are described as ethically valuable.[22] If, in contrast to Habermas, affective capabilities – as given, for instance, in empathy – are also counted among these communicative virtues, then the point has already been reached from where we can recognize in White's postmodern ethics the elaboration of an implication of discourse ethics: What he, in reference to Heidegger, described as the capacity for visualizing individual particularities is a central element of the communicative virtues that can be considered here as personal presuppositions of moral discourses.

III

The postmodern models of ethics so far encountered have not really gone beyond those normative thought horizons whose borders have been more or less clearly outlined since Kant by the universalist idea of equal treatment. Be it Lyotard's wish to bring the "silent" disputes to ethical awareness, or White's to argue the case of the specific particularity of the individual person, these attempts always remain bound to that moral-theoretic conception in which Habermas has continued Kant's project under intersubjectivity-theoretic premises: namely, that every subject must get an equal chance to articulate, free of constraint, his or her interests and claims in a practical discourse that must serve to resolve moral conflicts of action in a manner oriented toward reaching understanding. Neither Lyotard nor White can in any way eschew the idea thus outlined, though they themselves may view this differently. Both of them are dependent upon the universalist principle that finds application in discourse ethics, that is, dependent at the crucial point when they seek to defend in their respective models the heterogeneous and the particular against the general. What, over and above this, Lyotard and White have introduced into the debate in terms of new, postmodern insights can best be grasped as an immanent expansion of the moral perspective outlined in the idea of practical discourse: Lyotard, by making clear that the impediments to achieving an unconstrained understanding can reach right into the societal zones of incomprehensibility, zones hardly noticed by moral theory so far; and White, by pointing out that intersubjective openness to the particularity of the individual person is dependent upon communicative virtues, which extend right into affective conduct. But however penetrating the analyses of the two authors may be, however resolutely they may point out unsuspected barriers to human communication, it is always a matter of a minor expansion of the moral point of view already formulated with greater differentiation in discourse ethics: For one can speak – in a normative sense – of impediments to achieving intersubjective understanding, of the necessity for an affective openness to the particularity of the other only if one first defends the universalist idea that every subject in his or her individuality should get the chance of an unconstrained articulation of his or her claims. In their writings, neither Lyotard nor White goes beyond the thought horizons determined by this idea. Such a move, however, can be found in the approach to an ethics which Jacques Derrida has developed in broad outlines over the last few years. Supported by Levinas's reflections, his recent writings go beyond the scope of the theories sketched so far by attempting to counter the Kantian perspective of equal treatment with a second moral point of view.

If the transition to ethics in Lyotard is grounded – with a certain stringency – in the diagnosis of the times he had already developed, then the comparable form of internal motivation is completely absent in Derrida. True, it is not difficult indeed to recognize, in the early essay he wrote on the work of Emmanuel Levinas, references to moral motifs of an entirely unique kind;[23] and, certainly, the deconstructivist interpretations, in which he has examined philosophical texts in terms of uncontrollable meaning references, can be grasped as indirect evidence not only for a new theory of meaning but also for an ethics of correct understanding.[24] But all this is not sufficient in order to explain appropriately the transition to a normative conception that Derrida has consummated in his recent writings. Instead of merely negatively explicating the indeterminacy of moral rules – as all his previously developed reflections would have suggested – one finds here the thoroughly positive outlines of an ethics that is entirely untouched by deconstructivist self-reservation. The categorial link that nevertheless maintains the connection to the earlier writings is represented, as in the other sketches of a postmodern ethics, by the concept of "individual particularity." Thus, Derrida too is concerned with the attempt to identify the point within moral philosophy where the uniqueness of the individual person must be awarded greater theoretical attention. In contrast to White, he does not see this critical point of intervention as being located at the place occupied by the moral perspective of justice in the philosophical tradition since Kant. Rather, his thesis is that only a moral perspective that is in a relation of productive opposition to the idea of equal treatment can come to terms with the individual subject in his or her difference to all others. It is this relation of tension that Derrida attempts to elaborate in his ethics; its theoretical core is formed by a phenomenology of moral experience, which has to carry the entire burden of justification.

For Derrida, the basic features of the relevant form of moral experience are apparent in the phenomenon of friendship.[25] From Aristotle to Kant, this type of human interaction always enjoyed the special attention of practical philosophy, because in friendship, it was believed, one could study how two different attitudes to morality form a unity in a single social relationship. What was consistently viewed by the classical philosophers as the particular of friendship was the fact that affection and regard, sympathy and moral respect, flow together here without relinquishing much of their individual force. Derrida has this tradition in mind when, in his essay on "The Politics of Friendship," he sets about broaching the phenomenon of the moral from the perspective of the experience of friendship. What interests him primarily is the question of how two intersubjective attitudes that refer to different kinds of human responsibility form a synthesis. In every relation of friendship, Derrida claims, there is first a dimension of the relationship to the other in which he or she appears in the role of the concrete, unrepresentable individual person. A principle of responsibility governs here, one that has asymmetrical features because I am obligated to respond to my friend's pressing request or entreaty without considering reciprocal duties. But if the relationship were determined solely by such a principle of asymmetrical, one-sided obligation, it would no longer be friendship but already love. Only in affection, which is untroubled by any other considerations, do I experience the other as a person to whom I am obligated unconditionally, that is, beyond every moral responsibility. That is why, for Derrida, a second dimension of intersubjectivity is a factor in friendship, a dimension in which the other person appears in the role of the generalized other. In this moment of generality those institutionally embodied moral principles emerge which regulate within a society the responsibility – according to symmetrically distributed rights and duties – I have for all other persons.[26] Thus, in a relation of friendship I encounter my vis-à-vis in a double role in that he or she can appeal, on the one hand, at the affective level of sympathy and affection to my asymmetrical obligations, but simultaneously wants to be respected, on the other, as a moral person just like everyone else; and it is this irresolvable tension between two different forms of responsibility that establishes the bond of friendship in the first place. However, the chain of reasoning presented so far has only shown that there are two different ways of morally relating to human subjects. In a relation of loving concern, the other appears as the exclusive addressee of asymmetrical obligations, whereas from the standpoint of valid moral norms, he or she is the addressee of obligations shared in a symmetrical way with all other subjects. What has of course not been clarified by this is the question as to the extent to which these two patterns of recognition actually oppose each other on principle; an opposition, moreover, that supposedly determines, in the form of a tension, the entire experiential field of the moral. The philosophical deliberations Derrida undertakes in the remaining parts of his essay do not provide an answer to this. Essentially, they serve to justify the thesis that in the course of a friendship various sublevels are constantly being superimposed on one another, sublevels that result from maintaining one of the two responsibilities. Derrida's position does not become clear until his essay on modern law from a deconstructivist viewpoint.[27] Here he attempts to show what law – according to its innermost form – has to contribute to justice by analyzing the productive opposition of the two types of moral responsibility.

Derrida does not spend much time in his text on an examination of the universalist content that the legal relation has received under the conditions of modernity. Indeed, there are points in it where one gets the impression that the circumstance that modern law is anchored in the moral principle of equal treatment is not sufficiently clear to him. What is of interest to us here is thus not so much the difficulties Derrida has with the moral justification of formal law in modernity, as it is the reflections in which he considers the application of law to concrete cases. According to him, the situation of application shares with the relation of friendship the characteristic that two different principles of human responsibility confront each other, and both embody equally legitimate moral points of view.

In order to justify this thesis, Derrida outlines, in a first step, how the normative founding conditions of the formal legal relation in modernity are constituted. Every modern system of positive rights is accompanied by the prescription to regulate possible conflicts of interest according to the notion that all subjects are entitled to equal chances to exercise their legally restricted liberties. The practical application of this principle of equality implies, as we know, the task of clarifying anew in each individual case of a concrete legal dispute that, and in what respect, is to be regarded as equal and what as unequal. Because there are interpretative problems associated with this which must be solved not once and for all but over and over again, the application of law has an open, hermeneutical, and procedural character. According to its structure, it is the nonterminable process of checking again and again in the case of every new conflict what, in consideration of all the relevant aspects, must be regarded as equal and what as unequal.

So far, Derrida's presentation is still largely in agreement with leading currents in recent legal philosophy. It is only in the second step of his presentation that he veers away from them. It is not the principle of equality which he regards as the principle by which the practice of applying law should ideally be oriented; rather it is the idea of a justice that considers the "infinity" of the concrete other. What is meant by this in contrast to traditional views becomes tentatively clear when the consequences of the thesis are considered. The normative idea that should guide the practice-oriented interpretation of the equality prescription does not itself come from the moral foundations of the legal system, but approaches them from without in the form of a second moral principle. In the legal relation, just as in friendship, Derrida distinguishes two reference levels that are constituted by different, but reciprocally supplementing moral points of view. The demarcation line he suggests here runs "between justice (infinite, incalculable, rebellious to rule and foreign to symmetry, heterogeneous and heterotropic) and the exercise of justice as law or right, legitimacy or legality, stabilizable and statutory, calculable, a system of regulated and coded prescriptions."[28]

Everything of course depends on what Derrida specifically means by that moral point of view from which justice is to be done, in consideration of the "absolute difference" of the individual person. In the case of friendship, it is a matter of the perspective we adopt when we love another person and have a feeling of unconditional obligation to this person. But what corresponds to this pattern of recognition, namely, love, at the social level, where we are concerned with the modern system of formal rights? Here, a brief reference must be made to the basic ethical ideas Derrida takes from the work of the philosopher of religion, Emmanuel Levinas.

For Levinas, the ethical beliefs we have so far gotten to know as the late product of postmodernism's reflecting on its own foundations are already present at the start of the path into philosophy. The departure point of his theoretical work is the thesis that the intersubjective relationship to other persons possesses a normative content that the philosophical tradition has not been able to acknowledge because of its ontological premises. As with many Jewish philosophers of religion of his time, the religious tradition of the Bible represents for Levinas a theoretical source of the first order. That is why he takes from it, even before he turns systematically to philosophy, the normative models according to which communication between humans ought to be able to be determined ethically in concepts like goodness and empathy.[29] In attempting to articulate these moral contents of experience in the conceptual frame provided by his teachers, Husserl and Heidegger, it was inevitable that he quickly ran into systematic difficulties: For all their differences, both of them determined the realm of being (*Seiende*) in the same way in terms of a context of given, finite circumstances, so that there could not be any place for that experience which occurs in the direct communication between human subjects. In encounters of this kind – and there was no doubt about it for Levinas – the other human being always faces me as a person in need of protection and concern to such a degree that I am overburdened in all my finite possibilities to act and thus concurrently become aware of a dimension of infinity. Levinas concludes from this reflection, however, something more than merely the necessity to extend traditional ontology (which continues up to Husserl and Heidegger) by the appropriate categories. Rather, he draws the far-reaching conclusion that the relation between ontology and ethics must in the first place be reversed in order to give expression to the existential priority of the interpersonal encounter over all realms of being. The categorial construction of reality must be comprehended in terms of the leitmotif provided by the ethical experience of interaction, because here there is the inner-worldly reference to a transcendence, one in comparison to which all other occurrences and events appear as merely secondary, derivative, or reified.[30] Levinas found in this idea a theoretical basis on which he could further develop his religiously motivated ethics as the fundamental philosophical discipline.

The theoretical steps that were necessary to realize this program constitute today the various layers of Levinas's philosophical *oeuvre.* Its core must of course consist in a phenomenological demonstration of the fact that we, in encountering other persons, have precisely that moral experience which can be interpreted as the inner-worldly representative of a principle of infinity. For Levinas the starting point for such a description is the sentiment present in the visual perception of a human face. If this optical process is only described genuinely enough, then it should become evident that the experience of an ethical demand is also always given. At the sight of the "face" (Ger: *Antlitz;* Fr: *visage*) of another person, we have no choice but to feel obligated to help this person immediately and to assist him or her in coping with existential problems.[31] Levinas does not, however, clarify whether such a face refers only to the faces of those objectively in need of help, that is, "the poor" and "the strange,"[32] or to the faces of all other human subjects. Yet, the answer to this question would indicate to what degree we must regard as plausible the phenomenological claim that the cognitive reference to a moral obligation is also always included in the visually given meaning horizons of a face. If, therefore, the empirical core of Levinas's ethics remains somewhat obscure,[33] then determining the necessary consequences of that perception is all the more evident: Because, at the sight of the face of another person, I am said to have no choice but to feel obligated to care for this person, I must be aware that I am restricted in my individual autonomy in the sense that my own interests are only of subordinate significance. In this situation of an unintended deprivation of liberty, there is what Levinas believes to be an inner-worldly experience of infinity: My vis-à-vis is a person who, in his or her unrepresentable individuality, is so incalculable that I am presented with the demand to render help infinitely. To that extent, the intersubjective encounter is, for Levinas, structurally bound up with the experience of a moral responsibility that contains the infinite task of doing justice to the particularity of the other person by caring everlastingly. Furthermore, only by accepting such a boundless obligation, through which the egocentrism of interest-oriented action is broken, can the individual mature into a moral person.

It is not difficult to recognize in this basic conception of Levinas's ethics Derrida's references to the idea of a justice that considers the particularity of each individual subject. Like Levinas, though without the phenomenological foundation in an analysis of the "face to face," Derrida views as a central principle of morality the asymmetrical obligation to provide unlimited care and help for the human being in his or her individual need. But Levinas did not reduce the domain of the moral to a single perspective; rather he supplemented it at a second level with a further perspective that is supposed to be in permanent tension with the first. Here we again find a theoretical construction that anticipates one we have already come across in Derrida's recent writings. Levinas introduces into the process of interaction, which he has hitherto described in his phenomenological analysis, a second dimension, in that he expands this process by adding the role of a neutral observer. The latter's perspective constitutes an authority [*Instanz*] according to which, in the normal case of a conflict between a number of duties to care, I must decide how I have to act fairly.[34] It is easy to see that this authority of a generalized "third" represents the moral point of view which has always been designated as "justice" in the tradition going back to Kant; and what is meant by this here is the perspective we adopt as soon as we direct our action according to the standard of the universalizability of normative claims. Like Derrida later, Levinas does not hesitate to fully equate this standpoint of impartial justice with that sphere in which the principles of modern law are anchored: Legal norms, insofar as they are a component of the legal order founded on equality, reflect at the level of state institutions the moral perspective that urges us to bring about a fair compromise between conflicting duties to care. Thus, by means of the system of formal rights, what was formerly the infinite and asymmetrical responsibility for the well-being of the individual is demoted to a reciprocal duty to treat everyone equally. But in this way there emerges for the individual subject, indeed even for the legal order as a whole, a tension that permeates all morally relevant conflicts; for we cannot locate a superordinate perspective that could help us to decide which of the two principles of responsibility should direct us in a concrete case: "In reality, justice does not include me in the equilibrium of its universality; justice summons me to go beyond the straight line of justice, and henceforth nothing can mark the end of this march; behind the straight line of the law the land of goodness extends infinite and unexplored, necessitating all the resources of a singular presence."[35]

The point of this line of reasoning consists of course in the fact that, in accordance with his starting point, Levinas distinguishes two different perspectives on the moral, both of which he designates, however, as attitudes of "justice" in order to be able to formulate the surprising thesis that justice always pushes beyond justice itself. The moral orientation of goodness, which is concerned with boundless care for a single, unrepresentable individual, contains a viewpoint from which it becomes apparent that injustice is perpetuated on an individual whenever he or she is treated as an equal among equals within the framework of law's moral orientation. It is only from the perspective of this interim result that Levinas can reach, in the next step, that part of his philosophical work which is sketching to drafting a social ontology. This is assigned the task of deciphering the elementary constituents of social life in such a way that their emergence becomes clear as a process of violent abstraction from that primary experience which transpires in the intersubjective encounter with the other.[36] We can, however, refrain here from presenting the ideas Levinas develops in this domain of his ethics because the theoretical point has already been reached from where we can further pursue our question. This is so because, for Derrida to be able to reach his own determination of the domain of the moral, he only had to radicalize one degree further what Levinas designated (in the line of reasoning cited above) as a tension between two moral orientations – that of "law" and that of "goodness." For Derrida, the perspectives of equal treatment and of care represent two different sources of moral orientation, between which there is absolutely no possibility for the kind of continuum Levinas seems to assume. Rather, the application of law, that is, that normative sphere in which the idea of equal treatment is embodied, encounters again and again concrete cases whose "just" resolution can be attained only if the viewpoint of individual well-being is abruptly adopted. The perspective change that occurs in such situations bears

something violent insofar as it must transpire without any legitimation in a comprehensive idea of the moral.

As we shall presently see, a weakness of this thesis consists in its
having been developed exclusively along the guidelines of modern
legal relations; for it is here that there exists a series of special arrangements that see to it that, from within these legal relations
themselves, the individual case is considered as comprehensively as
possible and in a manner that Derrida can only imagine as the addition of a goodness or care perspective from without. For the moment, however, we need only point out that Derrida claims – reveal-
ingly – that a relation of violent and irresolvable, but at the same
time productive, conflict obtains between the two moral viewpoints
Levinas distinguishes in his ethics. This conflict is irresolvable because the idea of equal treatment necessitates a restriction of the
moral perspective from where the other person in his or her particularity can become the recipient of my care; for my showing him or
her boundless concern and providing unlimited help would mean
tending to neglect the moral duties that follow from the reciprocal
recognition of human beings as equals. And this conflict is productive because the viewpoint of care continually provides a moral ideal
from which the practical attempt to gradually realize equal treatment can take its orientation – in a self-corrective manner; for it is
only that kind of responsibility which is developed in loving concern for individual persons that brings about the moral sensorium
with which the possible suffering of all other human beings can also
be perceived. But with this line of reasoning Derrida has already
gone way beyond the limits drawn today in the tradition of justice
going back to Kant, because now the attempt is being made to inte-
grate the two different moral perspectives in a single frame of orientation.

IV

In the course of his elaborating discourse ethics, Habermas has had
to confront the question of the relation between the modern idea of
equal treatment and the moral principle of care. With the development of feminist moral theory in general and especially following
Carol Gilligan's research, the criticism was soon voiced that the
Kantian approach of discourse ethics neglects those moral attitudes

in which, without considering reciprocal obligations, we attend to the concrete other and, of our own free will, provide help and support.[37] If we reconstruct discourse ethics' program again up to that point at which it was a question of the significance of communicative virtues and capabilities, it will quickly become evident that this objection is justified in a trivial sense, without however initially having systematic relevance. Every person is indeed always included in a practical discourse only as an unrepresentable individual, but the presuppositions of symmetry obtaining in practical discourse necessitate that all particular bonds be disregarded and, accordingly, that viewpoints of care recede into the background. There is no problem in such an attitude as long as practical discourse is regarded as a procedure that serves the consensual resolution of intersubjective conflicts of interest. This is so because, in the case of conflicting interests, a just form of settlement can be reached only if all the persons involved show one another the same respect, without allowing feelings of sympathy and affection to come into play. To that extent, attitudes of asymmetrical responsibility, on which, for instance, care or benevolence is based, must remain excluded from the procedure of a practical discourse from the very beginning. This does not of course answer the question of how the moral perspective of discourse ethics is at all related to the principle invoked by feminist ethics today (and rightly so) under the heading "care." It can hardly be denied that our notion of the moral does not exhaust itself in the concept of equal treatment and reciprocal responsibility, but includes those modes of conduct that consist of asymmetrical acts of benevolence, helpfulness, and philanthropy. The theoretical conclusions that Derrida drew from his research on the application problem in law are not of any help here either, because they are in danger of locating the principle of benevolence at the wrong place. In a discourse ethics' view of law, it can easily be shown that there are now in law itself standpoints, such as that of "equity," which allow justice to be done to the particularity of an extremely difficult situation without, in the process, invalidating the basic norm of equal treatment.[38] Thus, for the question of how discourse ethics relates to the principle of "care," the moral foundations of modern law do not provide the appropriate departure point. On the other hand, however, Derrida's thesis – according to which the principle of equal treatment is always in a state of both irresolvable and productive tension with the principle of benevolence – retains some of its penetrating force, even if it proves to be false with regard to law. For in the light of this thesis, it becomes apparent that Habermas's attempt to mediate between the two moral principles has the features of a precipitate and inappropriate reconciliation.

Even if discourse ethics did not necessarily get into immediate difficulties as a result of the challenge of feminist ethics, it is nevertheless necessary to provide an answer to the question of how it relates on the whole to the principle of care. For that reason, Habermas has attempted to develop his own proposal for a response in an essay devoted to the then recent work of Lawrence Kohlberg.[39] His argument amounts to the notion that the communicative presuppositions of discourse do not indeed include the viewpoint of care, but they do encompass a related principle in which it is also a matter of the "welfare of one's fellow man": Taking one's orientation from the moral perspective of "solidarity" is built into every practical discourse because here the participants must recognize one another not only as equal persons but at the same time as unrepresentable individuals. This principle, which Habermas refers to as the "other" of justice,[40] is said to share with care the feature of a concern (*Anteilnahme*) for the existential fate of other human beings, a concern that extends into the affective. It is different from care in that individual concern applies to all human beings to the same degree, that is, free from any kind of privileging or asymmetry. For Habermas, solidarity is the other of justice because with it all subjects reciprocally attend to the welfare of the other, with whom they also share, as equal beings, the communicative form of human life.

What necessarily remains unclear in such a generalized form of concern is of course the particular motives and experiences that are said to be able to lead to its development in the first place. In this context Habermas speaks of a consciousness of one's "membership in an ideal communication community," and this consciousness arises from the "certainty of intimate relatedness in a shared life context."[41] However, such a feeling of social membership in a shared form of life can be formed in the first place only to the degree to which burdens, suffering, and tasks are experienced as something shared; and because such an experience of shared burdens and hardships can, for its part, develop only on the condition of collective goals, whose definition, however, is only possible in the light of commonly shared values, the development of a feeling of social membership remains necessarily bound to the presupposition of a value community. For this reason, solidarity – understood as the moral principle of reciprocal concern – cannot be conceived of without that element of particularism which is inherent in the development of every social community, insofar as its members understand themselves as being in agreement on particular, ethically defined goals and thereby share the experience of specific burdens.[42] The fixed point of a solidary humanity can indeed be located on a normatively graded scale, but only on the extremely idealizing assumption that all human beings have, over and above their cultural differences, a shared goal.[43] Hence, in contrast to the universalist idea of equal treatment, there is something abstractly utopian inherent in the notion of a solidarity encompassing humanity; but that is all the more reason for not being able to regard it as a universalist representative of that moral principle which, in the form of unilateral care and benevolence, has always constituted a transcending element of our social world.

What, following Levinas, Derrida referred to as a caring justice that considers the infinite particularity of the individual human being has, in contrast to both equal treatment and solidarity, the character of a completely unilateral, nonreciprocal concern. The obligation accompanying it will always tend to be so extensive that even one's own autonomy in action has to be restricted to a high degree.[44] To that extent, it cannot be expected of all human beings that they assume such a form of responsibility in the same way as respect for the dignity of each individual is morally expected of them. Genetically speaking, however, the experience of this moral principle precedes the encounter with all other moral points of view because, under favorable circumstances, it stands at the beginning of the child's developmental process. Indeed, it may be the case that a sensorium for what can be called, in an unrestricted sense, equal treatment can only be developed in the first place if one's own person has had the experience of unlimited care at some time.[45] Between the two principles, however, there is not only a relation of genetic primacy but also one of reciprocal exclusiveness: An obligation to care and to be benevolent can only exist where a person is in a state of such extreme need or hardship that the moral principle of equal treatment can no longer be applied to him or her in a balanced manner. Thus, human beings who are either physically or mentally unable to participate in practical discourses deserve at least the selfless care of those who are close to them via emotional ties. But, conversely, the moment the other person is recognized as an equal being among all others – in that he or she can participate in practical discourses – the unilateral relation of care must come to an end; an attitude of benevolence is not permissible toward subjects who are able to articulate their beliefs and views publicly.[46]

Yet, in no way may we draw from all this the conclusion – as Levinas does – that care or benevolence be declared not only the genetic but also the logical foundation of all principles of the moral. What we, under modern conditions, understand as the "moral point of view" is explained first and foremost by the universalist principle of equal treatment. But what has been said so far must also be accompanied by the conclusion that care be again awarded that place in the domain of the moral which it has all too frequently been denied in the tradition of moral philosophy going back to Kant: In the same way as solidarity constitutes a necessary counterpoint to the principle of justice, insofar as it furnishes it in a particularistic manner with the affective impulses of reciprocal recognition, care represents, on the other side, its equally necessary counterpoint because it supplements this principle of justice by a principle of unilateral, entirely disinterested help. The accomplishment of Derrida's recent writings is to have discovered the irresolvable but productive tension that prevails in the domain of the moral; ultimately, they reveal that postmodern ethics has indeed taken a small, but significant step beyond the normative horizons that, constituted by the idea of equal treatment, have hitherto been the determining factor for modernity.

NOTES

1 See, among others, Simon Critchley, *The Ethics of Deconstruction: Derrida and Levinas* (Oxford: Blackwell, 1992); Richard J. Bernstein, *The New Constellation: The Ethical-Political Horizons of Modernity/Postmodernity* (Cambridge: Polity Press, 1991); Stephen K. White, *Political Theory and Postmodernism* (Cambridge: Cambridge University Press, 1991); Andrew Benjamin, ed., *Judging Lyotard* (London/New York: Routledge, 1992).

2 Jean-Francois Lyotard, *The Postmodern Condition: A Report on Knowledge*, trans. Geoff Bennington and Brian Massumi (Minneapolis: University of Minnesota Press, 1984); *The Differend: Phrases in Dispute*, trans. George Van Den Abbeele (Minneapolis: University of Minnesota Press, 1988). On the philosophical context, see Wolfgang Welsch, *Unsere postmoderne Moderne* (Weinheim: VCH, Acta humaniora, 1988), chs. 7 and 8.

3 See, among others, Seyla Benhabib, "Epistemologies of Postmodernism: A Rejoinder to Jean-Francois Lyotard," *New German Critique* 33 (1984): 103–26; Axel Honneth, "An Aversion against the Universal: A Commentary on Lyotard's Postmodern Condition," *Theory, Culture & Society* 2, no. 3 (1985): 147–57.

4 Lyotard, *The Differend*, pp. xiff.

5 Translator's note: *"Der Widerstreit"* is the German title of Lyotard's *The Differend*.

6 Ibid., pp. xi and 3ff. [Translator's note: The French term *"tort"* is rendered as *"Unrecht"* in the German translation and as "wrong" in the English translation of Lyotard's book, see ibid.]

7 See Lyotard, *The Postmodern Condition*, pp. 66f.

8 Jürgen Habermas, "Morality and Ethical Life: Does Hegel's Critique of Kant Apply to Discourse Ethics?" in *Moral Consciousness and Communicative Action*, trans. Christian Lenhardt and Shierry Weber Nicholsen, intro. Thomas McCarthy (Cambridge, Mass.: MIT Press, 1990), pp. 195–215.

9 See, for instance, the impressive analysis by Albrecht Wellmer, "The Dialectic of Modernism and Postmodernism: The Critique of Reason since Adorno," in *The Persistence of Modernity: Essays on Aesthetics, Ethics, and Postmodernism*, trans. David Midgley (Cambridge, Mass.: MIT Press, 1991); Christoph Demmerling has now further developed this approach in an instructive manner, see *Sprache und Verdinglichung: Adorno und das Projekt einer kritischen Theorie* (Frankfurt: Suhrkamp, forthcoming). From a different perspective, Foucault presented such an analysis of communication barriers; see "The Discourse on Language," trans. Rupert Swyer, in *The Archeology of Knowledge*, trans. A. M. Sheridan Smith (New York, 1972), pp. 215–37.

10 Habermas, "Morality and Ethical Life," p. 205.

11 White, *Political Theory and Postmodernism*, pp. 20f.

12 Ibid., pp. 21f.

13 Translator's note: This is White's translation, ibid., p. 45; he also employs "releasement," the translation rendered by Anderson and Freund, see Martin Heidegger, *Discourse on Thinking*, trans. John H. Anderson and E. Hans Freund (New York: Harper & Row, 1966).

14 White, *Political Theory and Postmodernism*, pp. 99f.

15 Richard Rorty, *Contingency, Irony, and Solidarity* (Cambridge: Cambridge University Press, 1989), esp. pt. III.

16 Translator's note: That is, an individual who (or, whose interests) cannot be represented by another in a discourse.

17 Jürgen Habermas, "Justice and Solidarity: On the Discussion Concerning Stage 6," in *The Moral Domain: Essays in the Ongoing Discussion between Philosophy and the Social Sciences*, ed. Thomas E. Wren (Cambridge, Mass.: MIT Press, 1990), pp. 224–51, here pp. 232ff.

18 Thomas McCarthy points in this direction; see "Practical Discourse: on the Relation of Morality to Politics," in *Ideals and Illusions: On Reconstruction and Deconstruction in Contemporary Critical Theory* (Cambridge, Mass.: MIT Press, 1991), pp. 181–99.

19 Seyla Benhabib, "The Generalized and the Concrete Other: The Kohlberg–Gilligan Controversy and Feminist Theory," in *Feminism as Critique*, ed. Seyla Benhabib and Drucilla Cornell (Minneapolis: University of Minnesota Press, 1987), pp. 77–95, esp. pp. 91ff.

20 Habermas, "Morality and Ethical Life," p. 207.

21 Ibid., p. 207. [Translator's note: In the published translation, *"bedarf"* is rendered as "has to be."]

22 Within the context of various approaches to a further development of Kantian moral theory today, one also speaks in this formal sense of the necessity of reintroducing the category of virtue; a brief overview is offered by Mary Midgley, "Virtuous Circles. Gratitude, loyalty, responsibility and the solitary chooser," *Times Literary Supplement*, June 18, 1993, 3f. An interesting proposal of this kind is made by Peter Rinderle, "Liberale Integrität," *Deutsche Zeitschrift für Philosophie* (forthcoming).

23 Jacques Derrida, "Violence and Metaphysics: An Essay on the Thought of Emmanuel Levinas," in *Writing and Difference*, translated and with introduction by Alan Bass (Chicago: University of Chicago Press, 1978), pp. 79–153.

24 See Critchley, *The Ethics of Deconstruction*, esp. ch. 1; Richard Kearney, "Derrida and the Ethics of Dialogue," *Philosophy and Social Criticism* 19 (1993): 1–14. In a very instructive manner, Ruth Sonderegger also points in this direction, see (Un)making Sense: Zur Kritik des bedeutungstheoretischen Objektivismus bei Derrida und Wittgenstein, unpublished Master's thesis, Freie Universität, Berlin, 1993, pp. 157ff.

25 Jacques Derrida, "The Politics of Friendship," trans. Gabriel Motzkin, *Journal of Philosophy* 85 (1988): 632–45.

26 Ibid., pp. 640f.

27 Jacques Derrida, "Force of Law: The 'Mystical Foundations of Authority,'" *Cardozo Law Review* 11 (1990): 919–1045. See also the helpful

review of this article by Christoph Menke, "Für eine Politik der Dekons-truktion. Jacques Derrida über Recht und Gerechtigkeit," *Merkur* 47 (Jan. 1993): 65–9.

28 Derrida, "Force of Law," p. 959.

29 Emmanuel Levinas, *Ethics and Infinity*, trans. Richard Cohen (Pitts-burgh: Duquesne University Press, 1985).

30 In a very good and illuminating manner, Susan A. Handelman's study has reconstructed this program from its Jewish sources; see *Fragments of Redemption: Jewish Thought and Literary Theory in Benjamin, Scholem and Levinas* (Bloomington: Indiana University Press, 1991), pt. a. Stéphane Mosès's paper is also helpful, see "Gerechtigkeit und Ge-meinschaft bei Emmanuel Levinas," in *Gemeinschaft und Gerechtig-keit*, ed. M. Brumlik and H. Brunkhorst (Frankfurt: Fischer, 1993), pp. 364–84.

31 Emmanuel Levinas, *Totality and Infinity: An Essay on Exteriority*, trans. Alphonso Lingis (Pittsburgh: Duquesne University Press, 1969), esp. pp. 194ff.

32 See, as a typical example, ibid., p. 245.

33 In addition to this, it is also unclear at places whether the ethical con-tent of interaction is derived primarily from linguistic structures or from the visual components of the encounter with the other. To counterbal-ance those passages which refer to the optical experience, see, for in-stance, the comments on the ethical meaning of "discourse," ibid., pp. 195ff.

34 Ibid., pp. 212–15 ("The Other and the Others").

35 Ibid., p. 245.

36 See, above all, ibid., sec. II ("Interiority and Economy").

37 See the instructive overview provided by Herta Nagl-Docekal, "Jenseits der Geschlechtermoral. Eine Einführung," in *Jenseits der Geschlecht-ermoral*, ed. H. Nagl-Docekal and H. Pauer-Studer (Frankfurt: Fischer, 1993), pp. 7–32; a strong ethics of care is defended in the same anthology by, for instance, Nel Noddings, "Warum sollten wir uns ums Sorgen sorgen?" ibid., pp. 135–71. On the justification of an ethics of care, see also Annette Baier, "The Need for More Than Justice," in *Science, Mo-rality, and Feminist Theory*, ed. Marscha Hanen and Kai Nielsen, *Cana-dian Journal of Philosophy* Supplementary Vol. 13 (1987): 41–58.

38 On this, see esp. Klaus Günther, *The Sense of Appropriateness: Applica-tion Discourses in Morality and Law*, trans. J. Farrell (Albany: State Uni-versity of New York Press, 1993); a further development is presented in idem, "Universalistische Normbegründung und Normanwendung in Recht und Moral," in *Generalisierung und Individualisierung im*

Rechtsdenken, ed. M. Herberger, U. Neumann and H. Rüssmann (Stuttgart: Franz Steiner, 1992), pp. 36–76.

39 Habermas, "Justice and Solidarity."

40 Ibid., p. 244. [Translator's note: In the published translation *"Anderes"* is rendered as "the reverse side," ibid.]

41 Ibid., p. 246.

42 See my reflection on the concept of "solidarity" in *Kampf um Anerkennung: Zur moralischen Grammatik sozialer Konflikte* (Frankfurt: Suhrkamp, 1992), pp. 196ff.

43 This I see as a deficiency of the otherwise very clear reflections of Lutz Wingert, *Gemeinsinn und Moral: Elemente einer intersubjectivistischen Moralkonzeption* (Frankfurt: Suhrkamp, 1993), pp. 210ff.

44 Will Kymlika has made this very clear in his discussion of the feminist ethics of care, *Contemporary Political Philosophy: An Introduction* (Oxford: Clarendon, 1990), pp. 238–92, esp. p. 285.

45 The reflections of Justin Oakley are pointed in the direction of such an assumption, *Morality and the Emotions* (London/New York: Routledge, 1993), ch. 2.

46 This aspect is precipitously excluded by all those attempts that want to fuse the perspective of care with the principle of equal treatment in a single principle. See, as a paradigmatic example of this, Nagl-Docekal, "Jenseits der Geschlechtermoral. Eine Einführung."

SELECT BIBLIOGRAPHY

This bibliography is intended to provide, for an English-speaking audience, a basic orientation to Habermas's major works and the current state of the controversies they have spawned. The secondary literature emphasizes works published in the late 1980s and 1990s. Earlier select bibliographies are contained in McCarthy (1982; see entry in Section III) and Rasmussen (1990; see entry in Section III). A more exhaustive effort is René Görtzen, *Jürgen Habermas: Eine Bibliographie* (Frankfurt: Suhrkamp, 1982).

I. MAJOR WORKS BY HABERMAS IN GERMAN

1954. Das Absolute und die Geschichte: Von der Zweispaltigkeit in Schellings Denken. Unpublished dissertation, University of Bonn.

1961. *Student und Politik: Eine soziologische Untersuchung zum politischen Bewusstsein Frankfurter Studenten.* with Ludwig von Friedeburg, C. Oehler, Neuwied/Berlin: Luchterhand.

1962. *Strukturwandel der Öffentlichkeit: Untersuchungen zu einer Kategorie der bürgerlichen Gesellschaft.* Neuwied/Berlin: Luchterhand.

1963. *Theorie und Praxis.* Neuwied/Berlin: Luchterhand. Expanded edition, 1971 from Suhrkamp.

1967. "Zur Logik der Sozialwissenschaften" *Philosophische Rundshau* 14, Supplement 5. Expanded editions appeared in 1970 and 1982 from Suhrkamp.

1968. *Erkenntnis und Interesse.* Frankfurt: Suhrkamp.

1968. *Technik und Wissenschaft als "Ideologie."* Frankfurt: Suhrkamp.

1969. *Protestbewegung und Hochschulreform.* Frankfurt: Suhrkamp.

1971. *Philosophisch-politische Profile.* Frankfurt: Suhrkamp. Expanded edition, 1981.

I would like to thank Patricia White, Songbai He, Jochen Kirsch, and Mike Lipscomb for their help in compiling this bibliography.

325

1971. *Theorie der Gesellschaft oder Sozialtechnologie: Was leistet die Systemforschung?* with Niklas Luhmann. Frankfurt: Suhrkamp.

1973. *Kultur und Kritik: Verstreute Aufsätze.* Frankfurt: Suhrkamp.

1973. *Legitimationsprobleme im Spätkapitalismus.* Frankfurt: Suhrkamp.

1974. *Zwei Reden: Aus Anlass der Verleihung des Hegel – Preises 1973 der Stadt Stuttgart an Jürgen Habermas am 19. Januar 1974.* with Dieter Henrich. Frankfurt: Suhrkamp.

1976. *Zur Rekonstruktion des Historischen Materialismus.* Frankfurt: Suhrkamp.

1978. *Politik, Kunst, Religion: Essays über zeitgenössische Philosophen.* Stuttgart: Reclam.

1979. *Das Erbe Hegels: Zwei Reden aus Anlass der Verleihung des Hegel – Preises 1979 der Stadt Stuttgart an Hans-Georg Gadamer am 13. Juni 1979.* with Hans-Georg Gadamer. Frankfurt: Suhrkamp.

1981. *Kleine Politische Schriften (I – IV).* Frankfurt: Suhrkamp.

1981. *Theorie des kommunikativen Handelns.* Vol. 1: *Handlungsrationalität und gesellschaftliche Rationalisierung.* Vol. 2: *Zur Kritik der funktionalistische Verunft.* Frankfurt: Suhrkamp.

1983. *Moralbewusstsein und kommunikatives Handeln.* Frankfurt: Suhrkamp.

1984. *Vorstudien und Ergänzungen zur Theorie des kommunikativen Handelns.* Frankfurt: Suhrkamp.

1985. *Die Neue Unübersichtlichkeit: Kleine Politische Schriften V.* Frankfurt: Suhrkamp.

1987. *Eine Art Schadensabwicklung: Kleine Politische Schriften VI.* Frankfurt: Suhrkamp.

1988. *Nachmetaphysisches Denken: Philosophische Aufsätze.* Frankfurt: Suhrkamp.

1990. *Die Nachholende Revolution, Kleine Politische Schriften VII.* Frankfurt: Suhrkamp.

1991. *Texte und Contexte.* Frankfurt: Suhrkamp.

1991. *Erläuterungen zur Diskursethik.* Frankfurt: Suhrkamp.

1992. *Fakitizität und Geltung: Beiträge zur Diskurstheorie des Rechts und des Demokratischen Rechtsstaats.* Frankfurt: Suhrkamp.

II. MAJOR WORKS BY HAMERMAS IN ENGLISH TRANSLATION

Books

1971. *Knowledge and Human Interests.* Trans. Jeremy Shapiro. Boston: Beacon Press.

1971. *Toward a Rational Society: Student Protest, Science and Politics.* Trans. Jeremy Shapiro. Boston: Beacon Press.

1973. *Theory and Practice.* Trans. John Viertel. Boston: Beacon Press.

1975. *Legitimation Crisis.* Trans. Thomas McCarthy. Boston: Beacon Press.

1979. *Communication and the Evolution of Society.* Trans. Thomas McCarthy. Boston: Beacon Press.

1983. *Philosophical-Political Profiles.* Trans. Frederick Lawrence. Cambridge, Mass.: MIT Press.

1984. *The Theory of Communicative Action.* Vol. I. *Reason and the Rationalization of Society.* Trans. Thomas McCarthy. Boston: Beacon Press.

1987. *The Philosophical Discourse of Modernity: Twelve Lectures.* Trans. Frederick Lawrence. Cambridge, Mass.: MIT Press.

1987. *The Theory of Communicative Action.* Vol. 2. *Lifeworld and System: A Critique of Functionalist Reason.* Trans. Thomas McCarthy. Boston: Beacon Press.

1988. *On the Logic of the Social Sciences.* Trans. Shierry Weber Nicholsen and Jerry Stark. Cambridge, Mass.: MIT Press.

1989. *The Structural Transformation of the Public Sphere: An Inquiry into a Category of Bourgeois Society.* Trans. Thomas Burger. Cambridge, Mass.: MIT Press.

1989. *The New Conservatism: Cultural Criticism and the Historians' Debate.* Ed. and trans. Shierry Weber Nicholsen. Cambridge, Mass.: MIT Press.

1990. *Moral Consciousness and Communicative Action.* Trans. Christian Lenhardt and Shierry Weber Nicholsen. Cambridge, Mass.: MIT Press.

1992. *Postmetaphysical Thinking.* Trans. William Mark Hohengarten. Cambridge, Mass.: MIT Press.

1993. *Justification and Application: Remarks on Discourse Ethics.* Trans. Ciaran P. Cronin. Cambridge, Mass.: MIT Press.

1994. *The Past as Future.* Trans. Max Pensky. Lincoln: University of Nebraska Press.

Forthcoming. *Between Facts and Norms: Contributions to a Discourse Theory of Law and Democracy.* Trans. William Rehg. Cambridge, Mass.: MIT Press.

Selected recent interviews and articles

1989. "Work and Weltanschaung: The Heidegger Controversy from a German Perspective." *Critical Inquiry* 15: 431–56.

1990. "What Does Socialism Mean Today?" *New Left Review,* 183:3–21.

1991. "Comments on John Searle: 'Meaning, Communication, and Representation." In *John Searle and His Critics*, ed. Ernest Lepore and Robert Van Gulick, Cambridge, Mass.: Blackwell, pp. 17–55.

1992. *Autonomy and Solidarity: Interviews.* Edited and with introduction by Peter Dews. London: Verso, rev. ed.

1992. "Citizenship and National Identity: Some Reflections on the Future of Europe." *Praxis International* 12: 1–33.

1992. "Further Reflections on the Public Sphere." In *Habermas and the Public Sphere*, ed. Craig Calhoun. Cambridge, Mass.: MIT Press.

1992. "Jürgen Habermas on the Legacy of Jean-Paul Sartre: An Interview." Interviewed by Richard Wolin. *Political Theory* 20: 496–501.

1992. "Yet Again: German Identity – A Nation of Angry DM-Burghers?" In *When the Wall Came Down: Reactions to German Unification*, ed. Harold James and Maria Stone. New York: Routledge.

1993. "Remarks on the Development of Horkheimer's Work." In *On Max Horkheimer*, ed. Seyla Benhabib, Wolfgang Bonss, and John McCole. Cambridge, Mass.: MIT Press, pp. 49–65.

1993. "Struggles for Recognition in Constitutional States." *European Journal of Philosophy* 2:128–55.

1994. "Postscript to *Faktizität und Geltung.*" In *Habermas, Modernity and Law.* Special issue of *Philosophy and Social Criticism* 4:135–50.

1994. "Three Normative Models of Democracy." *Constellations* 1: 1–10.

1995. Forthcoming. "Reconciliation through the Public Use of Reason: Remarks on John Rawls's *Political Liberalism.*" *Journal of Philosophy.*

III. SELECTED BOOKS IN ENGLISH ON HABERMAS,
COMMUNICATIVE ETHICS, AND CRITICAL THEORY

Adorno, Theodor W., ed. *The Positivist Dispute in German Sociology.* New York: Harper & Row, 1976.

Alford, C. Fred. *Science and the Revenge of Nature.* Gainesville: University of Florida Press, 1985.

Baynes, Kenneth. *The Normative Grounds of Social Criticism: Kant, Rawls and Habermas.* Albany: State University of New York Press, 1992.

Benhabib, Seyla. *Critique, Norm, and Utopia: A Study of the Foundations of Critical Theory.* New York: Columbia University Press, 1986.
Situating the Self: Gender, Community and Postmodernism in Contemporary Ethics. New York: Routledge, 1992.

Benhabib, Seyla, and Fred Dallmayr, eds. *The Communicative Ethics Controversy.* Cambridge, Mass.: MIT Press, 1990.

Bernstein, Richard J., ed. *Habermas and Modernity.* Cambridge, Mass.: MIT Press, 1985.

Braaten, Jane. *Jürgen Habermas*. Albany: State University of New York Press. 1992.

Calhoun, Craig, ed. *Habermas and the Public Sphere*. Cambridge, Mass.: MIT Press, 1992.

Chambers, Simone. *Discourse and Procedural Ethics*. Ithaca, N.Y.: Cornell University Press, forthcoming.

Cohen, Jean, and Andrew Arato. *Civil Society and Political Theory*. Cambridge, Mass.: MIT Press, 1992.

Cooke, Maeve. *Language and Reason: A Study of Habermas' Pragmatics*. Cambridge, Mass.: MIT Press, 1994.

Dallmayr, Fred. *Between Freiburg and Frankfurt: Toward a Critical Ontology*. Amherst: University of Massachusetts Press, 1992.

Deflem, Mathieu. *Habermas, Modernity and Law*. Special issue of *Philosophy and Social Criticism*, 4 (1994).

DeHaven-Smith, Lance. *Philosophical Critique of Policy Analysis: Lindblom, Habermas and the Great Society*. Gainesville: University of Florida Press, 1988.

d'Entrèves, Maurizio Passerin, and Seyla Benhabib, ed. *Habermas and the Unfinished Project of Modernity: Critical Essays on "The Philosophical Discourse of Modernity."* Cambridge, U.K.: Polity Press, forthcoming.

Dryzek, John. *Discursive Democracy: Politics, Policy, and Political Science*. Cambridge: Cambridge University Press, 1990.

Fay, Brian. *Social Theory and Political Practice*. New York: Allen and Unwin, 1975.

Critical Social Science: Liberation and Its Limits. Ithaca, N.Y.: Cornell University Press, 1987.

Forester, John. *Critical Theory, Public Policy and Planning Practice*. Albany: State University of New York Press, 1993.

ed. *Critical Theory and Public Life*. Cambridge, Mass.: MIT Press, 1985.

Geuss, Raymond. *The Idea of a Critical Theory: Habermas and the Frankfurt School*. Cambridge: Cambridge University Press, 1981.

Günther, Klaus. *The Sense of Appropriateness: Discourses of Application in Morality and Law*. Albany: State University of New York Press, 1993.

Held, David. *Introduction to Critical Theory: Horkheimer to Habermas*. Berkeley: University of California Press, 1980.

Holub, Robert. *Jürgen Habermas: Critic in the Public Sphere*. New York: Routledge, 1991.

Honneth, Axel. *The Critique of Power: Reflective Stages in Critical Social Theory*. Trans. Kenneth Baynes. Cambridge, Mass.: MIT Press, 1991.

Honneth, Axel, and Hans Joas, eds. *Communicative Action*. Trans. Jeremy Gaines and Doris L. Jones. Cambridge, Mass.: MIT Press, 1991.

Honneth, Axel, and Hans Joas, eds. *Communicative Action*. Trans. Jeremy Gaines and Doris L. Jones. Cambridge, Mass.: MIT Press, 1991.

Honneth, Axel, Thomas McCarthy, Claus Offe, and Albrecht Wellmer, eds. *Cultural-Political Interventions in the Unfinished Project of Enlightenment*. Cambridge, Mass.: MIT Press, 1992. (One of a two-volume *Festschrift* for Habermas.)

eds. *Philosophical Interventions in the Unfinished Project of Enlightenment*. Cambridge, Mass.: MIT Press, 1992. (One of a two-volume *Festschrift* for Habermas.)

Ingram, David. *Habermas and the Dialectic of Reason*. New Haven, Conn.: Yale University Press, 1987.

Critical Theory and Philosophy. New York: Paragon, 1990.

Jay, Martin. *Marxism and Totality: The Adventures of a Concept from Lukács to Habermas*. Berkeley: University of California Press, 1984.

Fin de Siècle Socialism and Other Essays. New York: Routledge, 1988.

Keat, Russell. *The Politics of Social Theory: Habermas, Freud and the Critique of Positivism*. Chicago: University of Chicago Press, 1981.

Kelly, Michael, ed. *Hermeneutics and Critical Theory in Ethics and Politics*. Cambridge, Mass.: MIT Press, 1990.

Critique and Power: Recasting the Foucault/Habermas Debate. Cambridge, Mass.: MIT Press, 1994.

Kortian, Garbis. *Metacritique: The Philosophical Argument of Jürgen Habermas*. Cambridge: Cambridge University Press, 1980.

Leonard, Stephen. *Critical Theory in Political Practice*. Princeton, N.J.: Princeton University Press, 1990.

Matustik, Martin. *Postnational Identity: Critical Theory and Existential Philosophy in Habermas, Kierkegaard and Havel*. New York: Guilford, 1993.

McCarthy, Thomas A. *The Critical Theory of Jürgen Habermas*. Cambridge, Mass.: MIT Press, 1982, rev. ed.

Ideals and Illusions: On Reconstruction and Deconstruction in Contemporary Critical Theory. Cambridge, Mass.: MIT Press, 1991.

Meehan, Johanna, ed. *Habermas and Feminism*. New York: Routledge, forthcoming.

New German Critique. Special Issue on Jürgen Habermas. 35 (1985).

Poster, Mark. *Critical Theory and Poststructuralism: In Search of a Context*. Ithaca, N.Y.: Cornell University, 1989.

Pusey, Michael. *Jürgen Habermas*. London: Tavistock, 1987.

Raffel, Stanley. *Habermas, Lyotard and the Concept of Justice*. New York: St. Martin's Press, 1992.

Rasmussen, David. *Reading Habermas*. Cambridge, Mass.: Blackwell, 1990.

Rockmore, Tom. *Habermas on Historical Materialism*. Bloomington: Indiana University Press, 1989.

Roderick, Rick. *Habermas and the Foundations of Critical Theory.* New York: St. Martin's Press, 1986.

Sensat, Julius. *Habermas and Marxism: An Appraisal.* Beverly Hills, Calif.: Sage, 1979.

Siebert, Rudolph. *The Critical Theory of Religion: The Frankfurt School. From Universal Pragmatics to Political Theology.* Amsterdam: Mouton, 1985.

Thompson, John B. *Critical Hermeneutics: A Study in the Thought of Paul Ricoeur and Jürgen Habermas.* Cambridge: Cambridge University Press, 1981.

Thompson, John B., and David Held, eds. *Habermas: Critical Debates.* London: Macmillan, 1982.

Wellmer, Albrecht. *The Persistence of Modernity.* Trans. D. Midgley. Cambridge, Mass.: MIT Press, 1991.

White, Stephen K. *The Recent Work of Jürgen Habermas: Reason, Justice and Modernity.* Cambridge: Cambridge University Press, 1988.

Political Theory and Postmodernism. Cambridge: Cambridge University Press, 1991.

Wiggershaus, Rolf. *The Frankfurt School: Its History, Theories and Political Significance.* Trans. M. Robertson. Cambridge, Mass.: MIT Press, 1994.

IV. SELECTED WORKS IN ENGLISH ON SPECIFIC TOPICS

Context and intellectual heritage

Benhabib, Seyla (1986). See book entry, Section III.

Dallmayr, Fred. See book entry, Section III.

Fleming, Marie. "Habermas, Marx and the Question of Ethics." In *Die Frankfurter Schule und die Folgen,* ed. A. Honneth and A. Wellmer. Berlin: de Gruyter, 1986, pp. 139–50.

Held, David. See book entry, Section III.

Holub, Robert. See book entry, Section III.

Honneth, Axel. See book entry, Section III.

"Communication and Reconciliation: Habermas' Critique of Adorno." *Telos* 39 (1979): 45–61.

Ingram, David (1990). See book entry, Section III.

Jay, Martin (1984 and 1988). See book entries, Section III.

McCarthy, Thomas A. (1982). See book entry, Section III.

Nuyen, A. T. "Habermas, Adorno and the Possibility of Immanent Critique." *American Catholic Philosophical Quarterly* 66 (1992): 331–40.

Pensky, Max. "On the Use and Abuse of Memory: Habermas, Anamnestic

Solidarity and the *Historikerstreit.*" *Philosophy and Social Criticism* 15 (1989): 351–80.

Phelan, Shane. "Interpretation and Domination: Adorno and the Habermas–Lyotard Debate." *Polity* 25 (1993): 597–616.

Pulzer, Peter. "Germany: Whose History?" *Times Literary Supplement* 2–8 (Oct. 1987): 1076, 1088.

Scheuerman, Bill. "Neumann versus Habermas: The Frankfurt School and the Case of the Rule of Law." *Praxis International* 13 (1993): 50–67.

Schmidt, James. "Offensive Critical Theory." *Telos* 39 (1979): 62–70.

Sensat, Julius. See book entry, Section III.

Torpey, John. "Ethics and Critical Theory: From Horkheimer to Habermas." *Telos* 69 (1986): 68–84.

"Introduction: Habermas and the Historians." *New German Critique* 44 (1988): 5–24.

Vogel, Steven M. "New Science, New Nature: The Habermas–Marcuse Debate Revisited." *Research in Philosophy and Technology* 11 (1991): 157–78.

Wellmer, Albrecht. See book entry, Section III.

Wiggershaus, Rolf. See book entry, Section III.

Hermeneutics, epistemology, and social science

Adorno, Theodor W. See book entry, Section III.

Alford, C. Fred. See book entry, Section III.

Antonio, Robert J. "The Normative Foundations of Emancipatory Theory: Evolutionary versus Pragmatic Perspectives." *American Journal of Sociology* 94 (1989): 721–48.

Apel, Karl-Otto. "Types of Social Science in the Light of Human Interests of Knowledge." *Social Research* 44 (1977): 425–70.

Baynes, Kenneth. "Crisis and Life-World in Husserl and Habermas." in *Crises in Continental Philosophy*, ed. A. B. Dallery. Albany: State University of New York Press, 1990.

"Rational Reconstruction and Social Criticism: Habermas' Model of Interpretive Social Science." *Philosophical Forum* 21 (1989–90): 122–145.

Bernstein, Richard J. "Fred Dallmayr's Critique of Habermas." *Political Theory* 16 (1988): 580–93.

Bohman, James. "System and 'Lifeworld': Habermas and the Problem of Holism." *Philosophy and Social Criticism* 15 (1989): 381–401.

Dallmayr, Fred R. "Habermas and Rationality." *Political Theory* 16 (1988): 553–79.

Davey, Nicholas. "Habermas' Contribution to Hermeneutic Theory." *Journal of the British Society for Phenomenology* 16 (1985): 109–31.

Factor, Regis A., and Stephen J. Turner. "The Critique of Positivist Social Science in Leo Strauss and Jürgen Habermas." *Sociological Analysis and Theory* 7 (1977): 185–206.

Fay, Brian (1975 and 1987). See book entries, Section III.

Ferrara, Allessandro. "A Critique of Habermas' Consensus Theory of Truth." *Philosophy and Social Criticism* 13 (1987): 39–67.

Gadamer, Hans-Georg. "Hermeneutics and Social Science." *Cultural Hermeneutics* 2 (1975): 307–30.

"On the Scope and Function of Hermeneutical Reflection." *Continuum* 8 (1970): 77–95.

Geuss, Raymond. See book entry, Section III.

Giddens, Anthony. "Habermas' Critique of Hermeneutics." In Giddens, *Studies in Social and Political Theory*. Berkeley: University of California Press, 1977, pp. 135–64.

Hesse, Mary. "Habermas' Consensus Theory of Truth." In Hesse, *Revolutions and Reconstructions in the Philosophy of Science*. Brighton/Sussex: Harvester Press, 1980, pp. 206–31.

Johnson, James. "Is Talk Really Cheap? Prompting Conversation between Critical Theory and Rational Choice." *American Political Science Review* 87 (1993): 74–86.

Keat, Russell. See book entry, Section III.

Kolb, David. "Heidegger and Habermas on Criticism and Totality." *Philosophy and Phenomenological Research* 52 (1992): 683–93.

Leonard, Stephen. See book entry, Section III.

Mendelson, Jack. "The Habermas–Gadamer Debate." *New German Critique* 18 (1979): 44–73.

Mouzelis, Nicos. "Social Systems and Integration: Habermas' View." *British Journal of Sociology* 43 (1992): 267–88.

Nicholson, Graeme. "Answers to Critical Theory." In *Gadamer and Hermeneutics*, ed. Hugh J. Silverman. New York: Routledge, 1991.

Nielsen, Kai. "Skeptical Remarks on the Scope of Philosophy: Rorty v. Habermas." *Social Theory and Practice* 19 (1993).

Nussbaum, Charles. "Habermas and Grünbaum on the Logic of Psychoanalytic Explanations." *Philosophy and Social Criticism* 17 (1991): 193–216.

Olafson, Frederick. "Habermas as a Philosopher." *Ethics* 100 (1990).

Overend, Tronn. "Enquiry and Ideology: Habermas' Trichotomous Conception of Science." *Philosophy of the Social Sciences* 8 (1978): 1–13.

Parsons, Stephen D. "Explaining Technology and Society: The Problem of Nature in Habermas." *Philosophy and Social Criticism* 22 (1992): 218–30.

Power, Michael. "Habermas and Transcendental Arguments: A Reappraisal." *Philosophy and Social Criticism* 23 (1993): 26–49.

Ricoeur, Paul. "Ethics and Culture: Habermas and Gadamer in Dialogue." *Philosophy Today* 2 (1973): 153–65.

Rockmore, Tom. See book entry, Section III.

Shalin, Dimitri N. "Critical Theory and the Pragmatist Challenge." *American Journal of Sociology* 98 (1992): 237–79.

Thompson, John. See book entry, Section III.

Vogel, Steven. "Habermas and Science." *Praxis International* 8 (1988): 329–49.

White, Stephen K. "Toward a Critical Political Science." In Terence Ball, ed., *Idioms of Inquiry*. Albany: State University of New York Press, 1987.

Whitton, Brian J. "Universal Pragmatics and the Formation of Western Civilization: A critique of Habermas' Theory of Human Moral Evolution." *History and Theory* 31 (1992): 299–312.

Language, self, and communicative action

Alexander, Jeffrey C. "Review Essay: Habermas' New Critical Theory: Its Promises and Problems." *American Journal of Sociology* 91 (1985): 400–24.

Alford, C. Fred. "Habermas, Post-Freudian Psychoanalysis, and the End of the Individual." *Theory, Culture and Society* 4 (1987): 3–29.

Bohman, James. "Formal Pragmatics and Social Criticism: The Philosophy of Language and the Critique of Ideology in Habermas' Theory of Communicative Action." *Philosophy and Social Criticism* 11 (1986): 331–53.

Cheal, David. "Ritual: Communication in Action." *Sociological Analysis* 53 (1992): 363–74.

Cook, Maeve. See book entry, Section III.

Couture, Tony. "Habermas, Values, and the Rational, Internal Structure of Communication." *Journal of Value Inquiry* 27 (1993): 403–16.

Dallmayr, Fred R. "Life-World and Communicative Action." In Dallmayr, *Polis and Praxis*. Cambridge, Mass.: MIT Press, 1984, pp. 224–53.

Geiman, Kevin Paul. "Habermas' Early Lifeworld Appropriation: A Critical Assessment." *Man and World* 23 (1990): 63–83.

Giddens, Anthony. "Reason without Revolution? Habermas' *Theorie des kommunikativen Handelns.*" *Praxis International* 2 (1982): 318–28.

Gordon, David. "Reply to Chmielewski: Cooperation by Definition." *International Philosophical Quarterly* 31 (1991): 105–08.

Grünbaum, Adolf. "Critique of Habermas' Philosophy of Psychoanalysis."

In *The Foundations of Psychoanalysis: A Philosophical Critique*, ed. Grünbaum. Berkeley, Calif.: University of California Press, 1984, pp. 9–42.

Noam, Gil G. "Beyond Freud and Piaget: Biographical Worlds – Interpersonal Self." In Thomas Wren, ed., *The Moral Domain: Essays in the Ongoing Discussion between Philosophy and the Social Sciences*. Cambridge, Mass.: MIT Press, 1990.

Sciulli, David. "Foundations of Societal Constitutionalism: Principles from the Concepts of Communicative Action and Procedural Legality," *British Journal of Sociology* 39 (1988): 377–408.

Searle, John R. "Response: Meaning, Intentionality, and Speech Acts." In *John Searle and His Critics*, ed. Ernest LePore. Cambridge, Mass.: Blackwell, 1991.

Tugendhat, Ernst. "Habermas on Communicative Action." In *Social Action*, ed. G. Seebass and R. Tuomela. Dordrecht: Reidel, 1985, pp. 179–86.

Wagner, Gerhard, and Heinz Zipprian. "Intersubjectivity and Critical Consciousness: Remarks on Habermas' Theory of Communicative Action." *Inquiry* 34 (1991): 49–62.

Whitebook, Joel. "Intersubjectivity and the Monadic Core of the Psyche: Habermas and Castoriadis on the Unconscious." *Praxis International* 9 (1990): 347–64.

Young, R. E. "Habermas' Ontology of Learning: Reconstructing Dewey." *Education Theory* 40 (1990): 471–82.

Communicative ethics

Anderson, Heine. "Morality in Three Social Theories: Parsons, Analytical Marxism and Habermas." *Acta Sociologica* 33 (1990): 321–39.

Aragaki, Hiro. "Communicative Ethics and the Morality of Discourse." *Praxis International* 13 (1993): 154–71.

Baynes, Kenneth. See book entry, Section III.

Beiner, Ronald. "Do We Need a Philosophical Ethics? Theory, Prudence and the Primacy of Ethics." *Philosophical Forum* 20 (1989): 230–44.

Benhabib, Seyla (1986 and 1992). See book entries, Section III.

Benhabib, Seyla, and Fred R. Dallmayr, eds. (1990). See book entry, Section III.

Braaten, Jane. "The Succession of Theories and the Recession of Practice." *Social Theory and Practice* 18 (1992): 81–111.

Chambers, Simone. (1994) See book entry, Section III.

Clement, Grace. "Is the Moral Point of View Monological or Dialogical?

The Kantian Background of Habermas' Discourse Ethics." *Philosophy Today* 33 (1989): 159–73.

Coles, Romand. "Communicative Action and Dialogical Ethics: Habermas and Foucault." *Polity* 25 (1992): 71–94.

Doepke, Frederick. "The Endorsements of Interpretation." *Philosophy of the Social Sciences* 20 (1990): 277–94.

Doody, John. "MacIntyre and Habermas on Practical Reason." *American Catholic Philosophical Quarterly* 65 (1991): 143–58.

Funk, Nanette. "Habermas and Solidarity." *Philosophical Inquiry* 12 (1990): 17–31.

Günther, Klaus. See book entry, Section III.

Ingram, David. "The Limits and Possibilities of Communicative Ethics for Democratic Theory." *Political Theory* 21 (1993): 294–321.

Kelly, Michael. "The Gadamer–Habermas Debate Revisited: The Question of Ethics." *Philosophy and Social Criticism* 14 (1988): 369–89.

"MacIntyre, Habermas and Philosophical Ethics." *Philosophical Forum* 21 (1989–90): 70–93.

Levin, David. "The Body Politic: The Embodiment of Praxis in Foucault and Habermas." *Praxis International* 9 (1989): 112–32.

Nielsen, Kai. "The Generalized Other and the Concrete Other: A Response to Marie Fleming." *Indian Philosophical Quarterly* 17 (1990): 163–71.

Rehg, William. "Discourse and the Moral Point of View." *Inquiry* 34 (1991): 27–48.

"Discourse, Ethics and the Communitarian Critique of Neo-Kantianism." *Philosophical Forum* 22 (1990–91): 120–38.

Shearmur, Jeremy. "Habermas: A Critical Approach." *Critical Review* 2 (1988): 39–50.

Warnke, Georgia. "Rawls, Habermas and Real Talk: A Reply to Walzer." *Philosophical Forum* 21 (1990): 197–203.

Wellmer, Albrecht. See book entry, Section III.

White, Stephen K. (1988). See book entry, Section III.

Political theory, democracy, and capitalism

Baynes, Kenneth. See book entry, Section III.

Bohman, James. "Communication, Ideology and Democratic Theory." *American Political Science Review* 84 (1990): 93–109.

Calhoun, Craig. See book entry, Section III.

Chambers, Simone. See book entry, Section III.

Cohen, Jean. "Discourse Ethics and Civil Society." *Philosophy and Social Criticism* 14 (1988): 315–37.

Cohen, Jean, and Andrew Arato. See book entry, Section III.

Deflem, Mathieu. See book entry, Section III.

Doody, John A. "Radical Hermeneutics, Critical Theory and the Political." *International Philosophical Quarterly* 31 (1991): 329–41.

Dryzek, John. See book entry, Section III.

Eder, Klaus. "Critique of Habermas' Contribution to the Sociology of Law." *Law and Society Review* 22 (1988): 931–44.

Fleming, Marie. "Women and the 'Public Use of Reason'." *Social Theory and Practice* 19 (1993); 27–50.

Forester, John (1985 and 1993). See book entries, Section III.

Hager, Carol. "Citizen Movements and Technological Policymaking in Germany." *Annals of the American Academy of Political and Social Science* 528 (1993): 42–55.

Hanks, Craig. "Thinking about Democracy and Exclusion: Jürgen Habermas' *Theory of Communicative Action* and Contemporary Politics." *Southwest Philosophical Review* 8 (1992): 145–55.

Holton, R. J. "The Idea of Crisis in Modern Society." *British Journal of Sociology* 38 (1987): 502–20.

Ingram, David. "Habermas and the CLS Movement on Moral Criticism in Law." *Philosophy and Social Criticism* 16 (1990): 237–68.

Keane, John. "Elements of a Radical Theory of Public Life: From Tönnies to Habermas and Beyond." *Canadian Journal of Political and Social Theory* 6 (1982): 11–49, and 8 (1984): 139–62.

Kelly, Michael. See book entry, Section III.

Lakeland, Paul. "Providence and Political Responsibility: The Nature of Praxis in an Age of Apocalypse." *Modern Theology* 7 (1991): 351–62.

Landes, Joan. "Jürgen Habermas' *The Structural Transformation of the Public Sphere:* A Feminist Inquiry." *Praxis International* 12 (1992): 106–27.

Mara, Gerald. "After Virtue, Autonomy: Jürgen Habermas and Greek Political Theory." *Journal of Politics* 47 (1985): 1033–61.

Marshall, T. H. "Jürgen Habermas, Citizenship and Transition in Eastern Europe." *World Development* 21 (1993): 1313–28.

Martin, Bill. "The Enlightenment's Talking Cure: Habermas, *Legitimation Crisis,* and the Recent Political Landscape." *Southwest Philosophical Review* 4 (1988): 33–43.

Matustik, Martin J. See book entry, Section III.

"Havel and Habermas on Identity and Revolution." *Praxis International* 10 (1990–91): 261–77.

Miller, James. "Jürgen Habermas, Legitimation Crisis." *Telos* 25 (1975): 210–20.

Nagl, Ludwig. "The Enlightenment – a Stranded Project? Habermas on

Nietzsche as a 'Turning Point' to Postmodernity." *History of European Ideas* 11 (1989): 743–50.

Peters, John D. "Distrust of Representation: Habermas on the Public Sphere." *Media, Culture, and Society* 15 (1993): 541–71.

Piché, Claude. "Art and Democracy in Habermas." In Hugh J. Silverman, ed., *Writing the Politics of Difference*. Albany: State University of New York Press, 1991.

Plant, Raymond. "Jürgen Habermas and the Idea of Legitimation Crisis." *European Journal of Political Research* 10 (1982): 341–52.

Rasmussen, Douglas B. "Political Legitimacy and Discourse Ethics." *International Philosophical Quarterly* 32 (1992): 17–34.

Thorp, Thomas R. "Derrida and Habermas on the Subject of Political Philosophy." In A. B. Dallery, ed., *Crises in Continental Philosophy*. Albany: State University of New York Press, 1990.

Trey, George A. "Modern Normativity and the Politics of Deregulation." *Auslegung* 16 (1990): 137–47.

Tucker, Kenneth H. "Ideology and Social Movements: the Contributions of Habermas." *Sociological Inquiry* 59 (1989): 30–47.

Tuori, Kaarlo. "Discourse Ethics and the Legitimacy of Law." *Ratio Juris* 2 (1989): 125–43.

Walker, Brian. "Habermas and Pluralist Political Theory." *Philosophy and Social Criticism* 18 (1992): 81–102.

Warren, Mark. "Liberal Constitutionalism as Ideology: Marx and Habermas." *Political Theory* 17 (1989): 511–47.

Wells, George G. "Autonomy, Self-Consciousness and National Moral Responsibility." *History of European Ideas* 16 (1993): 949–55.

Modernism and postmodernism

Benhabib, Seyla (1992). See book entry, Section III.

"Epistemologies of Postmodernism: a Rejoinder to Jean François Lyotard." *New German Critique* 33 (1984): 103–26.

Bernstein, J. M. "The Causality of Fate: Modernity and Modernism in Habermas." *Praxis International* 8 (1989): 407–25.

"De-Divinization and the Vindication of Everyday-Life: Reply to Rorty." *Tijdschrift voor Filosofie* 54 (1992): 668–92.

Bernstein, Richard J. (1985). See book entry, Section III.

"An Allegory of Modernity/Postmodernity." In *Working through Derrida*, ed. Gary Madison. Evanston, Ill.: Northwestern University Press, 1993.

Cook, Deborah. "Remapping Modernity." *British Journal of Aesthetics* 30 (1990): 35–45.

Dallmayr, Fred R (1992). See book entry, Section III.

"The Discourse of Modernity: Hegel, Nietzsche, Heidegger (and Habermas)." *Praxis International* 8 (1989): 377–400.

Dumm, Thomas L. "The Trial of Postmodernism. The Politics of Postmodern Aesthetics – Habermas contra Foucault." *Political Theory* 16 (1988): 209–28.

d'Entrèves, Maurizio P. See book entry, Section III.

Esteban, Joseba I. "Habermas on Weber: Rationality, Rationalization and the Diagnosis of the Times." *Gnosis* 3 (1991): 93–115.

Gasché, Rodolphe. "Postmodernism and Rationality." *Journal of Philosophy* 85 (1988): 525–38.

Hayim, Gila. "Naturalism and the Crisis of Rationalism in Habermas." *Social Theory and Practice* 18 (1992): 187–209.

Hodge, Joanna. "Habermas and Foucault: Contesting Rationality." *Irish Philosophical Journal* 7 (1990): 60–78.

Hoy, David Couzens. "Splitting the Difference: Habermas' Critique of Derrida." *Praxis International* 8 (1989): 447–64.

Isenberg, Bo. "Habermas on Foucault." *Acta Sociologica* 34 (1991): 299–308.

Jay, Martin (1988). See book entry, Section III.

Kelly, Michael. See book entry, Section III.

Love, Nancy. "Habermas and Foucault on Discourse and Democracy." *Polity* 22 (1989): 269–93.

Margolis, Joseph. "Postscript on Modernism and Postmodernism, Both." *Theory, Culture and Society* 6 (1989): 5–30.

McCarthy, Thomas. (1991). See book entry, Section III.

Misgeld, Dieter. "Modernity and Hermeneutics in Gadamer and Habermas." In *Gadamer and Hermeneutics*, ed. Hugh J. Silverman. New York: Routledge, 1991.

Norris, Christopher. "Deconstruction, Postmodernism and Philosophy: Habermas on Derrida." In David Wood, ed., *Derrida: A Critical Reader*. Cambridge, Mass.: Blackwell, 1992.

Pickard, Dean. "Applied Nietzsche: The Problem of Reflexivity in Habermas, A Postmodern Critique." *Auslegung* 19 (1993): 1–21.

Pippin, Robert. "Hegel, Modernity and Habermas." *Monist* 74 (1991): 329–57.

Poster, Mark. See book entry, Section III.

Raffel, Stanley. See book entry, Section III.

Rasmussen, David. See book entry, Section III.

Rockmore, Tom. "Modernity and Reason: Habermas and Hegel." *Man and World* 22 (1989): 233–46.

Rorty, Richard. "Habermas, Derrida and the Functions of Philosophy." *Revue Internationale de Philosophie*, forthcoming.

Rorty, Richard. "Habermas, Derrida and the Functions of Philosophy." *Revue Internationale de Philosophie*, forthcoming.

Scharff, Robert C. "Habermas on Heidegger's *Being and Time.*" *International Philosophical Quarterly* 31 (1991): 189-20.

Schmidt, James. "Jürgen Habermas and the Difficulties of Enlightenment." *Social Research* 49 (1982): 181-208.

Smith, Nick. "The Spirit of Modernity in Habermas." *Radical Philosophy* 60 (1992): 23-29.

Steuerman, Emilia. "Habermas versus Lyotard." In *Judging Lyotard*, ed. Andrew Benjamin. New York: Routledge, 1992.

Villa, Dana. "Postmodernism and the Public Sphere." *American Political Science Review* 86 (1992): 712-21.

Visker, Rudi. "Habermas on Heidegger and Foucault: Meaning and Validity in the *Philosophical Discourse of Modernity.*" *Radical Philosophy* 61 (1992): 15-22.

Watson, Stephen. "Jürgen Habermas and Jean Francois Lyotard: Postmodernism and the Crisis of Rationality." *Philosophical and Social Criticism* 10 (1984): 1-24.

Weiner, Richard R. "Retrieving Civil Society in a Postmodern Epoch." *Social Science Journal* 28 (1991).

Wellbury, David. "Nietzsche – Art – Postmodernism: A Reply to Jürgen Habermas." In *Nietzsche in Italy*, ed. Thomas Harrison. Stanford, Calif.: Stanford University Press, 1988.

Wellmer, Albrecht. "Reason, Utopia and the Dialectic of Enlightenment." *Praxis International* 3 (1983): 83-107.

White, Stephen K. (1991). See book entry, Section III.

Wolin, Richard. "Modernism vs. Postmodernism." *Telos* 62 (1984-85): 9-29.

INDEX

abortion (issue), 130, 131–2, 135, 160
Ackerman, Bruce, 222
Acton, Lord, 167
Adenauer, Konrad, 73, 77, 82
administrative power, 8, 11, 12, 213
administrative rationality, 110
Adorno, Theodor, 3, 4–5, 6, 113, 290, 294, 299; Habermas's critique of, 20–2; identity and difference in ethical positions of Habermas and, 19–45
aesthetic criticism, 120, 140–1; Habermas's analysis of, 126–9
aesthetic-expressive attitude, 52–3
aesthetic judgments, 274–6, 278
Aesthetic Theory (Adorno), 34, 39
aestheticism, Nietzschean, 21
agency, 159–60, 173
agonism, 25, 32
agonistic conflict, pluralism and, 153–7
agonistic dimension, 144, 155, 157
agreement(s), 32, 157, 246, 247; as basis of society, 143; communicatively achieved, 8, 120–4; efficiency problem in, 248–50; mediated by reason, 304; in modern, postconventional societies, 251–3; universal, 128
Alembert, Jean d', 264
alienation, 24–5, 47, 52, 55–6; as exile, 47; labor and, 48–9
analytic moral philosophy, 9–10
Anthropology (Kant), 275, 277
Apel, Karl-Otto, 127, 296, 301
application of norms, 129–33
Arato, Andrew, 102, 199n55
Arendt, Hannah, 12, 212–13

argument(ation), 22, 23, 240; assumptions in, 127; conflict resolution through, 181; moral norms tested in, 157–8; principles in, 24; reasoned, 238
Aristotle, 130, 132, 308
art, 33, 39–40
association of free and equal consociates under law (*Rechtsgenossen*), 201, 221
asylum debate (Germany), 87–8, 89
Auschwitz, 266, 284
Austin, J. L., 22, 121
Australian politics, 103
authority: in democracy, 169, 170, 171; of generalized "third," 313; of moral rules, 177; in public spheres, 192–3; in therapy, 191–2
autonomous public spheres, 263
autonomy, 172–5, 188, 194, 220; as capacity for reason giving, 206; collective, 12; development of, 175–81, 184, 186, 189; in discursive democracy, 181–4; and happiness, 194; in Kant, 207–8; legal form and, 210; moral "ought" in, 281; in neurotics, 185; public/private, 12, 202, 211, 212, 214, 219, 221, 223–4, 225; social development of, 176–7; value of, 195

Babel, tower of, 47–8, 60
Ball, Terence, 98
Basic Law (*Grundgesetz*), 74–5, 85–7, 88–9
Bataille, Georges, 279, 280
Baynes, Kenneth, 11, 201–32

341